VAX C
Programmer's Guide

J. Ranade DEC Series

VAX C
Programmer's Guide

Jay Shah

McGraw-Hill, Inc.

York St. Louis San Francisco Blue Ridge Summit, Pa.
Auckland Bogotá Caracas Lisbon London Madrid
Mexico Milan Montreal New Delhi Paris San Juan
São Paulo Singapore Sydney Tokyo Toronto

Library of Congress Cataloging-in-Publication Data

Shah, Jay

    VAX C programmer's guide / by Jay Shah.
        p.   cm.
    Includes index.
    ISBN 0-07-056402-7 (h)
    1. VAX computers—Programming. 2. C (Computer program language)
    I. Title.
    QA76.8.V32S53 1992
    005.245—dc20   92-24335
                                                      CIP

0 0 0 0 0 0 0 0 0 AAAAAA 0 0 0 0 0 0 0

ISBN 0-07-056402-7

The editors for this book were Gerald T. Papke and Sally Anne Glover, and the director of production was Katherine G. Brown. This book was set in Century Schoolbook. It was composed by the McGraw-Hill Publishing Company Professional and Reference Division composition unit.

Printed and bound by R.R. Donnelly.

For more information about other McGraw-Hill materials, call 1-800-2-MCGRAW in the United States. In other countries, call your nearest McGraw-Hill office.

To S. Ramanujan, mathematician,
1887 to 1920.

Contents

Acknowledgments

I'd like to thank Bindoo Patel and Alan Pendley, with whom I have spent many a day discussing computer architectural issues. At Gujarat University in India, Kedar Bhatt and I developed courses on asssembly language programming, and I learned VAX/VMS internals then. My deep gratitude to Kedar and the University.

My guide for preparing the manuscript was Jay Ranade, whose expertise determined the style and contents of the book. Without his encouragement and advice, this book would not have been written.

My manuscript reviewers were David Alquist, Waldo Patton, and Ben Schwartz, whose recommendations I have heeded (more or less).

Finally, thanks to my colleagues at Chase Manhattan Bank: Jim Ghericich, Chia Hsu, Amy Lee, Felix Saget, and Luke Yee for the friendly discussions.

Preface

This book discusses the C programming language and how VAX C can be used to develop integrated applications in the VAX environment. The first C compiler was implemented around 1972 by Dennis Richie at AT&T Bell Labs. He used a PDP-11 computer running the UNIX operating system. Since the VAX-11 computer evolved from the PDP-11, the implementation of C on the VAX computer is one of the most efficient of all C compilers. C is a high-level or low-level language, depending on how it's used. C is like BASIC, COBOL, FORTRAN and Pascal, yet because of its efficiency and ability to perform low-level operations, C can be used to replace assembly language programs. (The VAX assembly language is MACRO-32). Because of its portability and dominance in the UNIX market, C will gain market share over other high-level languages as the move towards UNIX-like "open" systems accelerates.

Currently, the language specifications are defined by the ANSI C X3J11 standards committee. VAX C attempts to follows ANSI C; currently, VAXC is not completely ANSI C. To avoid losing the main focus of the book, differences between ANSI and VAX C are not highlighted in this manuscript.

VAX C is available on two operating systems: VAX/VMS and Ultrix (and OSF/1). Because Ultrix is a UNIX derivative and there are a number of "C under UNIX" books available, the emphasis in this book is on VAX C in the VAX/VMS environment.

The Intended Audience

This book is for application developers who want to explore and use C programs in VAX-based products. Application designers, programmers, potential programmers, and application maintenance staff should benefit from the book. Issues surrounding the use of C on the VAX are discussed at length. The book is also a handy desk reference.

Assembly language is popular among a certain coterie of programmers. It's true that a few programs have to be written in assembly language because of their intimate interaction with the machine. However, there are many programmers who write assembly language (MACRO-32) programs believing that these programs run fast and that the programs cannot be written in higher-level languages because low-level manipulations are performed within the programs.

Needless to say, MACRO code is not very understandable or maintainable. From personal experience, I estimate that about 75% of MACRO programs can, and should be, written in VAX C. C code is usually more easily understood, more easily documented, and more productive than MACRO code. There's little loss in efficiency when moving to VAX C, and often programs will execute faster. One of the main reasons for the popularity of MACRO-32 is simple inertia. A few years ago the C compilers on the VAX (and PDP-11) systems were of an inferior quality—with lots of limitations and bugs. Programmers used MACRO in many real applications, and since haven't bothered to learn another language. However, I hope this book is useful to assembly language programmers.

Many excellent C programmers don't know much about the operating system, which means they can't design complete real-life applications. A knowledge of VAX/VMS features is a must for anyone aspiring to be more than a junior programmer. Some of the VAX/VMS specific topics discussed in this book are:

- VAX hardware configurations.
- Basic VMS commands.
- Symbolic debugger.
- The file system.
- System routines.
- Using VMS features from C.
- Network and client/server programming.
- Project management tools.
- Designing professional-quality applications.

Prerequisites

Knowledge of basic programming concepts is assumed. The book will be easy reading if you know at least one other programming language under any operating system. The discussion on the C language is quite terse; the book focuses on the C environment on the VAX.

Why This Book is Complete

This book introduces C, the symbolic debugger, file handling, and system libraries. The book also covers peripheral issues like the operating system, VAXclusters, CASE tools, and DECnet. Where appropriate, examples and exercises are provided.

What's the Next Step?

This book should make you proficient and confident in developing applications on the VAX. Even complex online distributed transaction processing applications are based on concepts described in this book. The following products are mentioned in the book; however, when designing complex applications you might want to consult other books and manuals:

- VAX/VMS operating system.
- VAXclusters.
- High availability and fault-tolerant systems.
- DECnet.
- Transaction processing monitors.
- VAX connectivity with other computers.
- Other languages and layered products on VAX.

Introduction to C

A few reasons for C's popularity are:

- C has both high-level and low-level language features that can be used for commercial applications and systems software development.
- C compilers are available on most commercial computer systems.
- C is the dominant language on UNIX systems, and UNIX-like systems are gaining popularity as open systems.
- C code is portable among computers of many vendors when the code is written accordingly.

Many newcomers to C realize that it takes more time to learn C compared to other high-level languages like COBOL, BASIC, FORTRAN, and Pascal.

C has more esoteric features like pointers and unions. C doesn't have built-in I/O statements; even simple terminal I/O requires function calls. String manipulations require an understanding of pointers, and a good understanding of how data is stored and manipulated at the machine level is required when writing many applications. At times, seemingly simple tasks require elaborate programs, as, for example, when writing a record to an indexed file. Even simple programs contain calls to system services and other software products on the system, making the programs difficult to understand with just knowledge of C. This book takes these issues in account and should ease your transition to C.

C is the most versatile of the common languages. It can be used as a high-level or a low-level language; programs look like those of other high-level languages, yet operations that would normally be performed in assembly language can be performed in C. C has been used to write business and scientific applications, operating systems, compilers, databases, network servers, low-level device drivers, and transaction processing monitors. C programs, when written appropriately, can be moved among many operating systems with minor changes. C is often used for systems programming on new machines because the C compiler is usually more rugged than other software products on the system, and compiler bugs have been removed early.

This chapter gives an overview of VAX C features which, for most practical purposes, are standard C features.

1.1 A Simple Program

Here is a small VAX C program:

```
/* A demonstration C program. File: demo1.c */

main()
{
  printf("This is a small VAX C program\n");
}
```

When the program is executed, it prints:

```
This is a small VAX C program
```

The program file is created (by using a text editor), compiled, linked, and executed by commands such as:

```
$ EDIT/TPU DEMO1.C                          !Create the program file
$ CC DEMO1.C                                !Compile the program
$ LINK DEMO1, SYS$LIBRARY:VAXCRTL.OLB/LIB   !Link the program
$ RUN DEMO1                                 !Run the program
This is a small VAX C program
$
```

The VAX C compiler is invoked by the $CC command. VAX C program source files have a default filetype of .C. The LINKER is using the C runtime library, VAXCRTL.OLB. The commands will be explained later in more detail.

To be rigorous, the line:

```
#include <stdio.h>
```

should have been inserted at the top of the program. This would add the file sys$library:stdio.h within the program before the actual compilation. The file stdio.h contains information, called the function prototype, on the function printf(). The compiler will use the prototype to ensure that the use of the function in the program has the correct number of parameters, that each parameter has the proper data type, and so on. This allows errors to be detected at compile-time rather than runtime. If a prototype is not declared and a function call is encountered, the compiler uses defaults to generate code. In our example, the defaults work fine, hence the absence of the #include line. More on this later.

1.2 C Basics

C programs basically consist of a set of functions. Each executable program should contain the function main(). When the program is run, execution begins at this function. The main() function doesn't have to be the first function in the program. Here are some features that characterize C:

1. C is a free format language. Statements can start at any column and span multiple lines. Consecutive blanks, tabs and new lines are treated as one blank. The only exception is string constants that are processed literally. Program readability should be a prime consideration when creating source files.

2. Each C statement must be terminated by a semicolon.

3. Unlike most other computer languages, C is case sensitive. Uppercase and lowercase characters are considered distinct. Keywords must be entered in lowercase. Variables are also case sensitive. For example, in put_line, Input_line, and Input_Line are all different variables.

4. Basic C data types are characters, integers and floating point numbers. Aggregate and other data types are strings, arrays, structures, unions, enumerated data types and pointers.

5. All variables must be declared before use. However, C is not a strongly typed language. For example, an integer can be assigned to a character variable. The implications of such assignments will be discussed in this book. It should be noted that with the emerging ANSI standard, C is becoming more strongly typed.

6. Data (variables) can be static or automatic. Static data remains valid for the duration of complete program execution, while automatic data is valid only in the function where it's declared. The static data area is allocated when program execution starts, while the automatic data area is allocated at runtime when the function where it's declared is entered. The automatic data area is deallocated on function exit. Normally, the compiler allocates the automatic data area on the processor stack.

7. A block is a set of statements enclosed between two braces, { and }. The variable scope rules found in many block structured languages are valid for C. Generally, a variable can't be accessed outside the block in which it's declared.

8. C is not considered a block-structured language because functions can't be defined within other functions.

9. C pointers are variables pointing to other variables or memory locations. C supports arithmetic on pointers. One of the main reasons for C being considered a low-level language is that pointers allow C to manipulate data in memory via pointers, bypassing standard constraints of operations on C variables.

10. C has a set of bit manipulation operators. For example, | is the OR operator. It performs a bit-wise OR of two variables.

11. The body of each function is enclosed within braces, { and }.

12. Functions must be declared before they're used. Functions can be called recursively.

13. Many languages like Fortran have functions and subroutines. In these languages, a function returns a value, while subroutines change values of variables passed as parameters. C has only functions; however, C functions can both return a value and change values of variables passed as parameters.

14. Program flow control statements are: if, while, for, do and switch. Also, break and goto.

15. Comments within programs are enclosed between /* and */. Comments can span over multiple lines.

16. The basic C language has no input and output statements. However, as can be expected, all C compilers offer a standard I/O facility that mainly consists of a set of vendor-supplied functions.

17. Just about all useful C programs include other C files within the program. For compilation, the included file is effectively copied into the program by a part of the compiler called the preprocessor. Typically, such included files contain declarations of data and functions. For example, many programs include the file `stdio.h`, which contains declarations pertaining to the standard I/O facility. On the VAX/VMS operating system, this file resides in the directory `SYS$LIBRARY`, along with many other "include files" supplied with the VAX C compiler.

18. VAX C can call assembly language (MACRO-32) programs. Actually, VAX C adheres to the VAX calling standard, allowing VAX C programs to call programs in most other languages, and vice versa.

Question 1.1: The following program will not compile properly. Why? Hint: See item number five in the previous list.

```
main()
{
    result = 12;
}
```

The program shown in Fig. 1.1 multiplies two numbers and displays the result. The line numbers at the left are not part of the program; they have been inserted to aid in the following comments:

■ The program is compiled by a command like:

```
$ CC DEMO2.C
```

Here, the source file is DEMO2.c and the compilation output is the object file DEMO2.OBJ. The program can then be linked by:

```
$ LINK DEMO2.OBJ, SYS$LIBRARY:VAXCRTL.OLB/LIBRARY
```

```
1       /* Add two numbers. File: demo2.c
2        *
3        * The program multiplies two numbers and prints
4        * the result on the terminal.
5        *
6        * Usage of variables:
7        * number1 - multiplicand
8        * number2 - multiplier
9        * result  - of multiplication of number1 by number2
10       */
11
12      main()           /* main program function */
13      {
14      int  number1, number2, result; /* declare integer variables */
15
16          number1 = 123;    number2 = 32;
17          result = number1 * number2;
18          printf("123 multiply by 32 = %d",result);
19      }
```

Figure 1.1 A C program that multiplies two integers.

The output of the command is an executable image file, DEMO2.EXE. Here, the object library file, SYS$LIBRARY:VAXCRTL.OLB, contains routines like the printf function, which are included in the executable image file. The program is executed by running the executable image file as:

```
$ RUN DEMO2.EXE
```

Note that the filetypes are assumed by the commands, so they need not be specified. Hence, the simple commands are:

```
$ CC DEMO2
$ LINK DEMO2, SYS$LIBRARY:VAXCRTL/LIBRARY
$ RUN DEMO2
```

- Lines 1 to 10 are comment lines that are ignored by the compiler. The comment starts with a /* and ends with a */. The asterisks at the beginning of intermediate lines are not essential; nevertheless, they make it more clear that the lines contain comments. It's a good idea in many cases to explain how the variables in the program are used, as is done on lines seven to nine.

- C programs mainly consist of blocks of code called functions. In this program, execution will begin at the only function, main(), at line 12. Lines 13 through 19 constitute a block because they start and end with braces, { and }. The block is the body of function main().

- Function main() uses three integer variables, number1, number2, and result, declared at the top of the function. In line 14, int represents the data type integer. All declarations must precede executable statements in a block.

- Executable statements start at line 16. Line 16 contains two executable statements. The statement at line 18 is a call to the function printf(). The printf() function is included in the executable image during the linking phase of the program. Two parameters are passed to the function: address of the literal string 123 multiply by 32 = %d and address of the integer result. The function substitutes the value of result for %d and displays the resulting string: 123 multiply by 32 = 3936.

Consider the program in Fig. 1.2, which illustrates more elements of C programs. Here are a few comments on the program shown in Fig.1.2:

- The program consists of three functions: multiply at line 27, add at line 35 and main at line 43. Program execution will begin at function main().

- Lines 1 through 16 contain comments on the program.

- Line 18 includes a header file from the system directory SYS$LIBRARY:. The file, stdio.h, should be included when standard I/O is to be per-

Figure 1.2 A C program to add or multiply any two integers.

```
1       /* Add or multiply two numbers. File: demo3.c
2        * The program illustrates elements of typical C programs.
3        *
4        * The program accepts two integers from the terminal,
5        * adds or mutiplies them depending on the user's choice and
6        * prints the result on the terminal.
7        *
8        * Usage of variables:
9        * number1 - integer form of numeric string in number1_string
10       * number2 - integer form of numeric string in number2_string
11       * result  - of operation on number1 and number2
12       * number1_string - first number entered at terminal
13       * number2_string - second number entered at terminal
14       * choice  - character entered at terminal to represent
15       *           addition or multiplication of the two numbers.
16       */
17
18      #include stdio.h    /* include declarations file for input/output
19                           * from the directory SYS$LIBRARY:
20                           */
21
22      static int  number1, number2;    /* declare integer variables */
23      static char number1_string[80],
24          number2_string[80], choice; /* declare character variables */
25
26
27      void multiply(void)     /* function */
28      {
29      int result;
30
31          result = number1 * number2;
32          printf("Result of multiplication is %d",result);
33      }
34
35      void add(void)          /* function */
36      {
```

Figure 1.2 *Continued.*

```
37     int result;

38

39         result = number1 + number2;
40         printf("Sum is %d",result);
41     }

42

43     main()          /* main program function */
44     {
45         printf("Enter a number: ");
46         gets(number1_string);
47         number1 = atoi(number1_string);

48

49         printf("Enter another number: ");
50         gets(number2_string);
51         number2 = atoi(number2_string);

52

53         choice = ' ';
54         /* while choice not = 'm' and choice not = 'a' */
55         while (choice != 'm' && choice != 'a')

56            {
57            printf("\nEnter m to multiply, a to add the numbers: ");
58            choice = getchar();
59            };
60         /* call either one of the two functions: multiply or add*/
61         if (choice == 'm') multiply(); else add();
62     }
```

formed. The file mainly contains declarations of constants and functions used by I/O calls like `getchar`. The header file contains only declarations; actual code for I/O is inserted in the final image during linking. The lines

```
#include stdio
#include stdio.h
```

are equivalent because the default file type for header files is `.h`.

```
#include stdio.h
#include <stdio.h>
```

The first form of `#include` specifies that the include file is in the VMS text library file, `SYS$LIBRARY:VAXCDEF.TLB`. The second form specifies that the include file is `SYS$LIBRARY:STDIO.H`. When the VAX C compiler is installed, all modules in the text library file, `SYS$LIBRARY:VAXCDEF.TLB`, are extracted into `SYS$LIBRARY`. Hence, the two forms of `#include` are equivalent. However, many products create header files in `SYS$LIBRARY:` and don't put them in the library file. For this reason, the second form is preferable, although for simplicity, the first form is used in this book.

- Lines 22 through 24 declare variables used by all of the three functions. These are static variables as opposed to automatic variables. Static and automatic variables have significance to function recursion, which is discussed later in this book. The variables have a lifetime that is the same as that of the complete program execution. Each of the two variables `number1_string` and `number2_string` is an array of 80 characters.

- Lines 29 and 37 contain two automatic variables called result. Although they have the same name, they're two distinct variables. These variables don't share the same memory location because they're declared in different functions. The variables are given storage on the system stack when the corresponding functions are entered during program execution. The scope of the variables is their corresponding functions, multiply and add. The variables are effective when the corresponding function is entered during execution of the program; on function exit, the variables are not available to the program. Hence, the main function can't use either of the two variables called result.

- The functions at lines 27 and 35 have two `void`s each. The `void` can be interpreted as "no value." The `void` preceding the function name means that the function doesn't return a value, so a statement in the `main()` program such as

```
result = add();
```

will be flagged as an error by the compiler. The `void`s in parentheses mean that the functions must not be passed any parameters.

Question 1.2: Is the following line a complete and valid C program?

```
main() { }
```

ANSWERS:

1.1 Variable `result` is not declared before use.
1.2 Yes, though the program does nothing. The form is used as a stub for a function that will be filled out later.

Usually, answers are not provided in further chapters. This is to allow for some research and experimentation on your part.

2

The VAX/VMS Environment

Detailed knowledge of the environment in which programs will be running might not be required of C programmers; nevertheless, a basic understanding of the underlying computer's possible configurations is a prerequisite for any professional programmer. For example, the *ESE50* solid-state disk is a device that is accessed like other disk devices; however, the data is transferred very fast between the VAX and the disk. Knowing this, system analysts can decide whether to reengineer applications to increase performance by storing frequently used disk data on an *ESE50*. This chapter discusses the software and hardware components at VAX sites, which allow program designers to use judgment and make trade-offs when writing complete applications.

The VAX architecture is designed by *Digital Equipment Corporation* (DEC). The company was formed in 1957 with headquarters in Massachusetts. The VAX architecture evolved from DEC's older computer, the PDP (*Programmable Data Processor*). The PDP-11 is a 16-bit computer; the VAX-11 has a 32-bit architecture. "VAX" is derived from *Virtual Address eXtension*.

VAX systems are available as micro, mini or mainframe systems. Figure 2.1 shows a VAX 4000 cabinet. The cabinet is called a BA440 enclosure. The option module slots accept Qbus controllers. For example, the KRQ50 con-

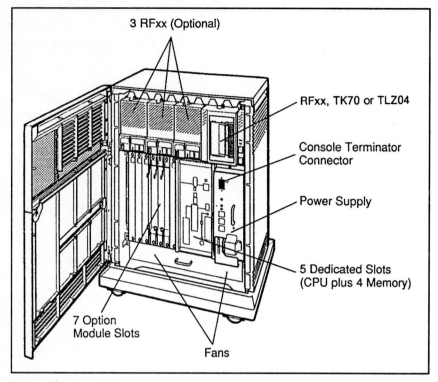

Figure 2.1 VAX 4000 Model 600. *(Copyright © 1990 Digital Equipment Corporation. All Rights Reserved. Reprinted by Permission.)*

troller for the RRD40 600 Mbyte CD-ROM reader occupies one slot. The RFxxs are disk drives. For example, the RF71 is a 400 Mbyte disk drive. There are two versions of the RF71: removable and fixed. The TK70 is a 270 Mbyte cartridge tape drive. The TLZ04 is a 4-mm DAT drive that can record 1.2 Gbytes per tape.

2.1 Vax Processors

A typical VAX CPU cabinet contains a card-cage. The card-cage holds a number of Printed Circuit Boards (PCBs). There are three major types of boards: CPU, Memory and Controllers.

The VAX CPU has *16 general-purpose data registers*, each of 32 bits. The machine uses *32-bit addressing* with a virtual addressing range of 4 Gbytes. The CPU supports more than 400 instructions, including character string manipulation, packed decimal arithmetic, floating point arithmetic, and variable-length bit-field instructions.

The 6000 and 9000 series VAXes support *vector processing* in hardware.

The basic instruction set is now extended to perform vector operations. There are about 63 vector processing instructions. When the vector processing hardware option is installed, the CPU has 64 vector registers. Each vector register has 64 elements (simple registers). Each element has 64 bits. Various instructions are provided to perform arithmetic in parallel on the contents of these registers.

While the instruction set is (nearly) the same for all VAXes, the hardware technology used to implement the CPU varies among the various VAX models. CPU speeds of the VAX models also vary. Figure 2.2 shows CPU characteristics of some VAX models.

There are four basic families of VAXes: VAX 9000, VAX 6000, VAX 4000 and MicroVAX 3000 series. The microVAX 3000 series will be gradually superseded by the VAX 4000 series computers. VAXes no longer in production (like the 8000 series, MicroVAX II, VAX 11/780 and VAX 11/750) are not discussed explicitly in this book, although many of them are supported by DEC and can be VAXcluster members.

Note that CPU speeds are normally not measured using standard MIPS (Millions of Instructions Per Second); rather, VUPs and microVUPs are used. DEC believes that MIPS, as a standard of measure, is misleading when applied to the VAX, which has a complex instruction set and a variety of intelligent I/O devices. The throughput of a complete system configuration is more indicative of system performance. One VUP (*VAX Unit of Processing*) is the speed of a VAX 11/780. Thus, a 3.7 VUP VAX has a CPU that is 3.7 times faster than a VAX 11/780 CPU. One microVUP is the speed of a microVAX II. Both the VAX 11/780 and microVAX II are no more in production; however, the standards of measure are still in use.

CPU model	CPU Speed	Implementation technology	Maximum memory Mbytes	I/O Bus	Max. bus I/O throughput Mbytes/sec
VAXstation 3100	2.7	CMOS	32	SCSI	1.5
MicroVAX 3900	3.8	CMOS	64	Qbus	3.3
				DSSI	4.0
VAX 4000-300	8.0	CMOS	128	Qbus	3.3
				DSSI	4.0
VAX 6000-520	25.0	CMOS	512	VAXBI	60.0
				XMI	80.0
VAX 9000-440	117.0	ECL	512	XMI	320.0

Figure 2.2 VAX models.

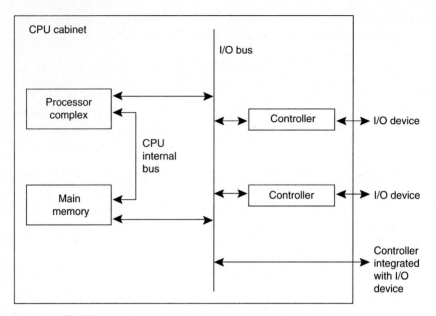

Figure 2.3   The I/O connection.

Memory on the smaller VAXes is 8 bit, with one bit parity; on the more expensive models ECC (*Error Correcting Code*) memory is used.

2.2   I/O Buses

A controller connects the CPU and memory to I/O devices via an I/O bus. Figure 2.3 shows this configuration. Usually, there is a separate internal bus connecting CPU with memory. This bus has a much higher speed than the I/O buses.

There are six major I/O buses used on VAXes:

- XMI. This is the fastest bus to date. Used on VAX 9000 series.
- VAXBI. Used on midrange and high-end systems like the VAX 6000 series.
- UNIBUS. Used on older midrange systems. Being phased out.
- Qbus. Used on low-end and midrange systems like the VAX 4000 and microVAX 3000 series
- SCSI. Used on VAXstations. SCSI is an acronym for Small Computer Systems Interface.
- DSSI. Used on some of the MicroVAXes and VAX 4000 series computers for disk I/O. Many of the disk controllers on this bus are integrated into

the device enclosure rather than in the CPU cabinet. DSSI is an acronym for Digital Standard Systems Interconnect.

The DSSI bus allows disk drives with integrated controllers to be connected to a VAX. The controllers have software that allows multiple VAXes to communicate with the drive. This allows VAXes in a CI-based VAXcluster to use common drives without resorting to the use of expensive Hierarchical Storage Controllers (HSCs) or, in the case of Local Area VAXclusters, to use common drives without resorting to the use of a VAX to serve a local disk as a cluster common disk.

Some VAXes can have more than one bus of the same type for better I/O performance. Many VAXes support more than one type of I/O bus. Figure 2.4 shows the characteristics of some of the general buses.

Controllers communicate with the CPU using hardware interrupts and Control and Status Registers (CSRs). CSRs are registers within the controller that can be accessed as memory locations by the CPU. This implies that the VAX uses memory-mapped I/O. Many controllers have Direct Memory Access (DMA) to the main memory.

2.3   Hardware Components

The VAX supports many I/O devices. Typically, the I/O device communicates with the CPU and memory via a controller. A controller's design depends on the type of bus that it can be used with and on the I/O devices it controls. The term "I/O device" is used generically, as controllers are also used to communicate with components (like Ethernet), which technically are not I/O devices. Figure 2.5 describes some common controllers.

A vast number of devices can be connected to VAX systems. Some of these are:

1. The *RA series disk drives* are the most common storage device on large systems. The RA92 has a capacity of 1.5 Gbytes and an average seek

Bus	Speed Mbytes/sec	Supporting Vaxes	Sample controllers used on the bus
XMI	80	6000, 9000 series	KDM70 disk controller
VAXBI	10	6000, 9000 series	KDB50 disk controller
Qbus	3.3	MicroVAX 3000 series	KDA50 disk controller
SCSI	1.2	VAXstation 3100	SCSI disk controller
DSSI	4.0	VAX 4000	DSSI disk controller

Figure 2.4   I/O buses on the VAX.

```
Controller   Bus required   Devices controlled
----------------------------------------------------------------
KDM70        XMI            RA series disk drives like RA92

KDB50        VAXBI          RA series disk drives

KDA50        Qbus           RA series disk drives

DSSI         DSSI           RF series disk drives

DEMNA        XMI            Ethernet interface

                           (DEC LANcontroller 400)

DESQA        Qbus           Ethernet interface

CIBCA        VAXBI          VAXcluster Port (CI interface)

CIBCD        XMI            VAXcluster Port (CI interface)

TQK70        Qbus           TK70 cartridge tape controller

SCSI         SCSI           Disk drives like RZ23 and

                           tape drives like TK50 drives

DMB32        VAXBI          Communication lines
----------------------------------------------------------------
```

Figure 2.5 Some common controllers.

time of 15.5 milliseconds. The RA90 has a capacity of 1.2 Gbytes and an average seek time of 18.5 milliseconds. The RA70 has a capacity of 280 Mbytes and an average seek time of 19.5 milliseconds. These drives are also packaged as storage arrays in units of four or more. These units are SA550, SA600, SA705, SA800, and SA850.

2. The *ESE20* is a solid state disk. On the system, it works like any RA series disk drive (Digital Storage architecture—DSA-compliant), however, instead of rotating magnetic media, it is made of volatile semiconductor memory. It has a capacity of 120 Mbytes and an access time of 1.3 milliseconds! Real throughput is at least four times more than an RA90 disk.

3. The *RF series disk drives* have controllers integrated with the disk drives (The controllers for RA series drives are inside the CPU cabinet of the host system). The drives use the DSSI bus and are ubiquitous on MicroVAX 3000s and VAX 4000s. The RF71 is a 5.25 inch drive with a capacity of 400 Mbytes and an average seek time of 21 milliseconds. The RF71 removable drive is similar to the standard RF71, except that it can be removed for safe storage when required. The RF72 has a 1.2 Gbyte capacity.

4. The *RZ series disk drives* are used on VAXes supporting the SCSI bus. The RZ24 has a capacity of 209 Mbytes and an average seek time of 24.3 milliseconds.

5. The RRD40 is a *Compact disk ROM* (CD ROM) reader. CD ROM capacity is 600 Mbytes and average seek time is 0.5 seconds.

6. The TA90 *Cartridge Tape Subsystem* is an IBM-3480 compatible unit. The cartridge has a capacity of 200 Mbytes. Six cartridges can be stacked for unattended backup of a RA90 drive.

7. A number of *8-mm and 4-mm magnetic* tape backup devices are available from DEC and third-party vendors. An 8-mm tape can hold more than 2 Gbytes per tape.

8. The *TA79 magnetic tape subsystem* is an industry standard ½-inch spool tape unit. It has a read/write speed of 125 inches/second. The TU81-Plus is a standard spool streaming tape drive. It has a streaming speed of 75 inches/second and a start/stop speed of 25 inches/second. Normally, VMS creates ANSI standard tapes. These tapes can be ported to computers of other manufacturers.

9. The *TK70* is a cartridge tape drive system. The cartridge capacity is 296 Mbytes. The TK50 is similar, except that it has a capacity of 95 Mbytes.

10. *PrintServer 40 PLUS* is a 40-pages-per-minute laser printer. The LN03 is an 8-pages-per-minute laser printer. The LN03R is a postscript laser printer. The LJ250 is an ink-jet color printer. The LA75 and LA210 are 250-characters-per-second dot matrix printers. The LA75 has a printing width of 80 characters; the LA210 prints 132 columns wide. The LA70 prints at 200 characters per second. LP29 is a 2000-lines-per-minute line printer. LG31 is a 300-lines-per-minute dot matrix printer. The LN03s are being superseded by the DEClaser 2000 family of printers. While both LN03 and DEClaser 2000s are similar in function, they differ in internal design (they are manufactured by different companies). The DEClaser 2000s print 8 pages per minute. The DEClaser 2100 prints single sides, the DEClaser 2200 prints both sides of pages.

11. *MD300 DECimage scanning subsystem* is a 300-dots-per-inch scanner.

12. A number of synchronous and asynchronous communications controllers are available. As VAXes are very common in process control and real-time monitoring and control environments, a number of real-time options like A/D and D/A controllers are also available.

We've seen the basic building blocks of a VAX system. Figure 2.6 shows a VAX 6000 Model 620 computer system with associated hardware.

2.4   Digital Command Language (DCL)

The user interface to VAX/VMS is the Digital Command Language (DCL). When a user logs in, a dollar sign prompt is issued by DCL:

```
$
```

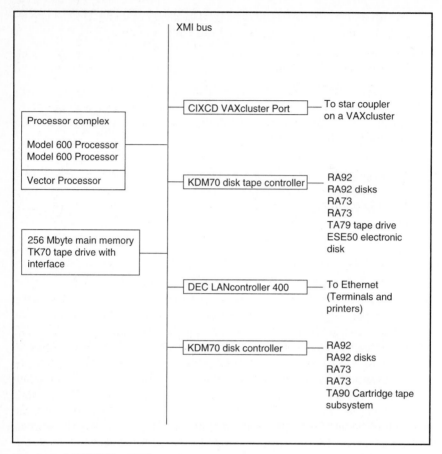

Figure 2.6 A VAX 6000—620 System.

DCL then waits for command input. DCL commands are written in a procedural language. DCL has a language interpreter for executing a string of commands, and powerful programs (procedures) can be written using DCL. A sequence of commands can be stored in a file and executed at a later stage. DCL supports parameter substitution, commonly used built-in functions and conditional execution of commands. Here is an example of a DCL command:

```
$ BACKUP/VERIFY DUA0:[TEST...] MUA0:TEST.BCK/SAVE
```

Here's an example command file that compiles and links a COBOL program:

```
$! File: COBOL_BUILD_1.COM
$ COBOL PROGA.COB
```

```
$ LINK PROGA.OBJ
$ EXIT
```

2.5 Program Development

VAX/VMS and ULTRIX-32 are the major operating systems used on the VAX computers. Third-party UNIX implementations are also used at many sites. ULTRIX-32 is DEC's implementation of UNIX System V. In this book, we'll be looking only at VAX/VMS.

Languages supported on the VAX/VMS include Ada, APL, BASIC, BLISS, C, COBOL, DIBOL, FORTRAN, LISP, VAX MACRO, OPS5, PASCAL, PL/1, RPG II, SCAN and VAX TPU. Of these, VAX TPU is the only language that comes bundled with the operating system. TPU (Text Processing Utility) is a programming language for manipulating textual data. Complex applications can be written in multiple languages with calls to programs written in other languages. The Run Time Library and System Services offer a collection of utility subroutines that can be called from programs. Because VAX/VMS uses virtual memory management techniques, program size is usually not a limitation.

Programs are created using an editor on the system. EVE (*Extensible VAX Editor*) is a popular editor. It's discussed in the next chapter. Other editors are EDT and LSE (*Language Sensitive Editor*). EDT was popular in the past; however, EVE is a more modern and versatile editor, hence EDT is not discussed in this book.

VMS has a *symbolic program debugger* that aids in program testing. The debugger displays multiple windows. Source code, program output and user commands are displayed in separate windows. The debugger can be used for testing programs in any language. Conditional execution of statements and other features make the debugger a powerful programming tool.

VAXset is a set of *CASE (Computer Aided Software Engineering) tools* that aid in software project management. The tool kit consists of :

- *Code Management System* (CMS). CMS manages source files for a project. It maintains a history of changes made to files by programmers.

- *Language Sensitive Editor* (LSE). The LSE can be used to create or edit programs in any language. The editor provides cues on entering code, which can be useful if you forget the syntax of statements. The program can be compiled within the editor. Compilation errors can be displayed and the source program corrected from the editor.

- *Source Code Analyzer* (SCA). SCA is a cross-referencing tool for analyzing usage of variables and routines. SCA can be used to search for variable declarations and usage in a set of source programs that constitute a complete application. The source programs are displayed to show the exact occurrence of the variable.

- *Module Management System* (MMS) MMS is used to build a software application from an interdependent set of source programs (which constitute the complete application). Programs can be modified, and then MMS can be used to generate the system. MMS checks revision dates on files and determines which parts of the application need to be regenerated. MMS can also be used on nonprogram files.

- *DEC Test Manager* (DTM). DTM automates the testing of a software system to determine if the system runs as expected. DTM is a regression analysis tool. The programmer runs the programs under DTM. DTM notes all input given by the programmer and all output generated by the application. This output is a benchmark. Later on, when some programs are modified, DTM can be used to rerun the test to ensure that results are the same as those of the benchmark.

- *Performance and Coverage Analyzer* (PCA). PCA shows how much time is spent by the CPU on each statement of a program during execution. It's an execution profiler that can be used to highlight bottlenecks in an application or to optimize programs. Statistics on I/O system calls are also collected.

Files used in programs can be sequential, relative or indexed. The *Record Management Services* (RMS) is used to manipulate files. RMS is normally available with the operating system. Many languages like COBOL automatically use RMS when files are handled within programs.

DECnet can be used to write distributed applications. Task-to-task communications are also supported by DECnet.

2.6 Layered Products

Most software products other than the operating system and DECnet are considered layered products, layered because they reside as a layer above the operating system. VAXset, mentioned previously, is a layered product. Some of the other products are mentioned here.

ALL-IN-1 is an integrated *office automation* package that supports word processing, graphics, spreadsheets and electronic mail. Many of the subpackages used within ALL-IN-1 are also available separately. WPS-PLUS is a word processor. DECspell can be used to check and correct spellings. VAX Grammar Checker proofreads a document for grammatical correctness. VAX DECalc is a spreadsheet package. DECgraph can be used to prepare presentation graphs.

DEC also offers a set of packages for application development:

- Two DBMSs are available from DEC: VAX DBMS, which adheres to the Codasyl standard and has a network architecture; and Rdb, a relational DBMS. Rdb has a SQL (Structured Query Language) interface.

- Datatrieve is a report writer. Datatrieve is an interpreter that aids fast program development at the expense of runtime efficiency. It's particularly useful for generating quick reports and graphical output.

- DECintact (DECtp) is a high volume *transaction processing* application development software. It supports distributed processing. It can be used for mission critical applications like electronic funds transfer where transaction integrity is required and where failure of hardware components could be disastrous.

- Applications Control Management System (ACMS). This is another transaction processing application development software that focuses on reduced application development time cycle.

Common Data Dictionary (CDD/PLUS) is a layered product that centralizes the storage and management of data definitions. CDD/PLUS keeps a description of the data, not the data itself. An application can have a large number of programs accessing a set of files. The record layouts of these files can be defined in a CDD. The definition can be included within programs. The definitions are translated into corresponding program statements by CDD/PLUS, depending on the programming language. The advantage of this is that changes to record formats (fields) can be made in the CDD without having to change the programs. CDD/PLUS also supports database products like Datatrieve, Rdb/VMS and VAX DBMS. CDD/PLUS will be superseded by a more extensive product called CDD/Repository.

Most end-user applications require *forms* to be displayed on screen and data to be accepted from fields within the form. While programmers can use standard input-output statements and perform data validation within programs, a number of packages are available for programming ease. DEC forms, Terminal Data Management System (TDMS) and Forms Management System (FMS) are used to design forms on screen. FMS is the oldest and currently the most commonly used screen design package. TDMS has most of the features of FMS; in addition, it can validate data without any programming. DECforms is the latest package conforming to ANSI/ISO FIMS (Form Interface Management System). The DECforms interface is being standardized by DEC for use with their DBMS's and other application development products.

VAX DOCUMENT is an *electronic publishing* package. Most of the VAX documentation from DEC is created using this package. It's a good tool for producing in-house pamphlets, proposals and other documents. Graphics can be integrated with text.

The DECtalk product consists of a hardware device and software programs. It can be used to create voice output and, when connected with a telephone system, it can recognize telephone key presses. In effect, an automated *interactive telephone system* can be designed.

VAX DEC/Shell is a *UNIX interface emulator*. It's an alternative to the standard DCL interface.

2.7 DECnet

One of the strengths of the VAX/VMS software is DECnet. DECnet is the networking component of VAXes for communications between VAXes (and other computers). For programmers, files residing on devices attached to other VAXes on the network are similar to files on the programmer's computer. Typical uses of a DECnet network are:

- Copying files.
- Logging into other VAXes.
- Sharing resources like files and fast line-printers.
- Running distributed applications.

Ethernet technology, though not essential to run DECnet, is extensively used for networking. Ethernet is a bus with a rated bandwidth of 10 Megabits/second. VAXes in the same building are usually interconnected by Ethernet. Ethernet is also used to support terminal servers. Terminal servers allow terminals to be logically connected to any VAX on the network. While Ethernet was designed for use in local area networks (LANs), Ethernet bridges allow the Ethernet to be extended over long distances, even from one continent to another.

Thinwire Ethernet is similar to standard Ethernet; the major difference is that the standard coaxial Ethernet cable is replaced by a thinner version. Thinwire Ethernet hardware is more convenient to handle physically. *10baseT twisted pair Ethernet* cables are also popular because the cables are handled like simple RS232 cables. Figure 2.7 shows a DECnet network using Ethernet and point-to-point communications lines.

VAXes can also be interconnected by point-to-point connections. The connections can be synchronous or asynchronous. These connections use the DDCMP protocol under DECnet. DDCMP stands for Digital Data Communications Protocol. Point-to-point connections are normally used when VAXes are far apart or if the connection is for a simple application where the installation of Ethernet products is not cost effective.

DECnet also has SNA connectivity products that allow VAXes to communicate with IBM mainframes. Some of these products are used for 3270 terminal emulation, APPC LU 6.2 task-to-task communications, RJE and file transfer. DECnet also has support for X.25 connectivity, which allows VAXes to communicate with other computers on packet-switched networks like Telenet and Tymnet.

DECnet phase V is also known as DECnet/OSI because it's compliant with

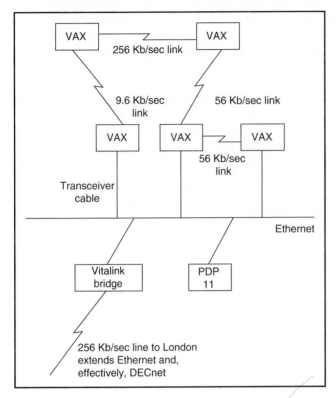

Figure 2.7 A DECnet network.

the ISO/OSI networking standard. It will replace DECnet phase IV over the next few years.

2.8 Fiber Optics

DEC was one of the first companies to announce commercial fiber optics products for networking. DEC's offerings closely follow the ANSI FDDI standard. FDDI (Fiber Distributed Data Interface) defines a standard for interconnecting computers and peripherals using fiber optics technology. The standard is being formulated by the American National Standards Institute (ANSI) committee X3T9.5. The committee was formed in 1982.

FDDI cables have a raw bandwidth of 100 Mbits/sec (contrast with Ethernet, which has a theoretical peak bandwidth of 10 Mbits/sec and a throughput of less than 4 Mbits/sec for most practical applications). An FDDI-based LAN can have a circumference of about 60 miles. As elaborated later, FDDI specifies a dual ring, token passing technique for communications. A tree structured configuration can also be designed.

A computer connects to a fiber optic cable via a concentrator. The computer (or device) connecting to the concentrator is called an attachment station. A station can be one of two types: a *single attachment station* (SAS) or a *dual attachment station* (DAS). A SAS connects to one of the dual rings (the primary ring) via the concentrator; the DAS, which is more complex and expensive, can connect to both the primary and backup rings, affording redundancy.

DEC's FDDI concentrator is DECconcentrator 500. At the time of writing, DEC doesn't have a SAS or DAS module that can plug into a VAX system and directly communicate with a concentrator. Such modules will soon be announced. (FDDIcontroller 700 allows a DECstation 5000, which is a RISC computer, to be directly connected to a concentrator). Meanwhile, the DECbridge 500 device allows Ethernet to be connected to the FDDI concentrator. The DECbridge is a SAS, and a set of Ethernet LANs can be interconnected by an FDDI backbone. Figure 2.8 shows a possible FDDI network.

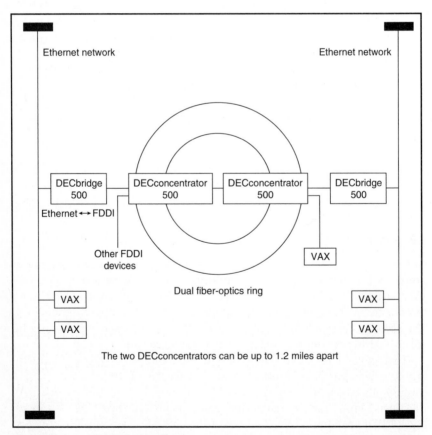

Figure 2.8 A simple FDDI network.

FDDI specifies a token ring network. Dual rings, called the primary and backup rings, are used for redundancy. A token circulates in the primary ring. A station will receive a token from an adjacent station. The station merely repeats the token for the next station unless it wishes to transmit data. A station can transmit data only if it has the token ("absorbed the token" is the phrase used in the literature). Once it has absorbed the token, the station sends out the data frame followed by the token. Intermediate stations repeat the data frames and the token. The destination station reads the frame (and processes it as required by the application), sets appropriate status flags in the frame and transmits it. It then receives and repeats the token. The transmitting station reads the frame returned by the destination station, checks the status bits, determines that the frame has been read by the destination station, and strips the frame off the ring. It then receives and repeats the token. This is the basic communication technique on FDDI.

For more efficient use of the high fiber optics bandwidth, FDDI allows more than one data frame to circulate in the ring. Consider a configuration that has four stations A, B, C and D, in that sequence on the ring. Station A is sending a data frame to station C, and station B wants to send a frame to station D. Station B will receive a data frame and the token from Station A, which it would repeat if it didn't have any data frame to transmit. But since it has data ready for transmission, it repeats A's data frame, receives the token, transmits its data frame and then transmits the token. This way, any station can transmit data frames when it has absorbed the token. (In effect, multiple frames can precede a token on the ring.)

2.9 VAXclusters

A *VAXcluster* is a collection of VAXes and peripherals connected together to form one synergetic system. Individual VAXes in the cluster run the VAX/VMS operating system. The words VAXcluster and cluster are used synonymously in this book. VAXclusters offer a number of additional features over independent (stand alone) VAX computers.

Figure 2.9 shows a sample VAXcluster. The components of this cluster are:

1. Three VAXes. VAX 6000-440 has 4 VAX processors. VAX 9000-210 and VAX 6000-610 are single processor computers. Each VAX has independent physical memory of 128 Mbytes each. VAX/VMS runs on each of the three VAXes. A separate set of processes are running within the VAXes.

2. *Computer Interconnect* (CI) bus. This bus is composed of a set of coaxial cables. The CI has a bandwidth of 70 Megabits/second. It's used for cluster communications. Maximum use of the CI bandwidth is for transferring disk and tape data between the physical memory of the

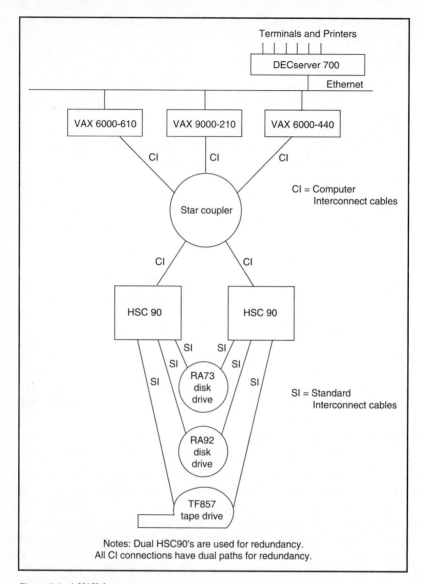

Terminals and Printers

DECserver 700

Ethernet

VAX 6000-610   VAX 9000-210   VAX 6000-440

CI   CI   CI

CI = Computer
Interconnect cables

Star coupler

CI   CI

HSC 90   HSC 90

SI   SI

SI   SI

SI   SI

RA73
disk
drive

SI = Standard
Interconnect cables

RA92
disk
drive

TF857
tape drive

Notes: Dual HSC90's are used for redundancy.
All CI connections have dual paths for redundancy.

Figure 2.9   A VAXcluster.

VAXes and the drives connected to HSC-90. Other uses of the CI will be mentioned later. Each CI connection has two paths for hardware redundancy.

3. A *star coupler*.   The star coupler is a junction box for interconnecting CI cables from the nodes on a cluster. The device doesn't have its own power supply.

4. Two *Hierarchical Storage Controller* (HSC) 90s. These are intelligent nodes on the cluster that manage I/O to disk and tape drives.

5. Disk and tape drives.

6. Ethernet. In this configuration, the Ethernet is used for DECnet communications and allowing terminals and the printer connected to terminal servers on the Ethernet to communicate with the VAXes (by the Local Area Transport protocol described later). Ethernet is not required to cluster VAXes; however, devices that can connect to it are ubiquitous in the VAX world; thus, most clusters have an Ethernet network.

7. A Terminal server. Terminals and printers are connected to it. The printers can be shared by all the VAXes.

This VAXcluster configuration has a number of advantages over three independent VAX computers:

1. *Resource sharing.* The three VAXes in the cluster can share the tape and disk drives. In fact, the same disk file can be accessed by all the VAXes, although it wouldn't make sense to have the VAXes simultaneously access the same record for updates. Also, the task of maintaining backups is less tedious because only one system's disks need to be backed up: the cluster's.

2. *High availability.* If one VAX has a hardware failure, the users can use one of the other VAXes. In fact, as will be explained later, users can be automatically switched to the other VAXes in the event of one VAX failing (or, using industry parlance, crashing). If an HSC-90 fails, the other HSC takes over automatically. Later, we will see how disks can be shadowed so that if a disk fails, other disks will automatically handle further disk I/Os.

3. *High throughput.* If, for example, a single online transaction processing application is running on all the VAXes on the cluster, the application can be sharing the same set of disk files. In this case, the processing speed for transactions is determined by the sum of the speeds of the VAX CPUs. As such applications are usually highly integrated internally, the common application will be inefficient when running from three independent VAX computers.

4. *Convenient system management.* System management is more efficient on a cluster than on a set of independent systems. Common databases can be maintained for user profiles (accounts), network databases, and so on. A common operator console can be created, and user activity can be monitored from one terminal. Most software products have to be installed only once for access by all the VAXes.

5. *Expandability.* If aggregate processing power doesn't meet the user

demand, more VAXes can be popped into the cluster. More HSCs and disk drives can also be easily added if I/O is a bottleneck.

VAXclusters have some disadvantages over independent VAX systems:

1. Normally, they're more *expensive* than independent VAX systems providing the same throughput. Also, software products for clusters cost more than for independent VAX systems. If the product is to be used by, for example, just two VAXes in a 6-VAX cluster, the cluster license may be more expensive than the license for two independent VAX systems.

2. *More system management expertise* is required. For example, because clusters have more drives than a single VAX system, more restrictions may have to be enforced on users. Improper management of votes and quorums (described later) can cause disks to be corrupted. Security management is more complex on a cluster than on independent VAX systems. Also, there are many options for implementing an application functional requirement; the system designer has to determine what the options are and judiciously select one.

3. Some sites use two separate VAX systems with each having a different power supply source. If clusters use two independent power sources, more *planning* is required to safeguard against failure of power from a single source.

4. Some sites have *security* audit requirements that the software development and online production applications be physically independent and that production applications not be available to the developers unless there's a critical software problem. A cluster doesn't meet these requirements. A solution could be to maintain separate clusters.

5. Local Area VAXclusters (LAVcs), which will be described later, use Ethernet instead of the CI for cluster communications. This may cause *congestion on the Ethernet*.

6. *Software bugs* on one computer may cause the whole cluster to crash.

7. VAXes on a cluster take *more time to boot* than if they were independent.

8. On CI-based VAXclusters, there's a trade-off to the high bandwidth (70 Megabits/second) CI cluster communications path: the cluster has to be *within a radius of about 45 meters*.

2.9.1 Homogeneous and heterogeneous clusters

As mentioned before, individual member VAXes on the cluster run the VAX/VMS operating system. The operating system is loaded from disk when a computer is brought up (or booted, as it's called). All the VAXes can share a common set of operating system files, thus saving disk space and simplifying system management. Such a cluster is called a *homogeneous VAXcluster*. Not all of the system files can be common. For example, many of the DECnet database files must be unique for each member VAX. These files contain node-specific information. The AUTHORIZE file, which contains profiles of each user, can be common to all the VAXes on the cluster, or it can be separate for each VAX. Normally, all of the operating system resides on one common system disk. Paging and Swap files are different for each VAX on the homogeneous cluster, though all of them can be on the same common disk.

Failure of the system disk can cause the whole cluster to stop functioning on a homogeneous VAXcluster. Disks can be shadowed to mitigate the effects of disk failures. Volume shadowing is described in its own chapter.

An *heterogeneous cluster* is one that has VAXes loading the operating system from different disks. Such clusters are also known as multiple-environment clusters. Such clusters are more customizable and, as a corollary, require more system management effort. For example, VAXes on the cluster can run different versions of the operating system.

2.9.2 VAXcluster Types: CI-Based, NI-Based and Mixed-Interconnect

A *CI-based cluster* uses the CI bus for cluster communications. CI is an acronym for Computer Interconnect. The bus was described before in this chapter. The CI has a high bandwidth of 70 Megabits/second, which only the larger VAXes can handle efficiently. The VAX 6000 and 9000 series VAXes can be members of a CI-based cluster; the MicroVAX 3000 series and VAX 4000 series VAXes can't.

A local Area VAXcluster (LAVc) uses Ethernet for cluster communications. LAVcs are also called NI-based VAXclusters; NI for Network Interconnect. Maximum theoretical Ethernet bandwidth is 10 Megabits/second; in practice, though, it's about 3 Megabits/second because of message collisions and wait states. Also, Ethernet will normally be used for DECnet and other kinds of traffic. Because of these reasons, LAVcs have a lesser throughput than CI-based clusters. Any VAX, including ones from the MicroVAX 3000 or VAX 4000 series, can be members of a LAVc.

Typically, in a LAVc, one node on the Ethernet is a *boot server*. The boot server is a VAX that has the operating system on one of its local disks and other VAXes on the LAVc boot with this copy of the operating system. VAXes booting off the boot server are called satellites. Satellites access system files from the boot server's system disk, while page and swap files are usually on local disks on the satellite node. Satellites can also have other disks for local files that are normally not required by other nodes. Because the boot server is handling disk I/O on behalf of a number of satellites, it's normally the VAX with the highest CPU speed on the LAVc. If a VAX serves

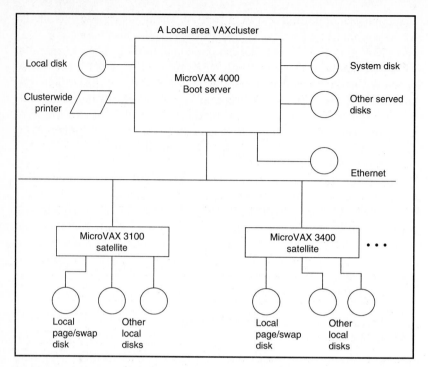

Figure 2.10 A local area VAXcluster.

disks to the cluster and the disks are used intensively by other VAXes, all Ethernet traffic will slow down. The hardware configuration has to be carefully analyzed for potential disk I/O bottlenecks when planning for a LAVc with a number of clusterwide disks. A LAVc can have multiple boot servers. Figure 2.10 shows a Local Area VAXcluster configuration.

A *Mixed-interconnect VAXcluster* is a hybrid of both CI-based and Local Area VAXcluster. Figure 2.11 shows a Mixed-interconnect VAXcluster. The discussions in this book are valid for all the three VAXcluster types mentioned here (unless specified otherwise).

2.10   DECwindows/Motif

DECwindows is a windowing environment that runs on VAX-based graphics workstations. DECwindows is based on The X-window System developed at the Massachusetts Institute of Technology. X in turn is based on W, which was developed at Stanford University. The first production version of X was X10. X10 was significantly modified to support a large class of applications, and the result was X version 11. Newer versions are enhancements to X11. The key components of X-windows are:

- X server that handles the display, keyboard, fonts and so on.
- Xlib, a library of low-level routines.
- Xtoolkit (Xt), a library of prepackaged routines for the convenience of application developers. Xtoolkit makes use of Xlib. Xt is also known as Xt intrinsics. DECwindows uses a tool kit called Motif (previously XUI), which is Xt intrinsics with some enhancements.

DECwindows offers the user a graphics-oriented interaction with the VAX. DCL can be used in terminal emulation windows, and multiple windows allow multiple sessions to be displayed simultaneously. Currently, a

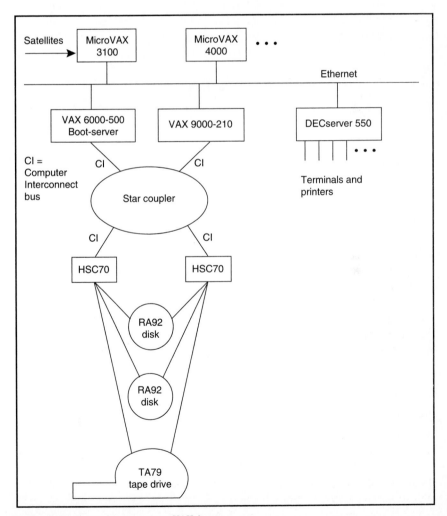

Figure 2.11   A mixed-interconnect VAXcluster.

number of VAX software products like VAX MAIL and VAXset software engineering tools have been enhanced to exploit DECwindows features.

X-windows may well become an industry standard for developing user interfaces. Motif, a user interface developed using X-windows, is being adopted as a standard by many companies. DECwindows supports Motif. Currently, without Motif, users accustomed to one vendor's products have to learn the new environment when moving over to another vendor's products. With Motif, this migration should become easy.

VAXstations are highly suitable for DECwindows applications. In particular, windowing applications are highly graphics oriented; parts of the screen have to be painted very quickly. VAXstations are suitable for this because the CPU is used mainly for handling the screen, although it can be used for running other applications. Basically, a VAXstation is a small VAX with a graphics terminal. The VAXstation normally connects to Ethernet and runs standard VAX/VMS. Of course, DECwindows will also work on other VAXes.

3

Getting Started With VAX/VMS

VMS is a highly interactive operating system. Program development functions, including compilations, are usually performed online. End-user applications also run online, with the user interface controlled by one of the form
management systems on VMS. Programs and commands can also be freely
used in submitted batch files. Batch is typically used for end-of-day processing of online applications and programs that run for a long time without
any user interaction.

Terminal interaction is similar to that on PCs. Each character entered at
the terminal is sent to the VAX, which in turn echoes it immediately, unlike
mainframe terminals where characters are buffered in the terminal until a
function key is pressed. VT220 and VT320 are the most common terminals.
Many installations use third-party terminals that normally emulate VT series terminals. The user interface after login is also very much like that of
most PCs. In fact, some of the commands like DIRECTORY and TYPE are
exactly the same in their basic form. The system, though, has far more functionality than a PC, as will be seen in this book. This chapter introduces basic system features for the novice user.

3.1 Logging In

A *username* and a *password* are required to gain access to the system. These are supplied by the systems administrator. To log in interactively, hit the RETURN key on the terminal. If the prompt `local>` is displayed, then enter `CONNECT nodename`, where nodename is the name of the system to log into. The `Username:` prompt should be displayed. Enter your username, followed by the RETURN key. The next prompt will be `Password:`. Enter your password. The password is not displayed. On successful log in, you should see the $ prompt. The prompt is issued by the component of the operating system called Digital Command Language (DCL). DCL is your interface to the system. DCL commands can now be issued. All DCL commands are terminated with the RETURN key. Except within strings, lowercase and uppercase characters are treated as the same.

Terminal servers are described in the chapter on VAX/VMS hardware environment. Here's a sample login from a terminal connected to a terminal server:

```
Local> Connect  SCUBA
        Welcome to VAX/VMS V5.5
Username: SHAH
Password:
        Welcome to VAX/VMS version V5.5 on node SCUBA
Last interactive login on Friday, 28-FEB-1992 12:51
Last noninteractive login on Thursday, 27-FEB-1992 14:04
$
```

3.2 Help

The HELP command is useful for seeing the list of commands that are recognized by DCL. HELP also displays usage information on the commands. Fig. 3.1 shows an example of HELP usage.

Figure 3.1 Sample online HELP usage.

```
$ SHOW  DEVICES

HELP
                                                                      T:

    The HELP command invokes the VAX-11 HELP Facility to display information    ⊃
    about a VMS command or topic.  In response to the "Topic?" prompt, you can


       Type the name of the command or topic for which you need help.


       Type PROCEDURES for information on commonly peformed tasks.
```

Figure 3.1 *(Continued)*

```
    Type HINTS if you are not sure of the name of the command or topic
    for which you need help.


    Type INSTRUCTIONS for more detailed instructions on how to use HELP.


    Type a question mark (?) to redisplay the most recently requested text.


    Press the RETURN key one or more times to exit from HELP.

 You can abbreviate any topic name, although ambiguous abbreviations result
 in all matches being displayed.



 Format:


 HELP [topic[subtopic]...]


  Additional information available:


  :=            =           @          ACCOUNTING ADVISE     ALLOCATE   ANALYZE

  APPEND        Ascii       ASSIGN     ATTACH     AUTHORIZE  AUTOGEN    BACKUP

  CALL          CANCEL      CC         CLOSE      Command_procedure     CMS

  CONNECT       CONTINUE    CONVERT    COPY       CREATE     DEALLOCATE DEASSIGN

  DEBUG         DECK        DEFINE     DELETE     DEPOSIT    DIFFERENCES

  DIRECTORY  DISCONNECT DISMOUNT     DUMP       EDIT       EOD        EXAMINE

  EXIT          Expressions           File_spec  GOSUB      GOTO       HELP

  Hints         IF          INITIALIZE INQUIRE    Instructions          Lexicals

  LIBRARY       LINK        LOGOUT     MAIL       MERGE      MESSAGE    MOUNT

  NCP           NCS         Numbers    ON         OPEN       PERFORMANCE

  PRINT         Privileges Procedures Protection PURGE      READ       RECALL

  RENAME        REPLY       REQUEST    RETURN     RUN        RUNOFF     SEARCH

  SET           SHOW        SNA_GM     SNA_Terminals         SORT       SPAWN

  SPM           START       STOP       Strings    SUBMIT     Symbol_assignment

  SYNCHRONIZE               THEN       Time       TYPE       UNLOCK     VPA

  WAIT          WRITE

 Topic? time
```

Figure 3.1 *(Continued)*

```
TIME


   Absolute time:


        dd-mmm-yyyy:hh:mm:ss.ss
        TODAY
        YESTERDAY
        TOMORROW


   Delta time:


        dd-hh:mm:ss.ss


   Combination time:


     An absolute time plus (+) or minus (-) a delta time.  Whenever a plus
     sign precedes the delta time value, the entire time specification must
     be enclosed in quotation marks.


     If a description states that a time can be expressed as an absolute time,
     a delta time, or a combination time, then you must specify a delta time
     as if it were part of a combination time.


Topic? wait



WAIT

   Puts your process into a wait state for the specified amount of time.


   Format
    WAIT time



   Additional information available:


   Parameters
```

Figure 3.1 *(Continued)*

```
   Parameters


WAIT Subtopic? para


WAIT


  Parameters


    time
      A time interval specified in the format hour:minute:second.hundredth,

      where hour is an integer in the range 0 through 59; minute is an

      integer in the range 0 through 59; second is an integer in the range 0

      through 59; hundredth (of a second) is an integer in the range 0

      through 99; the colons and period are required delimiters.   The

      format is hh:mm:ss.ss.


WAIT Subtopic? <RETURN>
Topic? <RETURN>
```

3.3 DCL Commands

DCL commands are terminated (and executed) by the RETURN key. Parameters for the command can be specified on the command line separated by spaces and/or tabs. If a required parameter is missing, DCL prompts for the parameter on the next line. For example, the TYPE command is used to display the contents of a file. It requires the file name as a parameter. To type the file MY.DOC the command is:

```
$ TYPE   MY.DOC
```

or

```
$ TYPE
_File: MY.DOC
```

The "_" indicates a continuation line. Most commands have qualifiers (also known as switches). Qualifiers specify options of the command. Qualifiers that apply to the command can be placed anywhere on the command line; qualifiers for particular parameters must follow the parameter. Qualifiers

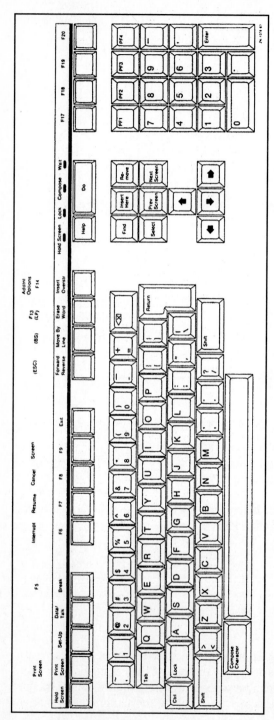

Figure 3.2   The VT series terminal keyboard. (*Copyright © 1990 Digital Equipment Corporation. All Rights Reserved.   Reprinted by Permission.*)

start with the slash character, /. For example, all of the following commands will copy the file MY.DOC to the file YOUR.DOC and perform a read of the output record after each record is copied.

```
$ COPY/WRITE_CHECK  MY.DOC  YOUR.DOC
$ COPY  MY.DOC  /WRITE_CHECK  YOUR.DOC
$ COPY  MY.DOC  YOUR.DOC/WRITE_CHECK
```

If a command takes a long time to execute, entering CTRL/T will display a one line status on the execution. Execution will not be interrupted. The status line displays the CPU time and I/Os performed. These should keep increasing every time CTRL/T is entered. A command execution can be aborted by CTRL/Y. If CTRL/Y is entered by mistake, execution can be resumed by entering the CONTINUE command.

Here's an example:

```
(Control-t display):
SCUBA::SHAH 15:07:38 VMSHELP   CPU=00:00:21.98 PF=4819 IO=236 MEM=623
```

The parameters displayed are nodename, process name, time, image name, CPU time used by the process, page faults, I/O count and working set size.

3.4 The Terminals

DEC terminals use the ASCII character set for communication with the host. The terminal-to-host communications protocol is RS232 or RS423. The two major types of terminals are hard-copy terminals like the DECwriter III (LA120) and video terminals like the VT300 series. DECwindow terminals also offer a VT terminal emulator that functions essentially as the standard VT terminals. The VT300 series terminals supersede the older VT200 and VT100 series terminals. These terminals have a screen display of 80 or 132 columns of 25 lines. The 25th line is used for status displays. The top 24 lines scroll up when new lines are displayed at the bottom of the screen. Fig. 3.2 shows the keyboard of a VT300 series terminal.

The VT420 supports all the features of a VT320 and, in addition, offers dual sessions and block mode data transfers (to reduce the number of interrupts generated on the host VAX). These terminals have a screen display of 80 or 132 columns of 25 lines. The 25th line is used for status displays. The top 24 lines scroll up when new lines are displayed at the bottom of the screen. The VT1000 series terminals are X-window terminals.

On the VT300 series terminal, the keys are classified into four groups:

1. Main keypad. This is similar to the keyboard on most other computer terminals. Some keys need special mention:
   Ctrl This key pressed with most other keys generates special codes. For example, pressing Ctrl, keeping it pressed and then pressing C gen-

erates the code 03. This two-key combination is written as CTRL/C.

Lock   Switches between uppercase and lowercase character mode for the alphabetic keys. The Lock indicator at the top right of the keyboard will be lit when the keyboard is in uppercase mode.

Compose Character   This key is used to generate extended ASCII characters. Typically, the compose key is pressed followed by two other keys to generate a code. It's used mainly to generate foreign language characters.

<X]   This key is at the top right of the keyboard. It's the DELETE key, usually used to delete the last character entered.

Conventionally, some of the control keys have special meanings:

CTRL/C   Abort the current application and exit.

CTRL/O   Continue program execution, but discard output sent to terminal. This feature is useful to stop verbose and useless output. Output continues when CTRL/O is pressed again.

CTRL/Q   Continue a display stopped by CTRL/S. An XOFF character is sent to the system by the terminal.

CTRL/S   Stop all display to the terminal. An XON character is sent to the system by the terminal. This is useful to "freeze" the screen to check what's displayed before allowing more information to be displayed. The HOLD-SCREEN key, F1, can also be used.

CTRL/T   Display a one-line summary of the process. For example, if you've issued the COPY command to copy a very large file, CTRL/T can be used every few seconds to see the CPU time going up. If the CPU time is not going up, there may be a problem with the copy operation or the system.

CTRL/U   Erase all characters entered up to the beginning of line.

CTRL/W   Refresh the screen if disturbed by, say, a power fluctuation.

CTRL/Y   Abort (interrupt) the current application and exit to DCL.

CTRL/Z   Exit from the current program.

2. Editing keypad. These keys are used by editors and screen-oriented forms and menus. The arrow keys are used by DCL also for command editing.

3. Numeric keypad. The keys PF1 to PF4 generate special codes. The other keys normally generate the codes displayed. Normally, the ENTER key is equivalent to the RETURN key. The numeric keypad can be programmed to transform into an application keypad. A different set of codes are generated when the keypad is in application mode. The keys are then interpreted in various ways, depending on the application.

4. Function keys. There are 20 of these, F1 to F20. F1 is the HOLD-SCREEN key. It's used to stop or continue a display that's scrolling up on the screen. F2 dumps the screen image to the printer port of the terminal. It's used to generate hard copies of displays. F3 is used to enter the

terminal SET-UP menu. The SET-UP menu allows you to change terminal characteristics like transmission speed and tab position settings. F4 is used to switch to the other session on dual session terminals like the VT330 and VT340. Note that the keys F1 to F4 don't send any codes to the computer. The F5 key generates the BREAK character, which is used by communications equipment. When the terminal is connected to terminal servers like the DECserver 200, 300 or 550, the BREAK key breaks the session temporarily and allows the terminal to issue DECserver commands. The session can be continued by the RESUME command issued to the DECserver.

The keys F6 to F20 generate codes that can be interpreted by the receiving application. Certain conventions are observed by most applications:

F6   is interpreted as CONTROL/C.

F10   is interpreted as EXIT (or CONTROL/Z).

F15   is used as a HELP key.

F16 (or DO)   is used to temporarily change the mode of operation. For example, the EVE editor changes the mode from text entry to command entry when the key is pressed.

3.5   Basic Commands

All DCL command and qualifier names can be abbreviated to the first four characters. Many commands and qualifiers can be abbreviated further if the name doesn't conflict with the abbreviation of a different command or qualifier. A complete DCL command is entered as:

```
$ cmdname /cmd_qual1/cmd_qual2...  parameter1/qual1/qual2...  parame
ter2...
```

Qualifiers to a parameter, or the command name can be specified in any order following the parameter or the command name. Most command name qualifiers can be specified anywhere on the command line.

3.5.1   TYPE

TYPE   is used to display the contents of one or more files. For example, to display files MY.DOC and PAYROLL.DATA the command is:

```
$ TYPE  MY.DOC,PAYROLL.DATA
```

or

```
$ TY  MY.DOC,PAYROLL.DATA
```

3.5.2 DIRECTORY

The DIRECTORY command is used to see the list of files in a directory on disk or tape. It displays the contents of the default directory on the default disk. If a disk name and/or directory is specified as a parameter, then the contents of that disk and/or directory is displayed. For example, to display the contents of directory [TEST] on the default disk, the command is:

```
$ DIR  [TEST]
```

The /SIZE qualifier lists the size of the specified files and the /DATE qualifier displays the creation dates of the files. For example:

```
$ DIR /SIZE /DATE      [BOOK]
Directory DUA5:[BOOK]
BOOK.INDEX;4   12      21-DEC-1990 04:22
SETHOST.LOG;2  7        3-MAR-1992 16:51
SETHOST.LOG;1 13        3-MAR-1992 16:43
START.DOC;3   17        3-MAR-1992 17:43
START.DOC;2   15        3-MAR-1992 17:32
START.DOC;1    2        3-MAR-1992 16:13
TMP.TMP;1      0        3-MAR-1992 17:44

Total of 6 files, 54 blocks.
```

Note that filenames are sorted in alphabetical order. Also, filenames contain a semicolon followed by a number called version. Typically, when a file is modified and written back by, say, the editor, a new version of the file is created. The new version is one higher than the old one. Version numbers are described in more detail later in this chapter.

3.5.3 COPY

The COPY command is used to make additional copies of files on disk or tape. For example, to copy MY.DOC to the directory [TEST] with a new name, YOUR.DOC the command is:

```
$ COPY  MY.DOC  [TEST]YOUR.DOC
```

3.5.4 RENAME

The RENAME command is used to change the names of existing files on disk. For example, to rename MY.DOC to JAY.DOC the command is:

```
$ RENAME  MY.DOC  JAY.DOC
```

The RENAME command is useful for moving a file from one directory to another. Move means to place the file in the new directory and remove it from the original directory. For example:

```
$ RENAME [APPLE]MY.DOC   [NEWDIR]MY.DOC
```

MY.DOC is removed from the directory [APPLE] and placed in the directory [NEWDIR]. In fact, this feature can be used to move a complete directory and its subdirectories. For example, suppose the directory [BOOK] is under the directory [PETER], and now it's to be removed from [PETER] and placed under the directory [SHANKER.PROJECTS]. The command would be:

```
$ RENAME [PETER]BOOK.DIR   [SHANKER.PROJECTS]BOOK.DIR
```

Now the directories and files that were under `[PETER.BOOK]` are accessed via the directory `[SHANKER.PROJECTS.BOOK]`.

Files cannot be moved from one disk to another using this command. The `COPY` command followed by the `DELETE` command will have to be used.

3.5.5 DELETE

The `DELETE` command is used to delete files. For example, the next command deletes version 2 of the file `MY.DOC`:

```
$ DELETE   MY.DOC;2
```

3.5.6 PURGE

Files on VAX/VMS have version numbers. When a file is edited, a new version of the file is created. The old version still exists. For example, editing `MY.DOC;8` (version 8 of `MY.DOC`) creates `MY.DOC;9`. If older versions are not deleted, many versions of files will exist on disk. Older versions should be periodically deleted to reduce cluttering of files and also to conserve disk space. The `DELETE` command can be used to delete files, but the `PURGE` command specifically deletes older versions of files. For example, to delete all except the latest version of the file `MY.DOC` the command is:

```
$ PURGE   MY.DOC
```

The `/KEEP:n` qualifier is useful for retaining the last n versions of a file. To delete all but the latest three versions of `MY.DOC`, the command is:

```
$ PURGE/KEEP:3   MY.DOC
```

or even,

```
$ PURGE   MY.DOC/KEEP:3
```

3.5.7 SET

The SET command is used to change various characteristics of the system or the current process. The SET PASSWORD command allows you to change your login password. The SET TIME command is used to change the system date and time. The command requires you to have OPER and LOG_IO privileges. The format for specifying time is:

```
dd-mmm-yyyy:hh:mm:ss.cc
```

where cc specifies hundredths of a second. Most of the fields are optional. Date fields not specified are filled in from the current date, while time fields not specified are set to zero. Examples:

```
$ SET   TIME=7-FEB-1990:18:30:15.12
$ SET   TIME=21-JAN-1992
$ SET   TIME=18:30
```

SET DEFAULT is used to change your defaults disk drive and/or directory. The defaults are used when accessing files on disks. For example:

```
$ SET   DEFAULT  DUB0:[TEST]
```

3.5.8 SHOW

The SHOW commands are used to display process or system characteristics. Commonly used SHOW commands are:

$ SHOW DEFAULT   displays the default disk and directory used when accessing files.

$ SHOW MEMORY   displays system memory usage statistics.

$ SHOW NETWORK   displays names and node-numbers of computers that the VAX can communicate with. If the node is not a router, only the current node name and its router node name are displayed.

$ SHOW PROCESS   displays process name, terminal name, process identification, default disk and directory, User Identification Code (UIC), and process priority. Additionally, the /ALL qualifier displays process quotas, accounting information, dynamic memory usage, privileges, and rights identifiers.

$ SHOW SYSTEM   displays all processes running in the system, along with their identification and resource usage information.

$ SHOW TIME   displays system data and time.

$ SHOW USERS   displays interactive users on the system (or cluster), along with their processes and terminal name.

3.5.9 `PRINT`

The `PRINT` command is used to queue files for printing. To print the files
`MY.DOC` and `YOUR.DOC`, the command is:

```
$ PRINT  MY.DOC,YOUR.DOC
```

The command has a number of qualifiers:

`/COPIES` number of printed copies of the file.
`/DELETE` delete the file after printing.
`/FLAG` print a banner page before printing the file.
`/FORM` use a specified form (paper type) to print the file. The list of forms
can be seen by `SHOW QUEUE/FORM`.
`/HEADER` print a header line on every page of output. The header contains the file name and page number.
`/PAGE` print specified pages of the file. For example, to print pages 5
through 20, the qualifier is `/PAGE:(5,20)`.
`/QUEUE` queue the file to a specified queue. Typically, each printer on the
system will have one associated queue. To see the queues on the system,
the command is `SHOW QUEUE`. If this qualifier is not specified, the file is
sent to the queue `SYS$PRINT`. For example:

```
$ PRINT  MY.DOC/COPIES=3/DELETE/FORM=LONG/QUEUE=LN03$PRINT
```

3.6 Command Editing

3.6.1 Command recall

DCL maintains a buffer for each terminal, where it stores up to 20 previously entered commands. These commands can be recalled, edited and re-executed. To recall all the commands use:

```
$ RECALL/ALL
```

To recall a particular command, say, the fifth one, use:

```
$ RECALL  5
```

The up and down arrow keys can also be used to scroll through the commands.

3.6.2 Editing the command line

Figure 3.3 lists the keys that are useful to edit the current or a recalled command line.

Key	Function
DELETE	Delete the last character entered
CTRL/A	Toggle between overstrike and insert modes. The mode applies to new characters entered on the command line.
left-arrow	Move cursor one character to the left.
CTRL/E	Move cursor to the end of line.
right-arrow	Move cursor one character to the right.
F12 or	Move cursor to the beginning of line.
CTRL/H or	
BS	
F13 or	Delete word to the left of the cursor.
CTRL/J	
CTRL/U	Delete all characters to the left of cursor.

Figure 3.3 Command line editing keys.

3.7 Error Messages

VAX/VMS software adheres to a convention for displaying error messages. The operating system, compilers, utilities and most other software display error messages in a uniform format. Here's an example of an error message when the TYPE command is not issued correctly:

```
$ TYPO   MY.DOC
%DCL-W-IVVERB, unrecognized command verb - check validity and spelling
\TYPO\
```

The syntax for a message is:

```
%FACILITY-L-IDENT, text
```

The fields are:

FACILITY   The name of the program issuing the message.
L   Severity level of the message:
  S - success
  I - informational
  W- warning
  E - error
  F - fatal or severe error

IDENT   Abbreviated description.
text   Description in plain English.

Note that messages can be merely informational or can depict successful operations; however, most messages are due to error conditions.

Here's an example of the TYPE command specifying a file that doesn't exist on disk:

```
$ TYPE ME.DOC
%TYPE-W-SEARCHFAIL, error searching for sys$SYSDEVICE:[SHAH]ME.DOC;
-RMS-E-FNF, file not found
```


3.8 Devices

Devices are usually attached to controllers, which are circuit boards in the CPU chassis (cabinet). A number of devices could be attached to one controller. An example of a device name is DUB2:. A device is identified as:

```
DDCnnn:
```

where

DD is the generic device name (sometimes this has three characters).
C is the controller designation.
nnn is the specific device on the controller.

Corresponding to controllers, the operating system has software device drivers. For example, the KDB50 disk controller consists of two boards that can be inserted in the backplane of a VAX 8700. This controller can handle up to four RA series disk drives. The generic device name of the disks is DU. The software device driver is called DUDRIVER. The controller is designated as "A." The four disks will be known as DUA0:, DUA1:, DUA2: and DUA3:. If another controller is added to the system, then it will be designated as "B" and the disks attached with this controller will be known as DUB0:, DUB1:, DUB2: and DUB3:. Figure 3.4 shows some devices and their mnemonic device names.

The system also supports software "devices." These have device drivers in the operating system but there's no hardware corresponding to them. An example is the mailbox device, MB, which is used for sending data from one process to another.

Device names on VAXcluster systems are preceded by the name of the computer on which the device resides, and a $ sign. For example:

```
SCUBA$DUB6: !VAXcluster device name for disk DUB6:
```

Device name	Device type	Typical devices
CS	Console floppy	RX02 floppy drive.
DJ	Disks	RA60 removable disk.
DU	Disks	RA90 fixed disk.
LI	Line printer	LP25 300 lines per minute line-printer.
LP	Line printer	LP29 2000 lines-per-minute line printer.
LT	LAT devices (terminals over Ethernet)	VT420 terminal or LN03 laser printer.
MU	Tapes	TA78 125 inch-per-second tape drive.
MS	Tapes	TU81-PLUS streaming tape drive.
MT	Tapes	TE16 tape drives.
MB	Mailbox (software device)	MBA12:
NET	Network communications (software device)	NET4:
NL	NULL device (software device)	
OP	Operator console (software device)	
TT	Terminals	VT420 terminal
TX	Terminals	VT420 terminal
VT	Virtual terminal (software device)	VTA2:
XE	Ethernet	DEBNT controller for VAXBI bus. Connects to Ethernet cable.
XQ	Ethernet	DELQA controller for Qbus bus. Connects to Ethernet cable.

Figure 3.4 Common devices on VAX/VMS.

3.9 Files

Here are some examples of file specifications:

```
SCUBA::DUA4:[TEST]PAYROLL.COB;27
SCUBA::PAYROLL.COB
DUA4:PAYROLL.COB
[TEST]PAYROLL.COB
PAYROLL.COB;-2
123_LONG_FILE_NAME.LONG_FILE_TYPE
```

Files can be created on disk or tape devices. The file specification syntax is:

```
nodename::device:[directory]filename.filetype;version
```

Fields not specified assume default values. Default values depend on the command used to operate on the file. Generally, if version number is not specified, then the latest version is assumed. Nodename is the computer on which the file resides. If it's not specified, the node is assumed to be the VAX you're currently using.

Each process has a default device and directory. These are specified by the system manager in the user authorization file. When specifying filenames, if the device and directory are not specified, the default values are assumed. To see the defaults use SHOW DEFAULT. To change the defaults use SET DEFAULT. For example:

```
$ SET  DEFAULT  DJA2:[TEST.PROGRAMS]
```

Usually, filename and filetype have no default values. Each of these fields can be up to 39 characters long.

Version numbers start at 1 and can go up to 32767. When not specified, it's assumed to be the latest version number. Version numbers are an extension of the .BAK method used on smaller computers for keeping previous versions of files. The latest version of the file can also be referred to as version 0. Versions can be specified going backwards, starting at the latest version, by using a minus sign before the version. For example, if a file has 12 versions, then version -1 is the same as version 11.

3.9.1 Wildcards

Suppose you want to create another copy of all the files in your directory that have a filetype of COB. The next command copies all the COB files in your directory to the directory [BACKUP]:

```
$ COPY  *.COB  [BACKUP]*.
```

The * is called a wildcard. It will match files with any filename and filetype of COB. Wildcards are used to select a subset of files. The percent sign, %, is another wildcard. It matches any single character at the position specified. The ... wildcard is used to search for files in all subdirectories of the specified subdirectory. Usually, wildcards can be used wherever a filespec is required in DCL commands. Wildcards are not valid on node names, and the percent wildcard is not valid on version numbers.

Here are some examples of file specifications with wildcards:

PAYROLL.COB;*	All versions of PAYROLL.COB.
.;*	All files in the default device and directory.
PAY%.COB	Files having four characters in the filename with the first three characters PAY and filetype as COB.
PAY*.COB	Files having the first three characters as PAY in the filename, and filetype as COB.
P*LL.COB	Files having filenames starting with P and ending with LL, and filetype as COB.
[*]PAYROLL.COB	PAYROLL.COB files in all directories on the default disk.
[TEST...]PAYROLL.COB	PAYROLL.COB files in the [TEST] directory, and all subdirectories of [TEST].

3.10 The Process

A *process* is the environment in which a program image executes. A number of processes are created when the system is brought up. Normally, the operating system creates a process for each user that's logged in. Processes can also be created by users.

The operating system maintains a list of parameters that define the environment in which each process is running. The SHOW PROCESS command displays some of the process parameters. The /ALL qualifier displays a more complete list of parameters. Figure 3.5 shows a sample use of the command.

Figure 3.5 SHOW PROCESS output.

```
$ SHOW  PROCESS /ALL
  5-JAN-1992 12:44:33.42                    User: SCOTT

Pid: 0000023D   Proc. name: SCOTT_2        UIC: [BOOKS,SCOTT]

Priority:   4   Default file spec: DUA3:[SCOTT.MEMO]

Devices mounted: DUB6:
Process Quotas:

 Account name: SCOTT

 CPU limit:                     Infinite  Direct I/O limit:     20000
Process Quotas:
```

Figure 3.5 *(Continued)*

```
Buffered I/O byte count quota:    108880  Buffered I/O limit:   20000

Timer queue entry quota:            1000  Open file quota:        995

Paging file quota:                 17533  Subprocess quota:         9

Default page fault cluster:           64  AST limit:              198

Enqueue quota:                      1000  Shared file limit:      900

Max detached processes:                0  Max active jobs:          0

Accounting information:

  Buffered I/O count:       138  Peak working set size:     388

  Direct I/O count:           9  Peak virtual size:        2467

  Page faults:              373  Mounted volumes:             0

  Images activated:           1

  Elapsed CPU time:       0 00:00:00.41

  Connect time:           0 00:00:09.05

Process privileges:

  CMKRNL              may change mode to kernel

  DETACH              may create detached processes

  ALTPRI              may set any priority value

  OPER                operator privilege

  EXQUOTA             may exceed quota

  SYSGBL              may create system wide global sections

  SHMEM               may create/delete objects in shared memory

  SHARE               may assign channels to non-shared device

  READALL             may read anything as the owner

Process rights identifiers:

  INTERACTIVE

  LOCAL

Process Dynamic Memory Area

      Current Size (bytes)      25600  Current Total Size (pages)      50

      Free Space (bytes)        21768  Space in Use (bytes)          3832

      Size of Largest Block     21712  Size of Smallest Block          16

      Number of Free Blocks         3  Free Blocks LEQU 32 Bytes        1

Processes in this tree:

SCOTT

  SCOTT_2 (*)
```

The display consists of seven groups:

- Summary of process.

- Quotas of system resources available to the process. This information is from the user authorization file (UAF).

- Accounting information. This group displays a summary of resource usage.

- Privileges the process owns. Privileges are generally required to access resources not assigned to you. For example, the READALL privilege allows you to read files that are owned by other users. There are about 30 privileges that can be assigned to each user by the system administrator.

- Rights Identifiers that the process owns. These are privileges that allow you to access objects like files and memory sections that are protected by these rights.

- Summary of memory use by the process.

- Subprocesses created by the top-level process using the SPAWN command. These processes normally inherit the parent's process parameters. The ATTACH command can be used to attach the terminal to any one of these processes. In this case, the process SCOTT created the subprocess SCOTT_2. The symbol (*) indicates that SCOTT_2 is the current process.

3.11   Operating System Basics

When you log into the system, a process is created that controls your terminal. The name of the process is the same as your username. More than one process in the system can have the same name, but each process has a unique identification number called PID. The RUN/DETACH command can be used to create additional processes. The process named JOB_CONTROL on many systems is a detached process that controls batch and print jobs. In fact, your process is a detached process created by the operating system when you log in.

The SHOW SYSTEM command displays the processes on the system. Figure 3.6 shows a sample use of the command. The SHOW USER command displays users logged in from terminals. Figure 3.7 shows a sample use of the command.

The SWAPPER process is created by the operating system. SWAPPER handles process swapping to and from disk when there are many processes on the system and not enough main memory, or when restructuring processes in memory. ERRFMT formats and logs errors like device malfunctions. EVL (Event Logger) formats and logs network errors. NETACP handles file access on other computers on the network. REMACP controls user logins on this system from other systems on the network. VAXsim_monitor performs system integrity checks and reports degradation in system perfor-

```
$ SHOW SYSTEM


VAX/VMS V5.4-2  on node SCUBA 4-JAN-1992 15:33:40.96   Uptime   5 19:18:05

  Pid     Process Name   State  Pri    I/O        CPU        Page flts Ph.Mem

00000081 SWAPPER          HIB   16      0     0 00:01:00.58       0      0

00000084 ERRFMT           HIB    8    5907    0 00:00:13.07      70    100

00000085 OPCOM            LEF    9    3060    0 00:00:08.29   11536    149

00000086 JOB_CONTROL      HIB    9    2983    0 00:00:06.24     129    260

00000087 VAXsim_Monitor   HIB    8    1560    0 00:00:03.46     345    204

00000088 NETACP           HIB   10   48295    0 00:12:36.72     401    301

00000089 EVL              HIB    6     293    0 00:00:00.90  123672     54  N

0000008A REMACP           HIB    9      63    0 00:00:00.11      77     53

0000008B SYMBIONT_0001    HIB    6      31    0 00:00:00.22     349    306

000001B2 _LTA63:          LEF    7    8486    0 00:02:16.65   77765   1000

000001B4 JANE             LEF    4  246446    0 00:39:15.96  568988    928

000001C1 SCOTT_1          CUR    4     148    0 00:00:00.41     355    370

000001C2 SCOTT            HIB    4   12018    0 00:00:26.42    4222   1271
```

Figure 3.6 SHOW SYSTEM output.

mance and devices. SYMBIONT processes send output from queues to printers connected to the system. OPCOM intercepts output for operators from the operating system and user processes. The output is sent to terminals designated as operator consoles and optionally logged to a disk file. The default disk log file is SYS$MANAGER:OPERATOR.LOG. The only other executable unit on the system is the operating system.

```
$ SHOW   USERS
           VAX/VMS Interactive Users
           4-JAN-1992 15:43:45.22
   Total number of interactive users = 3
 Username     Process Name     PID     Terminal
 JANE          _LTA67:       000001B4  LTA67:
 SCOTT         _LTA63:       000001B2  LTA63:
 SCOTT         SCOTT         000001C2  LTA70:
```

Figure 3.7 SHOW USERS output.

The two commands have given some other information. The system was up for more than five days. Process priority can be from 0 to 31. Lower priority processes get CPU time only if higher priority processes don't require it. User processes usually execute at priority 4. CPU and I/O use is displayed for each process. The other columns are explained in later chapters. User SCOTT has logged into the system from two terminals. The first time a user logs in, the operating system creates a process with the USERNAME of the user. Further logins by the same user create processes with the name of the terminal from where the login is performed, preceded by an underscore. The process with PID 000001C1 was created by the SPAWN command issued from the process SCOTT. The SPAWN command can be used to create a tree of subprocesses. The name of a spawned process is formed by using the process name of the top level process, followed by the underscore and a digit.

The SHOW MEMORY command displays a summary on system memory usage. Figure 3.8 shows a sample use of the command.

```
$ SHOW  MEMORY

              System Memory Resources on   4-JAN-1992 16:32:39.67

Physical Memory Usage (pages):     Total       Free       In Use     Modified

  Main Memory (32.00Mb)            65536       45379       19891         266

Slot Usage (slots):                Total       Free     Resident      Swapped

  Process Entry Slots                 70         44          26            0

  Balance Set Slots                   59         35          24            0

Fixed-Size Pool Areas (packets):   Total       Free       In Use        Size

Small Packet (SRP) List             826         93         733           96

I/O Request Packet (IRP) List       522        158         364          208

Large Packet (LRP) List              60          0          60         1584

Dynamic Memory Usage (bytes):      Total       Free       In Use     Largest

  Nonpaged Dynamic Memory         3072000     722528     2349472      703248

  Paged Dynamic Memory            276992       59008      217984       55584

Paging File Usage (pages):                     Free       In Use       Total

  DISK$FEDBEDISK:[SYS0.SYSEXE]SWAPFILE.SYS    39536       10464        50000

  DISK$FEDBEDISK:[SYS0.SYSEXE]PAGEFILE.SYS    83338        6662        90000

Of the physical pages in use, 10620 pages are permanently allocated to VMS.
```

Figure 3.8 SHOW MEMORY output.

The display indicates that about 69 percent (45379/65536) of main memory is unused. The process entry slots specify the number of processes that can be created on the system. The balance set slots specify the number of processes that can be in memory. If more processes than the maximum are created, some processes will be swapped out onto disk. Processes may also be swapped out if there's not enough physical memory to accommodate all the processes. The fixed-size pool areas contain fixed- size slots of memory which are used when quick allocation and deallocation of small chunks of memory are required. Dynamic Memory is where the processes and most of the operating system resides. Only a part of the operating system is in static memory. The paging files are used for swapped-out processes and pages. These files must be created using the SYSGEN procedure, and they must be large enough to accommodate any swapping and paging space requirements of the operating system.

The SHOW DEVICES command displays a summary of devices on the system, as shown in Fig. 3.9. It's useful to find out which devices are mounted, free space on disks, which devices are allocated to processes, and the number of device malfunction errors on devices.

The error count gives the number of errors that have occurred while accessing the device. Error details can be displayed by creating an error report using the command ANALYZE/ERROR. Devices having the alloc status are for exclusive use of the process that has issued the ALLOCATE command for the device. The devices are grouped by disks, tapes, terminals, printers and others. Further details on devices, like total disk space on a disk, can be displayed by using the /FULL qualifier. Figure 3.10 shows a sample use of the command.

The /FILES qualifier is useful for finding out all the files currently being accessed from a disk. Figure 3.11 shows a sample use of the command.

The MONITOR utility is a useful tool for observing system behavior. It sends output to a file or displays it to your terminal updating the information at specified intervals (by default, every 3 seconds). Figure 3.12 shows some examples of MONITOR use.The qualifiers are:

TOPCPU qualifier lists the processes that are consuming the most CPU time.

TOPDIO displays processes performing the most I/O, mainly to disks and tapes.

TOPBIO displays processes performing the most I/O, mainly to terminals, printers and over the network to other computers.

3.12 Conventions

Certain conventions need to be mentioned here because they're pervasive throughout software products for VMS.

```
$ SHOW  DEVICES


Device              Device         Error    Volume        Free  Trans Mnt
  Name              Status         Count    Label        Blocks Count Cnt
DJA1:               Mounted           0    SYSDEVICE     23697      4   1
DUA3:               Mounted           0    DEVELOP      342270    112   1
DUB2:               Online            0
DUB3:               Mounted           0    DEVELOP2    1057755      1   1


Device              Device         Error    Volume        Free  Trans Mnt
  Name              Status         Count    Label        Blocks Count Cnt
MUA0:               Online           92


Device              Device         Error
  Name              Status         Count
LTA0:               Offline           0
LTA23:              Online            0
OPA0:               Online            0
TXA7:               Online alloc      0


Device              Device         Error
  Name              Status         Count
LIA0:               Online alloc      0


Device              Device         Error
  Name              Status         Count
ETA0:               Online            0
PTA0:               Online            2
PUA0:               Online            1
```

Figure 3.9 SHOW DEVICES output.

3.12.1 Prompts and qualifiers

Utilities and other software products issue a prompt consisting of a few characters followed by >. Examples are:

```
UAF>      !issued by the AUTHORIZE utility
SYSGEN>   !issued by the SYSGEN utility
```

```
MAIL>     !issued by the MAIL utility
INSTALL> !issued by the INSTALL utility
```

The HELP command can be entered to see how to use the utility. Almost all the software products have the HELP facility. Commands entered at the prompt are analyzed by the utility. Many utilities will accept commands stored in another file. To execute command files, enter the file name preceded by the @ sign:

```
INSTALL> @INSCMD.COM
```

Control-Z is usually valid to exit from utilities.

Command qualifiers are specified after the command with the / sign. For example:

```
$ DIR/FULL
```

```
$ SHOW  DEVICE  DUB3:  /FULL

Disk DUB3:, device type RA82, is online, mounted, file-oriented device,
    shareable, available to cluster, error logging is enabled.


    Error count                0    Operations completed              64603

    Owner process             ""    Owner UIC               [SYSTEM,TEST]

    Owner process ID    00000000    Dev Prot    S:RWED,O:RWED,G:RWED,W:RWED

    Reference count            1    Default buffer size                 512

    Total blocks         1216665    Sectors per track                    57

    Total cylinders         1423    Tracks per cylinder                  15


    Volume label       "DEVELOP2"   Relative volume number                0

    Cluster size               3    Transaction count                     1

    Free blocks          1057755    Maximum files allowed            152083

    Extend quantity            5    Mount count          .                1

    Mount status          System    Cache name            "_DUA4:XQPCACHE"

    Extent cache size         64    Maximum blocks in extent cache   105768

    File ID cache size        64    Blocks currently in extent cache  50916

    Quota cache size           0    Maximum buffers in FCP cache        273


Volume status:  subject to mount verification, file high-water marking, write-
    through caching enabled.
```

Figure 3.10 SHOW DEVICES/FULL output.

```
$ SHOW  DEVICE  DUB3:  /FILES


Files accessed on device _DUB3: on  5-JAN-1992 12:35:37.46

Process name      PID       File name
                  00000000  [000000]INDEXF.SYS;1
SCOTT             000001B2  [SCOTT.DAT]TST_MESSAGES.DATA;1
SCOTT             000001B2  [SCOTT.DAT]SECURITY_FILE.DATA;1
SCOTT             000001B2  [SCOTT.TEST]POSITION_FILE.TEST;1
_LTA67:           000001B4  [JANE.DOC]MASTER_TABLE.DOCUMENT;1
```

Figure 3.11 SHOW DEVICES / FILES output.

Figure 3.12 MONITOR output.

```
$ MONITOR := $MONITOR            !required to use the monitor command


$ MONITOR  PROCESS/TOPCPU
                         VAX/VMS Monitor Utility
                         TOP CPU TIME PROCESSES
                            on node SCUBA::
                          10-JAN-1992 11:54:20


                           0        25       50       75      100
                           + - - - + - - - - + - - - + - - - -+
00000157  ANGELO         29 ***********
                           |         |        |        |        |
00000158  JULIE          17 ******
                           |         |        |        |        |
00000156  _RTA1:          1
                           |         |        |        |        |
0000010D  VPA_DC
                           |         |        |        |        |

                           |         |        |        |        |
```

Figure 3.12 *(Continued)*

```
                              |        |         |         |          |

                           + - - - + - - - - + - - - - + - - - - -+



$ MONITOR  PROCESS/TOPDIO
                         VAX/VMS Monitor Utility
                      TOP DIRECT I/O RATE PROCESSES
                          on node SCUBA::
                        10-JAN-1992 11:54:36


                              0        5        10        15        20
                           + - - - + - - - - + - - - - + - - - - -+
00000158  JULIE            12  ***********************
                              |        |         |         |          |
00000157  ANGELO           11  *********************
                              |        |         |         |          |


                              |        |         |         |          |


                              |        |         |         |          |


                              |        |         |         |          |
                              |        |         |         |          |


                              |        |         |         |          |

                           + - - - + - - - - + - - - - + - - - - -+



$ MONITOR  PROCESS/TOPBIO
                         VAX/VMS Monitor Utility
                      TOP BUFFERED I/O RATE PROCESSES
                          on node SCUBA::
```

Figure 3.12 *(Continued)*

```
                                    0       5      10      15      20
                                    + - - - + - - - + - - - + - - - -+

 00000158   JULIE             12    ************************
                                    I       I       I       I       I

 00000146   _LTA12:            9    ******************
                                    I       I       I       I       I

 00000156   _RTA1:             8    ****************
                                    I       I       I       I       I

 00000157   ANGELO             2    ****
                                    I       I       I       I       I
 00000140   O115               1    **
                                    I       I       I       I       I

 00000106   JOB_CONTROL        1    **
                                    I       I       I       I       I


                                    I       I       I       I       I


                                    + - - - + - - - + - - - + - - - -+
```

or

```
SYSGEN>SHOW /DRIVER
```

Command and qualifier names can usually be shortened as long as they're unique. For example, the MOUNT command can be shortened to MOU, but not to MO, because there's another command which starts with MO, the MONITOR command.

3.12.2 Execution status

To abort any running application, press the Control-Y key. DCL will be ready to accept the next command. If Control-Y was pressed by mistake, use the CONTINUE command to continue execution of the application.

When running any interactive application that doesn't display any data for a long time, the user at a terminal may want to be reassured that the application is running and not just "hung." Pressing Control-T causes a one-line status of CPU time, I/Os completed, and so on, to be displayed. The application continues normal execution. Control-T output is effective only after the following command is issued:

```
$ SET CONTROL=T
```

3.12.3 Time format

Date and time have to be specified in many commands. The standard format is

```
dd-mmm-yyyy:hh:mm:ss.ss
```

Most of the fields are optional. Examples are:

```
21-feb-1990:14:10
8:15              (8:15 am today)
31-jan-1990       (time is midnight of the date)
```

In most cases, the keywords YESTERDAY, TODAY or TOMORROW can also be specified. An example is:

```
$ DIRECTORY /SINCE:YESTERDAY
```

3.13 VMS Manuals

Basic documentation for VMS consists of the following kits:

- Base set. Overview of VMS, basic commands, system management and license management.
- General User Subkit. VMS basics, DCL, editors and system messages.
- System Management Subkit. System maintenance, security, performance and networking.
- Programming Subkit. Programming utilities (like debugger and linker), system routines, file system, system programming, device support and MACRO.

Other VMS documentation is on obsolete features and (new version) release notes. Each VAX has system-specific installation and operations manuals. Some other manuals are on RMS Journaling, Volume Shadowing, Parallel Programming and Layered Product Development.

VAX C documentation consists of two binders: "Guide to VAX C" and "Run Time Library Reference Manual." Each software-layered product has its own set of manuals, usually including a guide and a reference set. Hardware products also have separate manuals. A number of handbooks are also available.

4

VAX C Program Structure

Functions are building blocks of C programs. A complete program's functions can be compiled separately. The program-executable image is created by linking these functions, and functions in turn consist of blocks of statements. Syntactically, statements are made up of elements called *lexical tokens*. *Macros* are lines of text within C programs that are actually instructions to the compiler. The C preprocessor processes lines of text, which are instructions to the compiler rather than formal C language code. These topics are all discussed in this chapter.

4.1 Overall Structure

Here's the structure of a complete C program:

```
[external declarations]
[functions]

main()
{
[local declarations]
[statements];
}

[functions]
```

The elements between square brackets are optional. Here are some examples of complete programs.

Example 1: a simple program with variable number1 declared outside any function. In this example, the variable could have been declared within main().

```
int number1;

main()
{
number1 = 5;
printf("%d",number1);
}
```

Example 2: this program has two functions, main() and multiply(), in which main() calls multiply().

```
int multiply(int n1,int n2) /* function multiply */
{ return(n1*n2);
}

main()
{
int number1,number2,number3;

number1 = 5; number2 = 12;
number3 = multiply(number1,number2);
printf("%d",number3);
}
```

Example 3: this program is similar to the preceding one, except that the function multiply() is defined after main(). The function prototype (described later in this chapter) for multiply is required by the compiler to determine the datatypes of arguments and return value so that the appropriate conversions and checks can be performed when the call to multiply is encountered in main().

```
int number1,number2;

int multiply(int n1, int n2);    /* function prototype */
main() { int number3;

number1 = 5; number2 = 12;
number3 = multiply(number1,number2);    /* main program calls */
     /* function multiply */ printf("%d",number);
}

multiply(n1,n2) /* function multiply */
int n1,n2;
{
return(n1*n2);
}
```

Functions can't be nested. Library functions can be called from functions within the C program. To aid the compiler in data conversion of parameters, function prototypes should be included at the beginning of the C program.

4.2 Tokens

The compiler reads the input source file and converts the string of input characters into tokens. Examples of tokens are:

```
=
:=
==
int
number1
"abc xyz"
12.86
```

There are six classes of tokens: *identifiers*, *keywords*, *constants*, *strings*, *operators* and other *separators*. Blanks, tabs, new lines and comments are called *white spaces*. White spaces serve as token separators. They're ignored by the compiler, except when encountered within quoted strings.

4.3 Comments

Comments are enclosed within /* and */. They should be freely used as, in reality, most C programs tend to be difficult to read, compared to programs in languages like COBOL and PASCAL. Comments can't be nested.

Question 4.1: What are the advantages and disadvantages of allowing nesting of comments in a language? How would you comment out a block of code of about 50 lines that contain comments interspersed with C code?

4.4 Statements

A string of characters terminated by a semicolon is a statement in C.

4.5 Declarations

A declaration informs the C compiler about one or more identifiers and their characteristics. For example,

```
char ch1 = 'k';
```

is parsed to mean that ch1 is a character variable, and it has an initial value of 'k' (hexadecimal 6B). The compiler will allocate storage for this variable.

4.6 Identifiers and Keywords

Identifiers are names for constants, variables, functions and built-in keywords. VAX C identifiers can consist of letters, digits, a dollar sign ($) and the underscore character. The first character can't be a digit. Keywords that are shown in the following can't be redeclared. Conventionally, VAX C uses underscore as the first character of an identifier whose value is implementation specific. Some guidelines are:

- Identifiers can be up to 255 characters in length, but the LINKER uses only the first 31 characters. Moreover, ANSI C considers only the first 31 digits significant. Hence, it's recommended that identifiers be no longer than 31 characters.

- Variables should use lowercase characters only; constants should use uppercase characters only.

- All identifiers are passed to the LINKER with uppercase characters. Don't use identifiers that are the same when all characters are converted to uppercase.

- Don't use underscore as the first character.

- A dollar sign should be used within identifiers only for VMS global symbols.

VAX C keywords are identifiers that have specific meaning and usage. Unlike all other identifiers, they can't be redeclared. The keywords are also known as reserved words. Here are the VAX C keywords:

_align	auto	break
case	char	const
continue	default	do
double	else	enum
extern	float	for
globaldef	globalref	globalvalue
goto	if	int
long	noshare	register
readonly	return	sizeof
short	static	struct
switch	typedef	union
unsigned	variant_struct	variant_union
volatile	volatile	void

4.7   A Block

A *block* is zero or more statements enclosed within braces. Blocks can be nested. Here's a block with a block within:

```
{
int number1,number2;
number2 = number1 + 23;
  {
  int number3;
  number3 = number2 + number1;
  printf("%d\n",number3);
  }
printf("%d\n",number2);
}
```

A block is also known as a *compound statement*. The body of every function is a compound statement. All declarative statements within the block must precede any executable statement in a block. The scope of the variable is the block in which it's defined; once you exit the block, the variable can't be used. You'll notice most variable declarations at the start of function bodies in programs. A variable used in just a few statements within a function, like number3 in the block shown previously, can be declared locally within a nested block, as done in the example. This may be a good programming practice, but, in reality, programmers declare most variables at the top of the function rather than create local blocks for such variables. The two blocks in the previous example are equivalent to this single block:

```
{
int number1,number2,number3;
number2 = number1 + 23;
number3 = number2 + number1;
printf("%d\n",number3);
printf("%d\n",number2);
}
```

Note that declarations can be made outside blocks. The scope of variables is from the place of declaration to the end of the file. This program prints 4, then 7:

```
int a=4;      /* outside any block */


main()
{
printf("%d\n",a);
func1();
}
int b=7;      /* outside any block */

func1()
{
printf("%d\n",b);
}
```

4.8   Statement Types

4.8.1   Expressions and simple statements

Simple statements can be used as expressions (after removing the terminating semicolon), and expressions can be used as statements (after adding a semicolon). For example, the expression i++ can be used in a statement as:

```
i++;
```

When a = b is used in a statement, the value of b replaces the value of a:

```
a = b;
```

If a = b is used as an expression, the value of b replaces the value of a, and the expression then evaluates to the new value of a:

```
c = 4 + (a = b);
```

Question: Is this a valid statement?

```
c = a = b;
```

If before execution a, b, and c were 1, 2, and 3, what would their values be afterwards?

A block (compound statement) cannot be used as an expression:

```
a = {c=d;e=f;} /* illegal */
```

4.8.1.1 The comma operator. A statement can consist of comma-separated substatements without the semicolon. For example, this is one statement:

```
a = b, b = c;
```

The statement a = b is evaluated before b = c. Such statements are commonly found in loop test expressions of for, while and do statements.

4.8.2 The if statement

The if statement executes a statement if an expression evaluates to a nonzero value. Optionally, there may be an else part.

```
if (expression) statement
```

or

```
if (expression) statement else statement
```

Very often, statement in the if statements is actually a block of statements. For example:

```
if (a == b) printf("a and b are equal");

if (1) printf("This line always printed");

if (a == b) printf("a and b are equal");
else printf("a and are not equal");

if (a == b)
  {
  printf("a and b are equal\n");
  printf("This is a compound statement, if part");
  } /* Note, no semicolon here */
else
  {
  printf("a and b are not equal\n");
  printf("This is a compound statement, else part");
  };
```

Question: What's the difference between "a = b" and "a == b"?
Question: Consider the statement:

```
if (a = b) printf("Wrong?");
```

The expression, a = b, is an assignment statement. What does it evaluate to? Does the value of a change?

4.8.3 The switch statement

The switch statement executes one or more cases, depending on the condition of the expression.

```
switch ( expression ) statement
```

The switch statement is similar to the case statement of Pascal. For example:

```
int i;
switch ( i )
  {
  case 1:  printf("i is 1\n"); break;
  case 2:  printf("i is 2\n"); break;
  case 5:  printf("i is 5\n"); break;
  default: printf("i is not 1, 2 or 5\n"); break;
  }
```

The switch expression is evaluated and compared with the case expressions sequentially. If a match is found, the statements following the case label are executed. Execution continues right through further case statements unless a break or a similar control statement alters the flow of execution. The control statement break causes execution to continue after the switch statement. Other possible control statements are goto, return (if in a function), or continue (if in a loop). The default is executed if no case expression matches the switch expression. Each case expression must evaluate to a constant value during compilation. Nothing is executed if the switch expression doesn't match any case expression and there's no default.

Question: What's the output of this program?

```
main()
{
int i=2;
switch ( i )
  {
  case 1: printf("i is 1\n");
  case 2: printf("i is 2\n");
  case 5: printf("i is 5\n");
  }
}
```

4.8.4 The for statement

The for statement is useful for executing a set of statements a specified number of times.

```
for ( expression-1; expression-2; expression-3) statement
```

The expression-1 is evaluated once before the loop iterations begin. Typically, it specifies an initial value for a variable. The expression-2 is evaluated before each iteration. The loop is terminated if the expression evaluates to false (zero), or else the body of the loop is executed. The expression-3 is executed after each iteration. Typically, it increments a variable's value. The loop can also be exited by a break, goto or return (if in a function) statement. For example:

```
/* Loop prints the integers 1 through 50 *
/ for (i=1; i <= 50; i++) printf("%d\n",i);

/* Loop prints 50 values: 2, 4, 6 ... */
for (i=1,j=2; i <= 50; i++,j=j+2)
  {
  printf("%d\n");
  k = k + j;
  };
```

Question: What, if anything, gets printed by this statement?

```
for (;;) printf("Loop\n");
```

Question: What gets printed by this statement?

```
for (i=1; i <= 50; printf("%d\n",i), i++);
```

Question: Is this statement legal?

```
for (i=1; i <= 50; {int j;j=5;printf("%d\n",j+i);} );
```

4.8.5 The while statement

The while statement evaluates a specified expression, and if the expression is nonzero, the following statement is executed. The process is repeated until the expression evaluates to a zero.

```
while ( expression ) statement
```

The statement, called the *loop body*, is typically a compound statement. The loop can be interrupted by a break, goto or return (if in a function) statement. An example is:

```
i=0; found=0;
while ( (!found) && (i<10) )
   {
   if (array_values[i] == 35) found = 1;
   else i++;
   };
```

4.8.6 The do statement

The do statement executes a statement and then tests a while expression. If the expression evaluates to a nonzero value, the statement is executed again. The expression test and the execution of the expression continues until the expression evaluates to zero. The do statement resembles the while statement, except that the do statement body is executed at least once, and the while statement body may not be executed at all.

```
do statement while (expression );
```

For example:

```
i=0; found=0;
do
   {
   if (array_values[i] == 35) found = 1;
   else i++;
```

```
  }
while ( (!found) && (i<10) );
```

4.8.7 The break and continue statements

The break statements terminate the immediately enclosing switch, for, while, or do statement. Control passes to the statement following the loop body. For example:

```
while (i<10)
  {
  if (array_values[i] == 35) {found = 1; break};
  else i++;
  };
```

The continue statement passes control to the end of the enclosing for, while or do statement. The loop execution continues at the next iteration of the loop.

4.8.8 The label and goto statements

The label statement is used to identify a location for a goto statement.

```
identifier:
.
.
.
goto identifier
```

4.8.9 The null statement

The null statement is one that has only one character in it—the semicolon. The null statement can be used in a location where a statement is required, but nothing needs to be done. For example, this for loop initializes each element of a 25-element array to a value of 67. The body of the for loop is a null statement.

```
for (i=0; i<25; int_array[i++] = 67) ;
```

Question: This question illustrates a common mistake. If a=5 and b=7, what output is generated by the following two lines of valid C code?

```
if (a>b) printf("a greater than b\n");
if (a>b); printf("a greater than b\n");
```

4.9 Functions

Functions allow for modular programming. FUNCTIONs and SUBROU-TINEs of FORTRAN and *Functions* and *Procedures* of Pascal are all represented by *functions* in C. If a set of statements perform one logical task, then it should be put in a function. Function declarations can't be nested; a function declaration can't exist within another function declaration. This may reduce program complexity, but then C can't be called a block-structured language.

Some reasons for using functions are:

- A long main program is less readable than a small main program and a set of functions.

- A function may be appropriate if a similar set of statements are used at various places in the same program.

- A function highlights the fact that the enclosed statements are performing a closely related operation.

- Functions can be compiled separately from main programs and other functions, which allows for sharing of common routines, creation of function libraries, and uncluttered main programs. The VAX C Run Time Library is a collection of functions.

- Appropriate functions make an application easily maintainable.

- Functions are required for recursion.

4.9.1   Function usage

Here's a function that checks an integer and returns a character, +, −, or 0, depending on whether the integer is positive, negative, or 0:

```
char sign_of_int(input_int)
int input_int;
{
if (input_int < 0) return '-';
else if (input_int > 0) return '+';
else return '0';
}
```

The first two lines are the function header; the block enclosed between braces is the body of the function. The function `sign_of_int` is a character function, meaning it returns a character value. It has one parameter of type int. The value of a function is returned by:

```
return expression;
```

The function can be called, as in:

```
char sign_of_x;
int x;
sign_of_x = sign_of_int(x);
```

Note that there's no special CALL statement as found in COBOL and FORTRAN. The function is used as an expression in an assignment statement. Functions can also be used as statements. Consider the previous function rewritten so that rather than returning a value for the function, a parameter value is passed back.

```
sign_of_int(input_int, int_sign)
int input_int;
char int_sign;
{
if (input_int < 0) int_sign = '-';
else if (input_int > 0) int_sign = '+';
else int_sign = '0';
}
```

This function can be called, as in:

```
char sign_of_x;
int x;
sign_of_int(x, sign_of_x);
```

In many other languages like FORTRAN and Pascal, this form of a C function is called a subroutine or procedure. The function could have been called by a statement like:

```
var1 = sign_of_int(x, sign_of_x);
```

This is a valid statement, although it's likely to be a programmer's coding error. A better coding practice is to declare the function header as:

```
void sign_of_int(input_int, int_sign)
```

The word void signifies that the function doesn't return a value. The compiler then generates unfriendly messages when the function is used as an expression in an assignment statement.

4.9.2 Function parameters

Up to 253 parameters can be specified in parentheses after the function name. In the function declaration, the parameters are called formal arguments. In a function call, the parameters are called actual arguments. Some authors refer to the names in the function declarations as parameters and the names in the function calls as arguments. We will use the later convention.

The data type of each parameter must be specified following the closing parenthesis, as in:

```
char func(para1,para2)
int para1;
char para2;
```

```
{
...  /* function body */
}
```

Or, the data type can be specified in the parameter list, preceding each parameter name:

```
char func( int para1, char para2)
{
...  /* function body */
}
```

If a function has no parameters, the function can be declared as:

```
char func()
{
...  /* function body */
}
```

However, for compile-time type checking, it's better to write the function as:

```
char func(void)
{
...  /* function body */
}
```

Then, if the function is being inadvertently called with a parameter, the compiler will generate a warning message.

Question: All such forms of function headers

```
func()
```

should be replaced with

```
void func(void)
```

Why?

4.9.2.1 Parameters are values.

Many languages like Pascal allow a parameter to be passed to a function either by value or reference. Passing a parameter by reference means the address of the memory location of the parameter is sent to the function; the function then manipulates the original data rather than a copy of it. A copy of the data is manipulated when the parameter is passed by value.

Question: What are the advantages and disadvantages of passing parameters by value, as compared to passing them by reference?

In C, parameters are passed by value only. This is not a severe limitation, because if a parameter needs to be passed by reference, a pointer to the data (the data's address) can be passed as a parameter. Here's how the address of an array is passed to a function. Note that the name of the array is a pointer to the first element of the array.

```
void func(func_array)    /* array address is passed */
int func_array[]
{
  /* function body */
}

main()
{
int main_array[200];
...
func(main_array);
...
}
```

Many languages, like Pascal, allow parameters to be input to the subprogram or output from the subprogram. C doesn't. All parameters are input to the function; even if the function modifies the values, the values are not returned. Functions, however, can use the return statement to return a value to the calling program. Data in the calling program can be modified by a function, if a pointer to the data is passed to the function. Pointers are described in a later chapter.

Question: What's the output of this program? Here, &x means the address of the memory location x, and *x means the contents of memory location x.

```
func(x,y)
int x;
int *y;
{
x = 3; *y = 3;
}

main()
{
int a=5, b=5;
func(a,&b);  /* parameter 1 is value of a,
               parameter 2 is address of b */
printf("a=%d,b=%d", a, b);
}
```

Even structures are passed by value. (Structures are described in Chapter 8.) The complete structure is copied into another storage area, which is then used by the function. Consider this program, in which a main program passes a structure to a function:

```
struct two_paras_template
  { int x;
```

```
    char y;
  };

func(f_para)
struct two_paras_template  f_para
{
printf("%d , %c",f_para.x, f_para.y);
}

main()
{
struct two_paras_template  m_para;
m_para.x=5; m_para.y='p';
func(m_para);
}
```

The program output is:

```
5 , p
```

4.9.3 Return values

A function can return a value by the statement:

```
return expression;
```

A function return value can be used as an expression in a statement:

```
a = 4 + func(c,d);
```

The function call can also be a statement as:

```
func(c,d);
```

This would be of no use unless the function execution had some side effects; for instance, the function prints a message. Functions can also manipulate data in the main program if the address of the data is passed to the function as a parameter. This feature allows functions to behave like SUB-ROUTINEs of FORTRAN and Procedures of Pascal.

4.9.4 Function prototypes

The VAX C Run Time Library (VAX C RTL) contains a set of functions that can be called from C programs. Programmers can also create their own libraries. Each function in these libraries accepts a certain number of parameters of a certain type. To ensure that the function is called properly, the compiler is informed of the function by a prototype. The compiler then generates error messages if a function call doesn't have the same number of parameters and the parameters are not of the same type as specified in the prototype. The compiler also uses the prototype to generate code that converts data from the type of the argument to the type of the parameter in the prototype. The function prototype declares the function; the function definition is in the library. Consider the RTL function printf(). The prototype of this function is specified in sys$library:stdio.h as:

```
int printf (const char *format_spec, ...);
```

The function prototype specifies that printf() has one or more parameters of type character pointer. (The const implies that the value of this pointer can't be changed in the program.) If the file stdio.h is included in a program, the compiler will generate error messages if the function is not called properly. Because most programs use printf(), stdio.h is normally included at the top of most programs. In fact, most real-world programs include numerous .h files from sys$library at the beginning, partly because these files contain prototypes for functions in the VAX C RTL.

Question. Will there be compile-time or run time errors in these two programs?

```
/* program 1 */
main() { printf();  }

/* program 2 */
#include stdio
main() { printf();  }
```

Function prototypes are not required if a function is defined within the program before it's used. In many programs, functions are called before they're defined. In this case, function prototypes are required. Here are two similar programs, one with main() preceding the function definition, and the other with main() following the function. The main program is passing two floating point numbers, while the function accepts integer parameters. Because the compiler "knows" this, it generates code to convert the data from floating point to integer before the function uses the data.

```
/*    program 1 does not require a function prototype
      because the function is defined before use.

*/
func( int x, int y)
{
printf("%d , %d", x, y);
}

main()
{
float f1 = 10., f2 = 12.;
```

```
func(f1,f2);
}

/*   program 2 requires a function prototype
       because the function is not defined before use.
*/
func( int x, int y);    /* function prototype */
main()
{
float f1 = 10., f2 = 12.;
func(f1,f2);
}
func( int x,  int y)
{
printf("%d , %d", x, y);
}
```

Question: The two programs just shown generate the output:

```
10 , 12
```

What will be the output of the second program if the function prototype statement is removed?

4.9.5 Variable-length parameter lists

Programmers can write functions that handle a variable number of arguments passed to it. Note that calls to the function will pass a number of arguments known at compile time. Consider printf(), which is a VAX C run time library function for formatted display of data. It accepts a variable number of arguments. Example calls are:

```
printf("One argument, just this one");
printf("Two arguments, integer = %d", i_num);
printf("Three arguments, integer = %d, float = %f", i_num, f_num);
```

Here we discuss how you can write functions that accept a variable number of arguments. A variable number of parameters are depicted by an ellipsis at the end of the parameter list, in a function header as:

```
func(char c, int i, ...)
```

The ellipsis means that there may be more parameters of the datatype of the last specified parameter, int in this example. Here, the function's first parameter is a character, and subsequent parameters are integers. The first two parameters are accessed within the function by the variables c and i; the tricky part is accessing the unnamed parameters that follow. Visualize all the parameters stored sequentially in memory. The last parameter is followed by a null. Then if we declare a pointer to point to i, incrementing this pointer will allow us to access the next integer. All the following integers can be accessed with further increments of this pointer. There are no more parameters when the pointer is pointing to a `null`. Here's a program that illustrates this:

```
/*  Program to show access to variable number of parameters
    in a function. Do not use this program as it is
    machine dependent.
*/
void fn(char ch,int k_num, ...)  /* function parameters are
                                    one character followed
                                    by one or more integers
                                 */
{
int *ap;                        /* argument pointer */

printf("input character is %c\n",ch);

ap = &k_num;      /* point to first integer parameter */
/* print all the integer parameters values */
while (*ap != 0) /* if ap points to 0 then no more parameters */
  {
  printf("%d\n", *ap);
  ap++;           /* ap points to next integer parameter */
  };
}

main()
{
fn('a', 124, 6520, 3);
}
```

The program output is:

```
input character is a
124
6520
3
```

This is basically how variable parameter lists are handled in C. The program just shown is machine dependent, and it doesn't handle variable parameter types other than integers. To address these issues, there are three macros defined in the file sys$library:`stdarg.h` to facilitate access of variable parameter lists. These are `va_start`, `va_arg` and `va_end` (va for variable arguments). The macro `va_start` initializes a pointer to point to the first argument within the ellipses (the first unnamed argument). The pointer is of type `va_list`, which is defined in `stdarg.h` as:

```
typedef char * va_list;
```

The arguments are fetched by `va_arg`, which also increments the argument pointer to point to the next data item, so repeated use of `va_arg` returns further parameters. The macro va_end performs cleanups just before the function exits. Actually, it need not be used under VAX C. Here's the previously described program using these macros:

```
/*    Program to show access to variable number of parameters
      in a function.
*/

#include stdarg.h
void fn(char ch,int k_num, ...)  /* function parameters are one
                                    character followed by one or more
                                    integers
                                 */   ,
{
int *ap;                /* argument pointer */
int i_num;

printf("input character is %c\n",ch);
va_start(ap,k_num);  /* initialize ap to point to k_num */

/* print all the integer parameters values */
i_num = va_arg(ap,int);
while (i_num != 0)
  {
  printf("%d\n", i_num);
  i_num = va_arg(ap,int);
  };
va_end(ap);
}

main()
{
fn('a', 124, 6520, 3);
}
```

Question: If the function call in main were:

```
fn('a', 124, 0, 3);
```

the program output would be:

```
input character is a
124
```

Is this a bug, limitation or design feature of VAX C?

Question: Here are the three va_ macros as they are in the file sys$library:stdarg.h. Understand them. Hint: each parameter is aligned on a longword (4 byte) boundary.

```
#define va_start(ap, parmN)   \
   ap = (va_list) ((int) &parmN + ((sizeof (parmN) + 3) & 3))
#define va_arg(ap, type)      \
   (ap = (va_list) ((int) ap + ((sizeof (type) + 3) & 3)), \
   * (type *) ((int) ap - ((sizeof (type) + 3) & 3)))
#define va_end(ap)       ap = (va_list) 0
```

Question: The function prototype for `printf()` in `stdio.h` is:

```
int printf (const char *format_spec, ...);
```

This implies that the `printf()` function in the run time library has been
written to accept one or more arguments. The function basically performs a
`putchar(c)` for all the characters in the first argument string until a `NULL`
or a % sign is encountered. If a `NULL` is encountered, the function ends. If a
% sign is encountered, the next argument is printed in the format specified
in the % format specifier, and processing continues for the remaining characters in the input string. Write a version of `printf()` to handle only two
output format specifiers: `%c` and `%d`. Call the function `myprintf()`.

Exercise: Replace this set of statements by a single `for` statement:

```
va_start(ap,k_num);  /* initialize ap to point to k_num */

/* print all the integer parameters values */
i_num = va_arg(ap,int);
while (i_num != 0)
{
printf("%d\n", i_num);
i_num = va_arg(ap,int);
};
```

4.10   The C preprocessor

Preprocessor directives are instructions to the compiler rather than being C
statements. All preprocessor directives start on a new line with a #. For example:

```
#define TERMINATOR '.'
```

This directive tells the compiler to replace all occurrences of the token
`TERMINATOR` in the program by the string `'.'`. Unlike variables that are
valid within the block in which they're declared, C preprocessor directives
can be placed anywhere within a program, including within blocks, and
they'll be valid from the point of occurrence until the end of the program file
(compilation unit).

When C was invented, the preprocessor was a separate program that
scanned the input file to process the directives. Today, most compilers, including VAX C, process the directives during compilation for efficiency.
VAX C preprocessor directives are not completely portable with other C implementations. We will now consider the common directives.

4.10.1   Macro definitions—`#define` and `#undef`

The `#define` directive allows substitution of all occurrences of an identifier by a value. The most common use of the directive is to replace identi-

fiers by constants. For example, if the line:

```
#define BEEP printf("\07");
```

is put at the start of the program, and the line:

```
BEEP; BEEP;
```

is encountered, the second line effectively becomes:

```
printf("\07"); printf("\07");
```

This form of `#define` is useful:

- For making the program more readable.

- For defining a constant near the top of the program. The constant's identifier (like `BEEP` in the above example) can be used throughout the program. If the constant value changes, only the `#define` statement will have to be modified.

The syntax of such macro definitions is:

```
#define macro_name token_string
```

Macro definitions can be continued on the next line with a \ at the end of the line (which effectively allows the current line to be logically continued), but otherwise they can't span multiple lines.

To undefine a previously defined macro, the syntax is:

```
#undef macro_name
```

For example:

```
#undef BEEP
```

This way, if the macro is inadvertently used further on in the program, the compiler would flag an error. In practice, most programmers don't bother to undefine macros.

4.10.1.1 Substitution parameters. Consider the following statement, which assigns 1 to variable `whitespace` if variable `input_char` is a space or tab, but assigns 0 to `whitespace` if `input_char` is any other character:

```
whitespace = ((input_char == ' ') || (input_char == '\t'));
```

The \t represents the tab character and || is the logical OR operator. If the statement is used often in a program, it may be a good idea to define the macro:

```
#define iswhitespace(ch)  ((ch == ' ') || (ch == '\t'))
```

Here, the macro has a parameter, ch. When this macro is called in the program, the compiler replaces the macro parameter by the parameter actually present in the call. The assignment statement just shown can be written as:

```
whitespace = iswhitespace(input_char);
```

The compiler preprocessor will expand the macro call in this statement, substituting ch by input_char. The resulting assignment statement will be exactly the same as the one just shown. Macros can have multiple parameters, as:

```
#define macro_name(para1,para2...)  token_string
```

Calls to macros with parameters look similar to calls to functions. See the chapter on functions to differentiate between macros and functions.

4.10.1.2 Nested substitutions. Macro definitions can use previously defined macros. The VAX C compiler performs nested substitutions of macros. Hence, after a substitution, the program is scanned from the start of the substitution text for more substitutions, if any. For example:

```
#define iswhitespace(ch)  ((ch == ' ') || (ch == '\t'))
```

is equivalent to

```
#define TAB '\t'
#define SPACE ' '
#define iswhitespace(ch)  ((ch == SPACE) || (ch == TAB))
```

Obviously, the second form is more readable.

4.10.2 Conditional compilation—#if, #else and #endif

The directives #if, #ifdef, #ifndef, #else, #elif, and #endif are available for conditional compilation of a block of statements. Common uses for these directives are:

■ To write portable programs. Code can be included or excluded by conditional compilation, depending on whether the environment requires it or not.

■ For debugging programs. Debugging code can be included in the program image, but once the program is debugged, the code can be left within the program without being compiled.

For example, suppose a program is to be written so that it can be compiled on both VAX/VMS and Ultrix systems. One line at the top of the program could declare what system the program is compiling on:

```
#define VAX_VMS_SYSTEM 1
```

or

```
#define ULTRIX_SYSTEM 1
```

Now, within the program, operating system specific C code can be included by:

```
#ifdef VAX_VMS_SYSTEM
   .
   .
   .
   VMS specific C code
   .
   .
   .
#endif
   .
   .
   .
   Code common to VMS and Ultrix systems
   .
   .
   .
#ifdef ULTRIX_SYSTEM
   .
   .
   .
   Ultrix specific C code
   .
   .
   .
#endif
   .
   .
   .
```

Blocks of statements to be conditionally compiled start with #if, #ifdef, or #ifndef, and end with #endif. Optionally, there may be #else or #elif within. The #ifs can be nested. If there is no #elifdef, elif can be used instead.

The #if directive syntax is

```
#if expression
```

If the expression evaluates to a nonzero value, the if block is compiled, or else it's skipped.

The #ifdef directive syntax is

```
#ifdef identifier
```

The if block is compiled if the identifier is defined by a previous #define statement.

The #ifndef directive syntax is

```
#ifndef identifier
```

The if block is compiled if the identifier is not defined by a previous #de fine statement.

The #endif directive ends the scope of the most recent #if, #ifdef or #ifndef. The #else directive can be used to form an if-then-else type of block. The directive #elif can be used to test a condition for the else part of the block. Examples are:

```
#ifdef VAX_VMS_SYSTEM        #ifdef VAX_VMS_SYSTEM
  .                            .
  .                            .
  .                            .
#else                        #elif ULTRIX_SYSTEM
  .                            .
  .                            .
  .                            .
#endif                           #endif
                             #endif
```

4.10.3   File inclusion—#include

For compilation purposes, files can be included in the current program by the directive:

```
#include file_specification
```

This way, code or macros that are common among multiple programs can be put in a separate file and #included within each program. Nesting of #include is allowed.

The disk and directory where the file resides can be specified in the file specification. The include directory can also be specified on the C compilation command line by:

```
/INCLUDE_DIRECTORY as in: $ CC/INCLUDE_DIRECTORY=DUA0:[CFILES]    fname
```

The include directory can be specified as logical names VAXC$INCLUDE or C$INCLUDE.

4.10.3.1 Include file location. The include file specification can be optionally enclosed within angle brackets (< and >) or quotes ("). The disk and directory from which the file is retrieved will depend on how the file specification is specified. Note that a directive such as the following will not work!

```
#include DUA0:[SHAH]INCFILE.H
```

Complete VMS file-specs should be enclosed in quotes as:

```
#include "DUA0:[SHAH]INCFILE.H"
```

It's safest to specify complete VMS file specifications and enclose them within quotes. The rules for file inclusions are as follows.

If the filename is not enclosed within angle brackets or quotes, the file is searched for in the library SYS$LIBRARY:VAXCRTL>TLB (not in the current directory).

If the file specification is enclosed within angle brackets as:

```
#include <incfile.h>
```

then the compiler searches directories in the following order:

- The directory specified by the /INCLUDE_DIRECTORY qualifier on the compilation command line, if the qualifier is used.
- The directory specified by the logical name VAXC$INCLUDE, if defined.
- SYS$LIBRARY.

If the file specification is enclosed within quotes as

```
#include "incfile.h"
```

then the compiler searches directories in the following order:

- The directory containing the top-level source file.
- The directory specified by the /INCLUDE_DIRECTORY qualifier on the compilation command line, if the qualifier is used.
- The directory specified by the logical name C$INCLUDE, if defined.

4.10.4 Specifying the module name and identification #module

When multiple C modules are compiled together, the linker, by default, uses the filename as the module name for each module. Also, the final image contains a file identification field that contains "V1.0" by default. The file identification field can be displayed by a command like:

```
$ANALYZE/IMAGE TMP.EXE
    .
    .
    .
Image Identification Information

            image name: "TMP"
            image file identification: "V1.0"
            link date/time: 13-JAN-1992 13:57:31.57
            linker identification: "05-11"
    .
    .
    .
```

The #module directive allows the module name and identification to be specified as in

```
#module tmp V2.1
```

Here, the module name has not been changed, the identification has. The identification is a convenient means of specifying version numbers for different versions of the same program. The #module directive must precede all function and data declarations in a program. Only one #module directive can be present in a compilation unit. Normally, this directive is used to identify different versions of the same program.

Simple Data Types
and Storage Allocation

C has three simple data types: characters, integers, and floating point numbers. These will be discussed in this chapter. Arrays, structures (and unions), and pointers are compound data types that are discussed in other chapters. Strings are created and manipulated as arrays of characters. Of course, programmers can make their own data types using the C data types as a base.

5.1 Constants and Variables

Data in a C program is a constant value or a value in a variable. The value of a constant, once defined, cannot change in a program. Constants can be defined literally, as in:

```
cval = 24;
```

or with the #define directive, as in:

```
#define PI 3.1423

cval = PI;
```

or with the `const` keyword, as in:

```
const int suits 4;
```

Here, actually, `suits` is a read-only variable. All variables must be declared before use. In a block (delimited by { and }), all declarations must precede executable statements. Variables are declared by specifying the variable name preceded by the variables datatype. We have already used the `int` datatype in the programs. It represents a 4-byte integer storage.

Multiple variables can be declared in the same statement:

```
int a;
int b;
int c;
```

is equivalent to:

```
int a,b,c;
```

Values can be assigned to the variables in the declaration statement.

```
int var1 = 50;
```

This line declares a long integer variable called `var1` which will have an initial value of 50 when the program executes. Multiple variables each with a different initial value can be declared in the same statement:

```
int var1 = 34, var2 = 50;
```

Note that in this statement:

```
int var1, var2 = 50;
```

`var1` will have an initial value of 0; `var2` will have an initial value of 50.

5.2 Integers

Integers are classified as long and short. Long integers occupy 4 bytes of storage, short integers 2 bytes. Integers are also classified as signed and unsigned. Signed integers can be negative; unsigned integers can be 0 or a positive number. Examples of integer declarations are:

```
int a;          /* Long integer */
long int a;
long a;
```

```
short int a;
short a;
unsigned short int;
```

Table 5.1 lists the various integer data types and their storage allocation.

Understand integer constant specifications thoroughly; they are a common cause of obscure bugs. Decimal integer constants contain only the characters 0 to 9. If the integer begins with a 0, it's assumed to be octal. Hexadecimal integer constants begin with 0x and can contain the characters 0 to 9 and the hexadecimal digits A to F (and a to f). Examples are:

```
123      /* decimal integer */
0x1A     /* hexadecimal integer */
012      /* octal integer */
-012     /* octal integer */
```

5.3 Characters

Internally, characters are treated as 1-byte integers. That's why unsigned char is a datatype. A character variable can be assigned a value by a character enclosed within single quotes:

```
char ch;
ch = 'A';
```

TABLE 5.1 VAX C Simple Datatypes

Keyword	Size	Range of values
Integers		
int		
long		
long int	32 bits	-2,147,483,648 to 2,147,483,647
unsigned		
unsigned int	32 bits	0 to 4,294,967,295
short		
short int	16 bits	-32,768 to 32,767
unsigned short	16 bits	0 to 65,535
Characters		
char	8 bits	-128 to 127
unsigned char	8 bits	0 to 255
Floating point numbers		
float	32 bits	$0.29 * 10EXP\text{-}38$ to $1.7 * 10EXP38$
double	64 bits	D_floating
		$0.29 * 10EXP\text{-}38$ to $1.7 * 10EXP38$
		G_floating
		$0.56 * 10EXP\text{-}308$ to $0.90 * 10EXP308$

Here, the 1-byte variable, ch, contains the decimal value 65. Each character is stored in a byte, and not all byte values have a corresponding printable form. For example, 8 (commonly known as backspace) can be stored in a character variable, but there's no corresponding printable character.

How can such characters be conveniently assigned to integer variables within a program? This can be done by:

```
ch = '\b';
```

Here \b represents backspace. The character \b is called an *escape sequence*. An escape sequence is a sequence of characters that represent one character. The slash is the start of the escape sequence. Table 5.2 shows the possible escape sequences. Note that the integer value of the character can be specified by \nnn or \Xhh. The nnn is an octal value, and hh is a hexadecimal value. For example,

```
ch = '\010'   /* same as ch = '\b' */
ch = '\X41'   /* same as ch = 'A' */
ch = '\XDC'   /* hex DC is U with an umlaut */
```

Note that any character can be represented by the form \nnn or \Xnnn.

Though not recommended for reasons of clarity and portability, integers and other variables can be assigned one or more characters, as in:

```
int var1;
var1 = 'ABCD';
```

Here, the ASCII values of A, B, C and D are stored in each of the four bytes of the integer. Cute, but poor coding practice.

Strings of characters can be specified between double quotes, as in:

```
char *s;
s = "test data";
```

Here, s is not a character but a pointer to a character. When the assignment statement is encountered, the content of s will point to the string that is

TABLE 5.2 Storage Classes and Allocation.

Storage class	Storage location	Usage
auto	Stack or register	Within blocks only
register	Stack or register	Within blocks only
static	memory	Anywhere in the program
extern	memory	Anywhere in the program, the variable declaration must be outside of any block.

stored as consecutive characters in some memory location by the compiler/linker. C does not have special operators for string manipulations; a string is manipulated as a set of zero or more characters.

Question: What's the difference between these two statements?

```
x = '(';
x = "(";
```

5.4 Floating Point Numbers

VAX C supports three kinds of floating point numbers: F_floating, D_floating and G_floating. F_floating variables contain single precision numbers:

```
float var1;
```

D_floating and G_floating are double precision numbers. They differ in the number of bits allocated for the mantissa and the exponent. Both are represented by the same datatype keyword double:

```
double var2;
```

All double precision numbers in a compilation session are assumed to be D_floating unless the /G_FLOAT qualifier is specified on the command line in which case all the double precision numbers are assumed to be G_floating. D_floating and G_floating numbers cannot be mixed in the same program. Table 5.1 shows the storage allocation and range of values for floating point numbers. Long float can be used instead of double (though long float is not portable to other C compilers).

All floating point constants are interpreted as having datatype double. Examples are:

```
5.0
1.1e300
.42321752e-12
.1
```

5.5 The void Datatype Specifier

The void datatype specifier is like a datatype; it specifies that there is no data. It aids in type checking by the compiler and allows pointers to point to unspecified or unknown data types.

For example, a function that does not return a value can be declared as:

```
void func()
{
```

```
  printf("Test function\n");
}
```

The function is of type void. The function can be called, as in:

```
func();
```

However, if it is called as in:

```
a = func();   /* wrong */
```

the compiler will generate an error message. The void datatype specifier is also used to indicate that a function does not have any arguments, as in:

```
int func (void)
{
  return(426);
}
```

If this function is called, as in:

```
func(para1);  /* wrong */
```

the compiler will flag an error. The chapter on pointers shows how void pointers are used.

5.6   Type Conversions and the Cast Operator

When an operator has operands of different types, the "smaller" operand is converted to the type of the "larger" operand.

```
int i,j;
short k;
...
i = j+k;
```

Here, the + has a 2-byte and a 4-byte integer to operate on. The 2-byte short integer will be converted to a 4-byte long integer, and the addition will be performed on the two 4-byte integers.

Note that this statement is valid:

```
k = i;
```

Here, a 4-byte integer is assigned to a 2-byte integer. The program will run and possibly produce erroneous results. This is a limitation of the C language definition. The char variables can be used in arithmetic; they are treated as 1-byte integers. This program segment is legal:

```
int ch;
...
if (ch >= 'a' && ch <= 'z') printf("lowercase alphabet");
```

Here a and z are used as decimal 97 and 122.

When floating point and integers are mixed, the integers are converted to floating point numbers. At times, it may be necessary to force a data item to a particular data type. For example, to force a conversion of a variable j to type short, the syntax would be:

```
(short) j
```

Consider this program segment:

```
int i,j;
short k;
...
i = (short) j + k;
```

The j has been converted to short in the assignment statement. The plus sign now operates on two short operands, hence the addition is done without conversion on two short operands. If (short) were not present, k would be converted to a long integer, and the addition would be done on two long operands. To be precise, long integers mentioned above should be referred to as standard integers as the datatype int refers to standard integers; however, a standard integer on the VAX is the long integer, hence long integer and standard integer are equivalent on the VAX (though not necessarily on other machines). The process of forcing a variable or an expression to be of a particular data type is called *casting*. The syntax is:

```
(datatype) expression
```

Casts are used extensively when a pointer is used to point to data of different types at different locations in a program.

5.7 The `typedef` Keyword

The typedef can be used to give different names to existing data types.

```
typedef char byte;
```

The word byte becomes a synonym for char and can be used in casts or to define a character:

```
byte ch;
p = (byte) i;
```

Another example is:

```
typedef char *string;
```

The word `string` is a synonym for `char *`, or character pointer. These two statements are equivalent:

```
char *str;
string str;
```

A `typedef` does not create new data types; it just gives a new name to an existing datatype. The `typedef`s are somewhat like `#define`s, however, `typedef`s are processed by the compiler, and `#define`s are processed by the preprocessor. typedefs are useful to create more meaningful names for existing datatypes, like string in the above example.

5.8   Scope of Identifiers and Storage Classes

The *scope* of an identifier is that part of a program where the identifier is valid. For example, a variable identifier declaring a variable within a function is available to that function, but not to other functions. Each data item in a program has a storage class that determines its scope, location and the lifetime of the storage allocation. These are the issues discussed in this chapter.

5.8.1   Scope rules within a simple program

Let's consider a simple program that doesn't link with any other programs (except object libraries). Such a program is a compilation unit. A compilation unit is all the source files that are input to the compiler to produce one `.obj file`. Two files can be compiled as one compilation unit by a command like:

```
$cc file1+file2
```

The files can be concatenated into one file, and this file can be input to the compiler to produce the same `.obj file`. For example, here we append `prog1.c9` and `prog2.c` to an empty file, `prog3.c`. The `.obj file` produced is the same as the one produced by the command above.

```
$ append prog1.c, prog2.c prog3.c
$ cc prog3
```

In our discussion we'll assume a compilation unit to be one source file.

Here are some scope rules for identifiers in a compilation unit:

- The scope of an identifier declared at the top of the program outside any function, including `main()`, is the complete program.

- The scope of an identifier declared at the top of a block (including function bodies) is the entire block. If the same identifier is declared in an outer block, then that declaration is suspended until the end of the current block. The scope of labels (for `goto`s) is the entire block in which the label occurs. This implies that a `goto` cannot refer to a label in another block.

5.8.2   Scope rules for multiple compilation units

Parts of C programs can be compiled separately to produce multiple `.obj` files, which are then linked together by the linker. For example, functions can be compiled separately.

Consider the two files `prog1.c` and `prog2.c`, which together constitute a complete program:

```
/* This is prog1.c */
func(int a, int b);    /* function prototype */
main()
{
int a=5,b=6;
func(a,b);
}

/* This is prog2.c */
#include stdio        /* since printf() is used */
func(int x, int y)
{
printf("x=%d, y=%d",x,y);
}
```

The two files can be treated as one compilation unit. The commands would be:

```
$ cc prog1+prog2                    !output prog1.obj
$ link prog1, sys$share:vaxcrtl/olb  !output prog1.exe
```

Or, they can be treated as two compilation units:

```
$ cc prog1                          !output prog1.obj
$ cc prog2                          !output prog2.obj
$ link prog1,prog2, sys$share:vaxcrtl.olb
                                    !output prog1.exe
```

In the second case, the linker resolved the reference to function `func` in `prog2.obj` from `prog1.obj`. Function references are compiled as external if the function is not within the same compilation unit. The linker resolves the reference. But, if a variable were declared within main(), and func() attempts to access that variable, an error would be generated during compilation of prog2.c:

```
/* This is prog2.c with reference to variable c in main()*/
#include stdio        /* since printf() is used */
func(int x, int y)
{
printf("x=%d, y=%d",x,y);
printf("c=%d",c);
}

$ cc prog2
%CC-E-UNDECLARED, "c" is not declared within the scope of
                 this usage.
```

Two changes are required if a variable c is to be shared by various compilation units:

- In the main program, c must be defined outside any blocks, including the bodies of main() or functions. Variables defined within blocks are never accessible externally.

- In the function program, c needs to be declared as an *extern* variable. An extern variable is one that's referenced in this compilation unit, but is defined in another compilation unit. The extern variables cannot be given an initial value, as the compiler does not have the exact memory location for the variable; the linker knows the memory location; however, it does not initialize variables. The two programs should be:

```
/* This is prog1.c with variable c defined */

func(int a, int b);   /* function prototype */

int c=7;
main()
{
a=5,b=6;
func(a,b);
}

/* This is prog2.c with variable c declared */
#include stdio   /* since printf() is used */
func(int x, int y)
{
extern int c;
printf("xp=%d, y=%d\n",x,y);
printf("c=%d\n",c);
}
```

The compilation, link and execution commands are,

```
$ cc prog1                     !output prog1.obj
```

```
$ cc prog2                    !output prog2.obj
$ link prog1,prog2, sys$share:vaxcrtl.olb
$                             !output prog1.exe
$ run prog1
x=5,y=6
c=7
```

In summary, external function references are resolved by the linker automatically. External variables can be resolved by the linker only if the variable is defined in one compilation unit outside any block and the variable is
declared just like in the definition, except that the keyword `extern` is
added in the front to let the compiler generate appropriate information for
the linker to resolve the variable. The `extern` keyword is also useful for declaring variables that are defined later in the compilation unit.

Note that the variable can be defined in the middle of a compilation unit,
provided it's not within a block. In this case, the scope of the variable within
the compilation unit is the program text after the declaration. The scope of
the variable as referenced in the other compilation units is similar to the
scope of a local variable defined at that point.

Question: What's the difference between declaration and definition of a
variable?

5.8.3 Storage classes and allocation

Consider the definition of variable b within a function that's part of a large
program:

```
func()
{
int b;
...
}
```

Storage for b is allocated only when the function is entered for execution.
The storage area is deallocated when the function exits. The storage is actually allocated on the machine stack (or CPU register). If the function is
called recursively, a new storage area is allocated to b on the stack (or CPU
register). This method has two advantages over allocating the storage at
compile time.

- When there are lots of functions with lots of variables, pre-allocating storage for the variables may cause a memory overflow.

- Recursive calls to functions can be easily supported, since an invocation
  of the function does not overwrite data being manipulated by previous invocation.

Variables with space allocated this way are of class `auto`. By default, all defined variables within blocks have a storage class of `auto`. The storage class for a variable is defined by the appropriate keyword before the variable name in the declaration. Other keywords can also be specified; the order is not important:

```
auto int b;
int auto b;
```

A variable can be defined to be of class `static` as in:

```
func()
{
static int b;
...
}
```

Such variables have a constant location throughout program execution. While the scope rules apply for such variables, the variable value does not disappear when the block exits. In the above function, if b is set to a value, the value cannot be used outside the function, but on exiting the function and subsequent entry to it, the value of b will not have changed. The variable b, for example, can be used to keep a count of the number of times the function is entered. Variables that are `static` are not allocated on the stack; they are allocated in memory.

A simple variable can be defined to be of class `register`.

```
register int b;
```

The class `register` can be used within blocks only. It can be used wherever `auto` can be used. The compiler attempts to allocate the variable to a CPU register. The VAX has 16 General Purpose Registers of 4 bytes each. Because data in CPU registers can be processed quickly, commonly used variables can be assigned to registers. If too many variables are assigned to registers, some variables will be put in memory even if the `register` class is specified. Because the VAX C is an optimizing compiler, in general, the compiler will attempt to use unused registers for auto variables, even if not specified by the storage class. My recommendation to programmers: do not bother to use this storage class. Table 5.2 summarizes the storage classes mentioned up to now.

- The variables `auto` and `register` must be defined within functions; they cannot be defined, for example, at the top of a source file. They can be used only within the function in which they're defined.

- The variables `static` and `extern`, if defined within a function, are valid within the function only. If defined outside any function, they are valid throughout the compilation unit from that location onwards. All `extern` variables declarations must have corresponding variable definitions outside any functions, though not necessarily in the same compilation unit.

Question: Where is storage allocated for k in

```
main()
{
int i;
...
  {
  int k;
  ...
  };
  ...
} /* end of main program */
```

Question: Are the variables a, b, c, x, y, and z properly defined and declared? What's the scope of each? Both prog1.c and prog2.c are two compilation units of the same program.

```
/* prog1.c */        /* prog2.c */

static int x;        extern int y;
main()               func2()
{                    {
int z;               static int x;
...                  extern int z
}                    ...
                     }
static int a;
int y;
auto int b;

func1()
{
extern int c;
...

}
```

ANSWER: The scope of a is from the point of definition to the end of prog1.c. The b is outside any function yet because it is defined auto; it will generate a compile time error. The c has been declared extern within func1, but it is not defined anywhere; a link time error will be generated. The scope of x in prog1.c is the whole file. The scope of x in func2() is func2() only. The two x's are different variables. The variable y is valid in prog1 from the point of definition to the end of the file prog1.c. Within prog2.c, y is valid throughout the file. The z is valid in main(), but it cannot be exported to other compilation units because it is defined within a function (main, in this case). The use of z in prog2.c will generate a link time error.

5.7.4 The globaldef, globalref and globalvalue storage classes

These storage classes are specific to VAX C and hence, are not portable. The storage class globaldef defines a variable to be available to the com-

plete program, irrespective of where it is defined. The storage class glob
alref declares a variable that's pointing to the same value as the variable
that's defined by a globaldef:

```
globaldef int transaction_number;    /*variable definition*/
globalref int transaction_number;    /*variable declaration*/
```

These storage classes may seem somewhat like the C language extern
storage class; however, there are differences:

- When mixing languages in a program, globaldef and globalref can
  be used to exchange data between VAX C and other languages like
  MACRO, which support use of such variables. The storage class extern
  is to be used for communicating data among C compilation units.

- A globaldef can be put inside a block (or function). Another compilation unit can reference this variable by a globalref variable. A variable
  referenced by the extern class must be defined outside any block.

The storage class globalvalue can be used to share a constant integer
value among multiple compilation units:

```
globalvalue int debug_mode = 1;    /*  the linker notes this */
globalvalue int debug_mode;        /*  linker substitutes 1 for
                                       debug_mode in this
                                       compilation unit */
```

No storage is allocated for the identifier, debug_mode in this case. Instead, the linker defines a symbol debug_mode and assigns a value 1 to it,
and then substitutes all references to debug_mode with 1. If the value of
debug_mode is to be changed, then only the compilation unit where it is
defined has to be recompiled. The linker will then substitute the new value
wherever debug_mode is used. A globalvalue constant can be of up to
4 bytes; the variable type can be enum, int or pointer.

5.8.5 Datatype Modifiers: const and volatile

The const keyword can be placed in front of a variable definition to ensure
that it is not modified during program execution. The variable can be refer-
ring to an aggregate, in which case all members are treated as constants. At
the machine level, const data is put in NOWRT psects.

```
const int x;
const structure      {  int x;
                        char y;
                     }  struct1;
```

Structures are described in chapter 8. In the second example, both x and y
are constants.

The `volatile` keyword can be used to force a variable to be allocated in memory and not to a CPU register. This may be required when writing device drivers or other systems-level programs:

```
volatile int x;
```

Both `volatile` and `register` are mutually exclusive.

5.7.6 Storage class modifiers: `noshare,` `readonly` and `align`

If `noshare` is specified in front of a variable, the data is placed in a `psect` with the `noshare` attribute. This may be useful when creating sharable images that allow code to be shared, but not data.

The `readonly` storage class modifier is somewhat like `const`, which is a new ANSI C feature, while `readonly` was offered in VAX C much earlier. The `readonly` modifier should be replaced by `const`.

The `_align` modifier is used to force the alignment of data to a specified storage boundary. Alignment may lead to better performance, or it may be a requirement for some programs.

Here are the declarations for two characters that are (very likely) to be stored in two consecutive bytes of memory. Assume that the characters are not going to be stored in a CPU register.

```
char c1;
char c2;
```

The two characters can be forced into the next two longword boundaries by:

```
_align (longword) c1;    /*character starts at a
                           location 0,4,8,...*/
_align (longword) c2;    /*character is in the next
                           longword following c1 */
```

The alignment specifies the starting location, but depending on the size, the data may continue through several bytes of data.

TABLE 5.3

Alignment specifier	Startling location number divisible by
byte	1
word	2
longword	4
quadword	8
octaword	16
page	512
n	2**n

Possible alignments are shown in Table 5.3. Here, n is an integer, and these two declarations are equivalent:

```
_align (4) int x;
_align (octaword) int x;
```

Operators and Expressions

Everyone is familiar with the addition operator, +, which adds two numbers when an operator performs an operation on data. VAX C has about 42 operators.

6.1 Operators

Most programmers are familiar with the four basic arithmetic operators, +, -, *, and /. The unary operator, - is also commonly used, as in:

```
a = -b
```

Table 6.1 lists the C operators. Some of the operators are rarely used. Most programmers know that in an expression, the multiply and divide operators are evaluated before plus and minus operators. The operators * and / have a higher precedence than + and -. After the statement:

```
x = 3 + 2 * 5
```

is executed, variable x will contain 13. All C operators are ordered and evaluated by precedence. Table 6.2 shows this precedence. Operators on a line

TABLE 6.1 The VAX C Operators

Operator		Example	Description
–	unary minus	–x	
*	pointer	*x	reference to object at address x
&	address	&x	address of x
~	complement	~x	one's complement of x
++	increment	++x	increment x by 1, use the result
		x++	use xx, decrement xx by 1
—	decrement	—x	decrement x by 1, use the result
		x—	use xx, decrement xx by 1
sizeof		sizeof(d)	size in bytes of datatype d
		sizeof(e)	size in bytes of expression e
(datatype)	cast	(d) e	expression e converted to datatype d
+	plus	x + y	
–	minus	x–y	
*	multiply	x * y	
/	divide	x / y	
%	modulo	x % y	remainder of x/y
>>	right bit-shift	x >> y	x shifted right by y bits
<<	left bit-shift	x << y	x shifted left by x bits
>	greater	x > y	1 if x greater than y, else 0
<	less	x < y	1 if x less than y, else 0
>=	greater or equal	x >=y	1 if x greater than or equal to y, else 0
<=	less or equal	x <= y	1 if x less than or equal to y, else 0
==	comparison	x == y	1 if x equal to y , else 0
!=	not equal	x != y	1 if x not equal to y, else 0
&	bitwise AND	x & y	bitwise AND of x and y
|	bitwise OR	x | y	bitwise OR of x and y
^	bitwise XOR	x ^ y	Exclusive OR of x and y
&&	logical AND	x && y	1 if x and y both nonzero, else 0
||	logical OR	x || y	0 if x and y both zero, else 1
!	logical NOT	!x	1 if x is 0, else 0
?:	conditional expression	x ? el : e2	expression el if x is nonzero, expression e2 if x is zero
=	assignment	x = y	
+=		x += y	shorthand for x = y + x
–=		x –= y	shorthand for x = x – y
*=		x *= y+	shorthand for x = x * y
/*		x /= y	shorthand for x = x / y
%=		x %= y	shorthand for x = x % y
>>=		x >>= y	shorthand for x = x >> y
<<=		x <<= y	shorthand for x = x << y
&=		x &= y	shorthand for x = x & y
|=		x |= y	shorthand for x = x | y
^=		x^= y	x = x ^ y
,	comma	e1,e2	e2 after e1 has been evaluated
( )	function call	f1( )	call function f1
[]	array subscript	x[10]	10th element of array x
.	structure member	x.y	element of y structure x
->	structure member	p->y	element of y structure where p is a pointer to the structure

TABLE 6.2 VAX C Operator Precedence and Associativity

	Operators	Associativity
	( ) [] -> .	Left to right
	! ~ ++ — (type cast) * & sizeof	Right to left
	* / %	Left to right
|	+ –	Left to right
Decreasing |	<< >>	Left to right
order |	< <= > >=	Left to right
of |	== !=	Left to right
evaluation |	&	Left to right
priority |	^	Left to right
v |	|	Left to right
	&&	Left to right
	||	Left to right
	?:	Right to left
	+ += –=/= %= >>= <<= &= ^= !=	Right to left
	,	Left to right

are evaluated before operators shown in lines below. Multiple operators in the same line have the same precedence.

When one of the operators +, −, *, or / appears in sequence in an expression, the operators are processed left to right. In

```
x = a + b + c
```

a is added to b, the result of which is added c, the result of which is assigned to x. Note that the assignment operator, = is processed right to left. The order in which operators at the same precedence level are evaluated is known as *associativity*.

Question: If a=5, b=6, and c=7; what are the values of a, b, and c after this statement is executed?

```
a=b=c;
```

Table 6.2 also shows operator associativity. Note the comma operator. These are valid simple statements:

```
i++, j--;
a = b, c = d;
```

The compiler looks for the longest string of characters that can be considered a token. Hence, in the statement:

```
b++;
```

the compiler treats the two pluses as one token, –, the increment operator –, not as two binary + operators.

Question: x, y, and z are three integers with values 10, 8 and 6 respectively. What are their values after this statement is executed? (Yes, the statement is legal in C).

```
z = x --- y;
```

Question: Are these two statements equivalent?

```
if (x>='a' && x<='z') printf("alpha");
if ((x>='a') && (x<='z')) printf("alpha");
```

Question: What will be printed by this program?

```
main()
{
  {
  int a=1, b=2, c=3, d=4;
  d = a = b, c = d;
  printf("d=%d\n",d);
  };
  {
  int a=1, b=2, c=3, d=4;
  d = (a = b, c = d);
  printf("d=%d\n",d);
  };
}
```

Question: Differentiate among the three operators:

&   – pointer
&   – bitwise AND
&& – logical AND

6.2 Expressions

An *expression* is a series of tokens that produce a value. Expressions are fairly well understood by C programmers.
Two points of interest:

- An expression within parentheses has the same type and value as the expression. Parentheses are used to change precedence and associativity.

- A function name can be used as an expression. It represents the address of the function. A function name followed by zero or more parameters in parentheses is an expression. It represents the value returned by the function. For example, if there is a function declared as:

```
int func()
```

```
{
  return (5);
}
```

then

```
ast_rtn(func);
```

is a call to function `ast_rtn`, which passes the address of `func` as a parameter:

```
ast_rtn(func());
a = func();
```

are similar to

```
ast_rtn(5);
a = 5;
```

6.2.1 Datatype conversion

C is not strongly typed; data types can be mixed in expressions. In mixed datatype expressions the following conversion rules apply:

- An operand of type `char` or `short` is converted to `int`. An operand of type `unsigned char` or `unsigned short` is converted to type `unsigned int`.
- An operand of type `float` (4-byte floating point number) is converted to type double (8-byte floating point number), unless the `/PRECISION=SINGLE` qualifier is present on the compilation command line.
- In a binary expression, if either operand is of type `double`, the other is converted to type `double`.
- In a binary expression, if either operand is of type `unsigned`, the other is converted to type `unsigned`.

When long integers are converted to `char` or `short`, the integer is truncated at left. Shorter signed integers are converted to long integers by sign extension. Similar conversion rules apply when parameters are passed to functions.

Pointers and Arrays

Most beginning programmers find pointers the most difficult C topic. In VAX C, a *pointer* is a 32-bit variable that contains the address of a memory location. Data manipulation with pointers is one of C's most powerful and most abused features. Pointers allow data at any memory location to be conveniently accessed, but wanton use of pointers can defeat the C philosophy of data-type checking and can lead to unreadable code. Pointers are demystified in this chapter.

7.1 Pointers and Addresses

A pointer is declared by a statement like:

```
short int *var_address;
```

The variable `var_address` is a pointer variable that points to a memory location containing a variable of type `short int`.

Contrast the two declarations:

```
int x;
int *x;
```

The first causes the compiler to allocate storage for an integer that is referenced by x in the program. The second allocates storage for a memory address where the storage location is referenced by xm, and the storage contents point to a memory location containing an integer. On the VAX, the pointer can be visualized as a 4-byte integer, although it should be treated as a separate (pointer) data type. Typically in a program, an address is first put in var_address by a statement like:

```
var_address = &x;
```

The word var_address now contains the address of variable x. Assuming x is a variable of type short int, data can be stored by referencing x or the pointer. These two statements are equivalent:

```
x = 10;
*var_address = 10;
```

The unary operator * introduced here can be read as "contents of," and the unary operator & can be read as "address of."

Assuming the var_address is a short integer pointer as declared above, *var_address can be used any place a short integer can be used. For example, if var_address points to x by:

```
var_address = &x;
```

then the following two statements are equivalent:

```
x = x + 5;
*var_address = *var_address + 5;
```

Question: The following two statements are not equivalent. Why?

```
x++;
*var_address++;
```

7.2 The void Pointers

VAX C allows a pointer to be assigned to another pointer of a different type. For example, this is valid in VAX C:

```
int *int_address;
char *char_address;

...

int_address = char_address;   /* illegal in ANSI C */
```

ANSI C and some other C compilers do not allow such assignments so that type checking may be more strictly enforced. The qualifier /STANDARD= PORTABLE can be used on the $ CC compilation command line to produce informational messages when such assignments are made in VAX C.

Question: Can you use a cast within the assignment statement to make it legal?

The void pointer is a generic pointer that can point to data of any type. Any pointer can be assigned to a void pointer, and a void pointer can be assigned to any other type of pointer. ANSI C allows a void pointer to be used as an intermediary to allow a pointer to be assigned to a pointer of a different type. Previously, programmers created generic pointers with statements like:

```
char *generic_ptr;    /* illegal generic pointer in ANSI C */
```

The following pointer assignments are legal in ANSI C.

```
int *int_address;
char *char_address;
void *generic_ptr;

...

generic_ptr = char_address;
int_address = generic_ptr;
```

The void pointers are also used for function parameters and return values when their type is not known at compile time. Such functions are usually written to manipulate data of different datatypes. Here is the header of a function that sorts data at the memory location pointed to by inadr and leaves the output at the memory location pointed to by outadr. The datatype of the data is specified in the variable dtype, and the number of data elements is given by dcnt.

```
int sort_fn (void *inadr, void *outadr, char dtype, int dcnt)
```

7.3 Pointer Arithmetic

While it is useful to visualize pointers as integers within the VAX, pointers should never be treated as integers in C. A limited set of operations is permitted on pointer variables. For example, the value of a pointer can be incremented, as in:

```
var_address++;
```

Logically, the pointer is incremented to point to the next element the pointer is referencing. Internally, if the pointer is visualized as a 4-byte address, the address may not be incremented by one because addresses point to bytes of memory. For example, if the pointer were declared as:

```
short int *var_address;
```

the 4-byte address in the VAX representing the pointer will be incremented by 2 (in VAX C), so as to point to the next short integer. If the declaration were as:

```
char *var_address;
```

the pointer 4-byte address will be incremented by one.

A constant value may be added to a pointer, as in:

```
var_address = var_address + 10;
```

Here, a constant is added to the contents of `var_address` so that `var_address` points 10 elements ahead. If the elements were of type `short int`, then 20 would be added to the internal integer representation of `var_address`.

Question: How are these two statements different?

```
x = *var_address+1;
x = *(var_address+1);
```

The following are the only operations allowed on VAX C pointers:

- Assigning pointers of the same type to each other.

- Adding and subtracting a pointer and an integer. The `++` and `--` operators can be applied to pointers.

- Subtracting or comparing two pointers to members of the same array. Two pointers can never be added.

- Assigning or comparing to zero. Actually, a constant value can be assigned to a pointer, but a warning message is displayed if the `/STANDARD=PORTABLE` qualifier is used on the compilation command line.

- Assigning a pointer of any type to a `void` pointer.

- Assigning a `void` pointer to a pointer of any type.

Question: Why does C allow subtraction of one pointer from another, but not addition of two pointers?

Question: Why does C allow zero to be assigned to a pointer, but no other constant?

Question: Given the declaration:

```
int *var1_ptr, *var2_ptr, *var3_ptr;
```

which of the following statements are legal?

```
var2_ptr = var1_ptr + 25 - var3_ptr;
var2_ptr = var1_ptr * var3_ptr;
var2_ptr = *var1_ptr
var2_ptr = &(*var1_ptr);
var2_ptr = --var1_ptr - var3_ptr;
```

7.4 Arrays

A simple array is declared and used with a variable name followed by a number within square brackets. For example:

```
int counts[25];
```

Here, the array count has 25 elements, each of type `int`. The elements are count[0] to count[24]. Arrays can be initialized when declared by commands like:

```
int counts[5] = { 23, 0, 1000, -324, 4368};
```

Multidimensional arrays can be created in VAX C by declarations like:

```
char str[5][3];
```

The array elements are stored in row-major order, hence the preceding array will be stored in consecutive locations as:

```
str[0][0]
str[0][1]
str[0][2]
str[1][0]
  .
  .
  .
str[4][2]
```

When initializing this array, the initialization values are assigned in row-major order to the array elements.

Arrays of type `char` can be assigned by a string constant. The following two declarations are equivalent:

```
char x[4] = "ABC";
char x[4] = { 'A', 'B', 'C', '\0' };
```

Note that a NULL character is added as an array element at the end of the string.

If the declaration of the array includes initialization, then the size of the array can be omitted; the size is implied from the number of initialization elements. The following two declarations are equivalent:

```
char x[4] = "ABC";
char x[] = "ABC";
```

7.5   Pointers and Array Manipulations

An example array declaration is:

```
int a[35];
```

Here, a is an array of 25 integer elements. The array elements can be accessed with statements like:

```
a[12] = 650;
d = a[20];
```

A pointer can also be used to manipulate the array elements. If a_array_ptr is declared as:

```
int *a_array_ptr;
```

then the statement:

```
a_array_ptr = &a[0];
```

sets a_array_ptr to point to the first element (element 0) of array a. The statement is equivalent to:

```
a_array_ptr = a;
```

Now the first element of the array can be accessed by a[0] or *a_array_ptr. The next two statements are equivalent:

```
a[0] = 5;
*a_array_ptr = 5;
```

As explained in the previous section on pointer arithmetic, the elements of the array can be accessed simply by adding the element index to the pointer. The following two statements are equivalent:

```
a[12] = 546;
*(a_array_ptr + 12) = 546;
```

In the book *The C Programming Language* by the designers of C, Kernighan and Richie, the authors write: "In C, there is a strong relationship between pointer and arrays, strong enough that pointers and arrays should be discussed simultaneously."

I disagree with the authors. If possible, operations on arrays should be performed using standard array operators. Pointers tend to create more confusing code. The only exception may be when manipulating strings that can be considered as array of characters terminated by the null character, \0. In this case, pointers may produce concise-looking C code as, usually, these characters are accessed sequentially.

7.6 Pointer Misuse

Pointers make C a highly flexible language. A variable can be accessed by a declared variable name or by a pointer. If the variable names are used when manipulating the data, the compiler can perform extensive type-checking to weed out illegal operations. As the same data in memory can be pointed to by pointers of various types, manipulations on the data using pointers is difficult to validate during compilation.

Consider this program:

```
int x = 5, y = 10, z = 15;
int *var_address;

main()
{
var_address = &y;
var_address++;
*var_address = 13;
printf("%d %d %d",x,y,z);
}
```

The var_address is pointing to a simple element, and it was incremented. It then points to an undefined location. The number 13 is put in that location. This should not be allowed, but the compiler cannot trap the error, nor can it be trapped when the program runs. The program will run and either clobber a variable or generate a run time memory access violation. Under VAX C, the program sets z to 13. Such mistakes are common in C programs with pointers.

Pointers are convenient to use in many programs. But, inadvertently or not, programmers using pointers can create code that cannot be maintained and is full of surprises.

8

Structures and Unions

In real-world programming, many simple variables are logically related to other variables. For example, a sender, a destination, and an amount variable might be part of a funds transfer message. It would be convenient to group together the individual elements of a message. *Structures* allow such grouping. Structures are a collection of logically related variables. *Unions*, which are somewhat like structures, allow variables of different types to be stored in the same storage area. These are the topics of this chapter.

8.1 Simple Structures

Consider an example. In C, strings are a sequence of characters terminated by a NULL character. The length of the string can be found by counting all its characters. In many programs, it's more efficient to store the length of a string in a separate variable and use that variable rather than counting all the characters in the string. Because the string and its length are closely related variables, a structure can be used as:

```
struct string
  {   char str[100];
      short length;
  };
```

A structure is created by specifying struct, followed by an optional name (string in this example), followed by variable declarations within braces. The struct declaration defines a new data type, struct string in this example. The declaration is a template; no variable has been declared in this example. The string is called the structure tag. The tag is then referenced to create data of type struct string, as in:

```
struct string input_str;
struct string output_str;
```

or simply

```
struct string input_str, output_str;
```

Here, two variables, input_str and output_str have been created. Both are of data type struct string. The variables could have been created in the original struct declaration, as shown here:

```
struct string
  { char str[100];
    short length;
  } input_str, output_str;
```

The tag is optional when declaring structures; however, if defined, it can be used later on in the program to declare variables of that structure type. The preceding structure can be replaced by:

```
struct
  { char str[100];
    short length;
  } input_str, output_str;
```

provided no more variables of that structure type are going to be declared further in the program.

Variables within structures are accessed by constructs such as:

```
input_str.length
output_str.str[4]
```

The generic form is:

```
structure-name.member-name
```

where the . is a structure member operator.

8.2 More about Structures

Structures can be nested within other structures. Consider an example. A funds transfer message consists of a sender, a destination and an amount area. The sender consists of a person's name and an address. The destination consists of a bank name, address and account number. The amount is an integer. The templates for the sender and destination structures are straightforward:

```
struct sender_template
   { char name[30];
     char address[4][30];
   };
struct destination_template
   { char bank_name[50];
     char address[4][30];
     int  account_num;
   };
```

The template for the complete message includes the preceding constructs:

```
struct message
   { struct sender_template sender ;
     struct destination_template destination;
     int amount;
   };
```

which could have also been declared as:

```
struct message
   { struct
       { char name[30];
         char address[4][30];
       } sender;
     struct
       { char bank_name[50];
         char address[4][30];
         int  account_num;
       } destination;
     int amount;
   };
```

A variable of that structure type could be declared as:

```
struct message funds_message;
```

Structure members can be accessed with constructs like:

```
funds_message.sender.address
funds_message.amount
```

That address exists within two sub-structures within the top-level structure. This is allowed, as each can be uniquely identified.

Structures can be array elements. For example an array of 1000 variables of structure type message can be declared as:

```
struct message funds_message[1000];
```

Here, `funds_message` is an array of 1000 elements, each of which is a structure of type `struct` message. Structure members can be accessed using constructs like:

```
funds_message[16].destination.address
```

Structure variables can be initialized like other variables. Here, a funds transfer message is initialized:

```
struct message
   funds_message = { {  "John Doe",
                        { {"123, Maple street"},
                          {"Anytown, PA 07434"},
                          {""},
                          {""},
                        }
                     },
                     {  "Bank of Anytown",
                        { {"Anytown Plaza"},
                          {"Anytown, PA 07455"},
                          {""},
                          {""},
                        },
                        2348623
                     },
                     2500
                   };
```

Notice how the initialization structure mimics the original structure template. The output of the following statement:

```
printf("%s\n %d\n", funds_message.sender.address[1],
                    funds_message.amount);
```

would be

Anytown, PA 07434
2500

Pointers can point to structures. The following statement declares mes sage_ptr of type `struct` message. The declaration creates a pointer, but no storage is allocated for a message:

```
struct message *message_ptr;
```

Assuming that the initialized `find_message` previously shown has already been created, the following statement sets `message_ptr` to point to the contents of the `funds_message` variable:

```
message_ptr = &funds_message;
```

Now, the contents of `funds_message` can be accessed by constructs such as:

```
message_ptr->amount
```

The output of the following program would be

Anytown, PA 07434
2500

```
main()
{

/* program showing various aspects of structures */

struct message
    {   struct
            {  char name[30];
               char address[4][30];
            }  sender;
        struct destination
            {  char bank_name[50];
               char address[4][30];
               int   account_num;
            }  destination;
        int  amount;
    };

struct message funds_message =
                        {  {  "John Doe",
                            {  {"123, Maple street"},
                               {"Anytown, PA 07434"},
                               {""},
                               {""},
                            }
                           },
                           {  "Bank of Anytown",
                             {  {"Anytown Plaza"},
                                {"Anytown, PA 07434"},
                                {""},
                                {""},
                             },
                             2348623
                           },
                           2500
                        };
struct message *message_ptr;

message_ptr = &funds_message;
printf("%s, %d", message_ptr->sender.address[1],
```

```
                    message_ptr->amount);
}
```

Pointers to structures are commonly used when data of a particular structure is allocated dynamically, at runtime. Runtime allocation is usually used when the number of data items, messages in our example, are not known when the program is compiled. (If they were known, then an array of messages could be created in the program). Consider this example. The malloc function allocates a specified amount of memory from the process's unused virtual memory. In this statement:

```
message_ptr = malloc(sizeof (struct message));
```

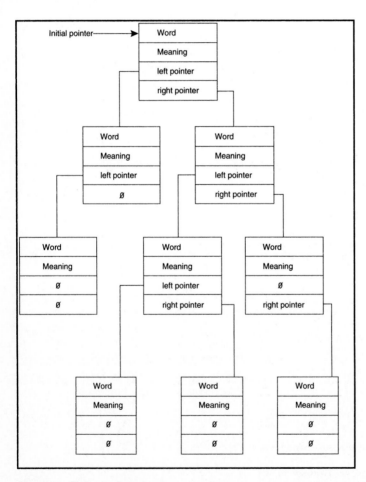

Figure 8.1 Dictionary layout.

enough memory is allocated for the contents of one variable of type
struct message. The memory is pointed to by message_ptr. These
mallocs can be called multiple times in the program. Instances of the
message data can be linked by pointers.

Structures can be recursively declared. Recursive structures are also
known as self-referential structures. Consider the classic example of a binary tree. A word dictionary could be sorted as a binary tree with each node
containing a word, its meaning, a left node pointer and a right node pointer
that point to a subtree. Each node can be declared as a structure:

```
struct tree_node
    { char              word[20];
      char              meaning[200];
      struct tree_node *left;
      struct tree_node *right;
    }
```

Note that struct tree_node contains a reference to itself. The outer
struct determines the storage required for each element. Although
tree_node is referenced within, the storage for left and right is one
pointer each, so the compiler associates with tree_node an array of 20
characters, another array of 200 characters and two pointers (each pointing
to a data of type struct tree_node).

The following program searches for a word in the binary tree dictionary.
Figure 8.1 shows the logical layout of the dictionary. To simplify the program, the code for creating the dictionary is not shown.

```
#include stdio.h
#include string.h
main()
{
/* this tree traversal program demonstrates recursive
   structures
*/
struct tree_node
    { char              word[20];
      char              meaning[200];
      struct tree_node *left;
      struct tree_node *right;
    };
struct tree_node *tree_node_ptr, *initial_ptr;
char response[250], found = 0;
/* the dictionary is set up here. The code is not shown
   initial_ptr points to the top of the tree.
*/

...

/* get a word to be searched */

printf("Enter a word: ");
gets(response);
```

```
tree_node_ptr = initial_ptr;

while (TRUE)   /* in stdio.h: "#define TRUE 1" */
{

  /* current node has the word? */
  /* strcmp() compares two strings and returns 1 if they are same */
     if (strcmp(tree_node_ptr->word, response) == 1)
         { found = 1; break; };
  /* go down left sub-tree? */
     if ((strcmp(tree_node_ptr->word, response) < 1) &&
         (tree_node_ptr->left != NULL))
         tree_node_ptr = tree_node_ptr->left;

  /* go down right sub-tree? */
     if ((strcmp(tree_node_ptr->word, response) < 1) &&
         (tree_node_ptr->right != NULL))
         tree_node_ptr = tree_node_ptr->right;

  /* word not in dictionary */
  break;
}; /* end while loop */

if (found) printf("%s\n",tree_node_ptr->meaning);
else printf("%s\n","*** Word not found in dictionary ***");
}
```

Exercise: Code the part of the preceding program where the tree is to be populated to set up the dictionary.

8.3 Unions

Data of different types can share the same storage location by means of *unions*. Unions are declared very much like structures. Consider:

```
union
    { int i;
      char c;
      double d;
    } var1;
```

The compiler scans the members of the union and allocates enough space to hold the largest element. The largest of i, c and d is d, which requires 8 bytes of storage. 8 bytes are reserved for the variable var1. The three members start at the same location; however, because of their differing size, they end at different locations. In the program, the members are referenced by:

```
var1.i
var2.c
var3.d
```

Figure 8.2 shows the variable contents.

Question: Suppose the keyword `union` was replaced by `struct`. How many bytes will the compiler allocate to `var1`?

The programmer has to have some means of determining what data resides in `var1` at various locations in the program. Members of a `union` can be structures. Consider that the sender of an electronic funds transfer message could be a person or a bank. Here is a `union` to depict this:

```
union
    {
    struct
        { char name[30];
          char address[4][30];
        } person;
    struct
        { char name[50];
          int  bank_num;
        } bank;
    } sender;
```

The `union` is of two members, which are structures. Elements in the structure are accessed by constructs such as:

```
sender.bank.bank_num
```

Question: What will be the output of the following statement in a program containing the preceding union?

```
printf("%d", sizeof sender);
```

Structures can contain unions. A structure similar to the following can be useful in a program processing IRS tax forms:

```
struct irs_forms_template
    { char person_name[30];
```

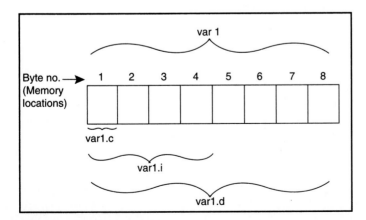

Figure 8.2 An example of a union.

```
      char ss_number[9];
      char address[4][30];
      char form_number[6];
      union
         {
         struct
         {
         ... Form 1040 fields ...
         } form1040;
      struct
         {
         ... Form 1040A fields ...
         } form1040a;
      struct
         {
         ... Form 1040EZ fields ...
         } form1040ez;
        ...
      } forms;
   };
```

This is one of the most common uses of unions. The structure contains a set of simple variables followed by variables sharing a common area. One of the variables in the beginning, form_number in this example, identifies the type of data residing in the common area.

At this stage, it may be obvious; structures and unions can contain nested structures and unions. A union can be initialized with a value of the type of its first member only, as shown here

```
union
   { int   i;
     char c;
     double d;
   } var1 = 345;  /* initialize i */
```

8.4   Passing Structures to Functions

When a structure name is specified in the parameter list of a function call, the structure is passed as an immediate value. Effectively, the structure's contents are copied to the function's structure declaration:

```
main()
{
struct string
   { char   str[1018];
     short length;
   } str_struct;

func(str_struct);      /* 1020-byte structure copied onto stack
                        * for the function to use as it's own
                        * copy.
                        */
```

```
func(&str_struct);    /* pass the address of the structure. */
}
```

The copy is performed by the efficient MOVC3 VAX instruction; however, the copy of a complete structure can be inefficient if done multiple times in a loop, and it may not be necessary. If possible, the address of structure should be passed to the function. If a complete structure is passed, the maximum length cannot exceed 1020 bytes.

Basic Input and Output

I/O is performed by function calls within C programs. The C language does not have any special constructs or statements for I/O. Traditionally, C compilers come bundled with standard I/O functions that are declared in the file stdio.h. On VAX/VMS, this file resides in SYS$LIBRARY:. The I/O functions are part of the C run time library, which is linked with the C programs. For portability, these functions are precisely defined by the ANSI C standard. The functions in this library are barely adequate for terminal and file I/O. Most professional-quality programs use a forms management package like DECforms for terminal I/O and Record Management Services (RMS) for file I/O. One major drawback of standard I/O in many applications is that it does not properly handle NULLs in files. Nevertheless, the standard I/O functions are useful and ubiquitous in most C programs, so they are discussed here. All programs using functions mentioned in this chapter must include the standard I/O header file, as:

```
#include stdio.h
```

9.1 Terminal I/O

The terminal input functions are:

```
getchar()
gets()
```

Terminal output functions are:

```
putchar()
puts()
printf()
```

The getchar() gets one character from the terminal, as in

```
char input_ch;
input_ch = getchar();
```

During program execution, getchar() causes the program to wait until a complete line of input (terminated by the RETURN key) is entered. The line can be edited with the line editing keys (like DELETE to delete the last character entered). The line is read into a work area, and just one character from this work area is returned to the program. The next getchar() will fetch the next character in the work area. The work area is used up before the user at the terminal is prompted for further input. The RETURN key is considered the character ASCII 10 (HEX 0D). The getchar() is not useful when the input is to be validated and processed one character at a time as, for example, in a form field where the user is not allowed to enter alphabetic characters in a numeric field.

The gets() function gets a line of input from the terminal, as in:

```
char input_line[250];
gets(input_line);
```

The input line is not read in until the RETURN key is pressed. The line is put in input_line without the RETURN character and, however, terminated with NULL.

The putchar() function writes one character to the terminal:

```
char output_ch;
putchar(output_ch);
```

The character is immediately displayed on the terminal at the current cursor position.

The puts() writes a string of characters to the terminal. A carriage return and line feed (CR and LF), also known as *newline*, are also sent to the terminal so the cursor moves to the next line:

```
char output_line[250] = "Test output line";
putchar(output_line);
```

The `putchar()` and `puts()` cannot be used to display integers and other datatypes, as this data is not formatted ASCII display characters. The `printf()` function performs formatted output for any datatype. The first argument is the format specifier, and further arguments are data to be printed. For example:

```
int x = 15;
char str[100] = "***test string***";
printf("Integer x is %d, string str is %s\n", x, s);
```

The format specifier is printed literally unless a % is encountered. The characters following % describe how an argument should be printed. The `%d` means that the next argument, x in the example, should be treated as a decimal number and printed as its `string` representation. The `%s` means that the next argument should be treated as a NULL terminated string. The output of the statement will be:

```
Integer x is 15, string str is ***test string***
```

Note that \n represents the newline character (actually, carriage return and line feed). See the chapter on data types for a list of such escape sequences. The formal syntax of a `printf` expression is:

```
printf( const char *format_specifier, argument, argument, ...);
```

Appendix A gives a list of formats that begin with % for converting internal representation of arguments into forms that can be displayed on the terminal. The appendix also shows some examples.

9.2   Basic File I/O

In most cases, file I/O refers to I/O to and from disk files. C treats terminal I/O and disk file I/O (or any other I/O) similarly. The same set functions are used for I/O with any device. The basic file manipulation functions are:

`fopen()`	Open a file.
`fgetc()`	Read one character from a file.
`fgets()`	Read a line (record) from a file.
`fputc()`	Write one character to a file.
`fputs()`	Write a character `string` to a file.

fprintf()	Write formatted output to a file.
fclose()	Close a file.
getc()	Exactly like fgetc().
puts()	Exactly like fputs().

The fopen() function opens a file, stores some information on the file in a work area, and returns a pointer to this area. This work area must be specified with the datatype FILE. FILE is declared in stdio.h using the statements:

```
extern  struct  _iobuf
                {
                int     _cnt;
                char    *_ptr;
                char    *_base;
                char    _flag;


#define _IOREAD          0x01
#define _IOWRT           0x02
#define _IONBF           0x04
#define _IOMYBUF         0x08
#define _IOEOF           0x10
#define _IOERR           0x20
#define _IOSTRG          0x40
#define _IORW            0x80
                char    _file;

                };


typedef struct _iobuf*    FILE;
```

Briefly, a variable declared with type FILE is merely a pointer to the structure _iobuf, which is manipulated internally by C when performing I/O operations. Here is an example of FILE usage:

```
FILE *file_ptr;
file_ptr = fopen("test.data","w");
```

Here, file_ptr is a pointer to file test.data. The w specifies that the file is to be opened for writing. The fopen() syntax is:

```
fopen( char *file_name, *access_mode);
```

Access modes can be combinations of the following characters

r	Open existing file for read.
w	Open a new file for write.

a   Open an existing file for appending to.

+   Open file for update access.

b   Open file for binary access (carriage controls are passed as is to the program).

Data can be read from files using statements like:

```
char input_ch;
char input_line[201];
input_ch = fgetc(file_ptr);     /* get one character from test.data */
fgets(input_line,200,file_ptr); /* get one line */
```

The `fgets()` specifies the input string, the maximum number of characters to be read into the input `string` and the file pointer. If the line is larger than 200 characters, only 200 characters are moved to the buffer; the rest of the line is discarded. The newline terminator is also put in in `put_line`.

Data can be written to files using statements like:

```
char output_ch;
char output_line[250] = "Test output line";
fputc(output_line, file_ptr);   /*  write one character */
fputs(output_line, file_ptr);   /*  write a string without
                                    the NULL at the end */
```

The `fprintf()` is similar to the `printf()`, except that `fprintf()` sends the output to a file whose pointer is the first argument:

```
int x = 15;
char str[100] = "***test string***";
fprintf(fileptr, "Integer x is %d, stringstr is %s\n", x, s);
```

The `fclose()` closes an open file:

```
fclose(file_ptr);
```

The `getc()` and `puts()` are not really functions; they're macros; within the file `stdio.h`, they are defined as `fgetc()` and `puts()`, as shown here:

```
#define getc(p)       fgetc(p)
#define putc(x,p)     fputc(x,p)
```

9.3 Error Processing

If a file open or close operation is not successful, a NULL is returned in the file pointer by the (VAX C run time library) function. The `perror()` function writes an error message to the standard error device (normally, the terminal), describing the last error encountered during a call to the VAX C run time library (RTL). A `string` pointer can be specified as a parameter to `perror()`, as in:

```
perror("Open error");
```

For example, here's how a file open error can be handled:

```
FILE *file_ptr;
file_ptr = fopen("test.data","w");
if  (file_ptr == NULL)
    { perror("test.data open error");
      exit();
    }
```

If `test.data` does not exist in the default disk and directory, the following error will be printed and the program will exit:

```
test.data open error: no such file or directory
```

Reading and writing errors can be checked by the macro `ferror`, which is used as in:

```
char input_line[200];
input_line = fgets( input_line, 200, file_ptr);
if  (ferror(file_ptr) != NULL)
    {  printf("read error\n");
       exit();
    }
```

The macro effectively generates code to look at a location in the file information area pointed to by `file_ptr`. If the location has a nonzero value, then there was an error.

Figure 9.1 shows a real-world program that reads a file with long lines and converts it into a file with lines longer than 80 characters wrapped around at the 80th column. Optionally, the wrap column position can be specified as some value other than 80. The program illustrates the I/O functions described here.

9.4   Terminal I/O Revisited

We mentioned that C uses the same functions for terminal and disk I/O, yet we have shown separate functions for each. Actually, terminal I/O is performed via three predefined files:

`stdin`   The file referred to by the logical name
SYS$INPUT.

Figure 9.1 Program to wrap long lines.

```
/* File: collapse.c        Author: Jay Shah
 * This program collapses long lines in a file down to 80 columns
 * or any other specified column position. The program can be used
 * when terminals and printers cannot display files with long lines.
 *
 * When the program is run, the user will be prompted for an
 * input file name, output file name and wrap column number.
 *
 * Usage of variables:
 *
 * infile         - attributes of input file, FILE variable
 * outfile        - attributes of output file, FILE variable
 * line_length    - length of a input line
 * last_line_length - length of last line to be written to
 *                    to output file for each input line

 * current_pos    - current position in input line buffer
 * wrap_width     - width at which lines from input file should
 *                    be wrapped if the lines exceed this width
 * inp_buffer     - buffer for each line from input file
 * out_buffer     - buffer for each line for output file
 * inp_filename   - buffer for input file name
 * out_filename   - buffer for output file name
 */


#include stdio            /* for the standard I/O performed here */
#include ssdef            /* system error messages */


main()
   {

    FILE *infile;          /* handler for input file */
    FILE *outfile;         /* handler for output file */
    int line_length, last_line_length;
    int current_pos, wrap_width;
    char inp_buffer[10000], out_buffer[10000];
```

Figure 9.1 *(Continued)*

```
  char inp_filename[80], out_filename[80];


  printf("Program to collapse long lines in a given file\n");

/* Get output file name and open the file in w]
 * Default file name is same as input file name
printf("output file (default %s): ",inp_filenar
gets(out_filename);
if (strlen(out_filename) == 0)
    { strcpy(out_filename,inp_filename);
    };
if ((outfile = fopen(out_filename,"w")) <= NUL]
    { perror("fopen:output");exit();
    };


/* Get column at which to wrap around long lin(
printf("Wrap at column (default 80): ");
wrap_width=atoi(gets(inp_filename));
if (wrap_width<=0) wrap_width=80;


/* Now process the input file */
 /* Repeat for each line in input file */
 while (fgets(inp_buffer,10000,infile) != NULL)
    {

    /* linefeed at end of input line is ignored */
    line_length = strlen(inp_buffer) - 1;
    current_pos = 0;

    /* Repeat for each line to be output,
```

Figure 9.1 *(Continued)*

```
   except for last output line */
 while (current_pos+wrap_width < line_length)

   {
   strncpy(&out_buffer,&inp_buffer[current_pos],wrap_width);
   fprintf(outfile,"%s\n",&out_buffer);
   current_pos = current_pos + wrap_width;
   }; /* end of while */


 /* last output line corresponding to the input line */
 last_line_length = line_length - current_pos;
 strncpy(out_buffer,&inp_buffer[current_pos],last_line_length);
 out_buffer[last_line_length] = NULL;
 fprintf(outfile,"%s\n",&out_buffer);
 } /* end of while */

}
```

stdout   The file referred to by the logical name
           SYS$OUTPUT.
stderr   The file referred to by the logical name
           SYS$ERROR.

Normally, the three logicals point to the terminal, tt:. getchar() and putchar() are actually macros in stdio.h.

```
#define getchar()     fgetc(stdin)
#define putchar(x)    fputc(x,stdout)
```

The other terminal I/O functions are different from file I/O functions, but very slightly. The gets(), puts(), and printf() are similar to fgets(), fputs(), and fprintf(), except that the former three use the default files stdin, stdout and stdout respectively. For example:

```
printf("test");      /* output to stdout */
fprintf(fp, "test"); /* output to fp */
```

The following two statements are equivalent:

```
printf("test");
fprintf(stdout,"test");
```

10

The Debugger

The VMS debugger is one of the most useful application development tools, yet it is rarely fully exploited. The debugger is symbolic and supports all the standard languages on VMS. The debugger has a rudimentary programming language that aids in debugging complex programs. It can be used with any terminal; however, on DECwindows-based workstations, the VMS debugger uses windowing features. This chapter discusses the various features of the debugger.

10.1 Overview

To run a program under the debugger, the program must be compiled and linked with the /DEBUG qualifier, as in:

```
$ CC/LIST/NOOPTIMIZE/DEBUG myprog
$ LINK/DEBUG myprog, sys$share:vaxcrtl/library
```

Note that the /NOOPTIMIZE qualifier must be used on the compilation command line because the compiler normally tightens code for efficient execution, and this can lead to inconsistencies in expected and actual values of variables within the debugger. The program should compile and link without errors. When the program is run, the DBG> prompt is displayed. Program execution is under the control of the debugger:

```
$ RUN myprog

     VAX DEBUG Version V5.4-02

%DEBUG-I-INITIAL, language is C, module set to MYPROG

DBG>
```

Debugger commands can then be entered. The GO command will cause the program to continue execution until the end of the program. The EXIT command terminates the debug session without further execution of the program. A program compiled and linked with the /DEBUG qualifier can be made to run through without any debugger prompting by a command like:

```
$ RUN/NODEBUG myprog
```

The DEBUG option causes the program to run slowly, so for better performance, once a program is debugged, the /DEBUG qualifier should not be used on the compile and link commands.

The basic features of the debugger are:

- The HELP command provides information on debugger operations.
- The STEP command causes (at least) one source line to be executed. If the line contains multiple C statements, all are executed. If the line contains a statement that continues on the following lines, this statement is executed, effectively executing multiple source lines. The STEP n command causes n source lines to be executed.
- The EXAMINE command can be used to display the value of a variable. The Deposit command can be used to change the value of a variable. As the debugger is symbolic, the variables are specified using the syntax of the source language.
- The EVALUATE command can be used to evaluate expressions.
- The SET BREAK command can be used to set breakpoints and suspend program execution at a specified location. Values of variables can be checked or changed when a breakpoint is reached.
- The SET TRACE command can be used to trace the flow of program execution. For example:

```
DBG> SET TRACE %LINE 910
```

will cause a message to be displayed when the line is reached during execution. Program execution continues.

- The SET WATCH command can be used to suspend program execution when the value of a variable changes.
- The FOR, IF, REPEAT and WHILE control structures are supported for conditional execution of commands.
- Multiple commands can be given on the same line, separated by semicolons. For example:

```
DBG> STEP; EXAMINE var1
```

- Debugger commands can be put in a file, which can later be run from the debugger.
- The source file (or files) of the executable image being debugged can be edited from within the editor.
- The sequence of nested function calls at the current point can be displayed by a command like:

```
DBG> SHOW CALLS
```

- To temporarily exit from the debugger to DCL, the command is:

```
DBG> SPAWN
```

To return to the debugger session, the command is:

```
$ EXIT
```

10.1.1 Expressions and supported C operators

Expressions can be entered as they are in C source programs; the debugger understands C language syntax. Example statements are:

```
DBG> deposit  position = 23 + 45
DBG> evaluate position % 20
8
```

The % is the *mod* operator, which returns the remainder of the position di-

Supported operators	
-	Unary arithmetic
+ - * / %	Binary arithmetic
== != < > <= >=	Relational
&& | | !	Logical
& | ^ ? ~	Bitwise logical
<< >>	Shift
sizeof	Size of a scalar
&	Address of
*	Contents of
Unsupported operators	
++ --	Increment/decrement
= += -= *= /=	Assignment
%= |= &= ^=	Assignment
?:	Conditional
(type)	Type cast

Figure 10.1 C operator support by the VMS debugger.

vided by 20. Not all operators are supported by the debugger, as many operators have side effects that can lead to incorrect debugger operations. Figure 10.1 shows the C operators supported and not supported by the debugger.

10.2 A Sample Debug Session

Figure 10.2 shows the output of a complete debugging session. The program is `collapse.c` from the chapter on basic input and output. The listing file generated by the compiler is shown in Fig. 10.3.

In order to keep the listing file small, the listing for `include files` is omitted by the compiler. The `include file` contents can also be listed with the `/SHOW=INCLUDE` compilation qualifier. In Fig. 10.2, the bold characters are input from the terminal. The line numbers on the left are not part of the debug session; rather, they're inserted to locate lines. Here are some

Figure 10.2 A debug session.

```
1       $ {CC/LIST/NOOPTIMIZE/DEBUG  COLLAPSE.C}

2       $ {LINK/DEBUG  COLLAPSE.OBJ,SYS$SHARE:VAXCRTL/LIBRARY}

3       $ {RUN COLLAPSE}

4

5             VAX DEBUG Version V5.4-02

6

7       %DEBUG-I-INITIAL, language is C, module set to COLLAPSE

8

9       DBG> {STEP}

10      stepped to COLLAPSE\main\%LINE 915

11         915:    printf("Program to collapse long lines in a given file\n");

12

13      DBG> {EXAMINE WRAP_WIDTH}

14      %DEBUG-E-NOSYMBOL, symbol 'WRAP_WIDTH' is not in the symbol table

15

16      DBG> {EXAMINE wrap_width}

17      COLLAPSE\main\wrap_width:        4

18

19      DBG> {SET WATCH wrap_width}

20      %DEBUG-I-WPTTRACE, non-static watchpoint, tracing every instruction

21

22      DBG> {GO}

23      Program to collapse long lines in a given file

24      input file: {tmp.input}

25      output file (default tmp.input): {tmp.tmp}

26      Wrap at column (default 80): {8}

27      watch of COLLAPSE\main\wrap_width at COLLAPSE\main\%LINE 936+22

28         936:    wrap_width=atoi(gets(inp_filename));

29         old value: 4

30         new value: 8

31      break at COLLAPSE\main\%LINE 937

32         937:    if (wrap_width<=0) wrap_width=80;

33

34      DBG> {DEPOSIT wrap_width = 7}

35

36      DBG> {SET BREAK %LINE 945}
```

Figure 10.2 *(Continued)*

```
37     %DEBUG-E-LINEINFO, no line 945, previous line is 943, next line is 946

38

39     DBG> {SET BREAK %LINE 946}

40

41     DBG> {GO}

42     break at COLLAPSE\main\main_4\%LINE 946

43        946:       line_length = strlen(inp_buffer) - 1;

44

45     DBG> EXAMINE/ASCIZ inp_buffer

46     COLLAPSE\main\inp_buffer

47        [0]:        "This is a test file."

48

49     DBG>  STEP{20}

50     break at COLLAPSE\main\main_4\%LINE 946

51        946:       line_length = strlen(inp_buffer) - 1;

52

53     DBG> {EXAMINE/ASCIZ inp_buffer}

54     COLLAPSE\main\inp_buffer

55        [0]:        "123456789 123456789 123456789 ."

56

57     DBG> {SHOW WATCH}

58     watchpoint of COLLAPSE\main\wrap_width [tracing every instruction]

59

60     DBG> {SHOW BREAK}

61     breakpoint at COLLAPSE\main\main_4\%LINE 946

62

63     DBG> {CANCEL BREAK %LINE 946}

64

65     DBG> {GO}

66     stepped to COLLAPSE\main\main_4\main_5\%LINE 954

67        954:          fprintf(outfile,"%s\n",&out_buffer);

68

69     DBG> {SHOW BREAK}

70     %DEBUG-I-NOBREAKS, no breakpoints are set

71

72     DBG> {GO}
```

Figure 10.2 *(Continued)*

```
73        %DEBUG-I-EXITSTATUS, is '%SYSTEM-S-NORMAL, normal successful completion'

74

75        DBG> {EXIT}

76

77        $ {TYPE TMP.INPUT}

78        This is a test file

79        123456789 123456789 123456789

80

81        $ {TYPE TMP.TMP}

82        This is

83         a test

84         file

85        1234567

86        89 1234

87        56789 1

88        2345678

89        9


        -----------------------------------------------------
```

Figure 10.3 Compilation listing file for collapse.c.

```
COLLAPSE                                       11-APR-1992 16:05:53    VAX C
V3.0-031                          Page 1

V1.0                                           11-APR-1992 15:48:16    $
1$DUS22:[TECH4]COLLAPSE.C;1 (1)




    1              /* File: collapse.c      Author: Jay Shah

    2               * This program collapses long lines in a file down to 80 columns

    3               * or any other specified column position. The program can be used

    4               * when terminals and printers cannot display files with long lines

    5               *

    6               * When the program is run, the user will be prompted for an
```

Figure 10.3 (*Continued*)

```
COLLAPSE                                                    11-APR-1992 16:05:53    VAX
V3.0-031                          Page 1

V1.0                                                        11-APR-1992 15:48:16    $
1$DUS22:[TECH4]COLLAPSE.C;1 (1)




     1              /* File: collapse.c      Author: Jay Shah
     2              * This program collapses long lines in a file down to 80 columns
     3              * or any other specified column position. The program can be used
    20              * out_buffer       - buffer for each line for output file
    21              * inp_filename     - buffer for input file name
    22              * out_filename     - buffer for output file name
    23              */
    24
    25              #include stdio              /* for the standard I/O performed here *
   267              #include ssdef             /* system error messages */
   904
   905              main()
   906                {
   907    1
   908    1              FILE *infile;              /* handler for input file */
   909    1              FILE *outfile;             /* handler for output file */
   910    1              int line_length, last_line_length;
   911    1              int current_pos, wrap_width;
   912    1              char inp_buffer[10000], out_buffer[10000];
   913    1              char inp_filename[80], out_filename[80];
   914    1
   915    1              printf("Program to collapse long lines in a given file\n");
   916    1
   917    1              /* Get input file name and open the file in read mode */
   918    1              printf("input file: ");
   919    1              if ((infile = fopen(gets(inp_filename),"r")) <= NULL)
   920    1                { perror("fopen:input");exit(); };
   921    2                };
   922    1
```

Figure 10.3 *(Continued)*

```
923    1                 /* Get output file name and open the file in write mode
924    1                  * Default file name is same as input file name. */
925    1                 printf("output file (default %s): ",inp_filename);
926    1                 gets(out_filename);
927    1                 if (strlen(out_filename) == 0)
928    1                     { strcpy(out_filename,inp_filename);
929    2                     };
930    1                 if ((outfile = fopen(out_filename,"w")) <= NULL)
931    1                     { perror("fopen:output");exit();
932    2                     };
```

```
COLLAPSE                                       11-APR-1992 16:05:53   V
AX C       V3.0-031            Page 2
V1.0                                           11-APR-1992 15:48:16   $
1$DUS22:[TECH4]COLLAPSE.C;1 (1)
```

```
933    1
934    1                 /* Get column at which to wrap around long lines */
935    1                 printf("Wrap at column (default 80): ");
936    1                 wrap_width=atoi(gets(inp_filename));
937    1                 if (wrap_width<=0) wrap_width=80;
938    1
939    1                 /* Now process the input file */
940    1
941    1                 /* Repeat for each line in input file */
942    1                 while (fgets(inp_buffer,10000,infile) != NULL)
943    1                     {
944    2
945    2                     /* linefeed at end of input line is ignored */
946    2                     line_length = strlen(inp_buffer) - 1;
947    2                     current_pos = 0;
948    2
949    2                     /* Repeat for each line to be output,
950    2                        except for last output line */
951    2                     while (current_pos+wrap_width  < line_length)
952    2                         {
953    3                         strncpy(&out_buffer,&inp_buffer[current_pos],wrap_width);
954    3                         fprintf(outfile,"%s\n",&out_buffer);
955    3                         current_pos = current_pos + wrap_width;
```

Figure 10.3 *(Continued)*

```
956   3                        }; /* end of while */

957   2

958   2              /* last output line corresponding to the input line */

959   2              last_line_length = line_length - current_pos;

960   2              strncpy(out_buffer,&inp_buffer[current_pos],last_line_length)
;

961   2              out_buffer[last_line_length] = NULL;

962   2              fprintf(outfile,"%s\n",&out_buffer);

963   2              } /* end of while */

964   1          }
```

comments on the session:

- Program execution under the debugger begins at line 3.

- No program statement is executed before the DBG> prompt at line 9. The STEP command causes an entry in main(). The next program line to be executed is displayed at line 11. Still, no program statements have been executed.

- The EXAMINE command at line 16 gives an error because the debugger knows that in C, lowercase and uppercase letters are considered separate. EXAMINE at line 16 shows the value of wrap_width to be 4, which is a garbage value from the point of view of the program.

- The wrap_width is WATCHed at line 19. Henceforth, during program execution, if the value of wrap_width changes, the program execution will be suspended and the DBG> prompt will be displayed. The comment on line 20 by the debugger is because the variable wrap_width has been allocated on the stack and not in program virtual memory. The comment is merely informational.

- The GO on line 22 causes program execution to continue until the end of program or until a break or watch point condition is satisfied.

- The wrap_width acquired a new value at program line 936, hence the break at line 27. The variable changed value inside the atoi function in the VAX C RTL, and because the debugger does not have the source code for the library, it shows the break location as %LINE 936+22. The break at line 31 is a consequence of the watchpoint condition being satisfied.

- The DEPOSIT at line 34 alters the value of wrap_width. DEPOSIT is useful for altering variable values "within" the program execution without having to recompile and link the program.

- At line 36, a BREAK is being set for program line 945; however, there is no executable statement on that program line, hence the debugger error message. The BREAK is then set for program line 946, and GO is issued at line 41. The program breaks at program line 946, as shown at line 43.

- The EXAMINE at line 45 is used to examine a string in memory. The string is assumed to be terminated by a zero byte. If the EXAMINE inp_buffer command had been issued, the debugger would display the array of 10,000 characters, one character per line, which would be time-consuming.

- The STEP 20 at line 49 will cause 20 source lines to be executed before suspending program execution. In this case however, as seen at line 51, the program breaks at program line 946 before executing 20 steps because a breakpoint has previously been set for line 946. The EXAMINE at line 53 shows the second line from the input file.

- The SHOW commands at lines 57 and 60 are to display for which locations and variables breakpoints have been set. The SHOW commands are useful in long debugging sessions. Breakpoints and watchpoints can be canceled by commands such as that shown on line 63.

- The GO at line 65 causes program execution to resume. The program breaks at program line 954 because 20 steps have been completed there. See line 66. Line 70 shows that there are no breakpoints set in the program. The GO at line 72 causes execution to continue until the program terminates. The input and output files for the program are typed at lines 77 and 81, which show the transformation performed by the program execution.

10.3   Scope of Symbols

Consider this C program, where the ellipses denote program statements:

```
main()
{
int xyz = 5;
...
  {
  int xyz = 3;
  ...
  }
...
}
```

Variable xyz is defined in two blocks. The scope rules used by C apply within the debugger. Hence, if during a debug session a breakpoint were set in the inner block, the EXAMINE command would show xyz = 3. In the outer block xyz would have a value of 5. Within the debugger (as in the program), there are two different variables with the same name xyz. To see multiple definitions of a variable, use SHOW SYMBOL, as in:

```
DBG>SHOW SYMBOL xyz
data prog1\main\xyz
data prog1\main\main_1\xyz
```

A particular symbol can be referenced by its full name, as in:

```
DBG>EXAMINE prog1\main\xyz
```

By default, when a variable is accessed by its simple name, the variable, as seen by the executing program at the current breakpoint, is assumed by the debugger. If a number of variables in another block are to be addressed, the default scope can be changed, as in:

```
DBG> SET SCOPE prog1\main\main_1
```

10.4   Screen-Oriented Debugging

The sample debug session in section 10.2 uses line-oriented input and output. This mode will work on any type of terminal, including hard-copy terminals. However, CRT terminals like the VT320 and the VT420 support screen mode debugging, which is usually more convenient and easy to use. (Screen mode should not be confused with DECwindows mode, which is discussed in the next section.) Screen mode can be entered from the debugger by the command:

```
DBG> Set Mode Screen
```

The screen divides into three windows:

1. The SRC window, which displays the source program.
2. The OUT window, which displays debugger output.
3. The PROMPT window, which is used for user input to debugger and program and program output.

Here's what would be seen if screen mode were entered when debugging the program used in section 10.2:

```
$ RUN COLLAPSE

    VAX DEBUG Version V5.4-02

%DEBUG-I-INITIAL, language is C, module set to COLLAPSE

DBG> Set Mode Screen
```

(See Fig. 10.4.) The arrow on the left in the SRC window points to the next statement to be executed. When the program is first run, the arrow is positioned just after `main()`. The cursor will be positioned in the prompt window after the `DBG>` prompt for further debug commands. The commands used in the debug session 10.2 can be entered in screen mode. A `STEP` command will cause the arrow in the SRC window to move to the first executable program statement. The output after the STEP command shown in Fig. 10.5.

Note that the next line to be executed is displayed in the SRC and the OUT windows. This double display is redundant. The command:

```
DBG> Set Step Nosource
```

will disable the display of the next line to be executed in the OUT window.

When a program is run under the debugger, the debugger senses the terminal characteristics. If the terminal is screen oriented, the debugger interprets the keys on the keypad at the right of the keyboard as a `string` of characters or macros that are commands to the debugger. For example, the PF3 key is interpreted as the string

```
Set Mode Screen; Set Step Nosource
```

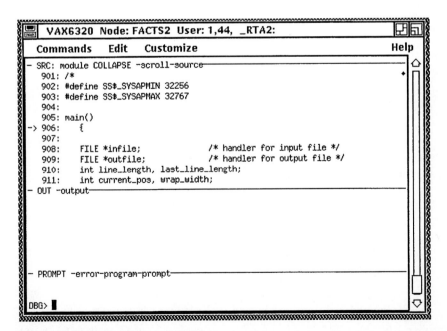

Figure 10.4 Debugger windows at startup.

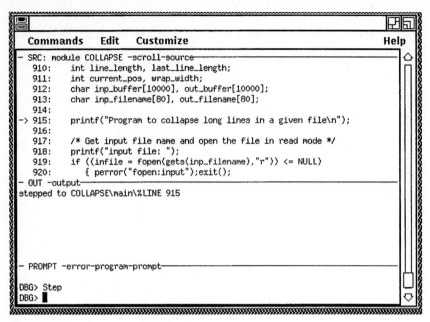

Figure 10.5   Main window pull-down menus. (*Copyright © 1990 Digital Equipment Corporation. All Rights Reserved. Reprinted by Permission*)

Hence, when PF3 is pressed from the debugger, the effect is exactly the same as entering:

```
DBG> Set Mode Screen; Set Step Nosource
```

The two commands were just explained. Many programmers enter PF3 just after entering the debugger. The keypad keys do not have any new commands; they are macro definitions of command strings that can be entered at the DBG prompt by typing out the complete string. Figure 10.6 shows some of the keypad commands. Keypad keys 2, 4, 6, and 8 are used to scroll the current window in the four directions. Initially, the current window is SRC; however, keypad key 3 can be used to change the current window.

Every keypad key has a definition within the debugger; however, not all keys are described here. Many keypad keys have a different meaning when preceded by PF1 (Gold) or PF4 (Blue). This way, many commands can be executed by a few keystrokes. For example,

Keypad 8	= Scroll/Up	Scroll window up one screen
PF1, keypad 8	= Scroll/Top	Scroll to top of file
PF4, keypad 8, w	= Scroll/Up w	Scroll up window w

Most keypad keys and function keys (at the top of the keyboard) can be redefined to a specified text. For example, if during a debugging session, the variable var1 is examined often, PF2, which is initially defined as "Help Keypad Default" by the debugger, can be redefined by:

```
DBG> DEFINE/KEY/TERMINATE PF2 "Examine var1"
```

The terminate means that a RETURN is added at the end when the key is pressed. The var1 can now be examined by merely pressing PF2.

10.5 Debugging Screen-Oriented Programs

Many C programs perform screen-oriented I/O with the aid of DECforms, SMG$, curses, or a similar package. When these programs are debugged

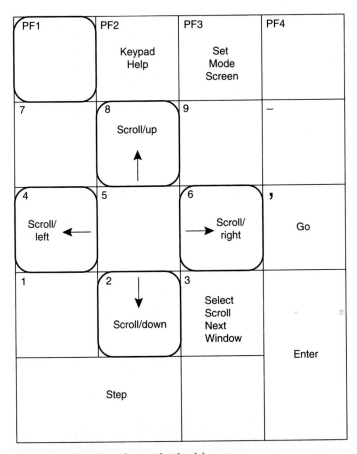

Figure 10.6 Basic keypad usage for the debugger.

from a terminal, program and debugger output is mixed up on the screen, making it difficult to visualize the screen as it would look when the program is run without the debug option. VMS Debugger allows debugger I/O to be performed on one terminal while program I/O is performed on another terminal. Here is how to achieve this:

- Suppose your terminal is LTA321:. Log into another terminal nearby. Suppose the terminal is LTA253:.

- Define two logicals at your terminal:

```
$ DEFINE DBG$INPUT LTA253:
$ DEFINE DBG$OUTPUT LTA253:
```

The debugger uses these logicals to direct debugger I/O to LTA253:.

- Enter a wait for 20 hours on LTA253: by:

```
$ WAIT 20:00
```

If this command is not entered, the terminal will send output to DCL and the debugger alternately, which can be confusing. The wait effectively causes DCL not to prompt for any more input (assuming you do not debug for 20 hours), so all I/O through LTA253: is via the debugger.

- Run the program to be debugged from your terminal, LTA321:. All program I/O will be to your terminal, while debugger I/O will be on the other terminal. This way, the debugger does not break any screen displays by the program.

Note that you must have appropriate privileges to access the second terminal. If you cannot access the terminal, the system manager can give you the SHARE privilege and allow WORLD access to the terminal by:

```
$ SET PROTECTION=WO:RWED/DEVICE LTA253:
```

Another solution is to define LTA253: using "MCR LATCP" to point to a particular port on a terminal server, allow free WORLD access to the device by the preceding command, and set that terminal as ACCESS=REMOTE on the terminal server. The sequence of commands can be:

```
$ MCR LATCP CREATE PORT LTA253:
$ MCR LATCP SET PORT LTA253:/NODE=SRVR15/PORT=PORT_6
$ SET PROTECTION=WO:RWED/DEVICE LTA253:
$ MCR NCP CONNECT NODE SRVR15 !get in the terminal server
USERNAME> shah
LOCAL> define port 6 access remote
```

```
LOCAL> logout port 6
LOCAL> (CTRL/D)
```

This is a more permanent solution that doesn't extensively compromise system security. The system manager may have other creative solutions.

10.6   DECwindows Mode Debugging

We've already discussed line mode and screen mode debugging, and now we'll discuss DECwindows mode debugging. Screen and DECwindows modes are similar; commands have to be typed in when using screen mode; commands are selected by moving the mouse, clicking mouse buttons and typing in some information. The program is compiled and linked as previously shown. On the DECwindows terminal, a DECterm window should be created so that DCL commands can be entered. On entering:

```
$ RUN myprog
```

three new windows will pop up on the screen, as shown in Fig. 10.7. The figure shows the `collapse` program being debugged.The three windows are:

- The main window. Commands are selected from the options presented in this window.

- The SRC window, which shows the source code. This window is similar to the SRC window of the screen-mode debugging described in the previous sections. The boxed line is the one that will be executed next.

- The OUT window, which shows debugger output. This window is similar to the OUT window of screen-mode debugging.

Program I/O is handled from the DECterm window from which the program was RUN. This is different from screen-mode, where the PROMPT window is used for program I/O. Programs using screen forms can be conveniently debugged using the DECwindows mode. (See Fig. 10.7.)

10.6.1   Executing commands

To execute a command, the mouse is moved over the corresponding box in the main window, and the left button is clicked. For example, the STEP command is displayed in a box in the main window. Clicking on the box causes one line of the source program to be executed. The top line of the main window offers a set of pull-down menu items that are displayed by clicking on the item. Figure 10.8 shows the pull-down menus. Some of these menus offer submenus.

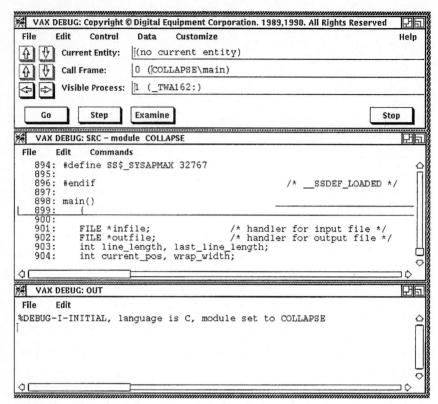

Figure 10.7   Initial DECwindows debugger screen.

Details of how to use each DECwindows debugging feature will not be discussed. In my opinion, the DECwindows mode is a fancy debugging style that doesn't offer much advantage over the screen-oriented mode of debugging. It is easier to type out most commands than to navigate the mouse through the various menus to perform a function. For example, to deposit a new value into a variable, the Data pull-down menu has to be selected, the Variable sub-menu has to be selected, and then the Deposit Variable sub-menu item has to be selected. After that, the variable name and the value have to be typed in! For a more challenging task, try using the FOR statement to control command execution.

It's possible to type commands during a DECwindows mode debugging session by entering the DO key. A command box is displayed within which a command can be entered at the DBG> prompt. The command box can be opened indefinitely by choosing the customized pull-down menu followed by the "Show Command..." option.

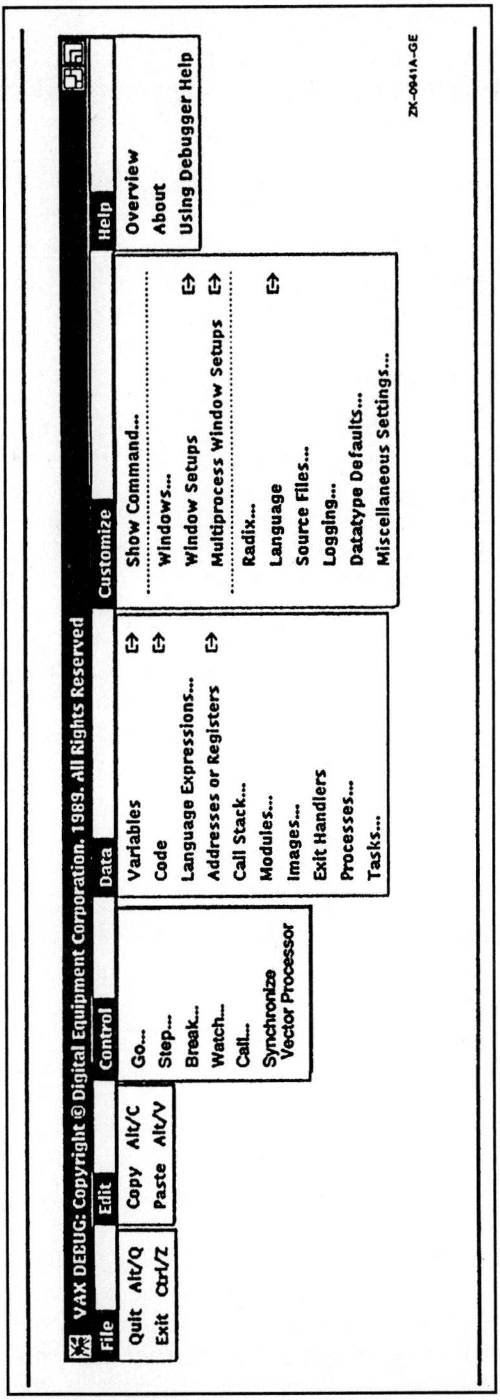

Figure 10.8 Main window pull-down menu.

10.6.2 Other features

The keypad keys are defined as they are for line- or screen-oriented modes. By default, DECwindows mode is used on a DECwindows terminal when the program is run from it. However, this mode can be disabled by:

```
$DEFINE/JOB DBG$DECW$DISPLAY " "      !A space between quotes
```

Later, when the RUN command is given from a DECterm window, the debugger will prompt from the same window, as in the case of line- and screen-modes.

10.7 Conditional Command Execution

The debugger allows for some commands to take effect when a specified condition expression is true. It also allows a set of commands to be executed when the condition expression is true. For example:

```
DBG> SET BREAK %LINE 951 WHEN (current_pos > 80)
                    DO (examine current_pos; go)
```

Here, the program will break at source line 951 if current_pos is greater than 80. The DO part will be executed when the program breaks. The DO part displays the value of current_pos and then continues program execution. Another example is conditional execution by control structures:

```
DBG> for tmpvar = 0 to 9 do ( examine current_pos[tmppar] )
```

Here, the contents of current_pos[0] through current_pos[9] will be displayed.

10.7.1 Conditions with commands

Some debugger statements support the WHEN clause as shown here:

```
DBG> SET BREAK address WHEN (condition-expression)
                    DO (command; command ...)

DBG> SET TRACE address WHEN (condition-expression)
                    DO (command; command ...)

DBG> SET WATCH address WHEN (condition-expression)
                    DO (command; command ...)
```

When the breakpoint or tracepoint address is reached or the contents of the watchpoint address location is modified, the condition-expression is executed. If the condition-expression evaluates to true, the DO commands are executed, and execution is suspended for further command input unless one of the DO commands cause execution to resume (like the GO command). If the condition-expression evaluates to false, execution continues without any action. The condition expression is a C language expression, for example:

```
current_pos == 5 || line_length > 80
```

10.7.2 Control structures

The control structures are:

```
DBG> IF condition-expression THEN (command; command ...)
                             ELSE (command; command ...)

DBG> FOR name = expression1 TO expression2 BY expression3
         DO (command; command ...)

DBG> REPEAT expression DO (command; command ...)

DBG> WHILE condition-expression DO (command; command ...)
```

The statements should be obvious to C programmers. The BY expres sion3 in the FOR statement is optional. The name is a program variable or an arbitrary debugger symbol. The EXITLOOP command can be used to break from an enclosing FOR, REPEAT or WHILE loop. EXITLOOP n can be used to exit from n enclosing loops. For example:

```
DBG> REPEAT 1000 (STEP; IF (current_pos == 0) THEN (EXITLOOP))
```

Here, the STEP command will be executed 1000 times unless current_pos is 0, in which case the REPEAT execution will be aborted, and the DBG> prompt will be displayed for further commands.

10.8   Other Debugger Features

10.8.1 CTRL/C Versus CTRL/Y

When a CTRL/C is entered within the debugger, the current command execution is suspended and control returns to the debugger. This feature is useful when, for example, the program is in an infinite loop or when a long array is being displayed unnecessarily.

When a CTRL/Y is entered within the debugger, the debugging session is terminated and the DCL $ prompt is displayed. VMS allows a command terminated by a CTRL/Y to resume execution if immediately followed by a:

```
$ continue
```

statement. Hence, $ continue can be entered to resume the debug session.

However, if the program were in an infinite loop, pressing CTRL/Y followed by a $ continue merely lets the program continue executing the infinite loop.

10.8.2 Using the DCL DEBUG command

After you give RUN a program and give the GO debugger command, sometimes a program goes into an infinite loop, and you may not know where you are in the program. Press CTRL/Y and then enter:

```
$ DEBUG
```

You will be in the debugger, and the DBG> prompt will be displayed. To see the current source line being executed, use:

```
DBG> show calls        !display nesting of function calls
```

The debugger can be used to determine the cause of the infinite loop.

10.8.3 Command files and debugger initialization

A sequence of commands can be stored in a file and executed from the debugger by a command like:

```
DBG> @cmds.com
```

where cmd.com contains debugger commands.

A set of debugger commands can be stored in a file and executed automatically whenever the debugger is run if the file is referenced by the dbg$init logical name:

```
$ define dbg$init myinit.com
```

This feature can be used to create a customized debugger configuration.

10.8.4 Debugging programs containing ASTs

ASTs are described in chapter 13. When a program is being debugged, at any instance either the debugger or the program is running. ASTs (asynchronous system traps) are enabled when the program is running but disabled when the debugger is running. Hence, ASTs cannot be delivered at the DBG> prompt. AST delivery can be disabled, even when the program is running, by previously issuing:

```
DBG> disable ast
```

ASTs can later be enabled by:

```
DBG> enable ast
```

It should be noted that ASTs are always disabled when the debugger is running; AST can be enabled or disabled when the program is running under the debugger.

10.8.5 Customized commands and debugger-defined symbols

Symbols can be defined within the debugger, as in:

```
DBG> define/value sym1 = 34 % 12
```

Here, symbol `sym1` is assigned a value of 2, which is the value of the expression on the right-hand side. The expression syntax is that of the current language, C in this case. These symbols can then be used within debugger expressions, but not within expressions assigning values to program variables. The value of a symbol can be examined by a statement like:

```
DBG> show symbol/define sym1
defined SYM1
      bound to: 2
      was defined /value
```

An example use of such symbols is:

```
DBG> define/value updates = 0
DBG> set watch current_pos do (define/value updates = updates +1; go)
```

Here, the value of updates will show how many times the value of program variable `current_pos` was changed during program execution.

New debugger commands can be defined by statements like:

```
DBG> define/command ss = "show symbol/define"
```

which can then be used as:

```
DBG> ss sym1
```

Address values can be assigned to a symbol by:

```
DBG> define/address sym2 = prog1\main
```

or

```
DBG> define   sym2 = prog1\main
```

The latter implies that /address is the default qualifier to the define command. The symbol can then be used as:

```
DBG> call sym2
```

10.8.6 The EXAMINE, DEPOSIT and EVALUATEcommands

A variable's contents can be examined by a command like:

```
DBG> EXAMINE current_pos
```

Any address location's longword (4-byte) contents can be displayed by a command like:

```
DBG> EXAMINE 2000
```

A string variable's contents can be displayed in ASCII by a command like:

```
DBG> EXAMINE/ASCIZ inp_buffer
```

Characters starting at the address inp_buffer will be displayed until an ASCII 0 (NULL) is encountered. This form of examine is convenient for viewing strings in C.

```
DBG> EXAMINE/ASCII:10 inp_buffer
```

This form of examine displays 10 ASCII characters starting at inp_buffer. This way, the initial part of a long string can be displayed.

When examining a C struct variable, the complete structure's content is displayed. For example, a source program can contain:

```
struct{int i;
      char c;
      }struct_var1 = { 12, 'A' };
```

The structure can be displayed during a debugging session by a command like:

```
DBG> EXAMINE struct_var1
COLLAPSE\struct_var1
      i:        12
      c:        65
```

C characters are actually 1-byte integers, so the debugger displays the integer value of 'A' when displaying the contents of struct_var1.c.

The DEPOSIT command is used to deposit values in memory locations, normally variables. Examples are:

```
DBG> DEPOSIT current_pos = 53
DBG> DEPOSIT/ASCIZ inp_buffer = "TEST123"
```

The value is converted to the datatype of the variable specified unless if the datatype is specified as a command qualifier as, for example, /ASCIZ in the second example given above. The right-hand side can be any valid C expression, as in:

```
DBG> DEPOSIT current_pos = (*addr1) + 24
```

The EVALUATE command displays the value of a C expression:

```
DBG> EVALUATE (*addr1) + current_pos
```

10.8.7 Typing source lines

A set of source lines can be typed by a command like:

```
DBG> TYPE 800:850
```

Here, lines 800 to 850 will be displayed. During screen mode debugging, the SRC window displays source lines at the point of program execution; however, the TYPE command can be used to display other lines within the source program.

10.8.8 Editing the source file

It's convenient to be able to edit the source file from the debugger so that changes can be made to the file while debugging it. To edit the source file from the debugger, the EDIT command can be used:

```
DBG> EDIT
```

The debugger spawns a subprocess that executes the Language Sensitive Editor (LSE) to edit the latest version of the source file. If a different editor is desired, the SET EDITOR command can be used before the EDIT command:

```
DBG> SET EDITOR /CALLABLE_EDT  !use EDT
```

or

```
DBG> SET EDITOR /CALLABLE_TPU  !use TPU
```

It may be convenient to put these commands in the debugger initialization file, defined by the logical dbg$init.

10.8.9   SEARCHing the source file

A line from the source file containing a specified string can be displayed by the SEARCH command. For example:

```
DBG> SEARCH "current_pos"
```

The line will be searched for from the current position until the end of the file. Consecutive SEARCH commands cause the search to proceed from the line where the immediately previous search string was found. A STEP or similar command that causes program execution will reset the search start point to the source line currently being executed. A range of search lines can be specified by a command like:

```
DBG> SEARCH 800:1000 "current_pos"
```

This command searches for current_pos between lines 800 and 1000.

10.8.10   SHOWing and CANCELing breakpoints

A breakpoint, tracepoint or watchpoint can be displayed by commands like:

```
DBG> SHOW BREAK
breakpoint at COLLAPSE\main\main_1\%LINE 920
breakpoint at COLLAPSE\main\%LINE 870
DBG> SHOW TRACE
tracepoint at COLLAPSE\main\main_1\%line 920
DBG> SHOW WATCH
watchpoint at COLLAPSE\main\current_pos
```

A breakpoint, tracepoint or watchpoint can be cancelled by commands like:

```
DBG> CANCEL BREAK %line 1000
DBG> CANCEL WATCH current_pos
```

All breakpoints of a type can be cancelled by a command like:

```
DBG> CANCEL WATCH/ALL
```

10.8.11 Features not covered

Some features of the debugger are not covered in this chapter because most programmers are not likely to use them, or the features are advanced. These features are:

- Multiprocess debugging. More than one process can be debugged in the same session.

- Vector debugging. Programs using vector instructions can be debugged.

- Sharable image debugging. Symbols in sharable images can be referenced by the SET IMAGE debugger command.

The debugger manual is *VMS Programming: Utilities—Debugger.*

11

VAX Procedure Calling Standard and Multiple Language Programs

VMS uses a standard method for calling routines from a program. The standard defines how arguments are passed, how values are returned, and so on. This allows a program in one language to call procedures in another language. Because of the standard, system library routines and subroutines in software packages can be used from any of the VAX languages. These are the topics of this chapter. In the initial sections, the discussion implicitly refers to operations performed at the VAX machine level.

11.1 The Standard

It's not necessary to know the VAX Procedure Calling Standard to call routines in other languages or any library; however, an understanding of the standard can help in finding some obscure bugs. The discussion here is at the machine level; each language will have a specified CALL format to adhere to this standard. The standard need not be followed when the program is not using any external library or other interface routines.

Some of the attributes the standard specifies are:

- Calling instructions.
- Arguments and how they're passed.
- Method for returning function values.
- CPU register usage.

11.1.1   The call and return instructions

The calling instructions must be CALLS or CALLG. CALLS is used when the arguments are passed on the stack, CALLG is used when the arguments are stored sequentially in memory.

Here's how CALLS is typically used,

```
PUSH   argumentn        ;put argument n on stack
 .
 .
 .
PUSH   argument1        ;put argument 1 on stack
CALLS  #n, procedure    ;call the procedure
```

Here, arguments 1 through n to be passed to the called procedure are pushed on the stack, and the CALLS specifies the number of parameters pushed. The CALLS causes the CPU to (along with some other activities) push the value n on the stack, set the *argument pointer* (AP) register to point to the top of the stack, and pass control to the location procedure.

Here's how CALLG is typically used:

```
CALLG argument_list_pointer, procedure
```

Here, the arguments are assumed to be in the memory location argu ment_list_pointer. The CPU (along with some other activities) sets the AP register to argument_pointer_list and transfers control to the location procedure. Unless there's an exception, the called routine must return by executing:

```
RET
```

11.1.2   The argument list

Figure 11.1 shows the structure of the argument list, whether it's on stack or in memory. Note that up to 255 arguments can be passed. Each argument is a long word that can be an immediate value or a memory address of the location that contains the data. The interpretation of the arguments will be found in the documentation for the called procedure.

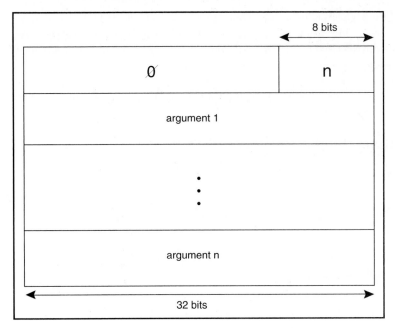

Figure 11.1 The argument list.

11.1.3 Function return values

The called procedure can return a value in registers R0. Registers R0 and R1 can be used if the value is up to 64 bits. Most system library procedures use this mechanism to return success or failure codes in register R0.

11.1.4 Register usage

Of the 16 general-purpose registers in the CPU, R0 through R11 can be freely used by the called procedure. (Registers R12 through R15 have specific uses as *Argument Pointer* (AP), *Frame Pointer* (FP), *Stack Pointer* (SP) and *Program Counter* (PC), respectively). However, the called procedure must restore the original value of registers R2 through R11 when returning the calling program. Typically, this is done by the .ENTRY MACRO directive and the RET statements. For example:

```
.ENTRY procedure_1,  ^m<R5,R7>
.
. (procedure body)
.
RET
```

The .ENTRY declares procedure_1 as a global symbol and generates a bit-mask, which effectively saves registers R5 and R7 on the stack when the procedure is called. The mask information is also stacked. The RET instruction automatically reads the mask and unstacks the registers before transferring control to the calling program. The ENTRY should only be used when the procedure is called by a CALLS or CALLG instructions; these instructions expect that the first 2 bytes at the beginning of the called procedure contain a register mask, and hence these two bytes are interpreted accordingly (rather than as machine instructions).

11.2   Using The Standard from C

No special consideration need to be given to C programs because the standard function calls and function definitions adhere to the VAX Procedure calling standard. For example, consider a main C program calling a function func1. The following C statement used in the main program:

```
status = func1( i1, &s2);
```

will generate assembly code like:

```
pushl i1            ;push value of i1 on stack
pushl -8(fp)        ;push long word address of s2 on stack
calls #2, func1     ;call func1 with the 2 parameters
```

The function:

```
func( v1,v2);
int v1;
char *v2;
{
  .
  .
  .
return (4);
}
```

will generate code like:

```
.entry func1,^m(r2,r5,r6)
  .
  .
  .
movl #4,r0
ret
```

The function func() can be in the same file as the main function main(), or it can be in a separate file.

11.3   Mixing Languages

Programs in other languages can be called from C, and vice versa. In fact, the library and system routines like printf() and strcpy() are written in the languages MACRO or Bliss. C programmers use these routines without being conscious of them as being written in non–C languages. As mentioned in the previous section, C functions adhere to the calling standard, so separately compiled functions can be called from other languages. Figure 11.2 shows a COBOL program, `main1.cob`, which calls a C function, `func1.c`, shown in Fig. 11.3. The program is compiled, linked and run with

```
Identification division.


* Demonstrating VAX Procedure Calling Standard usage for

* multi-language programs.

*

* This program, main1.cob, calls a C language

* function func1(). Note the CALL statement.


Program-id. main1.

Environment Division.

Data Division.


Working-storage Section.

01   int1     pic 9(9) comp value 253.

01   str2      pic x(10) value "Test 12345".


Procedure Division.

proc-start.

   display "int1: ",int1 with conversion.

       display "str2: ",str2.


       display "Entering C function...".

       call "func1" using int1, str2.

       display "Exiting C function...".


   display "int1: ",int1 with conversion.

       display "str2: ",str2.


       stop run.
```

Figure 11.2 Main program `main1.cob`.

```
/* func1.c. Can be called from any language adhering to
 * the VAX Procedure Calling Standard. A clause like the
 * following can be used,
 *    CALL func1(a,b)
 * where a and b are addresses of an integer and a 10
 * character string.
 */
#include stdio

func1(var1,var2)
int *var1;
char *var2;
{
    printf("var1: %d\n",*var1);
    printf("var2: %10s\n",var2);
    *var1 = 386;
    strncpy(var2, "From C   " ,10);
}
```

Figure 11.3 C function, `func1.c`, called by `main1.cob`.

the following commands:

```
$ COBOL     main1.cob
$ CC        func1.c
$ LINK      main1,func1,sys$library:vaxcrtl.olb/library
$ RUN       main1
int1:          253
str2: Test 12345
Entering C function...
var1:  253
var2:  Test 12345
Exiting C function...
int1:  386
str2: From C
```

A C program (or function) can call routines written in other languages. In that language, an understanding of how to write routines that can be called using the VAX Procedure Calling Standard is required. Normally, this information is provided in the language User Guide. Figure 11.4 shows a C program, `main2.c`, which calls a COBOL subprogram, `func2.cob`, shown in Fig. 11.5. The program is compiled, linked and run with the following commands:

```
$ CC       main2.c
$ COBOL    func2.c
$ LINK     main2,func2,sys$library:vaxcrtl.olb/library
$ RUN      main2
int1:      253
str2:      Test        12345
Entering   COBOL       sub-program...
var1:      253
var2:      Test        12345
Exiting    COBOL       sub-program...
int1:      386
str2:      From COBOL
```

```
/* Demonstrating VAX Procedure Calling Standard usage for
 * multi-language programs.
 *
 * This C program, main2.c, calls a COBOL program, func2.cob.
 */
#include stdio

main()
{
    int int1 = 253;
    char *str1 = "Test 12345";

    printf("int1: %d\n", int1);
    printf("str1: %s\n", str1);

    printf("Entering COBOL sub-program...\n");
    func2(&int1,str1);
    printf("Exiting COBOL sub-program...\n");

    printf("int1: %d\n", int1);
    printf("str1: %s\n", str1);
}
----------------------------------------------------
```

Figure 11.4 Main program main2.c.

```
Identification division.


* This program can be called by any language using the
* VAX Procedure Calling Standard with a clause like
*    call (variable1,variable2)
* Notes:
*    Arguments are defined in the linkage section and
*    declared in the Procedure Division Using phrase.
*    The return is via "exit program" not "stop run".
* By default, the arguments are received BY REFERENCE.


Program-id. func2.
Environment Division.
Data Division.


Linkage Section.
01  var1      pic 9(9) comp.
01  var2         pic x(10).


Procedure Division Using var1, var2.
 proc-start.
    display "var1: ",var1 with conversion.
        display "var2: ",var2.
        move 386 to var1.
        move "From COBOL" to var2.
        exit program.
--------------------------------------------------
```

Figure 11.5 COBOL subprogram func2.cob, called by main2.c.

RMS Files with VAX C

The C language does not define files or file structures on disk or tape. However, C compilers do come with a standard I/O library for performing I/O functions. These functions, declared in `stdio.h`, are the same for C compilers on all machines. As such, they do not adequately exploit the operating system architecture. For example, there is no direct support for indexed files, although the file systems on most operating systems allow manipulation of such files. On VMS, programmers normally use the Record Management Services (RMS) for file manipulations. RMS is a component of VMS that supports sequential, relative, and indexed disk file and sequential tape file manipulations. This chapter introduces RMS.

12.1 Introduction To RMS

Languages like COBOL and FORTRAN have built-in file manipulation statements. These statements implicitly use RMS. In VAX C, the standard I/O functions, when used to manipulate disk and tape files, implicitly use a subset of RMS file options. A special set of system services are used by C programmers to access RMS. Example programs are given later; first, let's understand the features of RMS. Since RMS is integrated with the operating system, no commands have to be issued to use it. RMS can be used over DECNET to manipulate files on other nodes by specifying the node-name in the file specifications.

Logically, files consist of a sequence of blocks on disk. Physically, these blocks may be scattered on the disk. Information about block usage in maintained in two files, INDEXF.SYS and BITMAP.SYS. These files are in directory [000000] on each disk. The block size (also known as sector size) on disk is 512 bytes. The record size can be defined to be variable or fixed when the file is created. For practical applications, files can be arbitrarily large, provided there's adequate free disk space.

Records in sequential files can be accessed sequentially from the beginning of the file. Once a record is skipped over, it can be accessed only by scanning the file from the first record. Records are created at the end of the file and cannot be deleted. Records can be updated as long as the new record's size does not exceed the size of the existing record.

Relative files, also known as random files, have fixed-size record cells. When the file is created, the cells may be defined to contain fixed- or variable-length records. Records can be accessed in any order. So, record number 50 can be accessed, followed by record 10, and then record 65. Records can be inserted, deleted or updated at any cell position.

Records in indexed files have keys. Records can be accessed randomly by specifying the key of the record. Records can also be accessed sequentially sorted by keys. Keys are defined by their position and length in the record. For example, an indexed file can have records each having 120 bytes and two keys, the first key of length 7 starting at position 5 and the second key of length 25 at position 50. An indexed file has at least one key called the primary key. The file can have up to 254 additional keys called alternate keys. Indexed files have two logical areas; one contains the data records and the other contains keys and data record pointers. The keys are stored sorted as a B-tree data structure. Actually, if an index file has more than one key, then a separate area can be created for each key.

To see file attributes of an existing file the command is:

```
$ DIR/FULL filename


Directory SYS$SYSDEVICE:[SHAH.RMS]


TEST-RMS.DOC;3     File ID:  (2692,10,0)
Size:          7/9 Owner:     [SYSTEM,MCG]
Created: 9-FEB-1992 15:03:41.58
Revised: 9-FEB-1992 15:03:41.79 (1)
Expires: <None specified>
Backup:   <No backup recorded>
File organization:   Sequential
File attributes:     Allocation: 9, Extend: 0,
                     Global buffer count: 0, No version limit
Record format:       Variable length, maximum 60 bytes
Record attributes:   Carriage return carriage control
```

```
RMS attributes:      None
Journaling enabled:  None
File protection:     System:RWED, Owner:RWED, Group:RE, World:
Access Cntrl List:   None
```

```
Total of 1 file, 7/9 blocks.
```

The file is `TEST-RMS.DOC` version 3. The number of blocks used is 7; the number of blocks allocated to the file is 9. The file is of type sequential, and the record format specifies that the file has variable-length records. The record attributes parameter specifies that a carriage return (and line feed) will be appended to every line when the file is displayed. The next few sections introduce RMS features.

12.2 Record Formats

RMS supports four record formats:

Fixed length	All records have the same length. The record length is stored in the file header.
Variable length	Records have variable lengths. Each record is preceded by a 2-byte header specifying the length of the record.
VFC	These are variable with fixed-length control records. Each record has a variable data area with a fixed control field in the front. The control field can be used as a "hidden" field for storing information pertaining to the record.
Stream	Records are variable length, delimited by a terminator. The terminator is usually a carriage return, line-feed, or a carriage return and a line-feed (specified as `Stream__CR`, `Stream__LF`, or `Stream`).

While the maximum record size depends on file attributes, RMS supports a size of at least 16,000 bytes for any format. Relative and indexed files support variable-length records, but the maximum record size must be specified for relative files when the file is created. Since relative files have fixed record cells, space is not conserved by storing records of sizes less than the maximum. Figure 12.1 shows various record formats.

Usually, fixed record format incurs the least processing overhead. Variable record formats also do not have a high overhead, but two bytes per record are used up to store the count of characters in the record. Figure 12.2 shows some of the file characteristics.

12.3 Initial Allocation

RMS allocates disk blocks dynamically as new records are added to files. This incurs the overhead of scanning for free blocks on disks. This overhead

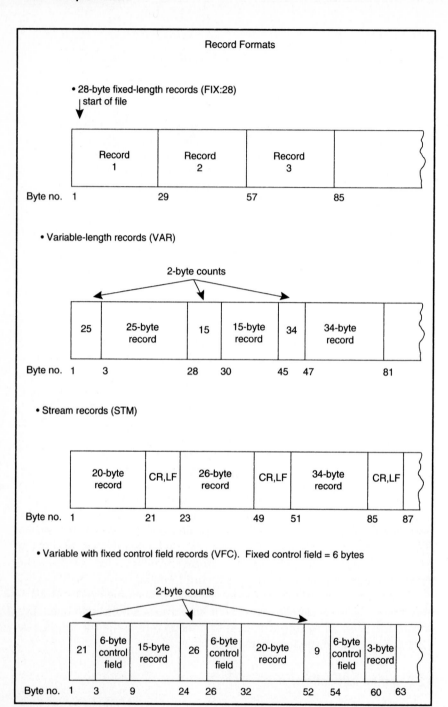

Figure 12.1 Record formats.

File organization	Record format	Maximum record size	Random access support
	FIX	32,767	No
Sequential	VAR	32,767	No
	VFC	32,767-FSZ	No
	STM	32,767	No
Sequential(tape)	VAR	9,995	No
	FIX	32,225	Yes
Relative	VAR	32,253	Yes
	VFC	32,253-FSZ	Yes
Indexed	FIX	32,224	Yes
	VAR	32,224	Yes

Abbreviations:
FIX - Fixed-length records
VAR - Variable-length records
STM - Stream records (including STM_CR and STM_LF)
VFC - Variable length with fixed control field records
FSZ - Fixed control field size of VFC records.

Figure 12.2 File characteristics.

can be eliminated if disk blocks are allocated to the file when it's created. Also, if disk blocks are allocated dynamically, there's a chance of the disk running out of free blocks. If the number of records to be stored is known when the file is created, then preallocating the required number of blocks ensures that the disk will not run out of space when creating records in the file. If more blocks are required when writing to the file at a later stage, RMS allocates them dynamically.

12.4 Extend Size

When a record is being added to a file and there are no more blocks in the file, RMS allocates just enough blocks from the disk's free block list to fit the new record. This allocation overhead can be reduced by allocating more blocks at a time than required for storing the record. That way, when additional records are created, RMS does not have to allocate new blocks for every record created. The number of new blocks allocated at a shot is called the *extend size*. The extend size can be specified when the file is created.

For example, if a file has fixed-size records, each 1000 bytes, and the extend size is 7, then when the first record is created RMS allocates 7 blocks ($7 \times 512 = 3584$ bytes) to the file. No blocks are allocated when the next two records are created. A set of 7 blocks will be allocated when the 4th record is created.

Large extend sizes may cause the last extend of the file to be mostly empty. The default extend quantity is defined when the disk is initialized. This can be overridden during the disk mount. For example:

```
$MOUNT /EXTENSION=10  DUA0: VMSUSER
```

sets an extend size of 10 blocks for disk `DUA0`. To see the disk's extend size, use the command:

```
$SHOW DEVICE DUA0: /FULL
```

12.5   Disk Cluster Size

The free/allocated information of every block on the disk is maintained in a table file called `BITMAP.SYS`. One entry would normally be required for each block. To reduce the size of this table, the minimum allocation quantity is a disk cluster (not to be confused with a VAXcluster) which is defined as one or more consecutive blocks. So, if the cluster size parameter is 4, then the size of the cluster allocation table would be one-fourth the size of a similar table maintaining block allocation information. When a file requires more blocks, RMS determines how many blocks the file should have as determined by the extend size parameter. Just enough clusters are allocated to fit the blocks to be allocated. In addition to fragmentation due to over allocation of blocks in the last extend of the file, there is further disk fragmentation due to over allocation of blocks in the last cluster of the file. As a trade-off, RMS speed increases. The cluster size parameter can be displayed by:

```
$SHOW DEVICE DUA0: /FULL
```

12.6   Buckets

A *bucket* is a sequence of blocks used by RMS for each transfer from disk to memory and memory to disk. If the bucket size of a file is defined as 5 during file creation and a block is required to be read by RMS, then RMS will read the complete bucket containing the block. Reading 5 blocks at a time is faster than reading 5 blocks one block at a time. Large bucket sizes are useful for sequential access in relative or indexed files since then the probability is high that the next record to be accessed has already been read in memory. More physical memory is used as file buffers for larger buckets. Records cannot span across buckets. If records will be accessed in random mode rather than sequentially, large bucket sizes may in fact slow down RMS. Bucket sizes can be up to 32 blocks in RMS. A default bucket size of 0 will cause the bucket size to be just large enough to hold one record.

12.7   Spanning

If a file contains records of 500 bytes, the first record will fit in the first block allocated to the file, while the second record will span over from the first block to the second. In fact, most records in the file will span blocks so that most reads and writes involve two blocks. To avoid this, the file can be defined to have no-spanning of records, which means records cannot continue across blocks, and maximum record size is limited to 512 bytes. (Actually, 510 bytes for variable record length files, since 2 bytes are used for storing the size of each record. Also, some more bytes may be used up in index files for index information). When a record is being created in a no-spanning file and the record cannot fit in the remaining space in the last block of the file, that space will be wasted, and the record will be stored in the beginning of the next block. No-spanning reduces file I/O at the expense of unutilized fragments in the file. See Fig. 12.3.

12.8   File Sharing and Record Locking

Many online applications require a number of programs to share the same set of disk files. The first program opening a file can allow:

> No access
> Read access or
> Read and write access

to other programs attempting to open the file.

When two programs share a file, there's a possibility of both of them attempting to update a particular record simultaneously. RMS supports two methods for record locking to avoid contention:

> Automatic record locking.
> Manual record locking.

In the case of automatic record locking, RMS handles record locking on behalf of the program accessing the file. If the file is opened for read access,

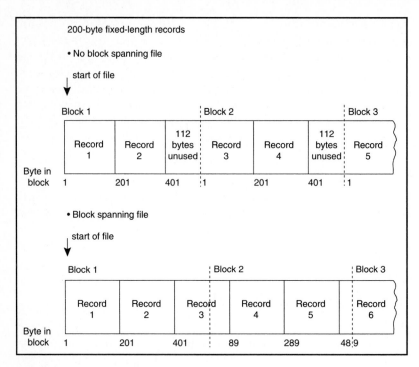

Figure 12.3 Record spanning.

then other programs are allowed read access to any record. If the file is opened for write or update, other programs cannot access records being read by the first program. This is the default locking method.

If the first program opening a file declares manual record locking, then the programs explicitly locks and unlocks records. Multiple records from the same file can be locked using this method. Any record can be locked so that other programs cannot access the record at all or can access it for reading only.

12.9 Indexed Files

Here are some terms used in the context of indexed files.

12.9.1 Duplicate keys

When an indexed file is created, the DUPLICATE KEY option can be specified for any key. Records with the same key value can be inserted in a file only if the DUPLICATE KEY option is specified for that key number. When accessing these records, only the first record can be retrieved by giving the key value. The other records have to be accessed sequentially.

12.9.2 Changeable keys

When the CHANGEABLE KEY option is specified for alternate keys, existing records can be updated with new values for these alternate keys, and RMS will update the alternate indexes accordingly. An update that changes the primary key has to be implemented as a DELETE, followed by an INSERT of the record.

12.9.3 Areas

By default, data and keys are intermingled in the data blocks of the index file. For better performance, they can be placed in separate areas within the same file. An *area* is simply an internal logical partition of the file for better performance when searching for keys. In fact, each key group (specified by key number) can be placed in separate areas. Separate areas can be specified when creating files using the EDIT/FDL utility.

12.9.4 Bucket size

A bucket is an integer multiple of 512 byte blocks. Each area in an area consists of a set of buckets. When records are inserted, keys are in key buckets. When a bucket is filled up and a new key has to be inserted in the bucket, the bucket is split, and the depth of the tree structure increases by 1. This reduces CPU performance. Larger bucket sizes should be specified when the file is created. The trade-off is that when keys are searched in buckets, whole buckets are brought in memory, and this in turn deteriorates performance if bucket sizes are large. Generally, bucket sizes should be increased if index depth levels exceed 1.

12.9.5 Fill factor

Usually, a number of records are inserted initially when index files are created. Records are then inserted randomly in the future. If key buckets are packed (with a fill factor of 100%) by the initial record load, there will be many bucket splits when records are inserted randomly later. This causes a deterioration in performance. If a lower fill factor (say 50%) is specified when the file is created, the initial record load will fill buckets only to the level specified. Later, when records are inserted randomly, the free space in the buckets is used to store key information reducing the amount of bucket splits. The trade-off for a lower fill factor is more disk space required for the initial loading of the file.

12.10 RMS with C

C programs set up RMS data structures and issue system calls to use RMS. Let's understand the data structures and then use them in programs.

12.10.1   RMS data structures

RMS associates four data structures with every file:

1. FAB (File Access Block)

   Contains file information like file organization. Some of the important fields and their possible values are:

fab$l__fna	for pointer to file name.
fab$b__fns	size of file name string.
fab$b__org	for file organization:
	FAB$C__SEQ9 for sequential,
	FAB$C__REL for relative, and
	FAB$C__IDX for indexed.
fab$b__fac	for file record operations:
	FAB$M__PUT for writes,
	FAB$M__GET for reads,
	FAB$M__DEL for deletes, and
	FAB$M__UPD for updates.
	Multiple operations can be specified by ORing the values.
fab$b__rfm	record format:
	FAB$C__FIX for fixed length records and
	FAB$C__VAR for variable length records.
fab$l__xab	points to the first of a linked list of xabs for the file.
fab$l__nam	points to NAM block.

2. RAB (Record Access Block)

   Contains record-level information such as record number for relative files. Some of the important fields and their possible values are:

rab$l__fab	points to a FAB block.
rab$b__rac	for record access mode:
	RAB$C__SEQ for sequential access, and
	RAB$C__KEY for keyed access of indexed files.
rab$l__ubf	User buffer where records will be read into.
rab$w__usz	Maximum size of this buffer (to avoid overflow).
rab$l__rbf	Buffer from which records will be written.
rab$w__rsz	Size of record to be written.
rab$b__krf	Key of reference in indexed files.

3. XAB (Extended Access Block)

   Contains additional information such as key length and position for indexed files. There are various types of XABs, each specifying one piece of information. The first XAB data structure of every file is pointed to by the FAB field fab$l__xab. The first XAB has one field that points to the next XAB, and so on. This linked list of XABs is terminated by a 0 in the next XAB pointer field of the last XAB. The XABs are:

XABALL   Allocation information like whether the file should be contiguous.

XABDAT   Date and time information like file expiration date.

XABFHC   File header information like end-of-file block within the file.

XABITM   Network file access items like the remote file system (RMS, Ultrix and so on).

XABJNL   Used with the RMS Journaling product.

XABKEY   Key information for indexed files.

XABPRO   Protection information and Access Control List (ACL) information.

XABRDT   Revision date and time information which can be specified when closing a file.

XABRU   Recovery Unit journaling information. Used with the RMS Journaling product.

XABSUM   Summary information of certain INDEXED file fields like number of keys.

XABTRM   Used to specify item lists to terminals to perform extended read operations.

4. NAM (Name block)

Optional block for storing complete file name specification when the FAB contains incomplete (wildcard) information. For example, the filespec in FAB may not contain version number (latest version assumed), however, RMS will store it in the NAM block when the file is opened. Similarly, the device can be assumed to be the default device when reading a file; however, RMS will store it in the NAM block.

Opening a file requires creation of these data structures, storing the file and record attributes in them, and issuing the RMS OPEN call. In C, the four data structures are defined by RMS.H. The basic C RMS calls for file operations are: sys$create, sys$open, sys$close, and sys$erase. These calls take the address of FAB as the only parameter and return RMS STATUS. The basic record operation calls are sysget, sysput, sys$update, and sys$delete. These calls take the address of RAB as the only parameter and returns RMS STATUS.

Since the four data structures contain a lot of fields, RMS.H provides prototypes for initializing them with default values. For example, the prototype to initialize the FAB data structure is cc$rms__fab. The file RMS.H is in the SYS$LIBRARY: directory. The fields of the four data blocks are described in the files NAM.H, FAB.H, RAB.H, and XAB.H within the directory SYS$LIBRARY:.

Figure 12.4   C program reading and displaying an RMS file.

```
/*      FILE_USE.C
 *      Program reads and displays file on terminal
 *      The compilation commands are:
 *              $ cc file_use
 *              $ link file_use,sys$input:/option
 *              sys$share:vaxcrtl.exe/share
 */
#include rms
#include stdio
#include ssdef

struct FAB fab;
struct RAB rab;
int rms_status;

main()
{

char *file name = "TEST_FILE.DAT";      /* the file to be read */
char inp_record[512];                   /* file records */

/* Initialize the fab and rab data structures */
fab = cc$rms_fab;                           /*default initialization*/
fab.fab$l_fna = file_name;
fab.fab$b_fns = strlen(file_name);          /* file name length */
fab.fab$b_org = FAB$C_SEQ;                  /* sequential file */
fab.fab$b_fac = FAB$M_GET;                  /*record operation on the
                                               file: only get */
rab = cc$rms_rab;                           /*initialize rab*/
rab.rab$l_fab = &fab;                       /*rab points to fab*/

rms_status = sys$open(&fab);                /*open the file*/
if (rms_status != RMS$_NORMAL)
    {
    printf("file: TEST_FILE.DAT open error\n");
    exit(rms_status);
```

Figure 12.4 *(Continued)*

```
        };
rms_status = sys$connect (&rab);                /*associate fab and rab*/
if (rms_status != RMS$_NORMAL)
        {
        printf("file: TEST_FILE.DAT open/connect error\n");
        exit(rms_status);
        };
rab.rab$l_ubf = inp_record;                 /*records read here */
rab.rab$w_usz = sizeof inp_record;          /*max size of records */


/* get records from file and display them on standard output*/
printf("Displaying file TEST_FILE.DAT\n");
for (;;)                                     /*forever*/
        {
        rms_status = sys$get (&rab);         /* get a record */
        if (rms_status == RMS$_EOF)
            {
            rms_status = sys$close(&fab);
            if (rms_status != RMS$_NORMAL)
                {
                printf("%s close error\n",file_name);
                lib$signal (rms_status);
                /* lib$signal is somewhat like exit(); however,
                    it supports conditional handling as
                    supported by VMS */
                };
            break;
            }
        else if (rms_status != RMS$_NORMAL)
            {
            printf("%s get error\n",file_name);
            lib$signal (rms_status);
            rms_status = sys$close(&fab);
            if (rms_status != RMS$_NORMAL)
                {
                printf("%s close error\n",file_name);
```

Figure 12.4 *(Continued)*

```
            lib$signal (rms_status);

            };

        break;

        }

    else

        {

        inp_record[rab.rab$w_rsz] = 0;

        printf("%s\n",inp_record);           /*print the record */

        };

    };


} /*end of main*/
```

Figure 12.4 shows a simple C program to read a sequential file and type it on the terminal. The typical steps involved in manipulating an RMS file are:

1. Create RMS data structures using the template structures NAM, FAB, RAB, and XAB. The program in Figure 12.4 does not need the NAM and XAB structures, hence they are not used.

2. Initialize the structures to default values by using the predefined structures, ccRMS__NAM, ccRMS__FAB, ccRMS__RAB and cc$RMS $__XAB*. Then initialize the individual fields within the structure to required values. All the possible values are in the header files mentioned previously.

3. Open an existing file (sys$open) or create a new file (sys$create). The FAB is specified in the call.

4. A RAB must be associated with an open file's FAB if records operations are to be performed on the file. Normally, a separate RAB is associated with each FAB. The call to achieve this is sys$connect.

5. Record operations can then be performed on the file. If records are to be read from the file, these two RAB fields must be defined correctly,

    RAB$l__ubf   User buffer where records will be read into.
    RAB$w__usz   Maximum size of this buffer (to avoid overflow).

If records are to be written to the file, these two RAB fields must be defined correctly,

    RAB$l__rbf   Buffer from which records will be written.

`RAB$w__rsz`   Size of record to be written.

Numerous other initializations will be required to specify various attributes of the file and file operations.

6. RMS status is returned by each call. This must be checked after every call. This checking increases the program code substantially but it is necessary in good quality programs.

Figure 12.5 is an example in C of how to create an indexed file and write one record in it. The optional NAM block is not used. The program illustrates use of the XAB data structures, specifically, the XABKEY structure.

Figure 12.5   Index file I/O from the C language.

```
/* INDEXIO.C
 * Program opens and populates a RMS indexed file.
 * The compilation commands are:
 *         $ cc indexio
 *         $ link indexio,sys$input:/option
 *         sys$share:vaxcrtl.exe/share
 *
 * Basic program steps are:
 *    . Set up data structures for indexed file, customer.dat. The
 *      file has two keys, dda_number and swift_address.
 *    . Create the file.
 *    . Loop
 *        Prompt for fields of the record.
 *        Write record to file.
 *      Until "OVER" is entered.
 *
 */
#include rms
#include stdio
#include ssdef
struct FAB fab;                          /* File data structure */
struct RAB rab;                          /* Record data structure */
struct XABKEY primary_key,alternate_key;   /* Keys data structure */
int rms_status;
```

Figure 12.5 *(Continued)*

```
struct {                                 /*Indexed file record layout*/

        char dda_number[9];

        char customer_address[35];

        char swift_address[11];

        } cif_record;


main()

{


char input_buffer[512];                         /*for terminal input*/


initialize("CUSTOMER.DAT");                     /*set up fab,rab,xab

                                                    data structures*/


rms_status = sys$create(&fab);          /*create the file*/

if (rms_status != RMS$_NORMAL)

    {

    printf("file: CUSTOMER.DAT create error\n");

    exit(rms_status);

    };

rms_status = sys$connect(&rab);                 /*associate fab and rab*/

if (rms_status != RMS$_NORMAL)

    {

    printf("file: CUSTOMER.DAT open error\n");

    exit(rms_status);

    };


/* get input from user and write records to file*/

printf("Creating and populating indexed file\n");

for (;;)                                        /*forever*/

    {

    printf("Enter dda number (OVER to terminate): ");

    gets(&input_buffer);

    if (strcmp("OVER",input_buffer) == 0) exit();
```

Figure 12.5 *(Continued)*

```
      /* move terminal input to file record buffer */
      strncpy(cif_record.dda_number,input_buffer,
               sizeof cif_record.dda_number);

printf("Enter customer address: ");
gets(&input_buffer);
/* move terminal input to file record buffer */
strncpy(cif_record.customer_address,input_buffer,
         sizeof cif_record.customer_address);


printf("Enter SWIFT address: ");
gets(&input_buffer);
/* move terminal input to file record buffer */
strncpy(cif_record.swift_address,input_buffer,
         sizeof cif_record.swift_address);



rab.rab$b_rac = RAB$C_KEY;       /* Keyed record access (as opposed
                                     to sequential) */
rab.rab$l_rbf = &cif_record;     /* file record buffer is here */
rab.rab$w_rsz = sizeof cif_record;


rms_status = sys$put(&rab);      /*write record to file*/
if (rms_status != RMS$_NORMAL &&
    rms_status != RMS$_OK_DUP)
    {
    printf("file: CUSTOMER.DAT write error\n");
    exit(rms_status);
        };
    }; /*for loop end*/
} /*end of main*/



initialize(file_name)
    char *file_name;
```

Figure 12.5 *(Continued)*

```
/* This routine is required to initialize the fab,rab and xab data
 * structures. The data structures are described in detail
 * in the VMS Programming Series: File System - Record Management
 * Services (RMS) manual.
 */
{
    fab = cc$rms_fab;                          /*default initializations*/
    fab.fab$b_fac = FAB$M_DEL |                /*record operations to be*/
                    FAB$M_GET |                /*performed: delete,read*/
                    FAB$M_PUT |                /*write and update */
                    FAB$M_UPD;
    fab.fab$l_fna = file_name;
    fab.fab$b_org = FAB$C_IDX;
                                               /*file organization indexed*/
    fab.fab$b_fns = strlen(file_name);
    fab.fab$l_xab = &primary_key;              /*pointer to first xab*/
    rab = cc$rms_rab;                          /*initialize rab*/
    rab.rab$l_fab = &fab;                      /*rab points to fab*/
                                               /*of the indexed file*/


    primary_key = cc$rms_xabkey;               /*first xab is for*/
                                               /*primary key*/
    primary_key.xab$w_pos0 = 0;                /*key position in record*/
    primary_key.xab$b_ref = 0;                 /*this is primary key*/
    primary_key.xab$b_siz0 = sizeof cif_record.dda_number;
                                               /*key size*/
    primary_key.xab$l_nxt = &alternate_key;
                                               /*pointer to second xab*/


    alternate_key = cc$rms_xabkey;
                                               /*initialize second xab
                                                 which is for the
                                                 secondary key*/
    alternate_key.xab$b_flg = XAB$M_DUP;
                                               /*allow duplicate keys*/
    alternate_key.xab$w_pos0 =
```

Figure 12.5 *(Continued)*

```
        (char *) &cif_record.swift_address

        -(char *) &cif_record;            /*position of this key*/

    alternate_key.xab$b_ref = 1;          /*this is key 1*/

    alternate_key.xab$b_siz0 =

        sizeof cif_record.swift_address;  /*key size*/

} /*end of initialize*/
```

12.11   RMS Utilities

The utilities FDL, CONVERT and DUMP aid in the maintenance of RMS files. These utilities are not strictly related with the C language, however, many programmers write unnecessary programs to emulate the functions performed by these utilities hence they are mentioned here. The utilities are also useful for debugging RMS programs. FDL is the File Definition Language facility. It is used to create specifications for RMS files and create the RMS files. CONVERT is used to copy records from one file to another of any organization. It can also be used to restructure files; say, change the position of keys. The records will change to reflect the organization of the output file. DUMP is used to display file contents in ascii, decimal, hexadecimal and octal representations.

12.11.1   FDL

While the OPEN statement in the VAX languages allows any existing file to be opened for update, not all RMS parameters can be specified when creating a file. The File Definition Language (FDL) facility can be used to create files with most RMS parameter specifications, and the file can then be opened for update by programs.

The FDL facility is also useful for modifying RMS parameters for existing files. For example a file contains 82-byte records and a new field of 6 bytes is to be added at the end of each record. An FDL file containing the RMS parameters of the original data file is created using the ANALYZE/RMS/FDL command. The FDL file is edited to reflect the new record length of 88 bytes. This can be done using any text editor or the EDIT/FDL command. The new data file is created using the CREATE/FDL command. Records from the old file are copied to the new file using the CONVERT command. The new records can be padded with blanks to the right by using the /PAD qualifier with the CONVERT command.

The FDL facility can be accessed by three commands:

1. EDIT/FDL.   Used to create a definition file containing specifications for RMS data files.
2. CREATE/FDL.   Used to create an empty data file from a previously created specifications file.
3. ANALYZE/RMS/FDL.   Used to create a specifications file using the RMS parameters of an existing data file.

Figure 12.6   Creating an INDEXED file with the FDL utility.

```
$ edit/fdl customer.fdl


                    Parsing Definition File
SYS$SYSDEVICE:[TECH4]CUSTOMER.FDL; will be created.


(Add Delete Exit Help Invoke Modify Quit Set View)
Main Editor Function            (Keyword)[Help] : I


(Add_Key Delete_Key Indexed Optimize
 Relative Sequential Touchup)
Editing Script Title            (Keyword)[-]    : I


Target disk volume Cluster Size (1-1Giga)[3]    :
Number of Keys to Define        (1-255)[1]      :


(Line Fill Key Record Init Add)
Graph type to display           (Keyword)[Line] :


Number of Records that will be Initially Loaded
into the File                   (0-1Giga)[-]    : 100
(Fast_Convert NoFast_Convert RMS_Puts)
Initial File Load Method        (Keyword)[Fast] : ?


Fast_Convert:   using the VAX-11 Convert/Fast_Load option
NoFast_Convert: using the VAX-11 Convert/NoFast_Load option
RMS_Puts:       writing to a file from a High Level Language
```

Figure 12.6 *(Continued)*

```
(Fast_Convert NoFast_Convert RMS_Puts)
Initial File Load Method         (Keyword)[Fast] :


Number of Additional Records to be Added After
the Initial File Load            (0-1Giga)[0]    :
Key  0 Load Fill Percent         (50-100)[100]   : 50
(Fixed Variable)
Record Format                    (Keyword)[Var]  : FIX
Record Size                      (1-32231)[-]    : 180


(Bin2  Bin4  Bin8  Int2  Int4  Int8  Decimal  String
 Dbin2 Dbin4 Dbin8 Dint2 Dint4 Dint8 Ddecimal Dstring)
Key  0 Data Type                 (Keyword)[Str]  :


Key  0 Segmentation desired      (Yes/No)[No]    :
Key  0 Length                    (1-180)[-]      : 4
Key  0 Position                  (0-176)[0]      : 9
Key  0 Duplicates allowed        (Yes/No)[No]    :
File Prolog Version              (0-3)[3]        :
Data Key Compression desired     (Yes/No)[Yes]   :
Data Record Compression desired  (Yes/No)[Yes]   :
Index Compression desired        (Yes/No)[Yes]   :


                *|
                9|
                8|
        Index   7|
                6|
        Depth   5|
                4|
                3|
                2|  2
                1|    1 1 1 1 1 1 1 1 1 1 1 1 1 1 1 1 1 1 1 1 1 1 1 1 1 1 1 1 1 1 1
                +- + - - - + - - - - + - - - - + - - - - + - - - - + - - - - + - +
                     1     5     10     15     20     25     30 32
                        Bucket Size (number of blocks)
```

Figure 12.6 *(Continued)*

```
Prolog Version        3 KT-Key  0 Type      String  EM-Emphasis  Flatter ( 3)

DK-Dup Key  0 Values   No KL-Key  0 Length        4 KP-Key  0 Position      9

RC-Data Record Comp    0% KC-Data Key Comp      0% IC-Index Record Comp   0%

BF-Bucket Fill        100% RF-Record Format   Fixed RS-Record Size        180

LM-Load Method  Fast_Conv IL-Initial Load       100 AR-Added Records        0

(Type "FD" to Finish Design)

Which File Parameter      (Mnemonic)[refresh]     : FD



Text for FDL Title Section      (1-126 chars)[null]:

Test for learning the FDL facility

Data File file-spec           (1-126 chars)[null]:

customer.dat

(Carriage_Return FORTRAN None Print)

Carriage Control              (Keyword)[Carr] :



Emphasis Used In Defining Default:     (    Flatter_files   )

Suggested Bucket Sizes:                (     3     3    12 )

Number of Levels in Index:             (     1     1     1 )

Number of Buckets in Index:            (     1     1     1 )

Pages Required to Cache Index:         (     3     3    12 )

Processing Used to Search Index:       (   126   126   510 )



Key  0 Bucket Size         (1-63)[3]      :

Key  0 Name                (1-32 chars)[null]:

Account number

Global Buffers desired     (Yes/No)[No]   :

The Depth of Key  0 is Estimated to be No Greater

than 1 Index levels, which is 2 Total levels.

Press RETURN to continue (^Z for Main Menu)

(Add Delete Exit Help Invoke Modify Quit Set View)

Main Editor Function          (Keyword)[Help] : exit


SYS$SYSDEVICE:[TECH4]CUSTOMER.FDL;1  44 lines
```

12.11.1.1 EDIT/FDL. The syntax for the EDIT/FDL command is:

```
$ EDIT/FDL fdl-file-spec
```

The command can be used to create a new FDL file or edit an existing one. Questions are asked depending on the response to previous questions. Here's an example for creating an indexed file with fixed-length records of 180 bytes, one key starting at position 4 (5th byte of the record) and length 9 bytes. Default values are specified for most answers. A question mark response to any question elicits help on that question. Figure 12.6 shows an example usage of the FDL utility. Here are some comments:

- Each question shows the possible responses in parentheses. Default values are specified in square brackets. A dash for the default value means the value has no defaults and must be specified.

- The index depth graph shows various bucket sizes and the depth of key indexes of the B-tree structure for the number of initial load records specified. If the graph shows a depth greater than 4 for the bucket size specified, then the bucket size should be increased.

- Key load fill percents should be less than 100 if records will be added randomly in the future. If initially the file will be empty and all records will be added randomly in the future, then this parameter is insignificant.

The definition file created, `customer.fdl`, is a text file. Minor changes can be made to it using a text editor like EVE. The recommended procedure for modifying the file is to use `EDIT/FDL` and select the `MODIFY` option from the main menu. The file is shown in Fig. 12.7.

Figure 12.7 An FDL file.

```
$ TYPE customer.fdl


TITLE    "Test for learning the FDL facility"


IDENT    "16-FEB-1989 17:26:37   VAX-11 FDL Editor"


SYSTEM

         SOURCE                VAX/VMS


FILE

         NAME                  "customer.dat"
         ORGANIZATION          indexed


RECORD

         CARRIAGE_CONTROL      carriage_return
         FORMAT                fixed
         SIZE                  180
```

Figure 12.7 *(Continued)*

```
AREA 0

        ALLOCATION              48

        BEST_TRY_CONTIGUOUS     yes

        BUCKET_SIZE             3

        EXTENSION               12


AREA 1

        ALLOCATION              3

        BEST_TRY_CONTIGUOUS     yes

        BUCKET_SIZE             3

        EXTENSION               3


KEY 0

        CHANGES                 no

        DATA_AREA               0

        DATA_FILL               100

        DATA_KEY_COMPRESSION    yes

        DATA_RECORD_COMPRESSION yes

        DUPLICATES              no

        INDEX_AREA              1

        INDEX_COMPRESSION       yes

        INDEX_FILL              100

        LEVEL1_INDEX_AREA       1

        NAME                    "Account number"

        PROLOG                  3

        SEG0_LENGTH             4

        SEG0_POSITION           9

        TYPE                    string
```

12.11.1.2 CREATE/FDL. The file described in the above FDL file can be created by the command:

```
$ CREATE/FDL=customer.fdl
```

The file created is `customer.dat`, as specified in the `fdl` file, `customer.fdl`. The file name of the created file can be overridden by giving it on the command line as:

```
$ CREATE/FDL=customer.fdl test.dat
```

The file specifications for the created file can be seen as:

```
$ DIR/FULL customer.dat

Directory SYS$SYSDEVICE:[TECH4]


CUSTOMER.DAT;1              File ID:   (5836,18,0)
Size:     52/52            Owner:     [1,1]
Created:  16-FEB-1989 17:28  Revised:  16-FEB-1989 17:28 (1)
Expires:  <None specified>  Backup:    <No backup recorded>
File organization: Indexed, Prolog: 3, Using 1 key
                            In 2 areas
File attributes:     Allocation: 52, Extend: 12, Maximum bucket size: 3
                     Global buffer count: 0, No version limit
                     Contiguous best try
Record format:       Fixed length 180 byte records
Record attributes:   Carriage return carriage control
Journaling enabled:  None
File protection:     System:RWED, Owner:RWED, Group:RE, World:
Access Cntrl List:   None

Total of 1 file, 52/52 blocks.
```

12.11.1.3 ANALYZE/RMS/FDL. This command is used to extract the FDL specification of an existing file. The FDL file can then be modified to create a new data file that has the same RMS parameters as the original file, except for the modifications performed on it. The command syntax is:

```
$ ANALYZE/RMS/FDL file-spec
```

File-spec is the data file. The FDL file created has the same file-spec, except for the filename extension, which is .fdl. For example:

```
$ ANALYZE/RMS/FDL account.dat
```

creates the file account.fdl.

12.11.2 DUMP

This command has the following qualifiers:

```
/ascii      |
/decimal    |Specifies display data representation.
/hex        |By default, hex and ascii values are displayed.
/octal      |
/byte       |
/longword   |Specifies grouping for the displayed data.
```

```
$ DUMP/RECORD=(START:2,COUNT=3) customer.fdl


Dump of file SYS$SYSDEVICE:[TESTING.DATA]CUSTOMER.FDL;2

on 17-FEB-1989 17:47:10.26

File ID (6510,3,0)   End of file block 2 / Allocated 2


Record number 2 (00000002), 48 (0030) bytes


 39312D42 45462D36 31220954 4E454449 IDENT."16-FEB-19 000000

 41562020 2037333A 36323A37 31203938 89 17:26:37   VA 000010

 22726F74 69644520 4C444620 31312D58 X-11 FDL Editor" 000020


Record number 3 (00000003), 6 (0006) bytes


                          4D45 54535953 SYSTEM......... 000000


Record number 4 (00000004), 17 (0011) bytes


 4D562F58 41560909 09454352 554F5309 .SOURCE...VAX/VM 000000

                                   53 S.............. 000010
```

Figure 12.8 DUMP command output.

/word	∣
/record	Specifies logical record display.
/block	Specifies display of blocks of the file. Optionally, the start-ing record or block number and the ending or count of the number of records or blocks can be specified. For example:

```
DUMP/RECORD=(START:3,END:5)   customer.dat
DUMP/RECORD=(START:3,COUNT:3) customer.dat
```

Figure 12.8 shows an example usage of the command.

12.11.3 CONVERT

The CONVERT command is used to convert (or restructure) a file of one or-ganization to another. The syntax of the command is :

```
$ CONVERT/qualifiers input-file-spec output-file-spec
```

Some of the qualifiers are:

/exceptions__file   Creates a file of records that could not be copied to the output file because of format errors. It's recommended that this qualifier be always used.

/fdl=file-spec   The output file is created using the FDL specifications from the file specified.

/merge   Specifies that records are to be inserted is an existing index file.

/pad=x
/pad=%by   If the output file has a fixed-length record format, the input record has a smaller record size, the records are padded with the character specified. The x is any ascii character. The y is a number in the base given by b. The b can be d for decimal, h for hex, or o for octal. For example, /pad= %h45 specifies the pad character to be hex 45 (or ascii E).

/statistics   Outputs summary information like number of records converted after the conversion is complete.

/truncate   If the output file has a fixed-length record format, and the input records have a larger record size, then the records are truncated to the output record size before writing.

Example: The file INPUT.DAT is sequential and contains 4 records that are to be loaded in the indexed file CUSTOMER.DAT created by the CRE ATE/FDL command. Here is the sequence of commands:

```
$ DIR/FULL input.dat

Directory SYS$SYSDEVICE:[TESTING.DATA]

INPUT.DAT;1                 File ID:  (6497,5,0)
Size:     1/2              Owner:    [1,1]
Created: 21-FEB-1989 11:56 Revised: 21-FEB-1989 11:56 (1)
Expires: <None specified>  Backup:   <No backup recorded>
File organization:  Sequential
File attributes:    Allocation: 2, Extend: 0, Global buffer count: 0,
No version limit
Record format:      Variable length, maximum 25 bytes
Record attributes:  Carriage return carriage control
Journaling enabled: None
File protection:    System:RWED, Owner:RWED, Group:RE, World:

Access Cntrl List:  None

Total of 1 file, 1/2 blocks.

$ TYPE input.dat
```

```
SMITH A.    2547 TEST DATA 1
BEY J.      7123 TEST DATA 2
BELL A.     8213 TEST DATA 3
HOLMES K.   3987 TEST DATA 4


$ CONVERT/MERGE/PAD=0 input.dat customer.dat


$ TYPE customer.dat

SMITH A.    2547 TEST DATA 1000000000...
HOLMES K.   3987 TEST DATA 4000000000...
BEY J.      7123 TEST DATA 2000000000...
BELL A.     8213 TEST DATA 3000000000...
```

Customer.dat is sorted by the key at position 9. The padding character is zero, so each record has zeros appended to make the record size 180 bytes. More records can be added to customer.dat by using the same CONVERT command line.

13

Using VMS Features from C

VMS has a rich set of features that are matched by few operating systems. Just about all C programs in production have calls to system features. Although these calls make the C programs nonportable, there are no effective alternatives for most applications. The features discussed in this chapter are:

- Mailboxes.
- Shared logical names.
- Global sections.
- Event flags.
- Locks.
- Object libraries.
- Shared images.
- Asynchronous System Traps (ASTs).

Most VMS system calls process strings in the form of string descriptors rather than a string of characters, as in C. A *string descriptor* is a data structure which contains information on a character string. String descriptors are described in chapter 15. The $DESCRIPTOR macro for declaring and initializing string descriptors, which is discussed extensively in this chapter, is also described in chapter 15.

13.1   Interprogram Communications

There are three main methods for transferring data among processes on a VAX:

- Mailboxes. These are used to send streams of data from one process to another. Normally, one or more processes would send data to a mailbox, and one process would process the data.
- Logical names. These are used to send small amounts of data like status and counts from one process to another. They can be thought of as common "registers."
- Global sections. These are common areas of memory for use by all or some processes.

The words "processes" and "programs" are used interchangeably since a program, when run, is an image in the context of a process. Most of the examples used in this section show communications between two processes; however, the techniques can be extended for communications among more processes. Also, processes are assumed to be running from terminals so that output can be displayed; however, the techniques apply to processes that don't have attached terminals (like detached or batch processes).

Mailboxes, logical names and global sections are (VAX) node specific, even if the nodes are part of a VAXcluster. DECnet and the Distributed Lock Manager can be used for communications between programs running on different nodes of the cluster.

13.2   Mailboxes

Mailboxes can be used for sending a stream of data from one process to another without resorting to disks as intermediate devices. Mailboxes are software devices. The device driver is SYS$SYSTEM:MBDRIVER.EXE, and the generic device name is MB:. A sample mailbox device is MBA12:. One process would normally create a mailbox and other processes would assign channels from their process to the mailbox. Processes can then use QIO functions (system services) to read from or write to the mailbox. Mailboxes are not available clusterwide. DECnet task-to-task communications or locks can be used for internode traffic.

Figures 13.1 and 13.2 show two programs, MAILBOX_WRITE.C and

MAILBOX_READ.C, where the first program creates the mailbox, writes to the mailbox, and waits for the data to be read by the second program while the second program reads the mailbox for data put in there by the first program, and sends the data to its terminal.

Figure 13.1 Mailbox demonstration: the writing program.

```
/* MAILBOX_WRITE.C          Jay Shah   15-DEC-1990
 * This mailbox demonstration programs works in conjunction with
 * MAILBOX_READ.C.
 *
 * The program
 *   . creates a mailbox
 *   . writes a message to it
 *   . and waits for the message to be read by MAILBOX_READ.C.
 */
#include stdio
#include descrip
#include iodef
#include ssdef


main()
{
int status;


/* variables used for creating mailbox */
char permanent_mbx = 1;       /* temporary mailbox */
short mbx_chan;               /* i/o channel to mailbox,
                               * returned by the $CREMBX call */
int  max_message_size = 0;    /* use VMS default */
int  max_buf_size = 0;        /* system dynamic memory for buffering
                                 messages to mailbox. Use default */
int  protection_mask = 0;     /* access for all users */
int  access_mode = 0;         /* most privileged access mode */


$DESCRIPTOR(mbx_logical_name,"MAILBOX_DEMO");
char tmp[100];
```

Figure 13.1 *(Continued)*

```
/* variables for QIO output to mailbox */
struct
    {short cond_value; short count; int info;}
        io_status_block;



char *message = "Test message to mailbox";
int tmp1;
/* system service call to create mailbox and assign
 * it a logical name
 */
status= sys$crembx(
            permanent_mbx,
            &mbx_chan,
            max_message_size,
            max_buf_size,
            protection_mask,
            access_mode,
            &mbx_logical_name
            );
if (status != SS$_NORMAL) lib$stop(status);
                    /* create mailbox error? */


/* send a message to the mailbox, wait until it is rea
tmp1 = strlen(message);
status = sys$qiow(
            0,                      /* event_flag */
            mbx_chan,
            IO$_WRITEVBLK | IO$M_NOW,
            &io_status_block,

            0,                      /* ast_address */
            0,                      /* ast_parameter */
            message,                /* parameter P1 */
            (int) strlen(message),  /* length, parameter P2 */
            0,0,0,0                 /* P3, P4, P5, P6 */
```

Figure 13.1 *(Continued)*

```
            );
if (status != SS$_NORMAL) lib$stop(status);      /* error? */
gets(tmp);
}
```

Figure 13.2 Mailbox demonstration: the reading program.

```
/* MAILBOX_READ.C             Jay Shah   16-DEC-1990
 * This program demonstrates use of mailboxes. It works in
 * conjunction with MAILBOX_WRITE.C.
 *
 * The program
 *   . opens an existing mailbox (created by MAILBOX_WRITE.C)
 *   . reads from it
 *   . and displays the data read onto the terminal.
 *
 * The mailbox is created by the program MAILBOX_WRITE.C

   * terminals.
   */

   #include stdio
   #include descrip
   #include iodef
   #include ssdef
   #include lnmdef
   #include psldef

   main()
   {
   int status;
   char response[255];
   char eqv_name[10];
   unsigned short ret_len;
   struct  { unsigned short eqv_length;
```

Figure 13.2 *(Continued)*

```
 * terminals.
 */


#include stdio
#include descrip
#include iodef
            &mbx_chan,
            0,                  /* access mode. Full access */
            0                   /* associated mailbox name.
                                 * Not used */
            );
if (status != SS$_NORMAL) lib$stop(status);     /* error? */


/* read a message from the mailbox */
status = sys$qiow(
            0,                  /* event_flag number 0*/
            mbx_chan,
            IO$_READVBLK,
            &io_status_block,
            0,                  /* ast_address   */
            0,                  /* ast_parameter */
            message,            /* parameter P1  */
            message_len,        /* buffer size,         ;
                                 * parameter P2   */
            0,0,0,0             /* P3, P4, P5, P6
                                 * ignored       */
            );
if (status != SS$_NORMAL) lib$stop(status);  /* error? */


printf ("%s",message);

}
```

Some notes on mailboxes:

■ Mailboxes are temporary or permanent. A temporary mailbox is deleted by VMS if no processes are accessing it. A permanent mailbox will remain in the computer until a reboot is performed or until the mailbox is explicitly deleted by the $DELMBX system service.

- Mailboxes can be written to and read from by multiple processes.
- Mailboxes are VMS devices, so device operations like setting access protections can be performed on them. To see mailboxes on the VAX, use: $ SHOW DEVICE MB or $ SHOW DEVICE/FULL MB.

13.3 Logical Names

Logical names were described in the chapter on the operating system. Logical names created at the group or system level can be shared by other users. Group logical names can be read by members of the same group, while system logical names can be accessed by all processes. Figure 13.3 shows a program, LOGICAL_NAMES_DEMO.C, which modifies or displays a group logical name called COMMON_LOGICAL_NAME. The program can be run by two users in the same UIC group from different terminals. Any modification made to the logical name by one user can be displayed by the other user. The users will require the GRPNAM privilege to modify group logical names.

Logical names can be manipulated using system calls or DCL commands:

Using logical names

Operation	How to perform the operation:	
	from a program	from DCL
Create a name	system call $CRELNM	DEFINE (or ASSIGN) command
Translate a name	system call $TRNLNM	F$TRNLNM lexical function
Delete a name	system call $DELLNM	DEASSIGN command

The logical name value can also be displayed by users in the same group at other terminals by using:

```
$ SHOW LOGICAL/GROUP *
```

or

```
$ SHOW LOGICAL/GROUP COMMON_LOGICAL_NAME
```

The logical name can be created in the SYSTEM table, in which case all processes on the computer will be able to read it. The privilege SYSNAM or SETPRV is required for this. If all the processes sharing the logical name are from the same job (created by using the SPAWN or a similar command), then the logical name can be placed in the job table. In this case, no special privileges are required to share the logical name.

Data exchange is limited by the size of logical names, which is 255 characters. Multiple logical names can be used; however, global sections may be

Figure 13.3 Interprocess communication with logical names.

```
/* LOGICAL_NAMES_DEMO.C        Jay Shah   1-DEC-1991
 *
 * This program demonstrates how small amounts of
 * data can be transferred from one process to
 * another; effectively performing task-to-task
 * communications. The program creates a group level
 * logical name, COMMON_LOGICAL_NAME, if it does not
 * exist. This requires the privilege GRPNAM. The
 * program then loops infinitely to allow the user to
 * display the equivalent name or enter a new
 * equivalent name for the logical name. The program
 * can be run by different users in the group.
 * Modifications made to the logical name by one user
 * will be displayed by the other users on their
 * terminals.
 */

#include stdio
#include descrip
#include iodef
#include ssdef
#include lnmdef
#include psldef

main()
{
int status;
char response[255];
char eqv_name[10];
unsigned short ret_len;
struct { unsigned short eqv_length;
         unsigned short item_code;
```

Figure 13.3 *(Continued)*

```
        int eqv_address;

        int ret_len_address;

        int terminator;

    }

    itemlist = { 10, LNM$_STRING, eqv_name, &ret_len, 0 };
$DESCRIPTOR(lognam_table, "LNM$GROUP");
$DESCRIPTOR(lognam, "COMMON_LOGICAL_NAME");


/* if COMMON_LOGICAL_NAME exists, get its value else create it

status = sys$trnlnm(

            0, /*&lognam_attributes,*/

            &lognam_table,

            &lognam,

            0, /*&access_mode,*/

            &itemlist

            );
if (status == SS$_NOLOGNAM)

    {

    status = sys$crelnm(

            0, /*&lognam_attributes,*/

            &lognam_table,

            &lognam,

            0, /*&access_mode,*/

            &itemlist

            );

    if ((status != SS$_NORMAL) && (status != SS$_SUPERSEDE))

        lib$stop(status);

    }
else if (status != SS$_NORMAL) lib$stop(status);

/* Display or change value of COMMON_LOGICAL_NAME */

while (TRUE)

    {

    eqv_name[ret_len] = 0;   /* terminate value with NULL */

    printf(

      "Group logical name COMMON_LOGICAL_NAME has a value of %s\n"

      , eqv_name);
```

Figure 13.3 *(Continued)*

```
printf(
  "Enter 1 to modify value, RETURN to see current value: ");
gets(response);
if (strcmp(response,"1") == 0)
  {
  printf("Enter new value for COMMON_LOGICAL_NAME: ");
  gets(eqv_name); itemlist.eqv_length = strlen(eqv_name);
  if (strlen(eqv_name) ==0)
    {
    printf("Value unchanged\n");
    itemlist.eqv_length = 10;
    }
  else
    {
    status = sys$crelnm(
                0, /*lognam_attributes,*/

                &lognam_table,

                &lognam,

                0, /*access_mode,*/

                &itemlist
                );
    if ((status != SS$_NORMAL) && (status != SS$_SUPERSEDE))
        lib$stop(status);
    };
  };
  status = sys$trnlnm(
              0, /*lognam_attributes,*/
              &lognam_table,
              &lognam,
              0, /*access_mode,*/
              &itemlist
              );
  if (status != SS$_NORMAL) lib$stop(status);
};
}
```

more appropriate for large amounts of data. Multiple DCL command procedures can also communicate using common logical names.

13.4 Global Sections

Global sections are a mechanism for sharing main memory among processes on the system. A logically contiguous piece of memory can be allocated to a global section for shared use by one or more processes. Some form of synchronization between the processes will be required to avoid multiple processes writing to the same shared area simultaneously. See the next section for a description of synchronization techniques.

Unfortunately, global sections are not available clusterwide. One node can have a common global section for all the nodes on a cluster; all the nodes access this global section when reading and writing. For redundancy, more than one node can have mirror images of the global section. This has to be implemented using transaction processing techniques, as a VAX might fail during a transfer of data from a global section's memory to a global section in another VAX's memory. DECnet task-to-task can be used to implement this scheme. Most clusters have DECnet running over Ethernet. This may be slow when a large amount of data is flowing between the VAXes. In this case, high-speed parallel interfaces can be used between the VAXes.

In some cases, it may be convenient to keep the data on disk files rather than in global sections. All the VAXes can have access to the common data on the disk. Since files are available clusterwide and the operating system assumes the task of access to the same records by multiple VAXes, no special synchronization is needed among the programs running on various VAXes on the cluster. This scheme simplifies program design.

Another method for sharing data in high-volume applications may be the use of electronic disks, which are described later in this chapter.

Figures 13.4 and 13.5 show two programs–GLOBAL_SECTION_WRITER and GLOBAL_SECTION_READER. GLOBAL_SECTION_WRITER creates a global section of 2048 bytes. The program then reads input from the terminal and writes it to the global section, repeating the terminal input until the 2048-byte limit of the global section has been reached. The program GLOBAL_SECTION_READER reads the global section from bytes 20 to 40 every 5 seconds and writes the output to its terminal. The programs should be run from two different terminals. The global section can be seen by:

```
$ INSTALL/LIST/GLOBAL !List all global sections on computer
```

Global sections are allocated pages of memory. Since a page is 512 bytes,

Figure 13.4   Global section demonstration: the writing program.

```
/* global_section_writer.c      Jay Shah    19-DEC-1990
 *
 * This program
 *   . creates a global section, GBL_SECTION_DEMO, of 2048 bytes
 *   . reads a string entered at the terminal
 *   . and writes the string to the global section.
 *     The string is repeated to fill-up the 2048 bytes
 *     of the global section.
 *
 * 2048 is a multiple of 512; global section main memory
 * is allocated in multiples of 512 bytes by the
 * operating system.
 */

#include stdio
#include descrip
#include secdef
#include ssdef

main()
{

char global_memory[2048];
$DESCRIPTOR ( gbl_secnam, "GBL_SECTION_DEMO" );
struct memrange { char *startaddress; char *endaddress; }
struct memrange inaddress =
                { global_memory, global_memory + 2047 };
struct memrange retaddress;


char ident[8] = { '\000','\000','\000','\000',
                  '\000','\000','\000','\000' };
char *tmpaddress, resp_len;


char response[80];
```

Figure 13.4 *(Continued)*

```
int status;


/* create the global section */
status = sys$crmpsc(

            &inaddress,      /* range of memory to be mapped */
            &retaddress,     /* actual memory mapped */
            0,               /* access mode.Full access by others */
            SEC$M_GBL        /* Global, not private, section */
            | SEC$M_WRT      /* Read/Write allowed */
            | SEC$M_EXPREG   /* Map into available space */
            | SEC$M_PAGFIL,  /* Page file not a disk file section */
            &gbl_secnam,
            &ident,          /* version number 0 */
            0,               /* first page of section to be mapped */
            (short) 0,       /* channel for file sections */
            4,               /* number of pages. all */
            0,               /* first virtual block number of file*/
            0,               /* protection. none */
            0                /* page fault cluster size */

            );
if (status == 1561) printf ("section created\n");
else if (status != SS$_NORMAL) lib$stop(status); /* error? */


while (TRUE)
    {
    puts("Input a string to be inserted in global section:");
    gets(response);


    /* insert the response in global memory, repeat response
     * until global memory is filled up.
     */
    tmpaddress = retaddress.startaddress;

                            /* start of global memory */
    resp_len = strlen(response);
    while (tmpaddress < (retaddress.endaddress - resp_len))
```

Figure 13.4 *(Continued)*

```
    {

    strcpy( tmpaddress, response);

    tmpaddress = tmpaddress + resp_len;

    };

  };


}
```

Figure 13.5 Global section demonstration: the reading
program.

```
/* global_section_reader.c      Jay Shah    19-DEC-1990
 *
 * This program
 *   . reads a part of the global section created by
 *     GLOBAL_SECTION_WRITER above
 *   . and displays the contents on the terminal.
 *
 * The two programs should run from two separate terminals.
 */

#include stdio
#include descrip
#include secdef
#include signal
#include ssdef

main()
{
char global_memory[2048];
$DESCRIPTOR ( gbl_secnam, "GBL_SECTION_DEMO" );
struct memrange { char *startaddress; char *endaddress; };
struct memrange inaddress =
                { global_memory, global_memory + 2047 };
struct memrange retaddress;
char ident[8] = { '\000','\000','\000','\000',
```

Figure 13.5 *(Continued)*

```
                  '\000','\000','\000','\000' };
char *tmpaddress, resp_len;


char response[80];
int status;


/* map the process to the global section created by the
 * execution of the program, GLOBAL_SECTION_WRITER.C
 */
status = sys$mgblsc(
            &inaddress,      /* range of memory to be mapped */
            &retaddress,     /* actual memory mapped */
            0,               /* access mode.Full access by others */
            SEC$M_GBL        /* Global, not private, section */
            | SEC$M_WRT      /* Read/Write allowed */
            | SEC$M_EXPREG   /* Map into available space */
            | SEC$M_PAGFIL,  /* Page file not a disk file section */
  /* EVENT_FLAG_WRITER.C         Jay Shah    20-DEC-1990

   *
   * This program demonstrates use of event flags
   * for synchronization between two processes. The
   * program maps to a global section created by
   * another program, EVENT_FLAG_READER.C and then
   * reads input from the terminal. It waits for a
   * common event flag to be set by the other program,
   * puts the terminal input in the global section and
   * resets the event flag so that the other program
   * can read the global section. The program then
   * reads more terminal input and the operation is
   * repeated.
   *
```

the section sizes will be multiples of 512 bytes. Disk file sections allow files to be mapped into memory. This way, a large file's contents can actually be manipulated as if it were memory locations in the program. Also, the section can be written out to disk automatically for use later.

Global sections can be created at the group or system level. Group global sections are accessible to processes within the group, while system global sections are accessible to all processes on the computer. The SYSGBL privilege is required to be able to create system global sections.

Global sections can be permanent or temporary. Temporary global sections are deleted by the operating system when no process is mapping to them. Permanent global sections can be deleted by the SYS$DGBLSC system call. The PRMGBL privilege is required to create permanent global sections. Note that if multiple processes are mapping to the same global section and one of them deletes the section, the section is actually marked for delete. In this case, the section is deleted only after all the processes release the mapping.

13.5 Synchronization

Synchronization between processes is required when they share common resources and there's a possibility of other processes accessing the resource when one process needs it for exclusive use. Many resources like disks and printer queues do not create contention among processes because the operating system handles synchronization issues for these resources. However, resources defined or created by cooperating processes may need to be shared amicably. An example of such a resource could be a common area in memory that's used by one or more processes.

There are two main program synchronization techniques:

1. *Event flags.* These are bit flags managed by the operating system. Processes can decide to wait until an event flag is set (or reset) by another process before continuing execution. When a process waits on an event flag, the operating system puts it in a wait state until the flag is modified. Event flags are not clusterwide. If internode synchronization is required, the Distributed Lock Manager (described later) can be used instead.

2. *Locks.* Locks are a few bytes of memory locations. These can be created by cooperating processes and then processes can queue up to use the lock. Once a process has a lock, other processes waiting for the lock will be put in a wait state by the operating system until the lock is released by the process which has acquired it. ASTs can be used to wait on a lock and continue program execution. ASTs are described later in this chapter. Locks can be used for synchronization between processes on different nodes on a VAX cluster; locks are clusterwide.

13.6 Event Flags

Event flags are bit data structures within the operating system which can be set by one process and tested by the same or another process on the same VAX. They can be used to signal the completion of an event by one process so that another process waiting for the event to be completed can continue execution.

Consider an example: Process 1 handles input from a terminal and stores it in a global section for processing by a "terminal command interpreter" process (Process 2). Every time process 1 receives a terminal input and

Figure 13.6 Synchronization with event flags: the writing program.

```
/* EVENT_FLAG_WRITER.C        Jay Shah    20-DEC-1990

 *

 * This program demonstrates use of event flags

 * for synchronization between two processes. The

 * program maps to a global section created by

 * another program, EVENT_FLAG_READER.C and then

 * reads input from the terminal. It waits for a

 * common event flag to be set by the other program,

 * puts the terminal input in the global section and

 * resets the event flag so that the other program

 * can read the global section. The program then

 * reads more terminal input and the operation is

 * repeated.

 *

 * See the Run-time library manual for a description

 * on how to acquire an event flag using the library

 * function LIB$GET_EF.

 */


#include stdio

#include descrip

#include secdef

#include signal

#include ssdef


#define event_flag_1 65

#define event_flag_2 66


main()
```

Figure 13.6 *(Continued)*

```
{

char global_memory[2048];

$DESCRIPTOR ( gbl_secnam, "GBL_SECTION_DEMO" );

struct memrange { char *startaddress; char *endaddress; };

struct memrange inaddress =

                { global_memory, global_memory + 2047 };

struct memrange retaddress;

char ident[8] = { '\000','\000','\000','\000',

                  '\000','\000','\000','\000' };


char response[80],resp_len;

int status;


$DESCRIPTOR( evflag_cluster_name, "EV_CLUSTER");


status = sys$mgblsc(

              &inaddress,      /* range of memory to be mapped */

              &retaddress,     /* actual memory mapped */

              0,               /* access mode.Full access by others */

              SEC$M_GBL        /* Global, not private, section */

              | SEC$M_WRT      /* Read/Write allowed */

              | SEC$M_EXPREG   /* Map into available space */

              | SEC$M_PAGFIL,  /* Page file not a disk file section */

              &gbl_secnam,

              &ident,          /* version number 0 */

              0                /* first page of section to be mapped */

              );

if (status != SS$_NORMAL) lib$stop(status);      /* error? */



/* Associate this process with common event

 * flag cluster EV_CLUSTER

   */

  status = sys$ascefc(

              event_flag_1,
```

Figure 13.6 *(Continued)*

```
            &evflag_cluster_name,
            (char) 0,        /* protection: group access  */
            (char) 0         /* temporary, not permanent cluster */
            );
if (status != SS$_NORMAL) lib$stop(status);      /* error? */


while (TRUE)
    {

    /* wait for event flag 2 to be set */
    status = sys$waitfr (event_flag_2);
    if (status != SS$_NORMAL) lib$stop(status);      /* error? */
    /* zero event flag 2 */
    status = sys$clref (event_flag_2);
    if ((status && 1) != 1) lib$stop(status);       /* error? */


    /* read terminal input */
    printf("Input a string to be inserted in global section:");
    gets(response);


    /* put terminal input in global section GBL_SECTION_DEMO */

    resp_len = strlen(response);
    strcpy( retaddress.startaddress, response);


    /* set event flag 1 */
    status = sys$setef (event_flag_1);
    if ((status && 1) != 1) lib$stop(status);       /* error? */


    };


}
```

stores it in the global section, it must inform process 2 that there's a string in the global section for processing. Of course, process 2 could continuously loop to check if a new string has arrived in the global section, but this would be a waste of CPU time. Instead, process 2 sets a flag and waits for process

Figure 13.7 Synchronization with event flags: the reading program.

```
/* EVENT_FLAG_READER.C          Jay Shah    20-DEC-1990
 *
 * This program demonstrates use of event flags
 * for synchronization between two tasks. The
 * program creates a global section and sets a
 * common event flag. Another program,
 * EVENT_FLAG_WRITER.C, puts data in the global
 * section and resets the event flag. This program
 * then processes the global section (in this case
 * it simply prints its contents out at the
 * terminal) and then sets the event flag to repeat
 * the operation.
 */

#include stdio
#include descrip
#include secdef
#include signal
#include ssdef

#define event_flag_1 65
#define event_flag_2 66

main()
{

char global_memory[2048];
$DESCRIPTOR ( gbl_secnam, "GBL_SECTION_DEMO" );
struct memrange { char *startaddress; char *endaddress; };
struct memrange inaddress =
                { global_memory, global_memory + 2047 };
struct memrange retaddress;

char ident[8] = { '\000','\000','\000','\000',
```

Figure 13.7 *(Continued)*

```
                    '\000','\000','\000','\000'  };


char response[80],resp_len;
int status;


$DESCRIPTOR( evflag_cluster_name, "EV_CLUSTER");


/* create the global section */
status = sys$crmpsc(
            &inaddress,      /* range of memory to be mapped */
            &retaddress,     /* actual memory mapped */
            0,               /* access mode.Full access by others */
            SEC$M_GBL        /* Global, not private, section */
            | SEC$M_WRT      /* Read/Write allowed */
            | SEC$M_EXPREG   /* Map into available space */
            | SEC$M_PAGFIL,  /* Page file not a disk file section */
            &gbl_secnam,
            &ident,          /* version number 0 */
            0,               /* first page of section to be mapped */
            (short) 0,       /* channel for file sections */
            4,               /* number of pages. all */
            0,               /* first virtual block number of file*/
            0,               /* protection. none */

            0                /* page fault cluster size */
            );
if (status == 1561) printf ("section created\n");
else if (status != 1) lib$stop(status); /* error? */


/* create a common event flag cluster called EV_CLUSTER */


status = sys$ascefc(
            event_flag_1,
            &evflag_cluster_name,
            (char) 0,      /* protection: group access  */
            (char) 0       /* temporary, not permanent cluster */
```

Figure 13-7 *(Continued)*

```
              );
    if (status != SS$_NORMAL) lib$stop(status);        /* error? */


    while (TRUE)

        {

        /* let other process know that it can
         * write to the global section
         */
        status = sys$clref (event_flag_1);
        if ((status && 1) != 1) lib$stop(status);        /* error? */
        status = sys$setef (event_flag_2);
        if ((status && 1) != 1) lib$stop(status);        /* error? */

        /* wait for the event flag 1 to be set by
         * EVENT_FLAG_WRITER.C When the flag is set,
         * EVENT_FLAG_WRITER.C has placed data in
         *the global section for this process to read
         */

        status = sys$waitfr(event_flag_1);
        if (status != SS$_NORMAL) lib$stop(status);        /* error? */

        /* read and display contents of global section */
        printf("New data in global section: %s \n ",retaddress.startaddress);


        }

    }
```

1 to zero it when there's a terminal string ready for processing. Figures 13.6 and 13.7 show two programs, EVENT_FLAG_WRITER and EVENT_FLAG_READER, which use event flags for synchronization.

Each process has four sets of 32 event flags. Each set is called a *cluster*. Clusters 0 and 1 (event flags 0 through 63) are local to the process, while clusters 2 and 3 (event flags 64 to 127) are common to processes in the same UIC group. Clusters 2 and 3 have to be given a name by the process that creates them. Cluster 0 and 1 event flags are automatically available to processes, while common event flags are available only by associating the process with the cluster name (by the $ASCEFC system service).

13.7 Locks

Locks can be used in place of event flags. Locks are more general than event flags; they can be used to synchronize usage of resources by multiple processes. In fact, locks are known across a cluster so they can be used to synchronize processes across a cluster. Event flags can be used when there are two processes with one process waiting for another to complete a task. Locks can be used when the input is from multiple processes (for example, a number of processes are writing terminal input to the global section) or multiple output processes (a number of processes are reading the global section and parsing the terminal input string).

The lock facility is provided by the system; however, locks are not controlled by the system. A cooperating set of processes defines and uses locks in an appropriate way. A process can acquire a lock and use the corresponding resource, but this doesn't stop another process from using the resource. The second process should wait for the lock to be released, acquire the lock, and then use the resource.

Figure 13.8 shows a program that reads and writes to a global section. The program can be run from multiple terminals; all the processes will then read and write to the same global section. The lock GBLSEC_LOCK will be used for synchronization. The process acquiring the lock can access the global section.

Some comments on locks:

- When a number of locks are being used by a set of processes, there's a possibility of a deadlock. For example, suppose process A has lock L1 and process B has lock L2. A deadlock occurs if process A waits for lock L2 and process B waits for lock L1 since the processes will be waiting forever. VMS monitors the system for such deadlocks; if it finds that there is a deadlock, it returns a status of SS$_DEADLOCK to one of the processes. Since VMS arbitrarily decides which programs should receive this message, programs using locks must be able to process this status appropriately.

- Locks in the system can be displayed using the System Dump Analyzer utility (although a good understanding of VMS internals is required to analyze the output):

```
$ ANALYZE/SYSTEM
VAX/VMS system analyzer

SDA> SHOW LOCKS
```

Figure 13.8 Demonstration of locks.

```
/* LOCK.C                       Jay Shah    22-DEC-1990
 *
 * This program illustrates use of the lock
 * management facility on VAX/VMS. The program
 * creates a global section and a lock, GBLSEC_LOCK.
 * The program then acquires the lock which allows
 * it to gain exclusive access to the global section.
 * The program prints the contents of the global
 * section, writes new data in the global section and
 * then releases the lock. The The program then waits
 * a random amount of time before reading and writing
 * the global section again.
 *
 * The program can be run from multiple terminals to
 * see varying output at each terminal depending on
 * the order in which processes acquire the lock.
 */


#include stdio
#include descrip
#include secdef
#include lckdef
#include ssdef


/* variables for global section */
char global_memory[2048];
$DESCRIPTOR ( gbl_secnam, "GBL_SECTION_DEMO" );
struct memrange { char *startaddress; char *endaddress; };
struct memrange inaddress =
                { global_memory, global_memory + 2047 };
struct memrange retaddress;
char ident[8] = { '\000','\000','\000','\000',
                  '\000','\000','\000','\000' };


int status;
```

Figure 13.8 *(Continued)*

```
main()

{

struct  {
        short vms_cond;
        short reserve;
        int   lock_id;
        char  lock_val[16];
        } lock_status_block;
$DESCRIPTOR (resource_name,"GBLSEC_LOCK");
char response[80],resp_len;
char this_process_id[80];


create_or_mapto_globalsection();


/* create a string to be put in the global section */
sprintf ( this_process_id,"process id = %d", getpid() );



/* loop forever: acquire lock,
 *               read global section,
 *               write global section,
 *               release lock.
 */
while (TRUE)
    {
    sleep ( rand() & 3); /* random wait between 0 and 3 seconds */
    status = sys$enqw(    /* acquire exclusive access to GBLSEC_LOCK */
              35,             /* event flag */
              LCK$K_EXMODE,   /* lock mode: exclusive */
              &lock_status_block,
              0,              /* flags: none */
              &resource_name,
              0,              /* parent lock: none */
              0,              /* AST address */
```

Figure 13.8 *(Continued)*

```
                0,              /* AST parameter */
                0,              /* blocking AST routine: none */
                0,              /* access mode: default */
                0               /* nullarg: reserved */
                );
if (status != SS$_NORMAL) lib$stop(status);     /* error? */
printf ("Global section contains: %s \n",retaddress.startaddress);
strcpy (retaddress.startaddress, this_process_id);
status = sys$deq(                    /* release lock */
            lock_status_block.lock_id,    /* lock id */
            &lock_status_block.lock_val,  /* value block */
            0,                            /* access mode */
                0                         /* flags */
                );
    if (status != SS$_NORMAL) lib$stop(status);     /* error? */
    };


};


create_or_mapto_globalsection()
{
/* create the global section (if it does not exist) */
status = sys$crmpsc(
            &inaddress,     /* range of memory to be mapped */
            &retaddress,    /* actual memory mapped */
            0,              /* access mode.Full access by others */
            SEC$M_GBL       /* Global, not private, section */
            | SEC$M_WRT     /* Read/Write allowed */
            | SEC$M_EXPREG  /* Map into available space */
            | SEC$M_PAGFIL, /* Page file not a disk file section */
            &gbl_secnam,
            &ident,         /* version number 0 */
            0,              /* first page of section to be mapped */
            (short) 0,      /* channel for file sections */
            4,              /* number of pages. all */
            0,              /* first virtual block number of file*/
```

Figure 13.8 *(Continued)*

```
                0,              /* protection. none */
                0               /* page fault cluster size */
                );
if (status == 1561)
    {
    printf ("section created\n");
    strcpy(retaddress.startaddress,"starting process");
    }
else if (status != SS$_NORMAL) lib$stop(status); /* error? */
    else
    {
    /* map to existing global section */
    status = sys$mgblsc(
                &inaddress,     /* range of memory to be mapped */
                &retaddress,    /* actual memory mapped */
                0,              /* access mode.Full access by others */
                SEC$M_GBL       /* Global, not private, section */
                | SEC$M_WRT     /* Read/Write allowed */
                | SEC$M_EXPREG  /* Map into available space */
                | SEC$M_PAGFIL, /* Page file not a disk file section */
                &gbl_secnam,
                &ident,         /* version number 0 */
                0               /* first page of section to be mapped */
                );
    if (status != SS$_NORMAL) lib$stop(status);    /* error? */
    };
};
```

The MONITOR utility can display a summary of lock usage on the system:

```
$ MONITOR LOCKS
```

13.7.1 The Distributed Lock Manager

The Distributed Lock Manager (DLM) is an extension of the lock manager on single-VAX computers. On a VAXcluster, all locks, even those defined and used on a single node, are available for clusterwide use.

Figure 13.9   Demonstration of clusterwide locks.

```
/* CLUSTER_LOCK.C             Jay Shah    22-DEC-1990
 * This program illustrates use of the
 * Distributed Lock Manager on a VAXcluster.
 *
 * The program creates (if not already created)
 * a lock called STUDY_LOCK. The program then
 * acquires the lock and prints a message on the
 * terminal. The program waits a random amount
 * of time and then release the lock.
 *
 * The program can be run from multiple terminals
 * on different nodes on a VAXcluster to see
 * varying output at each terminal depending on
 * the order in which processes acquire the lock.
 */
#include stdio
#include descrip
#include lckdef
#include ssdef

int status;
main()
{
struct {                        /* the lock data structure */
        short vms_cond;
        short reserve;
        int   lock_id;
        char  lock_val[16];
        } lock_status_block;
$DESCRIPTOR (resource_name,"STUDY_LOCK");

/* loop forever: acquire lock,
 *               read global section,
 *               write global section,
 *               release lock
 */
```

Figure 13.9 *(Continued)*

```
while (TRUE)              /* loop until a control-Y is entered */

   {

   status = sys$enqw(     /* acquire exclusive access to STUDY_LOCK */

               35,            /* event flag number, arbitrary*/

               LCK$K_EXMODE,  /* lock mode: exclusive */

               &lock_status_block,.

               0,             /* flags: none */

               &resource_name,

               0,             /* parent lock: none */

               0,             /* AST address: none */

               0,             /* AST parameter: none */

               0,             /* blocking AST routine: none*/

               0,             /* access mode: default */

               0              /* nullarg: reserved */

               );

   if (status != SS$_NORMAL) lib$stop(status);      /* error? */

   printf ("This process has the lock \n");

   sleep ( rand() & 10);  /* random wait between 0 and 10 seconds */

   printf ("This process is releasing the lock \n");

   status = sys$deq(       /* release lock */

               lock_status_block.lock_id,      /* lock id */

               &lock_status_block.lock_val,    /* value block */

               0,                              /* access mode */

               0                               /* flags */

               );

   if (status != SS$_NORMAL) lib$stop(status);      /* error? */

   }; /* while loop end */


}
```

Figure 13.9 shows program CLUSTER_LOCK.C, which loops to acquire a lock (called STUDY_LOCK), holds it for a random time interval, and then releases it. The program can be run from multiple terminals, on the same or different VAXes on a VAXcluster. The display indicates how locks can be used for synchronization among processes on different nodes on a cluster.

13.8   Object Libraries

An *object library* is a file containing commonly used routines in compiled form (not linked). The advantage is that programmers do not have to write code to perform the functions of these routines; instead, they just link their programs with the library. The routines can be used from a program by issuing calls to the routines. In most other respects, the routines can be treated as subroutines defined within the main program.

The main program must be linked with the object library. The next set of steps shows how to create an object library of two routines; one displays the current process id., and the other reverses an input string. The LIBRAR IAN utility is used to create library files.

Figures 13.10 and 13.11 show two subprograms (functions) that will be inserted in the library. To create the library, the commands are:

```
$CC PID        ! compile the two programs
$CC REVSTR
```

```
/* PID.C function to print process id */

pid()

{

printf("\nProcess identification is: %d\n", getpid() );

}
```

Figure 13.10   Subprogram one for the object library.

```
$LIBRARY/CREATE/OBJECT  CLIB.OLB
```

```
/* REV.C

    function to reverse an input string

*/


revstr (instr,outstr)

char instr[], outstr[];

{

int tmp,pos;

outstr[0] = '\000';

tmp = strlen(instr);

for (tmp=strlen(instr)-1, pos = 0;  tmp>=0;  tmp--, pos++ )

        outstr[pos] = instr[tmp];

}
```

Figure 13.11   Subprogram two for the object library.

```
/* mainpgm.c
*/


main()
{
char response[80],reversedstr[80];


pid();
printf("Input a string: "); gets(response);
revstr(response,reversedstr);
printf ("Input reversed is: %s", reversedstr);


}
```

Figure 13.12 A main program using the object library.

```
                ! Create library. File is CLIB.OLB
$LIBRARY/INSERT CLIB.OLB PID.OBJ, REVSTR.OBJ
                ! Insert the modules in the library
```

The program in Fig. 13.12 calls the two routines in the object library created above.

The next set of commands creates and runs the main program image. The library is specified in the LINK command line.

```
$CC MAINPGM
$LINK MAINPGM, CLIB.OLB/LIB, -
      SYS$INPUT:/OPTION !Create object module
SYS$SHARE:VAXCRTL/SHARE
<CTRL/Z>
$RUN MAINPGM
```

13.9 Shared Images

When, for example, 12 users run the same program, the program is loaded 12 times in memory. This may cause memory to be depleted. The program can be redesigned so that only one image (of the program) is in memory, while any number of other programs can use the image. In most cases, the programs do not have to be rewritten; only the LINKER options have to be changed. Note that the data area must be separate for each user using the shared image (and that the shared image must be re-entrant). Normally, this burden is assumed by the system. The linker creates separate sections (PSECTs) for program and data. When the sharable program image is run,

```
/* File: revpid.c
 * The file contains two functions which
 * will be used to create a sharable image.
 */


revstr (instr,outstr)
char instr[], outstr[];
/* the function reverses an input string */

{
int tmp,pos;
outstr[0] = '\000';
tmp = strlen(instr);
for (tmp=strlen(instr)-1, pos = 0;  tmp>=0;  tmp--, pos++ )
        outstr[pos] = instr[tmp];

}


pid()
/* display current process identification */

{
printf("\nProcess identification is: %X\n", getpid() );

}
```

Figure 13.13 Source program for a sharable image.

the loader maps the installed shared image's code into the user's process and then creates a separate area in memory for the user's data.

An image on disk that can be installed as a shared image is called a sharable image. To avoid loading multiple copies of the image, it must be installed using the INSTALL command.

Consider Fig. 13.13, which shows a C program containing two C functions. The first function reverses a specified input string. The second function displays the process-id of the current process (which can also be displayed from DCL by $SHOW PROCESS.

These routines are used by a number of other programs. The routines can be put in an object library; however, because code from object libraries is linked with the calling program, there is no saving in memory when a number of programs use the routines; the routines will be duplicated in each program's executable image. If the routines are put in a sharable image, other programs can still link to them, but the routines will be in memory only once. Here's how to create a sharable image of the routines:

```
$ cc revpid                         !compile the function file
$ link/notrace/share revpid,sys$input:/option
sys$share:vaxcrtl/share
universal=pid
universal=revstr

$ copy revpid.exe sys$share:    !move to the sharable image dir.
$ install sys$share:revpid.exe /share
```

The link command has the /share qualifier, so the image file is a shared image file. The options file (SYS$INPUT: in this case) contains the UNIVERSAL clause, which specifies that the function names are available to any other image linking against this image. Consider the C program in Fig. 13.14.

This program can be compiled and linked against the shared image by:

```
$link  mainpgm,sys$input:/option
sys$share:vaxcrtl/share
sys$share:revpid/share
```

Here's a sample execution of the main program:

```
$ run mainpgm
Process identification is: 1057
Input a string: This is a Test
Input reversed is: tseT a si sihT
```

Note that sharable images can contain a set of commonly used routines. They're similar to object libraries; the main difference is that programs link

```
/* mainpgm.c
*/
#include stdio


main()

{
char response[80],reversedstr[80];


pid();
printf("\nInput a string: "); gets(response);
revstr(response,reversedstr);
printf ("Input reversed is: %s", reversedstr);


}
```

Figure 13.14 A main program using a sharable image.

Figure 13.15   Asynchronous System Traps (ASTs).

```
/* AST.C                     Jay Shah    27-DEC-1990
 * This program demonstrates use of ASTs.
 * The program loops to accept input from
 * the terminal and then display it. A

  * timer will generate an AST every 5
  * seconds and the AST routine will display
  * a message.
  */
#include stdio
#include descrip
#include ssdef


int status;
char delta_time[8];
$DESCRIPTOR(timbuf,"0 00:00:05.00");    /* 5 seconds */
int ast_routine();          /* routine declared later */


main()
{
char response[80];


status = sys$bintim(       /* convert ascii time to internal form */
          &timbuf,
          delta_time
          );
if (status != SS$_NORMAL) lib$stop(status);


/* set timer to interrupt normal program after specified time */
status = sys$setimr(
            35,                  /* event flag */
            delta_time,          /* time before AST interrupt */
            &ast_routine,        /* ast addresss */
            0,                   /* timer id, ignore */
            0                    /* elapsed time, not CPU time */
```

Figure 13.15 *(Continued)*

```
                );
   if (status != SS$_NORMAL) lib$stop(status);


   while(TRUE)      /* This loop will be regularly
                       interrupted by the timer */

      {

      printf("Enter any input: "); gets(response);
      printf("You entered %s\n",response);

      };


   }
   ast_routine()    /* This routine is invoked by
                       timer interrupt AST */

   {
   printf("\nTimer interrupt\n\n");


   /* re-arm the timer */
   status = sys$setimr(

               35,                  /* event flag */

               delta_time,          /* time before AST interrupt */

               &ast_routine,        /* ast routine addresss */

               0,                   /* timer id, ignore */

               0                    /* elapsed time, not CPU time */

               );
   if (status != SS$_NORMAL) lib$stop(status);


   }
```

to one shared image of the common routines in memory, while routines from object libraries are included with the program.

Sharable images have another advantage; they can be installed with privileges, so they can be designed to perform functions that require privileges that are not assigned to the programs (processes) that link with these privileged-shared images. To see shared images installed in memory use:

```
$ install list
```

13.10 Asynchronous System Traps (ASTs)

An AST is an interruption to a program. The interruption is triggered by some event external to the program. Typically, the program services the interrupt by executing an interrupt service subprogram, and then continues where it left off in its normal flow of execution.

Consider a program that's required to loop indefinitely to accept a line of input from the terminal and display the line. The program is also required to display "Timer interrupt" every 5 seconds on the terminal. The program in Fig. 13.15 uses ASTs to achieve this.

To use ASTs in programs:

- Let the operating system know about the type of AST you wish to enable and the subroutine to be executed when the AST condition is satisfied.

- Continue program execution.

- When the AST condition is satisfied, the operating system will deliver the AST to your program. In effect, execution control will transfer to the address of the subroutine. When the subroutine completes executing, normal program execution will continue. Note that once an AST has been delivered, the AST is disabled until it is "re-armed" (reenabled) by the subroutine or the program.

- Since the timing of AST delivery is not known to the program (that's why it is called asynchronous), the program and the AST routine should not make assumptions about the state of execution of each other. Specifically, common data access should be synchronized by some means such as the AST routine setting a flag when it has data ready for the main program to process.

ASTs can be used to invoke a routine on completion of some system services like $QIO and $ENQ and $SETTIMR. In these calls, the address of the AST routine is given as a parameter. An AST routine can be explicitly invoked by the $DCLAST (declare AST) system service.

14

The VAX C Run-Time Library

All C implementations come bundled with a standard library of functions. Although this library is not part of the base C language, the functions are an integral part of all C environments. Hence, the ANSI C standard defines this library. Under VAX C, this library of functions is called the VAX C run-time library (VAX C RTL). Most, though not all, of the RTL functions are portable. This chapter discusses the VAX C RTL and how it can be used. Although the routines mentioned here are referred to as functions, some of them are actually macros defined in the header files.

14.1 Using the RTL Functions

Here's an example program using the RTL function printf():

```
#include stdio

main()
{
  printf("printf is a VAX C RTL function\n");
}
```

The function is linked with the compiled C program when the VAX C RTL is specified during LINKing, as shown in the next section. The printf()

function is used without being defined in this C program, hence the func tion prototype must be specified. The function prototype is specified in the included header file, stdio.h. The file is in SYS$LIBRARY:. The prototype for printf() is declared in SYS$LIBRARY:STDIO.H as:

```
int printf (const char *format_spec, ...);
```

Every RTL function has a prototype declaration in a header file that must be included in the program using the function. The prototype declaration is used by the compiler for checking the number of parameters passed and for type checking of arguments and return value. (The header files also contain other information like macros and constants.)

14.2   Using the Run-Time Libraries

VAX C has two types of RTLs, object libraries and shareable image libraries. When using an object library, a program using the RTL functions can be compiled and linked with commands like:

```
$ CC prog
$ LINK prog, SYS$LIBRARY:VAXCRTL.OLB/LIBRARY
```

Here, the RTL functions are extracted from the object library VAX CRTL.OLB and linked into the program image. When using a shareable image library, the program can be compiled and linked by a command like:

```
$ CC prog
$ LINK prog, SYS$INPUT:/OPTIONS
SYS$SHARE:VAXCRTL.EXE/SHARE
```

Here, the link command specifies an option file, which is SYS$INPUT: (whatever follows). The option file contains the name of a shareable image, VAXCRTL.EXE. (Currently, SYS$SHARE and SYS$LIBRARY are equivalent logical names.) The linker will generate code such that during program execution, when an RTL function is called, control is transferred to RTL VAXCRTL.EXE, which is memory resident. After execution of the function, control returns to the calling program. The advantage of a shareable image is that the programs are compact because they do not include the RTL function code. The INSTALL command is used by VAX/VMS when the system boots to make VAXCRTL.EXE (along with many other images) memory resident.

As mentioned in chapter 5, there are two formats for double precision floating point numbers on the VAX: D_FLOAT and G_FLOAT. They both have a size of 8 bytes; however, they differ in the precision and range of the floating point numbers. Any particular C program can use either one of these, but not both. By default, D_FLOAT is assumed when a declaration like this is made:

```
double float_num1, float_num2;
```

If G_FLOAT numbers are to be used, the compilation command line must be specified with the /G_FLOAT qualifier:

```
$ CC/G_FLOAT prog
```

Also, the RTLs to be used are different; VAXCRTLG.OLB must be used in place of VAXCRTL.OLB, and VAXCRTLG.EXE must be used in place of VAX CRTL.EXE as:

```
$ LINK prog, SYS$LIBRARY:VAXCRTLG.OLB/LIBRARY
```

or

```
$ LINK prog, SYS$INPUT:/OPTIONS
SYS$SHARE:VAXCRTLG.EXE/SHARE
```

The curses screen-oriented terminal I/O functions are defined in yet another object library, SYS$LIBRARY:VAXCCURSES.OLB. The curses do not have a corresponding shareable library. With curses, the link command would be

```
$ LINK prog, SYS$LIBRARY:VAXCRTLG.OLB/LIBRARY, -
  SYS$LIBRARY:VAXCCURSES.OLB/LIBRARY
```

In summary, VAX C comes with the following RTLs:

SYS$LIBRARY:VAXCRTL.OLB	Object library
SYS$LIBRARY:VAXCRTLG.OLB	Object library
SYS$LIBRARY:VAXCCURSES.OLB	Object library
SYS$LIBRARY:VAXCRTL.EXE	Shareable image library
SYS$LIBRARY:VAXCRTLG.EXE	Shareable image library

14.3 Character Manipulation Functions

Here's a brief description of the C character manipulation functions and macros:

Character classification function	Description
isalnum	Returns a nonzero integer if its argument is an alphanumeric character.
isalpha	Returns a nonzero integer if its argument is an alphabetic-character.
isascii	Returns a nonzero integer if its argument is an ASCII character between 0 and 127.
iscntrl	Returns a nonzero integer if its argument is DEL (127) or less than 32 (nonprintable characters).

Character classification function	Description
isdigit	Returns a nonzero integer if its argument is a decimal digit (0 to 9).
isgraph	Returns a nonzero integer if its argument is a printable character (33 to 126).
islower	Returns a nonzero integer if its argument is a lowercase alphabet.
isprint	Returns a nonzero integer if its argument is a printable character (33 to 126).
ispunct	Returns a nonzero integer if its argument is a punctuation (non-alphanumeric printable character).
isspace	Returns a nonzero integer if its argument is a white space: horizontal or vertical tab, CR, LF, or FF.
isupper	Returns a nonzero integer if its argument is an uppercase alphabet.
isxdigit	Returns a nonzero integer if its argument is a hexadecimal digit (0 to 9, a to f, or A to F).

Character conversion function	Description
ecvt	Converts a double precision floating point number argument to a NUL terminated string of ASCII digits. Returns address of the string. String is in a memory location created by the function.
fcvt	Similar to ecvt, except string is stored in specified location.
gcvt	Similar to ecvt; parameters are different.
toascii	Converts 8-bit ASCII argument to 7-bit ASCII.
tolower	Converts uppercase argument to lowercase.
_tolower	The function is tolower; The macro is _tolower.
toupper	Converts uppercase argument to uppercase.
_toupper	The function is toupper; the macro is _toupper.

Here's a program illustrating use of these functions:

```
/* character functions */

#include stdio
#include unixlib
#include ctype
```

```
main()
{
  {
  /*example 1*/
  int ch, stat;
  ch = '5';
  stat = isdigit (ch);
  if (stat) printf ("%c is a digit\n",ch);
  else printf ("%c is not a digit\n",ch);
  }


  {
  /*example 2*/
  double float_num;          /* number to be converted */
  int sign, dpoint;          /* sign and dec. point position */
  char converted_num[10];    /* output value */

  float_num= 324e-2;
  strcpy(converted_num,ecvt(float_num,6,&dpoint,&sign));
  printf("converted number: ");
  if (sign) printf ("-");
  printf ("%s\n",converted_num);
  printf("decimal point after %d digits\n",dpoint);
  }
}
```

The program output is:

```
$RUN prog
5 is a digit
converted number: 324000
decimal point after 1 digits
```

14.4 String Manipulation Functions

Here's a brief description of the C string manipulation functions and macros. Strings are assumed to be a NUL-terminated sequence of characters.

String manipulation function	Description
atof	Converts given string argument to a double precision floating point number.
atoi	Converts given string argument to an integer.
atol	Same as atoi.
strcat strncat	Appends one string to another.
strchr	Returns address of first occurrence of given character in a string.
strrchr	Returns address of last occurrence of given character in a string.
strcmp	Compares two strings and returns a negative, zero, or pos-

String manipulation function	Description
	itive integer, depending on whether the sort-sequence of the first string is less than, equal to, or greater than the second string.
strcpy	Copy one string to another.
strncpy	
strcspn	Searches a string for a character in a specified set of characters. Returns length of string up to the found character.
strlen	Return length of string (excluding the terminating NUL).
strpbrk	Searches a string for a character or a specified set of characters. Returns address of found character.
strspn	Searches a string for a character not in a specified set of characters.
strtol	Converts a string of characters to a long value. Conversion base of 2 to 36 can be specified.
strtod	Converts a string of characters to a double precision number.
strtok	Locates text tokens in a given string. The tokens are delimited by one or more specified delimiter(s).
strtoul	Converts a string of characters to an unsigned long value. Conversion base of 2 to 36 can be specified.

The mem* functions are similar to corresponding str* functions, except that they perform operations on bytes rather than characters, and they do not consider NUL as a terminating character. This may be significant on machines where one character is not equivalent to one byte. The mem* functions are:

memchr	Corresponds to strchr.
memcmp	Corresponds to strncmp.
memcpy	Corresponds to strncpy.
memmove	Is equivalent to memcpy on VAX.
memset	Sets a specified number of bytes starting at a specified address to a specified value.

The following functions are used to manipulate variable-length argument lists. Variable-length argument lists are described in the chapter on program structure.

```
va_arg, va_count, va_end, va_start, va_start_1, vfprintf,
vprintf, vsprintf.
```

14.5 I/O Functions

Many of the I/O functions are described in the chapter on basic input and output. Use of the Record Management Services for VAX/VMS specific file manipulations is shown in the chapter on RMS files. The I/O functions are mentioned here for the sake of completeness.

UNIX I/O function	Description
close	Close file associated with a file descriptor.
creat	Create a new file.
dup	Allocate a new descriptor that refers
dup2	to a file specified by a file descriptor.
fgetpos	Store the current value of the file position indicator for the stream.
fileno	Return an integer file descriptor of file.
fstat	
stat	Access file header information.
getname	Return file spec of file specified by descriptor.
isapipe	Return 1 if file is associated with mailbox, else return 0.
isatty	Return 1 if file is associated with a terminal, else return 0.
lseek	Position file to an arbitrary byte position (random search).
open	Open file.
read	Read from file.
ttyname	Return a pointer to the name of terminal device associated with descriptor 0 (standard input).
write	Write specified number of bytes to file.

Standard I/O function	Description
access	Check if specified access mode of file is allowed.
clearerr	Reset error and eof locations for specified file.
delete	Delete file.
fclose	Flush buffers, close file.
fdopen	Associate a file pointer with a file descriptor.
feof	Check if file is at eof.
ferror	Return nonzero integer if the previous file operation was a failure.
fflush	Write out buffers of specified file.
fgetc	Return characters from a specified file.
fgets	Return a line from specified file.
fgetname	Return filespec of file specified by file pointer.
fopen	Open file and return FILE structure.
fprintf	Perform formatted output to a file.
fputs	Write character string to file.
fread	Return specified number of items from specified file.

Standard I/O function	Description
freopen	Substitute a file, named by a file specification, with a file addressed by a file pointer.
fscanf	Perform formatted input from a specified file.
fseek	Position file to specified byte offset.
ftell	Return byte offset position of file.
fwrite	Write specified number of items to specified file.
getc	Same as fgetc.
getw	Return next 4 characters as integer from specified file.
mktemp	Create unique file name from given template.
putc	Same as fputc.
putw	Write 4 characters (representing an integer) to specified file.
remove	Delete file.
rename	Rename file.
rewind	Set file to beginning.
setbuf	Associate a buffer with a file.
setvbuf	Associate a buffer with a file. Buffer size is specified.
tmpfile	Create temporary file.
tmpnam	Create a character string that can be used in place of a file name argument in other function calls.
ungetc	Push back a character in the input stream of a file. It will be the next character returned.

Terminal I/O function	Description
getchar	Read a single character from standard input (stdin or SYS$INPUT).
gets	Read a line from standard input.
printf	Perform formatted output from standard input.
putchar	Write a single character to standard output.
puts	Write a character string to standard output, followed by a newline.
scanf	Perform formatted input from standard input.

14.6   Error- and Signal-Handling Functions

Error-handling function	Description
abort	Terminate process by executing an illegal machine instruction.
assert	Print file name and line number of current location if argument evaluates to zero.
atexit	Register a function that will be called without arguments when program terminates.
exit _exit	Terminate process.
perror	Display last error encountered during a call to the VAX C RTL.
strerror	Return error message string corresponding to error number.
alarm	Send signal SIGALARM after specified number of seconds.
gsignal	Generate specified software signal.
kill	Send signal to specified process.
longjmp	Jump to a specified location from within a nested series of function calls without performing returns.
pause	Wait until a signal is received.
raise	Generate specified software signal.
setjmp	Jump to a specified location from within a nested series of function calls without performing returns.
sigblock	Add the specified signals to the set of signals currently blocked for delivery.
signal	Catch or ignore a signal.
sigpause	Wait for a signal.
sigsetmask	Establish signals blocked from delivery.
sigstack	Define alternate stack for processing signals.
sigvec	Assign a handler for a specific signal.
sleep	Suspend execution for specified time.
ssignal	Specify action to be taken when a particular signal is raised.
VAXC$ESTABLISH	Establish a special VAX C RTL exception handler.

14.7 Subprocess and Process Communications Functions

Subprocess manipulation function	Description
system	Execute DCL command.
vfork	SPAWN child process.
execl,	
execle,	
execlp,	
execv,	
execve, execvp	Pass name of image to be executed by child process.
wait	Wait for child process to complete.
pipe	Communicate with another process via mailboxes.

The exec*() functions are used to create a child process. The system internally uses the system library function LIB$SPAWN to create the process. The first parameter is the name of the image file to be executed in the created process. Here is the syntax for these function calls:

```
int execl    (char *image_file_name, ...);
int execlp   (char *image_file_name, ...);
int execv    (char *image_file_name, char *argv[]);
int execvp   (char *image_file_name, char *argv[]);
int execle   (char *image_file_name, ...);
int execve   (char *image_file_name, char *argv[], char *envp[]);
```

The ellipsis represents further pointers, each pointing to a sequence of pointers to strings. The argv is an array of pointers that allows data to be passed between parent and child processes. The first string is always the name of the child image. The envp is an array of pointers to strings, each of the form:

```
HOME=home_dir
TERM=term_type
PATH=default_dev_and_dir
USER=parent_username
```

with the last pointer a Null.

The child program gets these parameters by declaring main() as:

```
main(int argc, char *argv[], char *envp[])
```

Here's an example:

```
* Parent program */
  ...
  char *my_argv[] = "child", "a1", "a2", 0;
  ...
```

```
    status = execv("child",my_argv);
    ...

/* child program */
main( int argc, char *argv[] )
{
    /* argc contains size of array argv */
    ...
    for (i=1; i< argc; i++)
        printf("Argument %d, value %s\n, i,argv[i]);
    ...
}
```

The `execlp()` and `execvp()` search for the child process in the directory pointed to by the logical name `VAXC$PATH`.

The `vfork()` function parallels the UNIX `fork()`. The `fork()` function creates an exact duplicate of the parent process, and execution continues in both the parent and the child process just after the `fork()` function. The `vfork()` on VAX/VMS sets up a child process context and returns a zero status. Later, a child process is created by one of the `exec*()` functions. On completion of the child process, control returns to the statement following the `vfork()` rather than the `exec*()`. The `wait()` function is used to check for completion of a child process. It returns the PID of the child process and it sets the location whose address is passed to it as the only parameter to the completion status of the child process. All of these are demonstrated in the two programs `parent.c` and `child.c`, shown in Figs. 14.1 and 14.2.

Figure 14.1 PARENT.C: process spawning demonstration.

```
/* PARENT.C            Jay Shah

 * This program uses vfork() and execl() to create a child

 * process. vfork() is a version of the UNIX fork(). It may

 * be helpful to see the system library function LIB$SPAWN.

 * The child process executes the program child.exe. wait()

 * is used to check status of a completed child process. It

 * returns the process id. of the child process or -1 for

 * an error.

 *

 * This is the parent process.
 */


#include stdio
#include processes
```

Figure 14.1 *(Continued)*

```
main()
{
    int status, child_status, child_pid;

    /* vfork() creates a child process context. The child
     * process is created by a subsequent execl(). When the
     * child process exits, control is returned to the
     * statement after the vfork(). Effectively, the
     * statements after vfork() are executed twice. The call
     * to vfork() returns a 0.
     */
    status = vfork();
    if (status == 0)
        { /* vfork() executed successfully */
        printf("Message from parent: starting child\n");
        status = execl("child",0);
        if (status == -1)
            {
            printf("Error from parent: execl() failed\n");
            exit(status);
            };
        }
    else
        {
        if (status < 0)
    {
    printf("Error from parent: Child process creation failed\n");
    exit(status);
    }
else
    { /* status > 0 , wait for child process */
    printf("Message from parent: waiting for child\n");
    child_pid = wait(&child_status);
    if (child_pid == -1)
        {
        printf("Error from parent: wait failed\n");
        exit(child_pid);
```

Figure 14.1 *(Continued)*

```
            };
        printf("Child process id: %d\n",child_pid);
        printf("Child status: %d\n",child_status);
        exit(child_status);
        };
    };
}
```

Here's a script created by execution of `parent`:

```
$ run parent
Message from parent: starting child
Message from parent: waiting for child
Message from child: exiting...
Child process id: 403
Child status: 1
$
```

14.8 The Screen Management Subpackage, `curses`—and Screen Manipulation Funtions

A portable screen management sub-package for VAX is `curses`. On VMS, the functions are implemented within the VAX C RTL using the VMS Screen Management Facility (`SMG$`). Most `curses` macros and functions are listed in pairs; the function is prefixed with a `w` for windows. For example, `[w]addch` represents the macro `addch` and the function `waddch`.

```
/* CHILD.C          Jay Shah
 * This program is a child process of the program PARENT.C.
 * The process is internally created LIB$SPAWN.
 */


main()
{
    int i;
    printf("Message from child: exiting...\n");
}
```

Figure 14.2 CHILD.C: process spawning demonstration.

Actually, within the header file, `curses.h`, addch is defined as:

```
# define   addch(ch)    waddch(stdscr, ch)
```

Consult the C Run-Time Library Reference Manual for further details.

14.9 Math Functions

The math functions and macros are:

Math function	Description
abs	Return absolute value of integer.
acos	Arc cosine.
asin	Arc sine.
atan	Arc tangent.
atan2	Arc tangent of y/x where x and y are arguments.
cabs	Absolute value of complex number. Square root of $(x*x + y*y)$.
ceil	Return smallest double integer greater than or equal to argument.
cos	Cosine.
cosh	Hyperbolic cosine.
exp	Return `e**argument`.
fabs	Return absolute value of floating point number.
floor	Return largest double integer less than or equal to argument.
fmod	Floating point remainder of first argument divided by second.
frexp	Return mantissa of a double value.
hypot	Square root of $(x*x + y*y)$.
labs	Return absolute value of integer as long integer.
ldexp	Return x * 2**y.
ldiv, div	Return quotient and remainder.
log, log 10	Logarithm.
modf	Return positive fraction of first argument. Assign integral part as double integer to location whose address is second argument.
pow	x**y
rand, srand	Return pseudorandom number in range 0 to 2**31 - 1.
sin	Sine.
sinh	Hyperbolic sine.
sqrt	Square root.
tan	Tangent.
tanh	Hyperbolic tangent.

14.10 Memory Allocation Functions

The memory allocation functions and macros are shown here. All memory references are to the program's virtual memory.

Memory allocation function	Description
brk, sbrk	Determine lowest virtual address not used.
calloc, malloc	Allocate an area of memory.
cfree, free	For reallocation, free up area of memory previously allocated by calloc, malloc, or realloc.
realloc	Change the size of the area pointed to by first argument to the number of bytes given by the second argument.
VAXC$CALLOC_OPT	Allocate an area of memory.
VAXC$CFREE_OPT	For reallocation, free up area of memory previously allocated by VAXC$CALLOC_OPT, VAXC$MALLOC_OPT, or VAXC$REALLOC_OPT.
VAXC$FREE_OPT	For reallocation, free up area of memory previously allocated by VAXC$CALLOC_OPT, VAXC$MALLOC_OPT, or VAXC$REALLOC_OPT.
VAXC$MALLOC_OPT	Allocate an area of memory.
VAXC$REALLOC_OPT	Change the size of the area pointed to by first argument to the number of bytes given by the second argument.

The functions malloc, calloc, realloc, free and cfree internally use the system library services, LIB$GET_VM and LIB$FREE_VM. The VAXC$ functions are very similar to the C language functions, except that they're more efficient, though not portable.

14.11 System Functions

This section shows the functions that manipulate the operating system objects, and miscellaneous functions.

System function	Description
asctime	Convert broken down time to form like Sun Nov 17 04:00:44 1991\n\0

System function	Description
bsearch	Binary search of a value in a given array of sorted values.
chdir	Change default directory.
chmod	Change file protection of file.
chown	Change UIC of file.
clock	Determine CPU time used since start of program execution.
ctermid	Return equivalent string for the logical name SYS$COMMAND.
ctime	Convert time in seconds to string like Sun Nov 17 04:00:44 1991\n\0
cuserid	Return pointer to string of username of current process.
difftime	Return difference in time between two times specified in arguments.
ftime	Return elapsed time in seconds since Jan 1, 1970.
getcwd	Return filespec of current default directory.
getegid, geteuid, getgid, getuid	Return group and member from user identification code (UIC).
getenv	Get user environment information. Possible values for argument are:
	HOME (login directory)
	TERM (terminal name)
	PATH (default device and directory)
	USER (username)
getpid	Return process id.
getppid	Return parent's process id.
localtime	Convert time specified as elapsed seconds since 1 Jan, 1970 into days, hours and so on.
mkdir	Create a directory.
qsort	Sort an array of values in place using the quick-sort algorithm.
time	Return elapsed time in seconds since Jan 1, 1970.
times	Return accumulated time of current process and terminated child processes.
umask	Create file protection mask.
VAXC$CRTL_INIT	Initialize VAX C RTL so that it can be called from other languages.

VMS System Services and Run-Time Libraries

VMS has hundreds of library routines that can be called from any language. VMS manuals differentiate between the basic routines as system services or run-time library (RTL) routines. *System services* are routines that perform operations that are closely tied with the operating system, like allocating devices and creating detached processes. The RTL routines perform utility functions like string manipulation and ASCII-to-EBCDIC character translation. Both types of routines can be treated similarly. This chapter introduces the system services and basic RTL routines.

15.1 Introduction

The system services are installed as shareable images when VMS boots. The routines are in the file `SYS$LIBRARY:IMAGELIB.OLB`. This library is automatically linked with when the `LINK` command is issued, so it need not be explicitly specified. The RTL routines are in the file `SYS$LIBRARY:STARLET.OLB`. These routines are in object form, so they're linked along with the program referencing them. Again, this library is automatically searched during linking, so it need not be explicitly specified. The library is searched after `SYS$LIBRARY:IMAGELIB.OLB`.

System services are described in volumes 3 and 4 of the VMS Programming set of manuals; the Run-Time Library is described in volume 5. At the DCL prompt, help for these routines can be elicited by the commands:

```
$ help RTL_routines
$ help System_Services
```

Figure 15.1 shows two examples of the help display.

Figure 15.1 HELP for system services and run-time library.

```
$ HELP  SYSTEM_SERVICE  $ASCTIM


System_Services


  $ASCTIM


      The Convert Binary Time to ASCII String service converts an absolute

      or delta time from 64-bit system time format to an ASCII string.

    Format:


      SYS$ASCTIM  [timlen] ,timbuf ,[timadr] ,[cvtflg]


    Arguments:


timlen


VMS usage: word_unsigned

type: word (unsigned)

access: write only

mechanism: by reference


Length (in bytes) of the ASCII  string  returned  by  $ASCTIM.    The
timlen argument is the address of a word containing this length.


timbuf


VMS usage: time_name

type: character-coded text string
```

Figure 15.1 *(Continued)*

```
access: write only

mechanism: by reference


Length (in bytes) of the ASCII  string  returned  by  $ASCTIM.    The
timlen argument is the address of a word containing this length.


timbuf


VMS usage: time_name
type: character-coded text string
access: write only
mechanism: by descriptor--fixed
length string descriptor


Buffer into which $ASCTIM  writes  the  ASCII  string.    The  timbuf
argument is the address of a character string descriptor pointing to
the buffer.


timadr


VMS usage: date_time
type: quadword (unsigned)
access: read only
mechanism: by reference


Time value that $ASCTIM is to convert.  The timadr argument  is  the
address of this 64-bit time value.  A positive time value represents
an absolute time.  A negative time value represents  a  delta  time.
If a delta time is specified, it must be less than 10,000 days.


cvtflg


VMS usage: longword_unsigned
type: longword (unsigned)
access: read only
mechanism: by value
```

Figure 15.1 *(Continued)*

```
         Conversion indicator specifying which date and time  fields  $ASCTIM
         should  return.   The  cvtflg argument is a longword value, which is
         interpreted as Boolean.  A value of 1 specifies that $ASCTIM  should
         return  only  the  hour,  minute,  second,  and  hundredth of second
         fields.  A value of 0 (the default) specifies  that  $ASCTIM  should
         return the full date and time.




$ HELP  RTL_ROUTINES  LIB$  LIB$GET_SYMBOL


RTL_ROUTINES


   LIB$


    LIB$GET_SYMBOL


        The Get Value of CLI Symbol routine requests the  calling  process's
        Command  Language  Interpreter  (CLI)  to  return the value of a CLI
        symbol as a string.  LIB$GET_SYMBOL then returns the string  to  the
        caller.   Optionally,  LIB$GET_SYMBOL  can  return the length of the
        returned value and the table in which the symbol was found.


            Format:


        LIB$GET_SYMBOL  symbol ,resultant-string [,resultant-length]
                   [,table-type-indicator]


    Arguments:


symbol


VMS usage: char_string
type: character string
access: read only
```

Figure 15.1 *(Continued)*

---

mechanism: by descriptor

Name of the symbol for which LIB$GET_SYMBOL searches. The symbol
argument is the address of a descriptor pointing to the name of the
symbol. LIB$GET_SYMBOL converts the symbol name to uppercase and
removes trailing blanks before the search. Symbol must begin with a
letter or dollar sign ($). The maximum length of symbol is 255
characters.

resultant-string

VMS usage: char_string
type: character string
access: write only
mechanism: by descriptor

Value of the returned symbol. The resultant-string argument is the
address of a descriptor pointing to a character string into which
LIB$GET_SYMBOL writes the value of the symbol.

resultant-length

VMS usage: word_unsigned
type: word (unsigned)
access: write only
mechanism: by reference

Length of the symbol value returned by LIB$GET_SYMBOL. The
resultant-length argument is the address of an unsigned word integer
into which LIB$GET_SYMBOL writes the length.

table-type-indicator

VMS usage: longword_signed
type: longword integer (signed)

Figure 15.1 *(Continued)*

```
access: write only
mechanism: by reference


Indicator   of   which   table   contained   the   symbol.   The
table-type-indicator   argument   is   the address of a signed longword
integer into which LIB$GET_SYMBOL writes the table indicator.
```

15.2 Routine Call Parameters

VAX/VMS has many data types; hence, a data structure has to be set up for each before the parameter can be passed to a system routine. In practice, there are three basic parameter-passing mechanisms: by *value*, by *reference* and by *descriptor*. By value is obvious. By reference means the address of the memory location containing the parameter is passed. By descriptor means the address of the descriptor of the parameter is passed.

Descriptors are usually used when passing string values. The descriptor gives the length of the string passed. Descriptors can be for various data types like arrays of integers or date and time, but string descriptors are the most common. A string descriptor has 8 bytes, as shown here:

```
A string descriptor:
length    —an unsigned word (2 bytes, length of string)
datatype  —an unsigned byte (value=14 for text strings)
class     —an unsigned byte (value=1 for text strings)
address   —an unsigned longword (4 bytes, address of string)
```

COBOL and most of the other languages set up string descriptors when declaring a string or array of characters. Here's how three different parameters are declared COBOL and passed to a routine:

```
*parameter passing in COBOL
working-storage section.
* parameter1 is a 2 byte integer.
* parameter2 is a string descriptor for a string of length 30.
* parameter3 is a 4 byte integer.

 01 parameter1   pic 9(4) comp value 8.
 01 parameter2   pic x(30).
 01 parameter3   pic 9(9) comp value 0.
 01 call-status  pic s9(9) comp.

procedure division.
* calling a system routine. parameter1 is passed by reference,
parameter2
```

```
* is a string descriptor passed by reference, parameter3 is passed by
value.

   call "sys$routine" using
                           by reference parameter1,
                           by reference parameter2,
                           by value parameter3
                           giving call-status.
   if call-status is failure then call "sys$exit" using
                           by value call-status.
```

Programmers using C have to make their own string descriptors. Here's an example that shows how to set up three parameters that are passed by value, reference, and descriptor, and call a system routine.

```
/* Parameter passing in C */

/* parameter1 is a 2-byte integer passed by reference.
 * parameter2 is a descriptor (for a 30 character string) and it
 * is passed by reference.
 * parameter3 is a 4-byte integer passed by value.
 */

   unsigned short parameter1;
   unsigned char str[30];
   struct
   {                              /*string descriptor*/
   unsigned short length;
   unsigned char  datatype;        /* value 14 for strings */
   unsigned char  descriptor_class; /* value 1 for strings */
   char           *str_address;
   }parameter2 = { 30, 14, 1, str};
   unsigned int parameter3;

main()
{

   status = sys$routine( &parameter1, &parameter2, parameter3);
   /* Note the missing & before parameter3 */
   if (status!=SS$_NORMAL) exit(status);
}
```

Each call returns a longword integer status. This status should be checked after every call in case the called routine did not execute properly.

15.2.1 The $DESCRIPTOR macro

A string descriptor for a constant string can be created in C by the use of the $DESCRIP macro declared in the header file SYS$SYSDEVICE:DE SCRIP.H. An example use is:

```
#include descrip.h
main()
{
$DESCRIPTOR(mailbox,"MBA21:");
printf("mailbox name length = %d\n", mailbox.dsc$w_length);
}
```

```
main()

{

#include stdio

#include descrip

#include ssdef


        unsigned char timbuf_internal[8],timbuf_ascii[30];

        int  timcvtflg = 0, status;

        struct

        {                                           /*string descriptor*/

        unsigned short  timlength;

        unsigned char   datatype;

        unsigned char   descriptor_class;

        char            *address;

        }   timbuf_ascii_descriptor =

                { 30, DSC$K_DTYPE_T, DSC$K_CLASS_S, timbuf_ascii};

                /* DSC$K_DTYPE_T, DSC$K_CLASS_S specify the

                    structure to be a constant string

                    descriptor */

        status = sys$gettim(&timbuf_internal);

        if (status!=SS$_NORMAL) exit(status);


        status = sys$asctim(    &timbuf_ascii_descriptor.timlength,

                                &timbuf_ascii_descriptor,

                                &timbuf_internal,

                                timcvtflg

                            );

        if (status!=SS$_NORMAL) exit(status);


        printf("%s",timbuf_ascii);

}
```

Figure 15.2 TIME.C: display current data and time.

The macro effectively declares the string descriptor C structure and
initializes it. The macro is declared in SYS$LIBRARY:DESCRIP.H some-
what like this:

```
#define $DESCRIPTOR(name,string)                                   \
         struct                                                     \
         { unsigned short  dsc$w_length;                            \
           unsigned char   dsc$b_dtype;                             \
           unsigned char   dsc$b_class;                             \
           char            *dsc$a_pointer;                          \
         } name = { size of(string)-1, 14, 1, string }
```

Hence, the code generated for

```
$DESCRIPTOR(mailbox,"MBA21:");
```

is

```
         struct                                                    \
         { unsigned short dsc$w_length;                            \
           unsigned char  dsc$b_dtype;                             \
           unsigned char  dsc$b_class;                             \
           char           *dsc$a_pointer;                          \
         } mailbox = { size of("MBA21:")-1, 14, 1, "MBA21:" }
```

15.3   Calling Routines from C

Figure 15.2 shows a simple program that displays the system data and time.
Two calls are made to the system: $GETTIM and $ASCTIM. $GETTIM gets
the current time from the system in binary form of 8 bytes. The $ASCTIM
routine converts this internal form of time to an ASCII displayable form.

To run this program the steps are:

```
$ !The C program
$ CC time
$ LINK TIME,sys$input/options
sys$share:vaxcrtl/share
$ RUN time
7-DEC-1989 11:30:30.60
```

15.4   Routine Classification

15.4.1   System services

VMS has about 150 system service routines. These routines can be broadly
classified as follows:

Security services
These routines allow a user to:

- Create and maintain the rights database (SYS$SYSTEM:RIGHTSLIST.DAT).
- Create and translate access control list (ACL) entries.

- Modify a process's rights list.
- Check access protection to an object by a user.
- Provide a security erase pattern for disks.

The rights database contains a list of identifiers and a list of user accounts that hold the identifier. Then programs can be written so that only holders of a particular identifier can perform certain operations. This way, the system manager can assign identifiers to users authorized to perform those operations. Example routines are:

$ADD_IDENT   Add an identifier to the rights database.
$FIND_HOLDER   Show holder(s) of an rights identifier.

Event flag services
These routines allow a user to:

- Associate or disassociate common event flag cluster.
- Delete common event flag cluster.
- Set or clear event flags.
- Wait for single event flag.
- Wait for Logical OR or Logical AND of event flags.

Some system services, like $ENQ and $QIOW, set an event flag to indicate completion of an event. Example routines are:

$SETEF   Set event flag.
$WAITFR   Wait for an event flag

Asynchronous System Trap (AST) services
These routines allow a user to:

- Enable an AST.
- Declare an AST.
- Set power recovery AST.

Some system services, like $ENQ and $QIOW, accept an AST service routine address as an argument and use the AST mechanism. Example routines are:

$SETAST   Enable AST.
$DCLAST   Declare AST.

Logical name services
These routines allow a user to:

- Create a logical name or logical name table.
- Delete a logical name.
- Translate a logical name.

  Example routines are:

  $CRELNM   Create a logical name.
  $TRNLNM   Translate a logical name.

Input/output services
These routines allow a user to:

- Assign and deassign channels.
- Queue I/O requests.
- Perform formatted I/O.
- Allocate and deallocate devices.
- Mount and dismount volumes.
- Get device and channel information.
- Cancel I/O on a channel.
- Create mailbox and assign a channel.
- Delete a mailbox.
- Breakthrough (and write to a terminal).
- Get queue information.
- Send message to job controller.
- Send message to operator.
- Send message to error logger.
- Get and put messages.
- Get job or process information.
- Get lock information.
- Get system information.
- Update section file on disk.

  Example routines are:

  $QIOW   Perform Queue I/O and wait for event flag.
  $GETQUI   Get queue information.

Process control services

These routines allow a user to:

- Create, delete, suspend or resume a process.
- Hibernate or wake up a process.
- Schedule or cancel waking up of a process.
- Exit or force exit of a process.
- Declare or cancel an exit handler.
- Set process name, priority or privileges.
- Set resource wait mode.
- Get job or process information.

Example routines are:

$CREPRC	Create a process.
$SETPRV	Set privileges of a process.

Timer and time conversion services

These routines allow a user to:

- Get current time.
- Convert binary (8-byte) time to numeric time.
- Convert binary time to ASCII string.
- Convert ASCII string to binary time.
- Set timer.
- Cancel timer request.
- Schedule and cancel wakeup.
- Set system time.

Example routines are:

$GETTIM	Get current time.
$SETIMR	Set timer.

Condition-handling services

These routines allow a user to:

- Set an exception vector specifying condition handlers
- Set system service failure exception mode.

- Unwind from condition handler frame.
- Declare change mode or compatibility mode handler.

  Example routines are:

  $SETSM   Set system service failure exception mode.
  $UNWIND   Unwind from condition handler frame.

Memory management services
These routines allow a user to:

- Expand program or control region.
- Create or delete virtual address space.
- Create and map a section.
- Map or delete a global section.
- Update section file on disk.
- Lock or unlock pages in working set.
- Adjust working set limit.
- Purge working set.
- Lock or unlock a page in memory.
- Set protection on pages.
- Set process swap mode.
- Set stack limits.

  Example routines are:

  $CRMPSC   Create and map a section.
  $LKWSET   Lock pages in working set.

Lock management services
There are two routines:

  $ENQ   Enqueue a lock.
  $DEQ   Dequeue a lock.

15.4.2   RTL routines
The RTL routines are broadly classified into the following groups:

  DNS$ Distributed Name Services routines. 13 routines.
  DTK$ DECtalk routines. 21 routines.

LIB$ Library of VMS routines. 153 routines.
MTH$ MATH routines. 83 routines.
OTS$ Object time system (binary-to-float conversion, etc.) 42 routines.
PPL$ Parallel Processing Library. 50 routines.
SMG$ Screen Management Routines. 116 routines.
STR$ String manipulation routines. 118 routines.

Example routines are:

DTK$DIAL_PHONE	Dial the telephone on the DECtalk device.
LIB$DAY_OF_WEEK	Return numeric day of week.
LIB$DELETE_LOGICAL	Delete logical name.
LIB$FIND_FILE	Find a file.
LIB$GETJPI	Get job or process information.
LIB$SET_SYMBOL	Set value of DCL symbol.
LIB$SPAWN	Spawn a subprocess.
LIB$WAIT	Wait a specified period of time.
MTH$ASIND	Return arc sine in radians.
MTH$CMPLX	Return complex number.
MTH$LOG2	Return base two logarithm.
OTS$CNVOUT	Convert D-, G- or H- floating number to character string.
OTS$CVT_TU_L	Convert unsigned decimal string to long integer.
PPL$INITIALIZE	Initialize the PPL$ facility.
PPL$CREATE_SPIN_LOCK	Create a spin lock.
PPL$SPAWN	Start parallel execution.
SMG$CREATE_VIRTUAL_DISPLAY	Create a virtual display.
SMG$DRAW_LINE	Draw a line.
SMG$PUT_CHARS	Write characters to a virtual display.
STR$ADD	Add two decimal strings.
STR$COMPARE	Compare two strings.
STR$DUPL_CHAR	Duplicate character string n times.
STR$TRIM	Trim trailing blanks and tabs.

15.5   A Tape-to-Tape Copy Utility

Figure 15.3 shows a system utility for making a duplicate copy of a tape. Blocks and tapemarks from the input tape are copied to the output tape until two consecutive tapemarks (signifying end-of-tape) have been processed. The input and output tapes could be of different types, like standard spool tapes and TK72s. The program illustrates usage of a number of system services. The program is typical of handy utilities written by programmers at VAX sites for their specific requirements.

Figure 15.3 A tape-to-tape copy utility.

```
/* File: tapecopy.c
 * Program duplicates the contents of one tape to another.
 * Tape header, tape marks, etc. are copied literally.
 *
 * Mount input and output tapes with a command like
 * $ mount mua0:/foreign/blocksize=33000
 *
 * Exercise: modify for one tape drive data center.
 *
 * Program logic:
 * Open input and output tape devices.
 * Loop forever
 *
 *     Read input tape
 *     If tape mark read then
 *         Write tape mark to output tape
 *         If previous tape read was also a tape mark read then
 *             End of tape. Exit program.
 *         End if
 *     End if
 *     If data block read then
 *         Write block to output tape
 *     End if
 * End of Loop forever
 *
 * Usage of variables and constants:
 * dummy_event_flag - arbitrarily chosen event flag for QIO calls
 * block_buffer    - buffer for data blocks from tape
 * tapemark_flag   - set to indicate last read was a tape mark. Used
 *                   to check for two consecutive tape marks which
 *                   signify end of tape
 * inpchan         - channel to input tape drive
 * outchan         - channel to output tape drive
 * status_block    - information returned by system service call, QIO.
 *                   cond_value is return status, count is bytes in
 *                   the block read off tape and info is unused
 * status          - return condition code for system calls
```

Figure 15.3 *(Continued)*

```
 * inptape_descriptor and outtape_descriptors of the tape device names.
 * These are required for the SYS$ASSIGN system service call.
 *
 */
#include rms
#include stdio
#include iodef
#include ssdef
#include descrip
#define dummy_event_flag   1

unsigned char block_buffer[33000], tapemark_flag = 0;
unsigned short inpchan, outchan;
struct {short cond_value; short count; int info;} status_block;
unsigned int status;


/* String descriptors for input and output tape device names. For
 * information on decriptors, see The VMS programming manual,
 * Introduction to system routines.
 *
 */
unsigned char inptape[80], outtape[80];
struct       string_descriptor                /* see sys$library:descrip.h */
   {
   unsigned short  length;
   unsigned char   string_type;
   unsigned char   string_class;
   char                *string_pointer;
   } inptape_descriptor = { 80 , DSC$K_DTYPE_T, DSC$K_CLASS_S, inptape },
     outtape_descriptor = { 80 , DSC$K_DTYPE_T, DSC$K_CLASS_S, outtape };


main()
   {
   printf("Utility to duplicate a tape\n");
   printf(
```

Figure 15.3 *(Continued)*

```
"The input and output tapes must be mounted with a command like:\n");
printf("$mount mua0:/foreign/blocksize=33000\n\n");


/* get input tape device name */
printf("Enter input tape name: ");
gets(inptape); inptape_descriptor.length = strlen(inptape);
/* assign an io channel to input tape drive */
status = SYS$ASSIGN(&inptape_descriptor, &inpchan, 0,0);
if (status != SS$_NORMAL) exit(status);


/* get output tape device name */
printf("Enter output tape name: ");
gets(outtape); outtape_descriptor.length = strlen(outtape);


/* assign an io channel to output tape drive */
status = SYS$ASSIGN(&outtape_descriptor, &outchan, 0,0);
if (status != SS$_NORMAL) exit(status);


/* Now move blocks and tapemarks from input tape to output tape.
 * Note that two condition values are checked after each tape
 * operation: status and status_block.cond_value. status will
 * indicates any problem with the call, status_block.cond_value
 * indicates any problem with the execution of the called code.
 */
while (TRUE) /*forever*/
   {
   /* get a tape block or tape mark */
   status = SYS$QIOW(dummy_event_flag, inpchan, IO$_READPBLK
                     ,&status_block, 0,0, block_buffer,
                     33000 ,0,0,0,0);
   if (status != SS$_NORMAL)
      {
      printf("tape read error\n");
      exit(status);
      }
```

Figure 15.3 *(Continued)*

```
if ((status_block.cond_value != SS$_NORMAL) &&
    (status_block.cond_value != SS$_ENDOFFILE))
   {
   printf("tape read error\n");
   exit(status_block.cond_value);
   }
/* tape mark from input tape? */
if (status_block.cond_value == SS$_ENDOFFILE)
   {
   printf("tape mark read\n");
   /* write tapemark to output tape */
   status = SYS$QIOW(dummy_event_flag, outchan, IO$_WRITEOF
                    ,&status_block,0,0,0,0,0,0,0);
   if (status != SS$_NORMAL)
      {
      printf("tape mark write error\n");
      exit(status);
      };
   if (status_block.cond_value != SS$_NORMAL)
      {
      printf("tape mark write error\n");
      exit(status_block.cond_value);
      };
   /* check for double tapemarks (end-of-tape) */
   if (tapemark_flag == 1)
      {
      /* second tapemark (end of tape) exit the program */

      printf("end of tape\n");
      exit();
      }
   else
      {
      tapemark_flag = 1;
      }
   }
else
```

Figure 15.3 *(Continued)*

```
        {  /* normal block, write it to output tape */
        printf("block read\n");
        status = SYS$QIOW(dummy_event_flag, outchan, IO$_WRITEPBLK
                        ,&status_block,0,0, block_buffer,
                        status_block.count, 0,0,0,0);
        if (status != SS$_NORMAL)
            {
            printf("tape write error\n");
            exit(status);
            };
        if (status_block.cond_value != SS$_NORMAL)
            {
            printf("tape write error\n");
            exit(status_block.cond_value);
            };
        tapemark_flag = 0;
        }
    }; /* while loop end */
} /* end of main */
```

16

DECnet and C: Designing Distributed Applications

DECnet was introduced in chapter 2, which covered the VAX/VMS environment. Many C programmers use the network for copying files from one VAX to another and running programs that perform cooperative processing functions among VAXes on the network. A typical distributed application is a client/server environment in which a powerful VAX acts as a database server, and a set of desktop VAXes perform local functions and provide access to the database on the server VAX. A good understanding of DECnet and DECnet programming is required when designing such distributed applications.

16.1 Basic Issues

Figure 16.1 shows a hypothetical network. Here are some notes on the network:

- Any of the six VAXes can communicate with each other. The communication path between VAXA to VAXF is VAXA to VAXB to VAXE to VAXF.

The network databases can be set up to disallow connections between any two VAXes.

- Users need not know the path their data takes from one node to another; only the source and destination node names are required. DECnet uses an adaptive routing algorithm to select intermediate nodes.

- Nodes that don't act as in-between nodes are called end nodes. Nodes that can receive messages from one node and send them to another are called *routers*. Routers also function as end nodes. VAXA, VAXD and VAXC are end-nodes (or nonrouters). VAXB, VAXE and VAXF must be routers.

- Ethernet bandwidth is 10 Megabits/second, so file transfer between, say, VAXB to VAXD is faster than file transfer between VAXA to VAXB.

- Any of the VAXes can be part of VAXclusters.

- Failure of VAXE will partition the network into two subnetworks whose nodes can communicate with other nodes within the subnetwork. Nodes send out messages at regular intervals that effectively say "I'm on the network." Other nodes make a note of nodes on the network by listening to these messages. Nodes can also determine if a particular node is on the network by sending out an inquiry message. The network database on each node is automatically updated when nodes enter or leave the network.

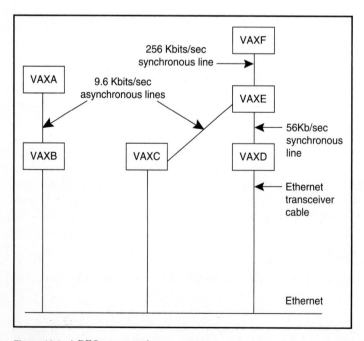

Figure 16.1 A DECnet network.

16.2 File Access across the Network

A user on one node can access another node provided he or she has an account on the node to be accessed. The node to be accessed is called a *host*. Here's the command to copy a file from node VAXE to the current node, which is VAXB:

```
$ COPY VAXE"username  password"::DUA1:[MYDIR]TEST.DATA  TEST.DATA
```

Node names are followed by two colons. The username and password are specified within double quotes. If a proxy account has been created on VAXE for the user, then the username and password need not be specified:

```
$ COPY VAXE::DUA1:TEST.DATA  *.*
```

Proxy accounts are described in chapter 14, which covers systems management.

Actually, most commands on the system that require a file name can access the file from another node if the node name is mentioned in the file specification. For example, this command displays the files in directory [TEST] on the logical device TEST_DRIVE:

```
$ DIRECTORY VAXD::TEST_DRIVE:[TEST]*.*;*>
```

The logical device name, TEST_DRIVE, is translated into a physical name by the node VAXD (and not the node from which the command is issued).

16.3 Login over the Network

To log into node VAXE:: from the current node VAXB::, the command is:

```
$ SET HOST VAXE::
```

Node VAXE:: will ask for your username and password. Once logged into the other node, the terminal works like a terminal on the new node. The LOGOUT command returns control to the original node.

When logged in across the network, the session can be logged into a file. All terminal input and output is logged in a file, SETHOST.LOG, on the original node, with the following login command:

```
$ SET HOST VAXE::/LOG
```

The log file can be printed out after logging off the host node. In fact, this method can be used to create a log file of a terminal session on the current node. The "0" in the next command means the current node:

```
$ SET HOST 0/LOG
```

In effect, you'll be logging into your system again, creating a second session. The log file can be accessed after logging off from the second session.

16.4   Networking Terminology and Concepts

16.4.1   Network control program (NCP)

NCP is used to configure the network database on each node and to monitor status of connections to other nodes. For example, to know the status of all nodes configured in the current VAX, the commands would be:

```
$ NCP :== $NCP
$ NCP SHOW KNOWN NODES

Known Node Volatile Summary as of 9-DEC-1989 17:56:07

Executor node = 1.5 (VAXNV5)

State          = on
Identification = DECnet-VAX V5.0,  VMS V5.1-1
Active links   = 1

      Node          State     Active Delay Circuit   Next node
                              Links


1.2  (VAXNE2)  reachable    1      1    BNA-0   1.2  (VAXNE2)
1.3            reachable              BNA-0   1.3
1.4            reachable              BNA-0   1.4
1.6  (VAXNE6)  reachable              BNA-0   1.9
1.9            reachable              BNA-0   1.9
1.421          reachable              BNA-0   1.421
```

Here are some notes on the output:

- Current node, called the executor node, is VAXNV5. Six other nodes are reachable. Two nodes, VAXNE2 and VAXNE6, were configured when setting up the database, so their node names are displayed. The other four nodes were found to be reachable by messages received from them.

- There is one session between the current node and node VAXNE2 as shown by active links. The session could be for file transfer, a network login from VAXNE2 to the current node, or from the current node to VAXNE2, or some other session.

- All the nodes are adjacent nodes, as they are all on Ethernet. Actually, the current node gathers information only on adjacent nodes by listening to other nodes. Information on nonadjacent nodes is displayed only if the network database is configured with nonadjacent node names and the DECnet addresses of these nodes.

■ The column headed by "next node" displays the node adjacent to the node at the left. Entering the NCP SHO KNOWN NODES command after logging into that node gives the adjacent nodes of that node. This way, it's possible to know all the nodes on the network.

16.4.2 Areas

In DECnet phase IV, the current implementation, a network can be divided into logical areas. Areas are numbered 1 through 63. Area 1 is assumed when not specified. Each area can have up to 1023 nodes. DECnet addresses of nodes are specified as area.node-number like 1.35, 4.32 and 32 (the last address is assumed to be 1.32).

I mentioned before that routers act as in-between nodes when they receive messages from one node and send it to another. There are two types of routers; intra-area routers (or just routers) and area routers. Area-routers can send messages received from a node in one area to a node in another area. Why segment a physically connected network into areas?

■ Messages directed within the area are not seen by nodes in other areas except by area routing nodes. This reduces the processing overhead of nodes in the network.

■ Networks can be logically partitioned for easier management.

■ Multiple areas are required if the number of nodes exceeds 1023.

Intra-area routers are also known as level-1 routers and inter-area routers are also known as level-2 routers.

The following command shows the areas that are accessible to the current node:

```
$ NCP SHOW KNOWN AREA

Known Area Volatile Summary as of 12-DEC-1989 12:35:13

Area    State      Circuit  Next node to area

 1    reachable             1.5 (SCOOP5)
 4    reachable    BNA-0    4.129 (TOPVAX)
```

In NCP commands, usually KNOWN NODES, KNOWN LINES, KNOWN CIR-CUITS can be replaced by the name of particular entities.
For example:

```
$ NCP SHOW KNOWN NODES
$ NCP SHOW NODE VAX5
$ NCP SHOW KNOWN CIRCUITS
$ NCP SHOW CIRCUIT BNA-0
```

16.4.3   Circuits and lines

A *circuit* is the logical path from a node to another node. A *line* is the low-level physical data path from a node to the network. For example, a VAX on the Ethernet may have a number of circuits, one for each adjacent node and each called BNA-1. The line could be called BNA-1. There is only one line per physical data path. To see all the circuits and lines on the current node, the commands are:

```
$NCP :== $NCP
$NCP SHOW KNOWN CIRCUITS

Known Circuit Volatile Summary as of 9-DEC-1989 18:19:38


Circuit State Loopback    Adjacent
                Name     Routing Node


  BNA-0     on        1.3
  BNA-0               1.4
  BNA-0               1.9
  BNA-0               1.2 (VAXNE2)
  BNA-1     on
$NCP SHOW KNOWN LINES

Known Line Volatile Summary as of 9-DEC-1989 18:19:45

 Line   State

 BNA-0   on

 BNA-1   on
```

Note multiple circuits to other nodes on line BNA-0. A circuit gets established whenever a new node is accessed. It remains even after the session is terminated. Lines are physical connections, so they'll be seen as soon as the system is booted. In this case, the VAX is connected to two separate Ethernets, so there are two lines BNA-0 and BNA-1.

16.4.4   Logical links

A *logical link* is a session between two nodes. For example, a user copying files from another node sets up a logical link between that node and the current node. Another user may have "set host" to the other node, in which case he or she also has set up a logical link. Both of these links may be over the same circuit and line. Logical links can be displayed by:

```
$ NCP SHOW KNOWN LINKS

Known Link Volatile Summary as of 9-DEC-1989 18:34:08
```

```
Link      Node        PID      Process Remote link Remote user

8209  1.5 (VAXNV5)  00000192  SHAH4      8210       CTERM
8195  4.200         00000109  REMACP     164        SYSTEM
```

Here, the first logical link was due to a SET HOST 0 command. The second one is a file transfer between the current node (1.5) and node 4.200. This is determined from the Remote user column.

16.5 Ethernet

Figure 16.2 shows a sample Ethernet-based network. Logically, each node has an Ethernet controller card, which is connected to the Ethernet cable by a transceiver cable. The H4005 allows a transceiver cable to be tapped into the Ethernet cable. The DELNI allows eight transceiver cables to be plugged into it and the corresponding nodes to communicate with each other.

Various pieces of hardware are available to support thin-wire Ethernet, Ethernet repeaters, LAN-bridges and so on. In fact, a DELNI can be used to interconnect the transceiver cables from various nodes without using any Ethernet backbone cable. The logical network is not changed by these products.

Logically, Ethernet can be considered a bus; each node on the network can communicate directly with any other node. The bus usage is quite straightforward. A node wishing to send out data, sends the data to the Ethernet controller card. The connection between the node CPU and the card is referred to as a LINE in NCP commands. The card "listens" to note if the Ethernet is in use. If no node is using the network, the card sends the data on the Ethernet. It listens again to note if another node also sent data on the Ethernet simultaneously. If there is such a collision, the data has to be retransmitted. This technique of usage is known as Carrier Sense, Multiple Access with Collision Detect (CSMA/CD). All Ethernet controllers continuously monitor the Ethernet to determine if there is any traffic for itself. If there is, the data is sent to the lower layers of DECnet software on that node. Ethernet bandwidth is 10 megabits/second, though collisions and other factors reduce the actual throughput to a much lesser value.

DEC has exploited Ethernet technology fully for DECnet and other uses like LAT (which is described later). An Ethernet node is identified by a 48-bit (12 hex digit) hardware address. This address is hardwired in the Ethernet controller card. This address is not used for DECnet communications. DECnet writes a new address in the controller card when DECnet is brought up on the node. This address, called the *physical address*, is calculated as a function of the DECnet area and node number of the node on which the card resides. The physical address is used when a node addresses another node on the network. The reason for doing this is that the transmitting node can determine the physical address of the Ethernet card on

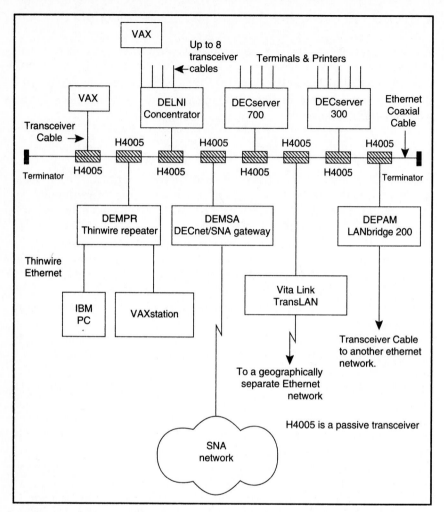

Figure 16.2 Ethernet devices.

the other node by looking up the DECnet address of the destination node from its NCP database. This way, nodes do not have to maintain (in their databases) a list of Ethernet addresses of other nodes on the network (although DECnet addresses have to be maintained).

16.6 DDCMP

DDCMP (Digital Data communications protocol) is used for point-to-point connections between nodes. Example connections are 1200 baud asynchronous (RS232C based) and 56K baud synchronous (using DMV11 cards). Modems can be installed at the two ends, but that's of no concern to DECnet.

To use permanently connected asnychronous terminal lines, the system managers on the systems at both ends must install the driver NODRIVER and set the terminal line as:

```
$ SYSGEN:==$SYSGEN                  !Enable SYSGEN as a command
$ SYSGEN CONNECT NOA0:/NOADAPTER    !Load driver NODRIVER
$ SET TERMINAL/PROTOCOL=DDCMP       TXA2:
```

The necessary line and circuit NCP commands must be issued on both systems:

```
$ SET LINE TX-0-2 STATE ON RECEIVE BUFFERS 4
$ SET CIRCUIT TX-0-2 STATE ON
```

The lines are then ready for communications.

For synchronous lines only, the line and circuit NCP commands are required. The line name is determined by the card used. For the DMV-11 card, the line name is DMP. Here's how to initialize the lines:

```
$ SET LINE DMP-0 PROTOCOL DDCMP POINT STATE ON
$ SET CIRCUIT DMP-0 STATE ON
```

The DEFINE commands can be used instead of SET to make the changes permanent in the network database on disk.

16.7 Distributed Programming across VAXes

VAXes can be connected to each other by a DECnet network over Ethernet (multidrop lines), direct DDCMP (point-to-point) lines or some other line type. VAXes could also be interconnected by a Computer Interconnect (CI) bus on a VAXcluster. All these VAXes can be used to develop distributed applications like:

- Distributed databases. Data is spread on files on disks attached to the various VAXes. Programs on the VAXes communicate to transfer data and perform other data manipulations.

- Distributed computing. Applications can be designed so that parts of it run on individual computers for a higher overall throughput. An example could be one VAX handling all terminal I/O, including input data validation, while another VAX acts as a database machine storing and managing data on disk.

- Resource sharing applications. One server VAX may have an expensive supercomputer connected to it locally. The server VAX can allow controlled access to the supercomputer by means of appropriate task-to-task communications between the VAXes. The following sections discuss how to write programs that interact with other programs over DECnet and VAXclusters.

16.8   Programming Using DECnet

The chapter on the DECnet network shows how to access files over the network and log into other nodes on the network. This section shows how to execute command files over the network and use task-to-task communications programs.

16.8.1   Executing command files over the network

A command file can be executed on another machine by simply specifying the node name in the file specification. Here's a command, issued on node MAYUR:: to execute a command file, NETCMD.COM, on node GANGES::

```
$ @GANGES"SHAH KELTUM"::[TEST]NETCMD.COM
```

Notes:

- The username and password (SHAH and KELTUM) have to be specified, as shown in the preceding command, unless GANGES has a proxy account for user SHAH.

- The command effectively performs a login on GANGES, executes the specified command file there, and then logs off the VAX.

- Output and error messages are displayed on the source node.

16.8.2   Task-to-task communications over the network by command files

A command file can initiate the execution of another command file on another node. The command files can then transfer data to each other, effectively allowing communications between the nodes.

Here's an example. GANGES is on a DECnet network of VAXes and has a high-speed laser printer attached to it. Users on other VAXes wish to print files on this printer. The command file NETCMD_CLIENT.COM (Fig. 16.3) can be on any node in a DECnet network. The command file NETSRV.COM (Fig. 16.4) is in the login directory of user SHAH on GANGES. SHAH must have an account on GANGES. When NETCMD_CLIENT is executed, it will execute the command file NETSRV.COM on GANGES. The process name would be like SERVER_0012. You will be prompted for the filename of the file to be printed

```
$!File: NETCMD_CLIENT.COM
$!
$! This command file can be used on any
$! node in a network to print a file on
$! that node to a printer attached to the
$! node GANGES::. The file NETSRV.COM must
$! be present on GANGES:: in your login
$! directory.
$!
$! The pair of command files can be modified
$! to write cooperating applications between
$! computers on a network.
$!
$ OPEN/READ/WRITE/ERROR=ERROR_EXIT NET_IO_CLIENT -
                  GANGES"SHAH KELTUM"::"TASK=NETSRV"
$ IF P1 .EQS. "" THEN -
      $INQUIRE/NOPUNCTUATION  P1 "File to be printed on GANGES: "
$ IF P1 .EQS. "" THEN $EXIT
$ COPY 'P1'  GANGES"SHAH KELTUM"::
$ WRITE/ERROR=ERROR_EXIT NET_IO_CLIENT  "''p1'"
$                  !Send file name of command file to be executed
$ DISPLAY:         ! Display input from the other node
$   READ/END=END_NET/ERROR=ERROR_EXIT NET_IO_CLIENT OUTPUT_LINE
$   WRITE SYS$OUTPUT OUTPUT_LINE
$ GOTO DISPLAY
$ END_NET:
$ CLOSE NET_IO_CLIENT
$ EXIT
$!
$ ERROR_EXIT:
$ WRITE SYS$OUTPUT F$MESSAGE($STATUS)
$ EXIT
```

Figure 16.3 DECnet client command file.

```
$!File: NETSRV.COM
$!
$! This file acts as a server for network
$! requests from other nodes. The file
$! works in conjunction with
$! NETCMD_CLIENT.COM on other VAXes on the
$! network. Presently, it copies and prints
$! a file from the client node onto this node.
$!
$ SET NOON
$ SET VERIFY
$
$ OPEN/READ/WRITE NET_IO SYS$NET:      !Open the channel to the process on
$                                      !the source VAX.
$ READ/END=EXIT NET_IO FIL            !Read filename
$ DEFINE/USER SYS$OUTPUT NET_IO       !Set output for the next command to
$                                      !go over the network to the process
$                                      !which executed this file.
$ PRINT 'FIL
$ CLOSE NET_IO
$ EXIT
```

Figure 16.4 A DECnet server command file.

on GANGES. The file is copied to GANGES by NETCMD_CLIENT.COM and printed by NETSRV.COM. The key command line is:

```
$ OPEN/READ/WRITE/ERROR=ERROR_EXIT NET_IO_CLIENT -
              GANGES"shah keltum"::"TASK=NETSRV"
```

Here, the open statement actually performs a network login from the current VAX to GANGES. The username and password are specified within double-quotes. After the login, the command file NETSRV.COM is run from the login directory. To see more information on the connection, use:

```
$ NCP:==$NCP
$ NCP show known links
```

The command files then communicate via

- The channel specified in the OPEN statement in the client VAX. In this case, the channel is NET_IO_CLIENT.

- The channel created by opening SYSNET: on the server VAX. In this case, the channel is NET_IO.

A file, NETSERVER.LOG, will be created in the login directory on GANGES. This file will contain the output from the execution of the command file. The output is similar to that produced by executing a file by the SUBMIT command. The file can be used to debug the application.

16.8.3   Task-to-task communications over the network by programs

Programs can communicate over the network in a way similar to command file communication described previously. Here's an example where two C programs on different nodes communicate with each other. INQ_CLIENT.C (Fig. 16.5) can reside on any node on a DECnet network. When its image is run, it executes the command file, INQSER.COM (Fig. 16.6) on node GANGES. The command file, INQSER.COM, is required on the server node to run the actual C program, INQ_SERVER.C (Fig. 16.7). The two C programs can pass data to each other. In this example, the client is asking for a table lookup in the server database.

The sequence of steps is:

- INQ_CLIENT.EXE is run on a VAX.

- The OPEN statement refers to another node, GANGES, so DECnet establishes a logical link with GANGES.

- The file SYS$SYSTEM:NETSERVER.COM is executed by DECnet on GANGES. This file in turn executes SYS$SYSTEM:NETSERVER.EXE. This file, in turn works in conjunction with the process NETACP and completes the connection. The execution of the command file specified, INQSER.COM, is logged in NETSERVER.LOG in the login directory.

- The device SYS$NET: on the server VAX is used to communicate back with the client VAX. This device is set up when the logical link is established.

Internode communications can be established by creating network objects. This method of communications does not require a command file to be executed on the server node, and it can offer more control of the link. For example, a network object can be set up to serve multiple nodes. Creating network objects is not discussed in this book.

```
/* This program, inq_client.c, performs
 * a database lookup on a server VAX on
 * the DECnet network. The server VAX runs
 * a command file, INQSER.COM, which in
 * turn runs a program, inq_server.c, which
 * performs the database lookup based on a
 * key passed by this program and returns
 * the accessed value to this program.
 */


#include stdio
#include file

main ()
{
int net_chan, stat;      /* channel to server VAX */
char *buf;
char inp_buf[80];

/* invoke INQSER.COM on the server VAX */
net_chan = open ("ganges\"shah keltum\"::\"task=inqser.com\"",O_RDWR);
if (net_chan < 0)
    {perror("network command file open error"); exit(SS$_NORMAL);};


buf = "7415";   /* search for this account on server VAX database */
stat = write(net_chan, buf, 4);
if (stat < 0) exit(SS$_NORMAL); /*end of file*/


stat = read(net_chan,inp_buf, 80);              /* read account title sent
                                                    by server VAX */
if (stat < 0) exit(SS$_NORMAL); /*end of file*/
printf ("%s",inp_buf);
if (stat == -1) exit(SS$_NORMAL); /*end of file*/
close (net_chan);
}
```

Figure 16.5 A DECnet client program.

```
$! File: INQSER.COM
$! Database server for lookup of information
$! on this node by other nodes.
$ SET VERIFY
$ RUN INQ_SERVER.EXE
$ EXIT
```

Figure 16.6 A DECnet server command file.

Figure 16.7 A DECnet server program.

```
/* This program, inq_server.c,is run by
 * the command file, INQSER.COM, which
 * is invoked by the program, inq_client.c,
 * on another VAX over the DECnet network.
 * The programs demonstrate a client-server
 * model for distributed applications on a
 * network.
 */


#include stdio
#include file
#include ssdef


main ()
{
int net_chan, chan_stat;        /* channel to client VAX */
char inp_buf[5];
char *tmp_title;


/* Create a database of account information.
 * In practice, the database would be on disk
 * files.
 */
```

Figure 16.7 *(Continued)*

```
struct acc_struct
        (
           char *no;
           char *title;
        );
struct acc_struct acc_info[5] =
                 (
                     ( "2543", "Mary Smith"       ),
                     ( "1234", "Peter Kak"        ),
                     ( "7415", "James Shneider"   ),
                     ( "8323", "John Bayer"       ),
                     ( "9231", "Gene Cortess"     ),
                 );


/* Open the channel to the client VAX */
net_chan = open ("sys$net:",O_RDWR);
if (net_chan == -1) {perror("SYS$NET: open error"); exit(SS$_NORMAL);};


/* Get account number from client VAX */
chan_stat = read(net_chan, inp_buf, 4);
if (chan_stat <= 0 ) {perror("Error on network read");exit(SS$_NORMAL);}


/* Given account number, find account title. In practice, this
   step would be a database lookup on disk. */
tmp_title = "Account does not exist";
if (strcmp(inp_buf,acc_info[0].no) == 0) tmp_title=acc_info[0].title;
else if (strcmp(inp_buf,acc_info[1].no) == 0) tmp_title=acc_info[1].title;
else if (strcmp(inp_buf,acc_info[2].no) == 0) tmp_title=acc_info[2].title;
else if (strcmp(inp_buf,acc_info[3].no) == 0) tmp_title=acc_info[3].title;
else if (strcmp(inp_buf,acc_info[4].no) == 0) tmp_title=acc_info[4].title;


/* Send account title to the client VAX */
chan_stat = write(net_chan, tmp_title, 512);
if (chan_stat <= 0 ) {perror("Error on network write");exit(SS$_NORMAL);}


close (net_chan);
}
```

Integrating C Applications with VMS

Good programs adhere to the standards and conventions of the system on which they're used. For example, there's a standard method for displaying error messages on VAX/VMS. The VMS operating system, utilities, and other programs use the same method for processing errors. Hence, C programmers should also use this method. This chapter discusses topics that aid in blending C programs with other VMS products. Specific issues covered are:

- Creating HELP.
- Error processing.
- Creating DCL commands using CDU.
- Distributing products in VMSINSTAL format.

17.1 Creating HELP

VMS users are accustomed to getting online information on products by using the HELP command. A help file can be created and inserted in the default help library, SYS$HELP:HELPLIB.HLB. The HELP command then provides information to the user.

```
1 key-1 name (for example: command name)

 .

 .

 .

  key-1 help text

 .

 .

 .

2 key-2 name (for example: parameters)

 .

 .

 .

  key-2 help text

 .

 .

 .



n key-n name

 .

 .

 .

  key-n help text

 .

 .

 .
```

Figure 17.1 Help text file structure.

17.1.1 Creating the HELP file

The help file is created as a text file using an editor like EVE. The file is then inserted into SYS$HELP:HELPLIB.HLB using the LIBRARIAN utility. The help file will contain a hierarchy of help subtopics, numbered by keys 1 through 9. Key 1 is the name of the DCL command. Keys 2 through 9 are subtopics like qualifiers for the command. Figure 17.1 shows the structure of the help file.

Help on qualifiers to commands can be placed with a / in the first column of the help text file. The qualifiers are treated like names at the same key level as the immediately preceding key level, except that they're listed along with their help text when the help is invoked for the preceding keyed name.

Figure 17.2 is an abbreviated version of the help file for the TYPE command. Note that if the first column contains a number or /, the line is assumed to be a key line.

Figure 17.2 Simplified TYPE command help text file.

```
1  TYPE

   Displays the contents of a file or group of files on the current

   output device.


   Format


     TYPE  filespec[,...]


2  PARAMETER


filespec[,...]

   Specifies one or more files to be displayed. If you specify a file

   name and not a file type, the file type defaults to LIS. The TYPE

   command displays all files that satisfy the file description.


   Wildcard characters (* and %)  are allowed in place of the

   directory name, file name, file type, or file version number

   field. If you specify more than one file, separate the file

   specifications with commas (,)  or plus signs (+). The files

   are displayed in the order listed.


2  QUALIFIERS


/BACKUP


   Modifies the time value specified with the /BEFORE or the /SINCE

   qualifier. The /BACKUP qualifier selects files according to the

   dates of their most recent backups. This qualifier is incompatible

   with the following qualifiers that also allow you to select files

   according to time attributes: /CREATED, /EXPIRED, and /MODIFIED.
```

Figure 17.2 *(Continued)*

If you specify none of these four time qualifiers, the default is
the /CREATED qualifier.

/BEFORE

    /BEFORE[=time]

Selects only those files dated prior to the specified time.
You can specify time as an absolute time, as a combination of
absolute and delta times, or as one of the following keywords:
TODAY (default), TOMORROW, or YESTERDAY. Specify one of the
following qualifiers with the /BEFORE qualifier to indicate the
time attribute to be used as the basis for selection: /BACKUP,
/CREATED (default), /EXPIRED, or /MODIFIED.

For complete information on specifying time values, see the VMS
DCL Concepts Manual.

/BY_OWNER

    /BY_OWNER[=uic]

Selects only those files whose owner user identification code
(UIC) matches the specified owner UIC. The default UIC is that of
the current process.

Specify the UIC by using standard UIC format as described in the
VMS DCL Concepts Manual.

2 EXAMPLE

1. $ TYPE COMMON.DAT

In this example, the TYPE command requests that the file
COMMON.DAT be displayed at the terminal.

If this help text file is `type.hlp`, it can be inserted in the system help library with a command like:

```
$ LIBRARY/INSERT/HELP SYS$HELP:HELPLIB.HLB TYPE.HLP
```

A sample usage of HELP for TYPE would be as shown in Fig. 17.3.

Figure 17.3 Sample use of HELP for the simple TYPE command.

```
$ help type

TYPE


    Displays the contents of a file or group of files on the current

    output device.


    Format


      TYPE  filespec[,...]




  Additional information available:


 PARAMETER   QUALIFIERS

 /BACKUP     /BEFORE     /BY_OWNER

 EXAMPLES

TYPE Subtopic? /before

TYPE


  /BEFORE


      /BEFORE[=time]


    Selects only those files dated prior to the specified time.

    You can specify time as an absolute time, as a combination of
```

Figure 17.3 *(Continued)*

```
    absolute and delta times, or as one of the following keywords:

    TODAY (default), TOMORROW, or YESTERDAY. Specify one of the

    following qualifiers with the /BEFORE qualifier to indicate the

    time attribute to be used as the basis for selection: /BACKUP,

    /CREATED (default), /EXPIRED, or /MODIFIED.


    For complete information on specifying time values, see the VMS

    DCL Concepts Manual.



TYPE Subtopic? quali


TYPE


  QUALIFIERS



    /BACKUP


      Modifies the time value specified with the /BEFORE or the /SINCE

      qualifier. The /BACKUP qualifier selects files according to the

      dates of their most recent backups. This qualifier is incompatible

      with the following qualifiers that also allow you to select files

      according to time attributes: /CREATED, /EXPIRED, and /MODIFIED.

      If you specify none of these four time qualifiers, the default is

      the /CREATED qualifier.


/BEFORE


    /BEFORE[=time]


  Selects only those files dated prior to the specified time.

  You can specify time as an absolute time, as a combination of

  absolute and delta times, or as one of the following keywords:

  TODAY (default), TOMORROW, or YESTERDAY. Specify one of the

  following qualifiers with the /BEFORE qualifier to indicate the
```

Figure 17.3 *(Continued)*

```
        time attribute to be used as the basis for selection: /BACKUP,

        /CREATED (default), /EXPIRED, or /MODIFIED.


        For complete information on specifying time values, see the VMS

        DCL Concepts Manual.


    /BY_OWNER


          /BY_OWNER[=uic]


        Selects only those files whose owner user identification code

        (UIC) matches the specified owner UIC. The default UIC is that of

        the current process.


        Specify the UIC by using standard UIC format as described in the

        VMS DCL Concepts Manual.



TYPE Subtopic? <return>

Topic? <return>

$
```

17.2 Error Processing

Chapter 3 shows the syntax of error messages that should be used for displaying errors. The syntax for a message is:

```
%FACILITY-L-IDENT, text
```

The fields are:

FACILITY   The name of the program issuing the message.
L   Severity level of the message:
          S - success
          I - informational
          W - warning
          E - error
          F - fatal or severe error

IDENT   Abbreviated description.

text   Description in plain English.

Actually, messages may signify a successful operation, or they may be informational; however, messages are often used to indicate an error, hence we'll refer to messages as error messages. Here's an example of the TYPE command specifying a file that doesn't exist on disk:

```
$ TYPE ME.DOC
%TYPE-W-SEARCHFAIL, error searching for SYS$SYSDEVICE:[SHAH]ME.DOC;
-RMS-E-FNF, file not found
```

It may seem that the TYPE program has to display a text string in the above preceding when an error occurs. That's partly correct. The symbol $STATUS is also set to a value reflecting the execution status of the command. The above TYPE command will set the $STATUS and the $SEVERITY value as:

```
$SHOW SYMBOL $STATUS
  $STATUS == "%X10951238"
$SHOW SYMBOL $SEVERITY
  $SEVERITY == "0"
```

These values are set by the TYPE program. DCL command procedures have ON ERROR statements that perform action depending on the execution status of commands within the procedure. Example statements are:

```
$ ON WARNING THEN $GOTO NEXTFILE
$ ON ERROR THEN $EXIT
$ ON SEVERE_ERROR THEN $CONTINUE
```

These statements use the $SEVERITY symbol value to determine error severity and to determine whether to perform the specified action. The MESSAGE utility will set the symbols if called to process an error.

Also, the user can disable the display of one or more fields of the message text. For example, the next command disables the display of the severity of all messages:

```
$ SET MESSAGE/NOSEVERITY
```

An example of a subsequent message display is:

```
$ TYPE ME.DOC
%TYPE-SEARCHFAIL, error searching for SYS$SYSDEVICE:[SHAH]ME.DOC;
-RMS-FNF, file not found
```

The following command will completely disable display of messages:

```
$ SET MESSAGE/NOFACILITY/NOIDENTIFICATION/NOSEVERITY/NOTEXT
```

This feature can be used to disable error messages and perform error processing in command files based on the $STATUS symbol value, which will be set to an appropriate value when a program completes execution. Messages can later be displayed by:

```
$ SET MESSAGE/FACILITY/IDENTIFICATION/SEVERITY/TEXT
```

This seems to indicate that a plain string display of messages is not sufficient for programs. To aid in message displays, VMS has the MESSAGE utility.

17.2.1 The MESSAGE utility

Messages to be displayed from a program are created in the MESSAGE utility format in a source file. This file is compiled with the MESSAGE command and linked with the program. The program displays error messages using the LIB$SIGNAL system service (or other system services like LIB$STOP and $PUTMSG). LIB$SIGNAL is somewhat like exit(); however, it supports conditional handling as supported by VMS. Refer to VMS system manual for a detailed description of the LIB$SIGNAL.

The message source file typically contains:

- The .TITLE directive. This specifies the link module name of the message file.

- The facility directive. A facility indicates which utility or program the message is from. For example, the facility for the error message in the TYPE command is TYPE.

- The message definition. A message name and an associated display text is specified as:

```
name  <message text>[/qualifier,...]
      qualifiers can be
      /IDENT=name  for the value of the IDENT field of the message.
      /FAO=n       for the count of variable arguments within the
                   message text.
      /SUCCESS     SEVERITY of error.
      /INFORMATIONAL
      /WARNING
      /ERROR
      /SEVERE
      /FATAL
```

- The .END directive. Terminates list of messages for the facility.

Consider an example. A C program is required to list the last line of a specified file. If the file is not present, a WARNING message should be displayed. If the file contains no lines, a SEVERE error should be displayed. Figure 17.4 shows the C program.

Figure 17.4 A C program using the MESSAGE utility.

```
/* Program illustrates use of the MESSAGE utility.
 * Program displays last line of a file.
 *
 * The compilation and link commands are:
 *    $ message last_messages.msg     !compile the message file
 *    $ cc last                       !compile this program
 *    $ link/notrace last, last_messages, sys$library:vaxcrtl/library
 *
 */


/* Symbols in the next line are defined in the message file: */
globalvalue last_nofile,last_norecord,last_ok;


#include stdio
#include ssdef
#include stsdef    /* contains STS$M_INHIB_MSG to inhibit
                     * message display but set symbols
                     * $STATUS and $SEVERITY. See the exit()
                     * statements in this program.
                     */
main()
{
FILE *infile;
char current_record[10000],last_record[10000],response[80];
int len;

struct    {   /* a string descriptor */
    unsigned short    length;
    unsigned char     dtype;
    unsigned char     dclass;
    char              *str;
    }
    filename_str = { 0, 14,1, response};


/* Get file name. The string descriptor filename_str
   is used with lib$signal().
*/
```

Figure 17.4 *(Continued)*

```
printf("Display last line of file: ");
gets(response); filename_str.length = strlen(response);


/* Open file. If no such file, display error.
   Error text from file LAST_MESSAGES.MSG. Note how a
   the file name is passed as a parameter in the message call.
   exit() can also be passed an error code as a parameter as in,
   exit(last_nofile);
   which will cause the corresponding error message to be displayed
   however, the file name cannot be passed hence the lib$signal
   followed by an exit which inhibits display of error messages
   although necessary status codes are set.


*/
if ((infile = fopen(response,"r")) <= 0)
   { lib$signal(last_nofile,1,&filename_str);
     exit (last_nofile | STS$M_INHIB_MSG);
   };


printf("Processing file %s\n",response);
/* Get first record. If no records, display error. */
if (fgets(current_record,10000,infile) == 0)
   { lib$signal(last_norecord);
     exit (last_norecord | STS$M_INHIB_MSG);
     /* the lib$signal and exit could have been replaced by
        exit (last_norecord);
     */
   };


/* Get records, keep last record */
while ( fgets(current_record,10000,infile) != 0)
  { len=strlen(current_record);
    strncpy(last_record,current_record,len);
  };
printf("Last record:\n");    /* print the last line of file */
printf("%s",last_record);
```

Figure 17.4 *(Continued)*

```
/* The success status message at end is optional */
lib$signal(last_ok);
exit (last_ok| STS$M_INHIB_MSG);
}
```

The messages used by the program are in the file LAST_MESSAGES .MSG. This file is shown in Fig. 17.5. The listing file created is LAST _MESSAGES.LIS. The file is shown in Fig. 17.6. Note how the messages are created, one per line with a name, text to be displayed, and severity of error. Message NOFILE contains a parameter that's supplied by the calling program. The parameter is in FAO (Formatted ASCII Output form). FAO usage is described in detail under the $FAO system service in the VMS System Services Reference Manual. In this example, the parameter, represented by !AS, is an ASCII string specifying a file name. The .FACILITY directive specifies a facility name that's displayed in the message line.

Here's a sample run of this program, using various files as input. Note how the set message/notext command disables text display. The $STA TUS symbol is set to the value of the message, as shown in the listing file.

```
$! Display last line of file tmp.tmp containing 3 lines:
$ type tmp.tmp
test a
test ab
test abc
$!
$ run last
Display last line of file: tmp.tmp
Processing file tmp.tmp
Last record: test abc
LAST-S-OK, last line displayed
$!
$! Display last line of file tmp.tmp containing no characters.
$!
$ type tmp.tmp
$ run last
Display last line of file: tmp.tmp
Processing file tmp.tmp
%LAST-F-NORECORD, no records in file
$!
$ run last
Display last line of file: gsfa
%LAST-W-NOFILE, error searching for file gsfa
$!
$! Disable display for text part of message
$!
$ set message/notext
$ run last
Display last line of file: gsfa
```

```
%LAST-W-NOFILE
$ set message/text
$!
$! Note how the symbols $severity and $status are set.
$!
$ run last
Display last line of file: gsfa
%LAST-W-NOFILE, error searching for file gsfa
$ show symbol $status
  $STATUS == "%X18018008"
$ show symbol $severity
  $SEVERITY == "0"
```

In the previous example, the message file was tested by using it with the
C program that makes use of the messages. The message file can be tested
independently by linking the MESSAGE object file and loading the image:

```
$ message last_messages.msg
$ link last_messages.obj !(ignore no transfer address error)
$ set message last_messages.exe
$ write sys$output f$message(%x08018014)
%LAST-F-RECORD, no records in file
```

17.2.1.1 The message argument vector. The value of the $STATUS sym-
bol is called the message code, also known as the *message argument vector*. This code is a unique identifier for the message, and it's used as an
index to search for messages. It has the format shown in Fig. 17.7.

```
      .TITLE Messages for the LAST program


! This is file LAST_MESSAGES.MSG. Although it can be used

! with any VAX program, here it is used in conjunction with

! the program LAST.C.

! This file is compiled by:

! $ message/list last_messages.msg

!

! Two files are created, last_messages.obj and last_messages.lis

!


      .FACILITY  LAST,1/PREFIX=LAST_

NOFILE          <error searching for file !AS>/FAO_COUNT=1/WARNING

NORECORD        <no records in file>/SEVERE

OK              <last line displayed>/SUCCESS

      .END
```

Figure 17.5 A MESSAGE file.

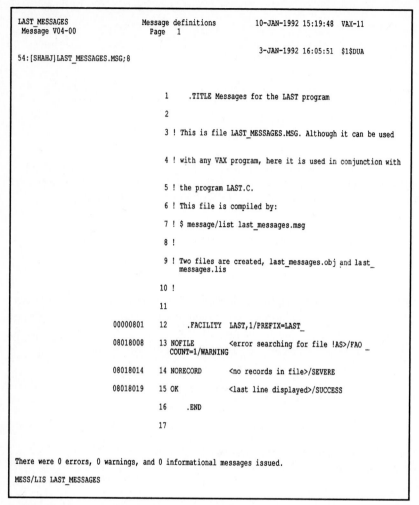

```
LAST_MESSAGES                  Message definitions          10-JAN-1992 15:19:48  VAX-11
  Message V04-00                 Page   1

                                                            3-JAN-1992 16:05:51  $1$DUA
54:[SHAHJ]LAST_MESSAGES.MSG;8


                              1      .TITLE Messages for the LAST program

                              2

                              3 ! This is file LAST_MESSAGES.MSG. Although it can be used

                              4 ! with any VAX program, here it is used in conjunction with

                              5 ! the program LAST.C.

                              6 ! This file is compiled by:

                              7 ! $ message/list last_messages.msg

                              8 !

                              9 ! Two files are created, last_messages.obj and last_
                                   messages.lis

                             10 !

                             11
                 00000801    12     .FACILITY  LAST,1/PREFIX=LAST_

                 08018008    13 NOFILE          <error searching for file !AS>/FAO _
                                   COUNT=1/WARNING

                 08018014    14 NORECORD        <no records in file>/SEVERE

                 08018019    15 OK              <last line displayed>/SUCCESS

                             16     .END

                             17

There were 0 errors, 0 warnings, and 0 informational messages issued.

MESS/LIS LAST_MESSAGES
```

Figure 17.6 Listing file created when MESSAGE file is compiled.

The message codes are shown in the message listing file. The severity codes depict whether the message represents WARNING, FATAL and so on. Message number is a unique number within the facility. This number is generated by the message utility. The facility number is specified in the .FACILITY directive. Since it has to be unique and there are many products on the system with their own facility number, the number should be registered with DEC so that there's no clash with other prod-

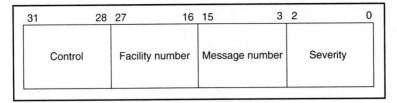

31	28	27	16	15	3	2	0
Control		Facility number		Message number		Severity	

Figure 17.7 The message code.

ucts using the MESSAGE utility. The default of 1 is acceptable for most simple user applications.

17.3 Command Language Definition: The CDU Utility

DCL commands have three major components: the verb, parameters and qualifiers. The verb is the name of the command, parameters are specified after a white space on the command line, and qualifiers are specified after a /. In $ copy /log a.a b.b, copy is the command verb, /log is a qualifier, and a.a and b.b are two parameters. C programs can be written to adhere to this format of command lines. CDU (Command Definition Utility) aids in creating commands and performing certain command line validations.

17.3.1 Defining command format

DCL commands are stored in the file SYS$LIBRARY:DCLTABLES.EXE. This file is loaded in each process' memory when the process is created. When a user enters commands, DCL calls the routine CLI$DCL_PARSE to check the command syntax. CLI$DCL_PARSE looks for the command syntax in the memory where DCLTABLES is loaded. If the command syntax is correct, DCL runs a program image (or internal DCL procedure) by calling CLI$DISPATCH. The program gets access to the command line entities by means of the routines CLI$PRESENT and CLI$GET_VALUE. A simple definition for the preceding copy command can be:

```
DEFINE  VERB COPY
        IMAGE "sys$system:copy.exe"
        qualifier LOG
        parameter P1, VALUE(TYPE=$FILE)
        parameter P2, VALUE(TYPE=$FILE)
```

17.3.2   Creating a command definition file

This file contains the syntax of the command that will be accepted on the command line. The command definition language has the following statements:

- DEFINE SYNTAX. This statement allows an alternate syntax for a command, depending on the parameters, qualifiers or keywords.

- DEFINE TYPE. Defines user-defined types that are used as VALUEs for parameters and qualifiers. Here's an example:

```
DEFINE  TYPE dir_keywords
        KEYWORD NORTH
        KEYWORD SOUTH
        KEYWORD EAST
        KEYWORD WEST
DEFINE  VERB MOVE
        IMAGE "sys$system:move"
        QUALIFIER DIRECTION, VALUE(TYPE=dir_keywords)
```

Possible commands are:

```
$ MOVE /SOUTH
$ MOVE /EAST
```

- DEFINE VERB. Defines the name of the command, along with information on its parameters and qualifiers. For example:

```
DEFINE  VERB COPY
        IMAGE "sys$system:copy.exe"
        qualifier LOG
        parameter P1, VALUE(TYPE=$FILE)
        parameter P2, VALUE(TYPE=$FILE)
```

Here, the verb is COPY; the file that will be run when the command is invoked is sys$system:copy.exe; the command has one qualifier, /LOG, and the command accepts two parameters, both of them filenames.

- IDENT. Used to identify object module. For example:

```
IDENT "V2.3"
```

- MODULE. Object module name for linker. For example:

```
MODULE COPY_TABLE
```

The Command Definition Utility manual, VMS programming volume 2B, should be consulted for other features of the command definition utility. Figure 17.8 shows the command definition for the TAIL program shown later in this book.

Once a command is created, it can be added to the process' table by:

```
$ set command tail.cld
```

The command is now available to the process that runs this command. However, the command can be inserted into DCLTABLES by a command like:

```
$ set command tail.cld -
      /table=sys$library:dcltables.exe -
      /output=sys$library:dcltables.exe
```

A command inserted in DCLTABLES is available whenever a user logs into the system.

Figure 17.8 Command definition for TAIL program.

```
!TAIL command. File TAIL.CLD
define type TAIL_FORMATS
   keyword PASSALL
   keyword TEXT
      default
   keyword NOFF
   keyword DUMP
   keyword NONULLS
define type HARDCOPY_MODES
   keyword OVERSTRIKE
   keyword UNDERLINE
      default
define type HIGHLIGHT_MODES
   keyword REVERSE
   keyword BOLD
      default
   keyword BLINK
   keyword UNDERLINE
   keyword HARDCOPY
      value (type=HARDCOPY_MODES)
define verb TAIL
   image sys$sysdevice:[shahj.tail]TAIL
   parameter P1 , label=TAILFILES , prompt="Filename(s)"
      value (required,list,type=$infile)
   qualifier BACKUP
```

Figure 17.8 *(Continued)*

```
qualifier BEFORE
    value (default="TODAY",type=$datetime)
qualifier BY_OWNER
    value (type=$uic)
qualifier CONFIRM
qualifier CREATED
qualifier EXACT
qualifier EXCLUDE
    value (required,list)
qualifier EXPIRED
qualifier FORMAT
    nonnegatable
    default
    value (default="TEXT",type=TAIL_FORMATS)
qualifier HEADING
    default
qualifier HIGHLIGHT
    value (type=HIGHLIGHT_MODES)
qualifier LOG
qualifier MODIFIED
qualifier NUMBERS
qualifier OUTPUT
    default
    value (default="SYS$OUTPUT",type=$outfile)
qualifier SINCE
    value (default="TODAY",type=$datetime)
qualifier STATISTICS
qualifier STARTLINE
    value (type=$number)
qualifier LINES
    value (default=10,type=$number)
disallow STARTLINE and LINES
-------------------------------------------------
```

17.3.3 Accessing command line information from programs

Once a command line syntax is defined in a .cld file and loaded with the SET COMMAND command, a user can use the command to invoke a program. The program can then use the CLI$PRESENT and CLI$GET_VALUE system services to access qualifiers and parameters. Figure 17.9 gives examples of usage of these calls from the TAIL program.

The TAIL program elsewhere in this book shows how all the parameters and qualifiers are handled for the TAIL command definition previously given.

17.4 The VMSINSTAL Facility

Software from DEC and many other companies is installed on the VAX/VMS system by the procedure SYS$UPDATE:VMSINSTAL.COM. When creating a product for distribution, it should be installable with the VMSINSTAL utility. In a typical product installation, the following operations are performed:

- Release notes containing latest information are moved to SYS$HELP:.
- Executable images are moved to SYS$SYSTEM:.
- Error message files are moved to SYS$MESSAGE:.

Figure 17.9 Getting command line information from programs.

```
/* This is partial code from a program which can be invoked
 * by a command like,
 *
 * $ TAIL a.a /OUTPUT=b.b
 */


#include climsgdef.h  /* Contains values for constants like CLI$_PRESENT */
#include descrip.h    /* string descriptor definitions */
int cli_status;


/*string descriptor of value part of a qualifier */
char cli_value[255];
short cli_val_len;


/* dsc$descriptor_s is a structure defining the layout of
```

Figure 17.9 *(Continued)*

```
   a string descriptor. String descriptors are described in
   chapter 15.
*/
struct dsc$descriptor_s cli_value_str = { 255,14,1, cli_value };


/* possible TAIL qualifiers*/

$DESCRIPTOR (cli_backup  ,"BACKUP");
$DESCRIPTOR (cli_output  ,"OUTPUT");
...


cli_status = cli$present(&cli_output);  /* /OUTPUT present? */
if (cli_status == CLI$_PRESENT)

    {
    /* get value (filename) part of /OUTPUT=filename */
    cli_status = cli$get_value ( &cli_output, &cli_value_str, &cli_val_len);
...

    }

...
```

- Library files are moved to SYS$LIBRARY:.

- The file SYS$LIBRARY:DCLTABLES.EXE is modified to incorporate one or more DCL commands.

- The file SYS$HELP:HELPLIB.HLB is modified to incorporate help on the product. (See the HELP command.)

- Sample examples on using the product are stored in SYS$EXAMPLES:.

- A startup command file is moved to SYS$STARTUP:.

- Directories and accounts may be created for the product's use.

- An installation verification procedure is run to confirm that the product is properly installed.

Here's a sample installation for the product Datatrieve:

```
SYS$UPDATE:VMSINSTAL
```

```
          VAX/VMS Software Product Installation Procedure V5.4-1


It is 21-JAN-1992 at 14:11.
Enter a question mark (?) at any time for help.

%VMSINSTAL-W-DECNET, Your DECnet network is up and running.
* Do you want to continue anyway [NO]? y
* Are you satisfied with the backup of your system disk [YES]?
* Where will the distribution volumes be mounted: MUA1:

Enter the products to be processed from the first distribution volume
set.
* Products: dtr
* Options:
The following products will be processed:
  DTR V4.2
       Beginning installation of DTR V4.2 at 14:11


%VMSINSTAL-I-RESTORE, Restoring product saveset A ...
%VMSINSTAL-I-RELMOVED , The product's release notes have been
                                successfully moved to SYS$HELP.
       Product:      DTR or DTR-USER
       Producer:     DEC
       Version:      4.2
       Release Date: 1-MAY-1988


* Does this product have an authorization key registered and loaded? y
* Do you want to use default answers for all questions [NO]? y

       **********************************************************

       The Language-Sensitive Editor is not installed on your
       system. To have the Language-Sensitive Editor support,
       you must:

           1. Install the Language-Sensitive Editor
           2. Install or reinstall this product

       **********************************************************


* Do you want to continue the installation [NO]? y

       The installation of VAX DATATRIEVE will now continue for
       10 minutes to 30 minutes.

%VMSINSTAL-I-RESTORE, Restoring product saveset B ...
%VMSINSTAL-I-SYSDIR, This product creates system
                                disk directory VMI$ROOT:[DTR].
%VMSINSTAL-I-SYSDIR, This product creates system
                                disk directory VMI$ROOT:[SYSTEST.DTR].


   During the installation, a file called
   DTRSTUP.COM has been added to SYS$MANAGER:
   The site-dependent start-up file, SYS$MANAGER:SYSTARTUP.COM
   (if you are running under VMS V4.x) or
   SYS$MANAGER:SYSTARTUP_V5.COM
```

(if you are running under VMS V5.0) should have the following
line added:

```
$    @SYS$MANAGER:DTRSTUP.COM
```

```
*****************************************************************
```

VAX DATATRIEVE User Environment Test Packages (UETPs)
have been provided and can be run after the installation is
complete. They are invoked from VAX DATATRIEVE as follows:

```
DTR> @sys$common:[systest.dtr]dtr    ! The general test
DTR> @sys$common:[systest.dtr]plots  ! The plots test
DTR> @sys$common:[systest.dtr]rdb    ! The Rdb test
```

```
*****************************************************************
```

%VMSINSTAL-I-MOVEFILES, Files will now be moved to their target direc
tories...

Executing IVP for: VAX DATATRIEVE V4.2-1

Running the general IVP test ...
    Test completed successfully

```
***************************************
```

    VAX DATATRIEVE V4.2-1
    IVP COMPLETED SUCCESSFULLY

```
***************************************
```

IVP completed for: VAX DATATRIEVE V4.2-1

Restoring VAX DATATRIEVE demonstration RDB/VMS database

Exported by Rdb/VMS V2.1-5 Backup/Restore utility
A component of Rdb/VMS V2.1-5
Previous name was DTR$LIBRARY:PERSONNEL.RDB
It was logically exported on 3-JUN-1989 12:22
IMPORTing relation COLLEGES
IMPORTing relation DEGREES
IMPORTing relation DEPARTMENTS
IMPORTing relation EMPLOYEES
IMPORTing relation JOBS
IMPORTing relation JOB_HISTORY
IMPORTing relation SALARY_HISTORY
IMPORTing relation WORK_STATUS
    Installation of DTR V4.2 completed at 14:30

Enter the products to be processed from the next distribution volume set.
* Products: <CTRL/Z>

    VMSINSTAL procedure done at 14:35

The product to be installed is created as a set of BACKUP savesets and
copied to a tape or directory. For example, Datatrieve is stored in the tape
MUA1: and a listing of the tape shows:

```
$ MOUNT MUA1: /OVERRIDE=IDENTIFICATION
%MOUNT-I-MOUNTED, DTR mounted on MUA1:
$ DIRECTORY MUA1:

DTR042.A;1
DTR042.B;1
DTRO42.C;1
```

There are three savesets on the tape. The product name is DTR, and 042 signifies a version number of 4.2. For any product, the first saveset always contains a file, KITINSTAL.COM. When the product is being installed, VMSINSTAL reads this file and executes it. KITINSTAL.COM must contain all the necessary commands to install the product. The manual "VMS Developer's Guide to VMSINSTAL" describes in detail how to create a product tape. Let's look at an example. Consider the SUBSTITUTE utility described elsewhere in this manual. Here's a sample script of the product installation:

```
$ @sys$update:vmsinstal

        VAX/VMS Software Product Installation Procedure V5.4-2
It is 16-JAN-1992 at 13:08.

Enter a question mark (?) at any time for help.

* Are you satisfied with the backup of your system disk [YES]?
* Where will the distribution volumes be mounted: mua0:

Enter the products to be processed from the first distribution volume
set.
* Products: sub011
*Enter installation options you wish to use (none):
The following products will be processed:

  SUB V1.1

    Beginning installation of SUB V1.1 at 13:09

%VMSINSTAL-I-RESTORE, Restoring product save set A ...
%VMSINSTAL-I-RELMOVED, Product's release notes have been moved to
SYS$HELP.
* Do you want to purge files replaced by this installation [YES]?
%VMSINSTAL-I-MOVEFILES, Files will now be moved to their target direc
tories...
    Installation of SUB V1.1 completed at 13:10

Enter the products to be processed from the next distribution volume set.
* Products: <control-z>
    VMSINSTAL procedure done at 13:10
```

The tape, mua0:, contains one BACKUP saveset, sub011.a. The contents of this saveset are:

```
KITINSTAL.COM;6
SUBSTITUTE.CLD;7
SUBSTITUTE.HLP;8
SUBSTITUTE.OBJ;13
SUBSTITUTE011.RELEASE_NOTES;1
```

During installation, the individual files in the saveset are restored to disk, and KITINSTAL.COM is executed. The .CLD file is used (by KIT INSTAL.COM) to install the command in the system's DCL table. The .HLP is used to insert HELP within the system help library. The .OBJ is linked to create the image SYS$SYSTEM:SUBSTITUTE.EXE (the linking is required because a .EXE created on another version of VMS may not run on the system on which the product is being installed). The .RELEASE _NOTES file is moved to SYS$HELP. These are the basic operations performed during the install. Here is KITINSTAL.COM. (The line numbers at left are not part of the file):

```
 1 $!Jay Shah 2-JAN-1992
 2 $!KITINSTAL.COM for the substitute utility
 3 $!
 4 $on control_y then vmi$callback control_y
 5 $on warning then exit $status
 6 $if p1 .eqs. "VMI$_INSTALL" then goto subst_install
 7 $exit vmi$unsupported
 8 $subst_install:
 9 $vmi$callback set purge ask
10 $link/executable=vmi$kwd: vmi$kwd:substitute, sys$input:/opt/notrace
11 sys$share:vaxcrtl/share
12 $vmi$callback provide_image subexe substitute.exe vmi$root:[sysexe]
13 $vmi$callback provide_dcl_command  substitute.cld
14 $vmi$callback provide_dcl_help     substitute.hlp
15 $exit $status
```

The developer has to basically create a set of callbacks when creating KITINSTAL. The vmicallback statement effectively "calls" a subroutine within VMSINSTAL.COM to interpret the remainder of the line. The basic callbacks are:

- Line 9 in effect asks a question and accepts a response: Do you want to purge files replaced by this installation [YES]? VMSINSTAL purges installed files if the response is YES.

- Line 12 copies the file substitute.exe into sys$syscommon: [sysexe].

- Line 13 adds the command in substitute.cld into SYS$SYS TEM:DCLTABLES.EXE so that the SUBSTITUTE command is available systemwide.

- Line 14 adds HELP on the SUBSTITUTE utility to the system HELP library.

Note that KITINSTAL also performs a LINK of the SUBSTITUTE utility at lines 10 and 11. This product had just one saveset on tape, and this was restored by VMSINSTAL; however, if the product has other savesets, these will have to be restored from KITINSTAL.COM. Also, an installation verification procedure, if it exists, must be executed from KITINSTAL.COM. All

other functions to be performed for a product installation must be placed in
KITINSTAL.COM. To create the tape, the system has a command proce-
dure, SYS$UPDATE:SPKITBLD.COM. For example, if the files: KIT
INSTAL.COM;6, SUBSTITUTE.CLD;7, SUBSTITUTE.HLP;8, SUBSTI
TUTE.OBJ;13, and SUBSTITUTE011.RELEASE_NOTES;1 are stored in
[shahj.files], the next command will create the file SUB011.A (which
is a BACKUP saveset) and store it in [shahj.kit]. The file can then be
COPIED to tapes for distribution.

```
$@sys$update:spkitbld   sub011   [shahj.kit]   [shahj.files]
```

The general usage of this command is:

```
$@sys$update:spkitbld  saveset-name  kit-destination  kit-source-files
```

18

VAXset: Software Project Management Tools

VAXset is a collection of six utilities that aid in the software development cycle. These utilities are also known as CASE (Computer Aided Software Engineering) tools. The tools are:

- Code Management System (CMS).
- DEC Test Manager (DTM).
- Language Sensitive Editor (LSE).
- Module Management System (MMS).
- Performance and Coverage Analyzer (PCA).
- Source Code Analyzer (SCA).

These tools support all the VMS languages and, when used properly, can substantially reduce development and maintenance efforts in large projects. All the tools can run under DECwindows using windowing functionality. The windowing aspect of the tools is not covered in this book. The tools are introduced here and described in detail in later sections.

Code Management System (CMS) is used to create a central repository for a project's program and other files. CMS maintains a history of program modifications and handles concurrent access of source files by more than one programmer. CMS also maintains all present and previous versions of all files in a compressed form.

Before the final version of an application is released, various intermediate versions may also be released. At times, it may be necessary to revert back to an older version of the application. CMS can be used to note the version numbers of programs corresponding to an application release. The release level is called a Class. CMS can be used to revert back to a Class, if required.

DEC Test Manager (DTM) automates the application testing process, making use of the regression testing method. A test is set up by running the application under DTM. DTM notes all keyboard input and screen output. This information is stored in benchmark files. In the future, to confirm the original functioning of the application, DTM is invoked to run the test. DTM repeats the set of input keystrokes generated during test set up, and compares the output generated with the benchmark output. Any discrepancy is displayed on the screen. A battery of tests can be set up to rigorously test an application. The tests can be automatically run when new features are added to the application. This way, if the modifications have introduced any bugs in the application functionality, DTM will catch those bugs.

In its basic form, Language Sensitive Editor (LSE) can be used to create programs (or other files) much like any other editor on the system. LSE provides extensive online HELP on language syntax and generates program statement templates where only the variable information in the statement need be filled out. This feature may be useful to novice programmers. LSE allows compilation of programs, review of compilation errors and correction of source programs, all within the same edit session. LSE supports all of the standard languages.

In a large project, modifications to some programs may require the compilation and linking of these programs and possibly other programs that refer to code in these programs. Interdependencies of files can be described within Module Management System (MMS) files. When source files are modified, MMS can be used to re-create the application. MMS will perform only the required minimum steps to generate the application. MMS does this by noting the interdependencies and file creation or revision time. MMS can also be used for small projects because it saves time to create the final application, and it's consistent.

Performance and Coverage Analyzer (PCA) generates a run time profile of application execution. The main statistics generated are CPU time spent on each program statement and I/O counts. PCA is a powerful tool for identifying execution bottlenecks and for increasing execution efficiency. PCA displays statistics for program source statements of the standard languages on VMS.

Given a symbol (like a variable name), Source Code Analyzer (SCA) can display the source program statements where the symbol is referenced. SCA can be useful when multiple source program files generate a single executable image. The product is an extended cross-referencing tool. The point in the source program where the symbol is used can be displayed within an editor, and the source program can be edited if required.

18.1   Code Management System (CMS)

Consider a small application of eight C programs and six form (FMS) files used by the C programs to display forms on screen. The application is handled by three programmers. A programmer may modify any of the files. Without CMS, a programmer would notify other programmers when he or she is working on a particular file. This way, concurrent access can be avoided. Also, a brief comment can be inserted at the top of source files explaining modifications performed to the file. With CMS, these two operations can be made more efficient. CMS would store the files in its own library. CMS does not allow other programmers to access a file reserved by one programmer. Also, every time a programmer reserves a file or inserts a file into the CMS library, a comment can be entered. The comments make up the history of program changes.

18.1.1   Setting up a project under CMS

To run CMS, the command is simply:

```
$ CMS
CMS>
```

The first step is the creation of a CMS library. The library is a normal disk directory. The directory must be created before the CMS library can be created. CMS stores source file information, history and other information in this library. A separate library should be maintained for each project.

```
$ CREATE/DIRECTORY    [test.cmslib]
CMS> create library   [test.cmslib]  "PAYROLL application"
```

Note that a remark is entered within quotes. Many CMS commands have a remark that can be displayed at a later stage to chart the history of a project. The CREATE command is used initially to create the CMS library. Once created, the library can be used by the SET LIBRARY command. Initially, the library will contain two files:

00CMS.CMS   Maintains various CMS information on the project.
00CMS.HIS   Maintains history information.

Files that are to be maintained by CMS have to be first created in your own directory and then inserted into the CMS library. Files inserted in CMS are called *elements*. For example, if a file PROG3.C exists in the current directory, the next command will remove the file from the current directory and create an element in the CMS library:

```
CMS> create element PROG3.C "PAYROLL deductions"
```

Files in the CMS library directory should be accessed by CMS commands only, as these files are stored in a CMS internal format. The CREATE command should be used to enter all the project files in the CMS library.

The files in the CMS Library directory are protected by standard UIC- and ACL-based protection (not explained further in this book). CMS also has its own ACLs, which can be set to restrict or allow selected commands to specified users. For convenience, members of a project team can have the same UIC group.

18.1.2   Accessing the CMS library

Typically, programmers will copy elements from the CMS library into their directories, modify them, and re-insert them in the library. Once the CMS library is set up, programmers can use one of two commands to copy an element in their directory:

```
CMS> reserve PROG3.C "to look into invalid date bug"
```

or

```
CMS> fetch PROG3.C "to look into invalid date bug"
```

If the RESERVE command is used, CMS will not allow other programmers to access the element until the programmer re-inserts the element by the REPLACE command or the reservation is removed by the UNRESERVE command:

```
CMS> replace PROG3.C "changed date validation routine"
CMS> unreserve PROG3.C "cannot locate the problem"
```

The elements reserved can be displayed by

```
CMS> show reservations
```

The FETCH command can be used to create a copy of an element without reserving it so that other programmers may access it if required.

The history of operations performed on an element can be displayed by:

```
CMS> show history PROG3.C

History of DEC/CMS Library DISK$USER:[TEST.CMSLIB]

18-FEB-1990 12:27:50 ALAN CREATE ELEMENT PROG3.C "Payroll deductions"
18-FEB-1990 12:50:36 ALAN RESERVE PROG3.C(1) "to look into invalid
date bug
18-FEB-1990 12:51:06 ALAN REPLACE PROG3.C(2) "cannot locate the prob
lem"
```

The numbers within parentheses are generation numbers that are described shortly. A complete project history can be displayed by using:

```
CMS> show history
```

18.1.3   Other CMS features

Just as VMS maintains version numbers of files, CMS maintains generation numbers of elements. Generation numbers are specified like version numbers, and the default is the latest generation.

Elements can be placed in groups within a CMS library:

```
CMS> create group PAY_STUB "PAYROLL paystub related programs"
CMS> insert element PROG2.C, PROG4.C, STUB.FRM PAY_STUB
```

CMS has various commands to manipulate elements in a group:

```
CMS> show history PAY_STUB
CMS> show group PAY_STUB/contents
```

CMS can be used to create a CLASS of elements. Classes are useful for noting the generation numbers of elements corresponding to old releases of the application. Suppose the current set of element generations were used to release V2.1 of the PAYROLL application. These generations can be noted as class PAY_V21:

```
CMS> create class PAY_V21 "Release with medical deductions"
CMS> insert generation PROG1.C, PROG2.C, STUB.FRM PAY_V21 "main code"
```

The elements can be modified to create new generations in the library. Later, to retrieve a generation of an element corresponding to release V2.1, the command could be:

```
CMS> FETCH PROG2.C /generation=PAY_V21 "to see the old date routine"
```

Note that a CLASS can contain only one generation of any one element.

18.2   DEC/Test Manager (DTM)

Consider a simple requirement: The command $DIRECTORY[TMP] should always display the same output. A DTM test can be set up for this purpose. The test can be run any time later to confirm that no files have been deleted or created in that directory.

18.2.1   Interactive test setup

Run DTM by issuing the DTM command:

```
$ DTM
DTM>
```

DTM stores information on tests in a library. The library is actually a disk directory (and its subdirectories). The library has to be created once:

```
$ create/directory      [test.dtmlib]
DTM> create library     [test.dtmlib]
```

Once the library is created, the SET LIBRARY command has to be issued at the start of a DTM session:

```
DTM> set library [test.dtmlib]
```

The test description is created by:

```
DTM> create test_description dirtest /interactive  "Sample test"
```

Most DTM commands accept remarks within double quotes. The remarks are displayed by the various SHOW commands. An interactive test is one that's actually run from a terminal, while a noninteractive test is one that's specified in a command file. To set up the test the RECORD command is used. This command creates a benchmark file within the DTM library:

```
DTM> record dirtest  "directory [tmp] should not change"
```

After the RECORD command is issued, whatever is entered at the terminal and whatever is displayed is recorded by DTM in the library. In a practical test, a judiciously chosen set of operations should be performed so that what is displayed reflects proper functioning of the application. The recording session is terminated by entering two control-Ps:

```
$ dir [tmp]
^P^P
```

The test has been set up. Various tests can be set up for a particular application, and these tests can be placed together in a collection. DTM runs collections, not individual tests, so a collection of one test has to be formed in our example:

```
DTM> create collection dirtest_coll dirtest "simple collection"
```

18.2.2 Running tests

Once a collection of one or more tests is set up under DTM, the collection can be run to ensure that the output does not change for the same operations performed during test setup:

```
DTM> run dirtest_coll
```

DTM will run the test (or tests) in the collection, compare the output generated with the benchmark output, and display a status message specifying whether the comparison was successful or not. The differences can be displayed by entering the REVIEW subsystem:

```
DTM> review dirtest_coll
DTM_REVIEW> show/differences
```

The screen is split horizontally into two halves; the top half shows the benchmark (expected) output, and the bottom half shows the output from the current execution of the test. Differences are highlighted in reverse video. The keypad 0 key can be used to display further screens.

18.2.3 Noninteractive tests

A *noninteractive test* is one where input comes from a command file rather than the terminal. The RECORD command is not valid for noninteractive tests. Instead, the benchmark file is created by running the test once and then issuing the UPDATE command during the review process. Here's an example:

```
$ dtm
DTM> set library [test.dtmlib]
%DTM-S-LIBIS, DEC/Test Manager library is SYS$SYSDEVICE:[TEST.DTMLIB]
DTM> create test_description dirtest "sample
test"/template=[tmp]tmp.com
%DTM-I-DEFAULTED, benchmark file name defaulted to DIRTEST.BMK
%DTM-S-CREATED, test description DIRTEST created
DTM> create collection dirtest_coll dirtest "directory test"
%DTM-S-CREATED, collection DIRTEST_COLL created
DTM> run dirtest_coll

Starting DIRTEST test run...

Directory SYS$SYSDEVICE:[TMP]

BAT.COM;3     BLISSKEY.DOC;2  CC.COM;4        CMSLIB.DIR;1
```

```
COMPAQKEY.DOC;1        COMS.DIR;1        COVERLET.TXT;3  CUTOVER.COM;1

Total of 8 files.

Performing post-run cleanup with comparison...

%DTM-I-NEWTEST, test DIRTEST is a New test
%DTM-S-COMPARED, collection DIRTEST_COLL compared
DTM> review dirtest_coll
Collection DIRTEST_COLL with 1 test was created on 19-SEP-1989 12:43:34
by the command:
     CREATE COLLECTION DIRTEST_COLL DIRTEST "directory test"
     Last Review Status = not previously reviewed
     Success count = 0
     Unsuccessful count = 0
     New test count = 1
     Updated test count = 0
     Comparisons aborted = 0
     Test not run count = 0

Result Description DIRTEST      Comparison Status : New Test

DTM_REVIEW> update
%DTM-I-UPDATED, the benchmark for test DIRTEST has been updated
DTM_REVIEW> exit
%DTM-S-EXIT, leaving Review subsystem
DTM> run
DTM> run dirtest_coll

Starting DIRTEST test run...


Directory SYS$SYSDEVICE:[TMP]

BAT.COM;3        BLISSKEY.DOC;2    CC.COM;4          CMSLIB.DIR;1
COMPAQKEY.DOC;1  COMS.DIR;1        COVERLET.TXT;3    CUTOVER.COM;1

Total of 8 files.


Performing post-run cleanup with comparison...

%DTM-I-SUCCEEDED, the comparison for the test DIRTEST succeeded
%DTM-S-COMPARED, collection DIRTEST_COLL compared
DTM> exit
```

In the example, the test is noninteractive by default when the CREATE
TEST_DESCRIPTION command is issued. The /TEMPLATE qualifier
specifies the command file to be executed by the test. The command file
(tmp.com) contains just one statement:

```
$ dir [tmp]
```

18.2.4 Other DTM features

A set of SHOW commands displays various information:

```
DTM> show collection dirtest_coll
DTM> show history dirtest
```

```
DTM> show history dirtest_coll
DTM> show test_description dirtest
```

At times, it may be necessary to perform a set of steps before or after the actual execution of a test. In these cases, a prologue or epilogue command file can be specified when creating a test. The prologue is executed before the actual test, and the epilogue after the test; the output of these files is not included in the test comparison. For example:

```
DTM>> create test_description dirtest "sample test" -
      /template=[tmp]tmp.com -
      /prologue=[tmp]start.com/epilogue=[tmp]end.com
```

The prologue and epilogue files can be specified for a collection also.

Some applications are highly screen oriented. Normally, the test comparisons are done character by character, but screen comparisons may be more appropriate during an interactive test run for screen-oriented applications. This can be achieved by using `control-P` escape sequences during the `RECORD` phase of setting up a test. After the `RECORD` command is issued, entering `control-P` twice terminates the test-setup session. Actually, there are other `control-P` sequences interpreted by DTM. Entering `control-P` followed by the letter `E` will stop the comparison at that stage when the test is run. Then, whenever a screen that's displayed has to be compared, a `control-P` and `C` has to be entered during test setup. Just that screen will be compared during test run, and comparison will be disabled again. Character-by-character comparison can be enabled at any stage by entering `control-P` and `B`.

18.3 Language Sensitive Editor (LSE)

Although LSE can be used as a text editor, its major use lies in the additional functionality:

- LSE can be used to generate program templates. LSE has a database of language elements and syntactical structure. The editor can be used to, for example, generate a template for the `FOR` statement in C. This template is inserted in the program at the point specified; the programmer then has to insert the variable portion of the statement. This feature is useful for novice programmers, and to "recall" statement syntax during the edit session.

- Program compilation errors can be removed while in the edit session, as LSE supports compilation, error display and source program edit.

LSE is implemented using the Text Processing Utility (TPU) and has the "feel" of the EVE editor, also implemented using TPU. Some experience with EVE would help when learning LSE usage.

18.3.1 Language sensitivity

Suppose a C program is to be created. The editor is invoked by a command like:

```
$LSE PROG1.C
```

The screen is shown in Fig. 18.1. LSE determines the language from the edit file type specified, in this case .C. In this example, the cursor is on the letter p of the word program. At this stage, the COBOL program can be entered as if this were an ordinary editor. Or a template for the program can be created by entering control-E (for Expand). If control-E is entered, the screen looks like Fig. 18.2.

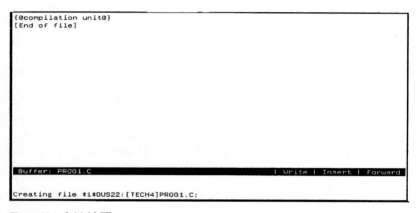

```
{@compilation unit@}
[End of file]
```

```
Buffer: PROG1.C                           | Write | Insert | Forward
```

```
Creating file $1$DUS22:[TECH4]PROG1.C;
```

Figure 18.1 Initial LSE screen.

```
[@module@]
[@module level comments@]
[@include files@]
[@macro definitions@]

[@preprocessor directive@]...

[@data type or declaration@]...

[@function definition@]...
[End of file]
```

```
Buffer: PROG1.C                           | Write | Insert | Forward
```

```
Creating file $1$DUS22:[TECH4]PROG1.C;
```

Figure 18.2 Screen after Control-E is entered.

Moving the cursor over the tokens and entering `control-E` expands the token into more program text and tokens. A complete program can be expanded using `control-E` iteratively and filling out some fields.

Items, like {@compilation unit@}, inserted in the edit buffer by LSE are called *placeholders*. Placeholders expand to other placeholders or to actual language statements. Placeholders within braces, { and }, expand to text that's required in the program; placeholders within brackets, [and], are optional.

Here's a brief list of the keys for manipulating placeholders:

Key or keys	Function
CTRL/E	When pressed over a placeholder, the placeholder is expanded to further placeholders or tokens that are actual program text.
PF1 - CTRL/E	Undo the last EXPAND (UNEXPAND).
CTRL/K	Remove current placeholder.
PF1 - CTRL/K	Re-insert the last removed placeholder.
CTRL/N	Goto next placeholder.
CTRL/P	Goto previous placeholder.

A statement template can be created by entering the statement keyword and then entering CTRL/E. For example, the FOR statement template can be created by entering FOR followed by CTRL/E. Figure 18.3 illustrates this.

18.3.2   A compilation session

The compilation and review feature of LSE can be very useful for correcting compilation errors quickly. Once a program is created, it can be

```
main()
{

for ([@expression@];   [@expression@];   [@expression@])
{
    {@statement@}...
}


}
[End of file]




  Buffer: PROG1.C                         | Write | Insert | Forward

Creating file $1$DUS22:[TECH4]PROG1.C;
Attempt to move past the beginning of buffer PROG1.C
```

Figure 18.3 Expanded FOR statement.

compiled by entering the LSE command mode (pressing CTRL/Z or the DO key) and entering COMPILE:

```
LSE Command> COMPILE
```

To continue editing the source program, CTRL/Z can be entered when on the command line.

The program is written out to disk and compiled with the /DIAGNOS TICS qualifier specified to the compilation command. The /DIAGNOSTICS qualifier causes a .DIA file to be produced. This file is used by LSE during the REVIEW phase which is entered by:

```
LSE Command> REVIEW
```

The screen is split into two windows; the top window displays the listing file with errors in reverse video, and the bottom window displays the source program.

Pressing CTRL/F causes the next error to be displayed. Pressing CTRL/G causes the cursor to move to the bottom window at the point in the source program where the error occurred. The source program can be corrected before checking out other errors. CTRL/F can be used to display further errors, and CTRL/B can be used to display previous errors. Once all errors have been corrected, the COMPILE/REVIEW cycle can be repeated. CTRL/Z can be entered to terminate the edit session.

A sample screen showing LSE compilation errors is shown in Fig. 18.4. The program is chop.c. The error is a missing quote in the printf statement. The sequence of commands used is:

```
$ LSE CHOP.C
(DO key to enter command mode)
LSE Command> COMPILE
(DO key to enter command mode)
LSE Command> REVIEW
(control-G to go to error position in source file)
```

18.4 Module Management System (MMS)

MMS can be used to rebuild a complete application when changes are made to various portions of the application source programs and other files. MMS reduces errors; it doesn't "forget" to compile a module, which could happen if the system is built using commands. MMS is consistent; once a proper description is provided to MMS, it follows the same set of steps to build the application. MMS saves time; it rebuilds only those components of the system that are modified since the last build. MMS is similar to the MAKE utility on UNIX systems.

```
Line  902:        printf(Chop to column (default 80): ");
%CC-E-UNDECLARED, "Chop" is not declared within the scope of
                this usage.

Line  902:        printf(Chop to column (default 80): ");
%CC-W-NONTERMSTRING, Nonterminated string constant;
                quotes added at end of line.

 Buffer: $REVIEW                          | Read-only | Insert | Forward
if ((outfile = fopen(response2,"w")) <= 0)
          {perror("fopen:output");exit();};
printf(Chop to column (default 80): ");
wid=atoi(gets(response)); if (wid<=0) wid=80;

while (fgets(inbuffer,10000,infile) != 0);
          {
          len = strlen(inbuffer) - 1; /* linefeed at end is ignored */
          i = (len/wid) * wid;
          outbuffer[wid]  = 0;
 Buffer: CHOP.C                           | Write  | Insert | Forward

Starting compilation: CC $1$DUS22:[TECH4]CHOP.C;40 /DIAGNOSTICS=$1$DUS22:[TECH4◆
Compilation of buffer CHOP.C completed with error status
```

Figure 18.4   Reviewing compilation errors.

An MMS description file has to be created. The file contains dependency rules for all the files in the application. MMS is then run with the description file as input.

Consider two programs, PROG1.C and PROG2.C, which are compiled and linked by the following commands:

```
$ C prog
$ LINK prog
```

The prog is either PROG1 or PROG2.

An MMS description file can be set up to create the executable images:

```
!File: APPLIC.MMS
!The file describes to MMS the compilation and link process for
! two programs, PROG1 and PROG2.
!
application DEPENDS_ON prog1.exe, prog2.exe
        !no action
!
prog1.obj DEPENDS_ON prog1.c
    CC prog1
prog1.exe DEPENDS_ON prog1.obj
    LINK prog1, sys$share:vaxcrtl.olb/library
!
prog2.obj DEPENDS_ON prog2.c
    CC prog2
prog2.exe DEPENDS_ON prog2.obj
    LINK prog2, sys$share:vaxcrtl.olb/library
```

The statement:

```
prog1.obj DEPENDS_ON>\f>prog1.c
```

is a dependency rule. The following statement, CC prog1, is executed if the modification date on the file prog1.c is later than the modification date on the file `prog1.obj`. The `DIR/DATE=MODIFIED` command can be used to display the modification date on a file. Only one target can be specified in a description file. This target is the first file name mentioned in the first dependency rule. In many applications, like in this example, there are a number of final target `.EXE` files. In the example, the target is `applica tion` which is a dummy file name causing MMS to ensure that `prog1.exe` and `prog2.exe` are up-to-date.

To rebuild the application, the command is:

```
$ MMS/DESCRIPTION=APPLIC.MMS
```

If, for example, `PROG2.C` is modified before the MMS rebuild command is executed, the command `CC prog2` will be executed. This in turn will create a new `prog2.obj` file, which will cause the next dependency rule to be fired, executing `LINK prog2, sys$share:vaxcrtl.olb/library`.

The format of a dependency rule is:

```
target-file, target-file ... DEPENDS_ON source-file, source-file ...
      action-line
      action-line
         .
         .
         .
```

If any of the source-files are newer than any of the target files, the action lines following the rule are executed.

The `DEPENDS_ON` keyword can be interchanged with a colon. For example:

```
main.exe : module1.obj, module2.obj
      LINK/EXE=main module1, module2
```

The action lines follow the dependency rule without any intervening blank lines and are indented by at least one space or tab. A line starting with a nonspace (or tab) character is considered a dependency rule. Note that MMS builds an internal tree from these dependency rules before proceeding to build the system, so the order in which the rules are specified is not crucial.

This basic information is sufficient for the creation of MMS description files. The key is to develop an accurate dependency tree for the application (a diagram can help visualize the dependencies) and then write the appropriate MMS dependency rules.

18.4.1 MMS macros

MMS macros are short names for strings of characters. An example is:

```
objects = module1.obj, module2.obj
```

The macro can be used in the MMS description file by enclosing it within parenthesies and preceding the result with a dollar sign. For example:

```
main.exe : $(objects)
        LINK/EXE=main module1, module2
```

MMS has some special macros. For example, MMS$SOURCE refers to the file at the right of the preceding dependency rule, while MMS$TARGET_NAME refers to all file names (without the type) of the files at the left of the preceding dependency rule.

18.4.2 MMS built-in rules

MMS has a set of built-in rules that are used in case action lines are not specified for dependency rules. Consider the next dependency rule specified in an MMS description file without any action line (the rule is immediately followed by another dependency rule):

```
prog1.obj DEPENDS_ON prog1.cob
```

MMS will invoke the following built-in command to execute:

```
$(cobol) $(cobflags) $(mms$source)
```

The command actually consists of references to three built-in macros. The built-in definitions are specified in the file SYS$SYSROOT:[SYSHLP.EXAM PLES.MMS]MMS$DEFAULT_RULES.MMS. The relevant lines in this file are:

```
COBOL          = COBOL
COBFLAGS       =/NOLIST/OBJECT=$(MMS$TARGET_NAME).OBJ
.COB.OBJ :
        $(COBOL) $(COBFLAGS) $(MMS$SOURCE)
```

Here, the built-in rule is:

```
.COB.OBJ :
        $(COBOL) $(COBFLAGS) $(MMS$SOURCE)
```

The rule effectively says that if the source file of a dependency rule is of type .COB and the target file is of type .OBJ and there is no action line specified then use the second line as the action line for the rule.

The final command executed by DCL is:

```
COBOL /NOLIST/OBJECT=prog1.obj prog1.cob
```

The built-in rules and macros can be overridden by redefining them within the description file, as done in the example description file shown to compile and link `prog1` and `prog2`.

18.5 Performance and Coverage Analyzer (PCA)

PCA consists of two components:

- The collector gathers data on a running program and stores it in a file.
- The analyzer reads this file and displays program execution statistics.

Statistics can be gathered on:

- CPU time spent on each statement. The program counter is sampled every 10 milliseconds. This sample is used to estimate the CPU time per statement, since PCA knows the range of program counter values for each source statement.
- PC. This is CPU time, time spent in I/O, and all other time during program execution.
- Page faults. This shows which statement caused how many page faults.
- System service calls.
- I/O calls.
- Program coverage. This can be used to remove unreachable source code.

18.5.1 Collecting data

Consider the C language program shown in Fig. 18.5. This program takes a file, converts long lines to a set of 80 (or specified number of) column lines and creates an output file.

Figure 18.5 Program to wrap around long lines.

```
/* File: chop.c

   This program:

   . accepts an input file name.

   . accepts an output file name.

   . accepts a number which specifies the column position

     at which long lines from the input file are to be

     wrapped around. Default column position is 80.
*/
#include stdio
#include ssdef
```

Figure 18.5 *(Continued)*

```
FILE *infile;
FILE *outfile;

main()
{
int len,tmp;
int i,j,wid;
char inbuffer[10000],outbuffer[10000];
char response[80],response2[80];
printf("Chops and wraps lines from input file down to specified length\n");
printf("input file:");
if ((infile = fopen(gets(response),"r")) <= 0)
   {perror("fopen:input");exit();};
printf("output file (default %s): ",response);
gets(response2); if (strlen(response2) == 0) { strcpy(response2,response); };
if ((outfile = fopen(response2,"w")) <= 0)
   {perror("fopen:output");exit();};
printf("Chop to column (default 80): ");
wid=atoi(gets(response)); if (wid<=0) wid=80;
while (fgets(inbuffer,10000,infile) != 0)
   {
   len = strlen(inbuffer) - 1; /* linefeed at end is ignored */
   i = (len/wid) * wid;
        outbuffer[wid]  = 0;
   for (j=0;j<i;j=j+wid)
           {
           strncpy(&outbuffer,&inbuffer[j],wid);
           fprintf(outfile,"%s\n",&outbuffer);
           };
   tmp = len -i;
   strncpy(outbuffer,&inbuffer[i],tmp);
   outbuffer[tmp] = 0;
   fprintf(outfile,"%s",&outbuffer);
   };
}
------------------------------------------------------------------------
```

To analyze the execution of this program, the program must be compiled and linked using the /DEBUG qualifier, as shown here. Note that a PCA debugger is specified during the LINK phase.

```
$cc/debug CHOP
$link/debug=sys$library:pca$obj CHOP,sys$input:/opt
sys$share:vaxcrtl/share
```

When the program is run, the data collector component of PCA will take control. The data to be recorded can be selected by SET commands. In this example, CPU samples and I/O counts are specified. The collected data is stored in a file with a file type of .PCA (CHOP.PCA is the file in this example).

Here's the execution of the program:

```
$ run chop
      VAX PCA Collector Version 3.1-9

PCAC> set cpu_sampling
PCAC> set io_service
%PCA-I-CPUDISTOR,  CPU sampling data may be distorted by collection of
other data
PCAC> go
%PCA-I-DEFDATFIL,  set  datafile  required  in  this  context,  creating
'[]CHOP.PCA'
%PCA-I-BEGINCOL,  data collection begins
Chops and wraps long lines from input file down to specified length
input file: long.fil
output file (default long.fil): short.fil
Chop to column (default 80):
%PCA-I-ENDCOL, data collection ends
$
```

The collected data is displayed by the PCA Analyzer. The analyzer is invoked by the PCA command. Here is an analyze session where the CPU time spent on each statement of the source program is displayed.

```
$ pca chop
      VAX Performance and Coverage Analyzer Version 3.1-9

PCAA> plot/source/cpu_sampling routine main by line
```

(See Fig. 18.6 for output.)

The PLOT and TABULATE are the analyzer commands to display statistics. PLOT draws a graph, while TABULATE gives counts. Otherwise, the two types of commands are similar. The routine name was specified in this example, as a lot of definitions from the .H files were being included in the display. Routine names can be displayed by the SHOW SYMBOL * command. In this example, line 898 uses the most CPU time.

Figure 18.6 Percent of total CPU time spent at each C statement.

```
VAX Performance and Coverage Analyzer Page 1


CPU Sampling Data (3967 data points total) - "*"


Percen   Count   Line
CHOP\main\
  0.0%           880: {
                 881: int len,tmp;
                 882: int i,j,wid;
                 883: char inbuffer[10000],outbuffer[10000];
                 884: char response[80],response2[80];
                 885:
  0.1%           886: printf("Chops and wraps lines from input file down to specified length\n");
  0.0%           887: printf("input file:");
  0.1%           888: if ((infile = fopen(gets(response),"r")) <= 0)
  0.0%           889:        {perror("fopen:input");exit();};
                 890:
  0.0%           891: printf("output file (default %s): ",response);
  0.0%           892: gets(response2); if (strlen(response2) == 0) { strcpy(response2,response); };
  0.2%           893: if ((outfile = fopen(response2,"w")) <= 0)
  0.0%           894:        {perror("fopen:output");exit();};
  0.0%           895: printf("Chop to column (default 80): ");
  0.0%           896: wid=atoi(gets(response)); if (wid<=0) wid=80;
                 897:
 99.5% ******** 898: while (fgets(inbuffer,10000,infile) != 0);
                 899:        {
  0.0%           900:        len = strlen(inbuffer) - 1; /* linefeed at end is ignored */
  0.0%           901:        i = (len/wid) * wid;
  0.0%           902:        outbuffer[wid]  = 0;
  0.0%           903:        for (j=0;j<i;j=j+wid)
                 904:            {
  0.0%           905:            strncpy(&outbuffer,&inbuffer[j],wid);
  0.0%           906:            fprintf(outfile,"%s\n",&outbuffer);
  0.0%           907:            };
  0.0%           908:        tmp = len -i;
  0.0%           909:        strncpy(outbuffer,&inbuffer[i],tmp);
```

Figure 18.6 *(Continued)*

```
0.0%         910:          outbuffer[tmp] = 0;

0.0%         911:          fprintf(outfile,"%s",&outbuffer);

             912:          };

0.0%         913: }
```
  VAX Performance and Coverage Analyzer Page 2

CPU Sampling Data (3967 data points total) - "*"

VAX PCA Version 3.1-9   20-DEC-1991 14:22:55

PLOT Command Summary Information:

Number of buckets tallied: 24

CPU Sampling Data - "*"

Data count in largest defined bucket:	3947	99.5%
Data count in all defined buckets:	3962	99.9%
Data count not in defined buckets:	0	0.0%
Portion of above count in P0 space:	0	0.0%
Number of PC values in P1 space:	0	0.0%
Number of PC values in system space:	0	0.0%
Data points failing /STACK_DEPTH or /MAIN_IMAGE:	5	0.1%
Total number of data values collected:	3967	100.0%

Command qualifiers and parameters used:

  Qualifiers:

    /CPU_SAMPLING /NOSORT /NOMINIMUM /NOMAXIMUM

    /NOCUMULATIVE /SOURCE /ZEROS /NOSCALE /NOCREATOR_PC

    /NOPATHNAME /NOCHAIN_NAME /WRAP /NOPARENT_TASK /NOKEEP /NOTREE

    /FILL=("*","O","x","@",":","#","/","+")

    /NOSTACK_DEPTH /MAIN_IMAGE

  Node specifications:

    ROUTINE CHOP\main BY LINE

No filters are defined

18.6 Source Code Analyzer (SCA)

SCA is an extended cross-referencing tool. All the programs that constitute a project have to be compiled with the /ANALYSIS_DATA qualifier:

```
$ CC/ANALYSIS_DATA prog1.c
```

The qualifier causes an .ANA file to be created. This file contains the necessary cross-referencing information used by SCA.

All the .ANA files have to be loaded in an SCA library. Normally, all the files for one project are stored in a single SCA library. The following two commands create an SCA library:

```
$ CREATE/DIRECTORY [TEST.SCALIB]
$ SCA CREATE LIBRARY [TEST.SCALIB]
```

All .ANA files belonging to a project can be loaded in the library:

```
$ SCA SET LIBRARY [TEST.SCALIB]
$ SCA LOAD /LIBRARY=[TEST.SCALIB] prog1, prog2, prog3, prog4
```

Now, inquiries can be made on the symbols defined in the programs. Typical inquiries will display the place where a symbol is defined and the nesting structure of modules in the program.

Here's a C language program that opens and reads data from an existing RMS indexed file:

```
/*RMS.C
 This program illustrates RMS usage in C.
 Opening and reading an existing RMS indexed file in C. The file
 is INPUT.IDX, indexed with the first 3 characters as index,
 total record length is 228.

 The compilation and link commands are:

$cc/nooptimize rms
$link rms, sys$input/option
sys$share:vaxcrtl/share

*/
#include rms
#include stdio
#include ssdef
struct FAB fab;
struct RAB rab;
struct XABKEY primary_key;
struct        {
                char filkey[3];
                char fildata[225];
                } record;/* each record in the file:
                                3 character as key
                                225 characters as data
```

```
                                        */
       int rms_status;

       initialize(fn)
       /* initializes RMS structures to open the file */
               char *fn;
       {
                       fab = cc$rms_fab;
                       fab.fab$b_fac = FAB$M_DEL | FAB$M_GET |
                                       FAB$M_PUT | FAB$M_UPD;
                       fab.fab$l_fna = fn;
                       fab.fab$b_fns = strlen(fn);
                       fab.fab$l_xab = &primary_key;

                       rab = cc$rms_rab;
                       rab.rab$l_fab = &fab;

                       primary_key = cc$rms_xabkey;
       };

       main()
       {
       int i,j;
       initialize("INPUT.IDX");       /* set up rms FAB and RAB */
       rms_status = sys$open(&fab);  /* open the file */
       if (rms_status != RMS$_NORMAL){
                                       printf("file open errorn");
                                       exit(rms_status);
                                       };
       rms_status = sys$connect(&rab);
       if (rms_status != RMS$_NORMAL){
                                       printf("rab connect error\n");
                                       exit(rms_status);
                                       };

       /* run time initializations */
       rab.rab$b_rac = RAB$C_KEY;
       rab.rab$b_ksz = 3;
       rab.rab$l_kbf = "mno";
       rab.rab$l_ubf = &record;
       rab.rab$w_usz = 228;

       /* read one record */
       rms_status = sys$get(&rab);
       if (rms_status != RMS$_NORMAL){
                                       printf("read error\n");
                                       exit(rms_status);
                                       };

       printf("key is mno, record data is %s ",record.fildata);
       }
```

Here's a sample SCA session using the previous C program:

```
$ CC/ANALYSIS_DATA  RMS.C
$
$ CREATE/DIRECTORY  [TEST.SCALIB]
$ SCA CREATE LIBRARY  [TEST.SCALIB]
%SCA-S-NEWLIB, SCA Library created in DISK$USERS:[TEST.SCALIB]
%SCA-S-LIB, your SCA Library is DISK$USERS:[TEST.SCALIB]
```

```
$ SCA LOAD /LIBRARY=[TEST.SCALIB] RMS
%SCA-S-LOADED, module RMS loaded
%SCA-S-COUNT, 1 module loaded (1 new, 0 replaced)
$
$ SCA SET LIBRARY [TEST.SCALIB]
%SCA-S-LIB, your SCA Library is DISK$USERS:[TEST.SCALIB]
$ SCA FIND rms_status
Symbol          Class     Module\Line    Type of Occurrence

RMS_STATUS     variable    RMS\2446       variable definition declaration
                           RMS\2469       write reference
                           RMS\2470       read reference
                           RMS\2472       read reference
                           RMS\2474       write reference
                           RMS\2475       read reference
                           RMS\2477       read reference
                           RMS\2488       write reference
                           RMS\2489       read reference
                           RMS\2491       read reference
%SCA-S-OCCURS, 10 occurrences found (1 symbol, 1 name)
$ SCA VIEW CALL_TREE MAIN
1    RMS\MAIN calls
2    .  RMS\INITIALIZE
3    .  unknown\SYS$OPEN
4    .  unknown\PRINTF
5    .  unknown\EXIT
6    .  unknown\SYS$CONNECT
7    .  unknown\SYS$GET
%SCA-S-ROUTINES, 6 routines found (no recursive, depth = 1)
```

The VIEW CALL_TREE command is used to see the static call structure of modules. It displays all the modules calling and all the modules called by the specified module. The module in this case is the C language main program.

SCA commands can be issued from LSE also. This way, SCA is integrated with LSE. The symbols are displayed in a window during an LSE session. The up and down arrow keys can be used to scroll through the symbol1 references. The command:

```
LSE Command> GOTO SOURCE
```

can be issued from LSE. This causes the source code corresponding to the symbol reference to be displayed. The source can be edited if required.

19

Useful VMS
Products and Features

Programmers should be aware of the hardware and software environment in which their programs will be running. This allows them to write more effective applications. This chapter discusses VMS issues that are not relevant to C programming but are, nevertheless, issues that should be given some thought when designing complete applications. Topics covered are:

- Volume shadowing.
- Electronic disk drives.
- Disk striping.
- RMS Journaling.
- DECdtm—distributed transaction manager.
- Fault-tolerant VAXes.
- Symmetric multiprocessing.
- Vector processing.
- Assembly language (MACRO) code of C programs.

19.1   Volume Shadowing

Failure of disk drives can have catastrophic effects on many online applications. The volume shadowing facility on VAX/VMS allows a logical disk to consist of multiple physical disks, with the physical disks being mirror images of each other. In case a disk fails, I/O is performed on the remaining disks. Applications using shadowed disks will not be impacted by such disk failures.

VMS has two flavors of shadowing; one is host-based (VAX-based) and the other is HSC-based. The discussion here applies to both types of shadowing, although most of the examples assume HSC-based shadowing.

19.1.1   How does it work?

The requirements for volume shadowing are:

1. The disk drives that will be used as one shadow set must be of the same geometry; they must have the same number of sectors per track, tracks per cylinder and cylinders per volume. Also, the disk drives must conform to the Digital Storage Architecture (DSA) and Mass Storage Control Protocol (MSCP). Currently, most disk drives conform to DSA and MSCP.

2. The VAX Volume Shadowing software license must be installed on all the VAXes that will be using the facility. If a cluster license is purchased, the license has to be installed only once on the common system disk for use by all the member VAXes.

3. For HSC-based shadowing, an HSC is required. If there are multiple VAXes in a cluster, the cluster must have at least one VAX connected to the HSC via the Computer Interconnect (CI) bus. Usually, this requirement is met by CI-based and mixed- interconnect VAXclusters.

Figure 19.1 shows the minimal requirements for volume shadowing with an HSC. Figure 19.2 shows a host-based shadowing configuration.

In the case of HSC-based shadowing, programs on the VAX perform I/O to the logical disk, also called *virtual unit*, $HSC1$DUS5:. Usually, this I/O will be done by using high-level language statements. The I/O is routed to the Record Management Services (RMS), which in turn decides which disk blocks have to be accessed. For I/O optimization, multiple contiguous disk blocks will be accessed even when a single block is to be used. This fact is irrelevent in this discussion. RMS conveys the disk block I/O information to the I/O driver on the VAX, which in turn conveys it to the HSC software. The HSC receives the disk block I/O information for the virtual unit (not a physical disk). The HSC maintains a table that lists each physical disk corresponding to a virtual unit. This table was updated when the shadow set was created by the DCL MOUNT command. If a write block operation is to be per-

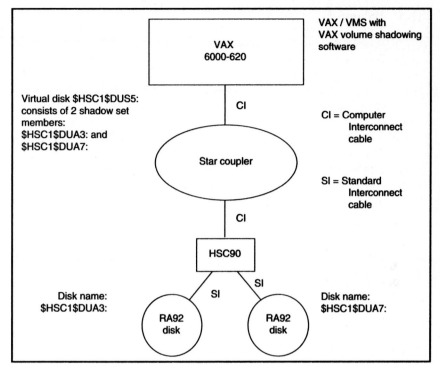

Figure 19.1 An HSC-based volume shadowing configuration.

formed, the HSC writes the block to each of the physical disks, which are shadow members of that virtual unit. If a read disk block operation is to be performed, the HSC reads the block from one of the disks, which are members of the shadow set.

HSC-based volume shadowing has little overhead on a VAX performing I/O because the VAX issues a single disk I/O command to the HSC, irrespective of whether the I/O is to a nonshadowed disk or to a virtual unit, which actually consists of multiple physical disks. The HSC incurs overhead when writing to multiple disks in a shadow set. When a disk block is to be read, the HSC reads it from only one disk, whether the logical disk is shadowed or not. So, reads do not incur any overhead. In fact, continuous read operations will be faster on a shadow set because the HSC's disk I/O optimizing algorithm uses the disk that will have the lowest seek time among the shadow set members. As a rule of thumb, sustained I/O performance will be poorer on multiple disk shadow sets than on single disks if more than 25% of the I/O operations are writes.

In the case of host-based shadowing, programs issue I/Os to disk 3DSA2:. For writes, the VAX translates an output request to 3DSA2:

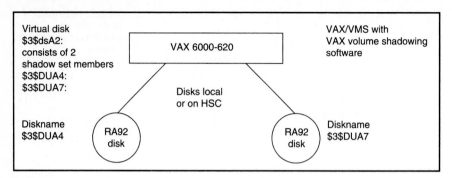

Figure 19.2 A host-based volume shadowing configuration.

into two writes, one to DUA4: and the other to DUA7:. The driver software performs two writes. This does require more CPU time than in the case of a single disk write. Reads are from only one drive; hence, no additional CPU time is used.

Physical disks can be added to a shadow set after a shadow set has been operational. Disk blocks from the existing shadowed disks are copied to the new disk in the shadow set.

19.1.2 What volume shadowing cannot do

Hardware redundancy is required for critical online applications. Since disk drives are key components of most of these applications, well-planned disk-drive configurations and use of the volume shadowing facility on a cluster eliminate problems associated with disk drive (or disk) failures. Some system analysts and programmers believe that if logical disks are adequately shadowed, no special transaction processing considerations are required when developing crucial applications. This is not true.

Due to system software bugs or power supply glitches, a set of shadowed disks may be inoperational temporarily. The application must be designed so that, with minimum impact to users, it can be restarted on other disks or it can re-use the shadowed disks after they're properly functioning. A particular challenge is to ensure that integrity of the disk databases is maintained when the application recovers. Many times, the application was in the process of updating a series of files, and the disks failed after a few of these files were actually updated. In this case, the databases may be in an inconsistent state after the application recovers. The application must be able to back out such partial updates before the users perform any operations to the databases.

A power supply problem can cause the complete system to be brought down involuntarily. In most such situations, proper power supply is restored within a short time. In this case, when proper power supply is restored and the operating system is brought up, the application should be able to recover in a short time.

The volume shadowing facility treats the disks as consisting of a sequence of 512-byte blocks and is oblivious of the higher-level logical disk structure. Sometimes, a disk's logical file structure becomes corrupt because of software bugs and improper file design. If a disk file is corrupt, the file will be corrupt on all the disks that are members of a shadow set. Indexed files are prone to file corruption in case of power failures, and volume shadowing does not mitigate the problem.

The issues mentioned here are addressed in the realm of transaction processing. A particular challenge is to develop fail-safe and resilient databases whose integrity is not compromised by various kinds of system and software failures. Currently, most critical commercial applications are written in standard languages with transaction processing extensions. These extensions are usually calls to subroutines that are part of a separate software package. Many vendors offer such transaction processing packages. A detailed discussion on how to design transaction processing applications is not within the scope of this book.

The shadow sets are created with commands like:

```
$ MOUNT /SYSTEM $HSC1$DUS5: -
         /SHADOW=($HSC1$DUA3:,$1HSC1$DUA7:) TESTDISK

$ MOUNT /SYSTEM $3$DSA2: -
         /SHADOW=($3$DUA4:,$3$DUA7:) TESTDISK
```

The DCL SHOW DEVICES command will produce a display like:

```
$ SHOW DEVICES DUA5
Device                 Device          Error  Volume      Free    Trans  Mnt
Name                   Status          Count  Label      Blocks   Count  Cnt
$HSC1$DUA3: (HSC1)     ShadowSetMember     0  (member of $HSC1$DUS5:)
$HSC1$DUA7: (HSC1)     ShadowSetMember     0  (member of $HSC1$DUS5:)
$HSC1$DUS5: (HSC1)     Mounted             0  TESTDISK  193560      1     1
```

19.2 Electronic Disks

In most major applications, there will be a need to share data among processes on the system. Disk files can be shared; however, they may be too slow for high-volume online applications. On an independent VAX computer, the application database can be stored in global sections in main memory. This way, fairly large amounts of data, which can be efficiently accessed, can be shared by multiple processes. Of course, system failures can cause data in global sections to be erased. Moreover, global sections cannot be used for storing more than a few megabytes of data (depending on the amount of available main memory). So most applications would make judicious use of global sections and disk files.

VAXclusters do not have global sections that can be shared by processes on different VAXes in the cluster. Since disk files can be shared, most applications resort to putting shared data on magnetic disks, causing the application to run inefficiently. A simple solution, though possibly expensive, is to use electronic disks. These disk devices are accessed like any other disk on the VAXcluster. Instead of storing data on a rotating magnetic medium, these disk devices store data in semiconductor memory similar to that used as main memory on the VAX systems. The semiconductor memory is also known as Random Access Memory (RAM).

Currently, DEC offers one electronic disk—the Electronic Storage Element 20 (ESE20). For most practical purposes, it's an ordinary RA series disk drive, except that it's fast. The disk has an access time of 1.3 milliseconds and can handle over 300 I/Os per second. Theoretically, on a VAXcluster the electronic disk can be up to 10 times faster than a typical magnetic disk. A speed-up of 4 times can be achieved with little or no changes to the applications, provided all disk files are moved to the electronic disk.

The formatted storage capacity of the ESE20 is 120 Mbytes. The disk is compliant with Digital Storage Architecture (DSA). The disk has a backup magnetic disk and a rechargeable battery power supply. In case of power failure, data in the disk's RAM memory is written out to the magnetic disk. When power resumes, the data in the magnetic disk is copied back to the semiconductor memory.

Data that's common to processes on the VAXcluster and that requires fast access by the application can be stored on the ESE20 disk. On an independent VAX computer, global sections can be accessed more quickly than electronic disks. The application designer will have to make trade-offs among using global sections, electronic disks and magnetic disks.

19.3 The Disk Striping Driver

The disk striping driver software can be used to create one large logical disk from a set of physical disks. The logical blocks are spread over the physical disks such that the first few blocks are on the first physical disk, the next few on the next physical disk, and so on. This way, a typical file will have data blocks spread over multiple disks. The advantage here is that file access requests will be serviced by multiple physical disks, resulting in faster I/O response time. This may be important for reasons given in the previous section. Performance can significantly improve with applications that have heavily accessed, large data files if these files are placed on striped disks.

The STRIPE command is used for disk striping operations. Here are a series of commands for mounting three RA92s as a disk striping set:

```
$ STRIP/INITIALIZE/CHUNK_SIZE=50 -
    $2$DUA3:,$1$DUA12:,$1$DUA5: 1,2,3
```

```
          !The three volumes are volumes 1,2 and 3 in sequence.
  $  STRIP/BIND $2$DUA3:,$1$DUA12:,$1$DUA5:  STRIP$DEV1
  $  INITIALIZE STRIP$DEV1 STRIP$DISK1
  $  MOUNT/SYSTEM STRIP$DEV1 STRIP$DISK1
  $!Here is an example command:
  $  COPY DISK$USERS:TMP.DATA  STRIP$DISK1:TMP.DATA
```

The chunk_size specifies that the first 50 logical blocks of the stripe disk will be on physical disk 1, the next 50 on physical disk 2, and so on. The overall storage capacity of the stripe set volume is about three times the capacity of one RA92. Individual volumes in the stripe set can be shadowed. Disks with different geometries cannot be mixed in a stripe set. So, for example, RA90s and RA92s cannot be part of the same stripe set.

Multivolume disk-striping logical disks are not to be confused with multivolume volume sets. VMS allows a set of disks to be mounted as one large logical disk without using the disk striping driver. This large logical disk is called a volume set. When files are created on this logical disk, any free space on a physical disk is allocated before the next physical disk is used. Overall, I/O throughput will be about the same as when the individual physical disks are mounted as separate logical disks.

19.4   RMS Journaling

RMS Journaling is a layered product that minimizes the impact of system failures, disk crashes and file corruptions on RMS files. The product is particularly suitable for online transaction processing applications. Basically, the product keeps track of updates to data files in a separate set of journal files and uses these journal files for recovery in case the original files become corrupt. RMS journaling could be considered for use on VAXclusters when designing fail-safe applications.

19.4.1   RMS journaling features

Many programmers use RMS sequential, relative and indexed files without realizing the impact of disk and system power failures on these files. RMS files, particularly indexed files, can be corrupted if, for example, the system fails when the files are being written into. Keeping critical files on shadowed disk volumes doesn't help, since a file corruption due to power failure is a logical corruption of the internal file pointers, which implies that the file on all shadowed disks will be corrupt. See the discussion in the chapter on volume shadowing. Effective with VMS Version 5.4, RMS Journaling is supported across DECnet, which allows the development of robust distributed transaction processing systems. RMS Journaling uses three techniques to safeguard data: after-image (roll forward) journaling, before-image (roll back) journaling and recovery-unit (transaction) journaling. For most transaction processing applications, recovery-unit journaling is the most important.

After-image journaling allows a data file to be recovered in case the file gets corrupted due to disk head crashes, system failures, and so on. *Before-image journaling* allows modifications to a data file to be backed out. Modifications may need to be backed out if, for example, records have been inserted or updated incorrectly. *Recovery-unit journaling* allows a set of operations on a set of data files to be treated as a transaction. In case the system fails while the operations are being performed, the operations are either completed when the system reboots, or completely backed out. In effect, database integrity is maintained by recovery-unit journaling.

It should be noted that not all operations to a journaled RMS file are recoverable. For example, a RENAME of a journaled file is not journaled and hence cannot be redone by RMS Journaling if the file has to be recovered. The RMS Journaling manual should be consulted to determine exactly which RMS operations are recoverable. Usually, operations that change file contents, like record deletes, writes and updates, are journaled. This journaling is sufficient for data recovery. Just about any RMS file can be journaled. It should be anticipated that journaling incurs overheads in terms of CPU time and disk space for journal files. We will now study the three journaling techniques in detail.

19.4.2   After-image journaling

To set up a data file for after-image (AI) journaling, the file must be marked as such by the $SET FILE command. The file must then be backed up using the BACKUP utility. The COPY command cannot be used because it doesn't set appropriate flags in the file header of the copied file. The journal file and the data file can later be used for recovery of the data file in case the original file is lost. Here's an example of journaling of a savings account file of bank customers:

```
$ SET  FILE    /AI_JOURNAL=(FILE=BACKUP_DISK:, CREATE) -
               database_disk:savings.account
$ BACKUP/RECORD      database_disk:savings.account -
               backup_disk:savings.bck
```

Record operations to the data file database_disk:savings.ac count will now be journaled. The journal is in the file backup_ disk:savings.rms$journal. The CREATE option in the $SET FILE command specifies that a new version of the file should be created rather than using an existing journal file. The BACKUP command must be issued after (and not before) the $SET FILE /AI_JOURNAL command is used. The /RECORD qualifier notes the date and time of backup of the data file. This information is used during the recovery process. If the /RECORD qualifier is not used, the recovery process will work; but it may take more time.

In case the original data file, savings.account, is corrupt, it can be recovered by:

```
$ RECOVER/RMS_FILE/FORWARD  backup_disk:savings.bck
```

The qualifier /RMS_file is optional. The /FORWARD qualifier is required (/BACKWARD is used for before-image recovery, which is described later). During recovery, RMS journaling automatically uses the journal file noted in the file header of savings.bck. The recovery process updates sav ings.bck using the journal file to recreate the contents of the original file within savings.bck. The original file can then be restored by:

```
$ COPY  backup_disk:savings.bck  database_disk:savings.account
```

If the recovered data file is to be journaled, the $SET FILE /AI_JOURNAL and the $BACKUP commands must be issued again on the recovered data file.

19.4.3 Before-image journaling

To set up a data file for before-image (BI) journaling only one command is required:

```
$ SET  FILE    /BI_JOURNAL=(FILE=BACKUP_DISK:, CREATE) -
               database_disk:savings.account
```

Unlike AI journaling, the data file does not have to be backed up.

During recovery, the /BACKWARD instead of the /FORWARD qualifier is used. The /UNTIL qualifier allows the file to be recovered up to a particular time. For example:

```
$ RECOVER/RMS_FILE/BACKWARD/UNTIL=15:30  database_disk:savings.account
```

will restore the contents of the data file to the state they were in at 3.30 p.m. It should be noted that the recovery is performed on the original data file by undoing (in reverse chronological order) all RMS operations after 3.30 p.m.

19.4.4 Recovery-unit journaling

A *recoverable unit* is a group of operations on one or more RMS files. The operations, normally performed from one program, constitute one logical transaction. This transaction is treated as one atomic operation. Recovery-unit (RU) journaling ensures that these operations are either all completely performed on the data files, or none are performed. RU journaling protects against loss of database integrity and consistency. RU journaling, along with the other journaling techniques, are supported on files residing on VAXes on a DECnet network, provided that RMS journaling software is loaded on all the participating nodes. This facilitates design of distributed database applications.

To appreciate the power of RU journaling, consider the quintessential debit/credit transaction. A bank has two RMS indexed files for customer savings and checking accounts. Suppose a customer uses an ATM connected to our VAX system and transfers $500 from his checking to his savings account. The program running on the VAX would subtract $500 from the balance field of the customer's record in the checking file and then add $500 to the corresponding field in the savings file. Obviously, this constitutes two separate RMS operations. If the system fails after the checking file is updated but before the savings file is updated, the files would be in an inconsistent state—the customer "loses" $500 from his savings account. This problem can be alleviated if RU journaling is used on these two files and the program is written appropriately. Note that AI and BI journaling do not solve the problem. To use RU journaling, the two files should be marked by:

```
$ SET  FILE  /RU_JOURNAL  database_disk:savings.account
$ SET  FILE  /RU_JOURNAL  database_disk:checking.account
```

The programmer then encloses the set of RMS operations, which constitute a transaction within the two system service calls:

```
$START_TRANS
```

and

```
$END_TRANS
```

The RMS journaling software (working with the distributed transaction manager—DECdtm) will consider all journalable RMS operations between the two system service calls to be one atomic operation. The system guarantees that the transaction will be either completely done or not done at all, even if the system fails during the operation.

19.4.5 Other issues

- More than one type of journaling can be applied to data files.
- The same journal file can be used for multiple data files.

- The /UNTIL qualifier can be used during recovery for any type of journaling.

- If RU journaling is combined with AI and/or BU journaling, the data files are restored during recovery in such a way that transaction consistency is maintained.

- The $ABORT_TRANS system service allows a transaction started by a $START_TRANS to be logically aborted so that the transaction operations are rolled back.

- RMS Journaling cooperates with DECdtm software to support distributed transaction processing.

- RMS Journaling is supported on a VAXcluster where multiple nodes may update common database files.

- The DIR/FULL command applied to a data file displays journaling flags on the file. See Fig. 19.3.

19.5 DECdtm—Distributed Transaction Manager

DECdtm is a software component of VMS. It uses the standard two-phase commit protocol (2pc) for ensuring integrity of databases distributed on VAXes interconnected by a DECnet network. DECdtm is just a *transaction manager*; it works in close conjunction with resource managers on individual VAXes on the network. Currently supported resource managers are RMS journaling, Rdb, VAX DBMS, ACMS, DECintact, RALLY, and VAX

Figure 19.3 Attributes on a file with AI, BI and RU RMS journaling enabled.

```
$ DIR/FULL  RMSJNL.TMP


Directory SYS$SYSDEVICE:[SHAHJ]


RMSJNL.TMP;1                   File ID:  (544,18,0)

Size:          3/3       Owner:    [1,1]

Created:   19-MAR-1991 12:05:24.38

Revised:   19-MAR-1991 12:05:27.84 (2)

Expires:   <None specified>

Backup:    19-MAR-1991 12:05:34.07

File organization:  Indexed, Prolog: 3, Using 1 key

File attributes:    Allocation: 3, Extend: 0, Maximum bucket size: 2

                    Global buffer count: 0. No version limit
```

Figure 19.3 (*Continued*)

```
Record format:        Fixed length 18 byte records

Record attributes:    Carriage return carriage control

RMS attributes:       None

Journaling enabled:   AI, BI, RU

AI journal file:      DISK$VAXVMSRL054:[SHAHJ]RMSJNL$AI.RMS$JOURNAL;1

BI journal file:      DISK$VAXVMSRL054:[SHAHJ]RMSJNL$BI.RMS$JOURNAL;1

File protection:      System:RWED, Owner:RWED, Group:RE, World:

Access Cntrl List:    (RMS_AI_JOURNAL,JOURNAL_FILE=DISK$VAXVMSRL054:[SHAHJ]

                      RMSJNL$AI.RMS$JOURNAL;1,JOURNAL_LEVEL=1,

                      JOURNAL_CREATION_DATE=19-MAR-1991:12:05:26.50,

                      JOURNAL_STREAM_INDEX=1,BACKUP_SEQUENCE_NUMBER=1,

                      JOURNAL_CONSISTENCY_DATE=17-NOV-1858:00:00:00.00,

                      JOURNALING_OPTIONS=BACKUP_PERFORMED,OPTIONS=HIDDEN+

                      PROTECTED+NOPROPAGATE)

                      (RMS_BI_JOURNAL,JOURNAL_FILE=DISK$VAXVMSRL054:[SHAHJ]

                      RMSJNL$BI.RMS$JOURNAL;1,JOURNAL_LEVEL=1,

                      JOURNAL_CREATION_DATE=19-MAR-1991:12:05:27.19,

                      JOURNAL_STREAM_INDEX=1,BACKUP_SEQUENCE_NUMBER=1,

                      JOURNAL_CONSISTENCY_DATE=17-NOV-1858:00:00:00.00,

                      JOURNALING_OPTIONS=BACKUP_PERFORMED,OPTIONS=HIDDEN+

                      PROTECTED+NOPROPAGATE)
```

SQL. Third-party database systems cannot be converted for distributed applications using DECdtm because the design of DECdtm is proprietary.

From a programmer's point of view, DECdtm comes into play when the following system services are used:

```
$START_TRANS  !Start a transaction
$END_TRANS    !Commit the transaction
$ABORT_TRANS  !Backout current transaction
```

Synchronous forms of the three system services can also be used:

```
$START_TRANSW !Start a transaction
$END_TRANSW   !Commit the transaction
$ABORT_TRANSW !Backout current transaction
```

These three services are similar to the corresponding ones shown previously, except that the program using a service waits until the service has completed execution. It's somewhat like the QIO and QIOW system services for I/O.

DECdtm generates a unique transaction identifier (TID) for each $START_TRANS or $START_TRANSW call issued from any program on the VAX. Transactions are tracked by TIDs. Each node on the network (and VAXcluster) has a separate log file where transaction information is maintained by DECdtm.

Programmers can convert current simple RMS applications on single nodes for operation in a transaction-processing-oriented, high-availability distributed environment by using RMS journaling. RMS journaling can be used on files across a network by specifying the node name in the data file specifications, as in:

```
VAX3::database_disk:savings.account
```

19.6   VAXft Fault-Tolerant VAXes

In 1990, DEC announced a fault-tolerant series of VAX systems called the VAX*ft*. These systems are truly fault tolerant in the sense that all critical hardware is completely duplicated and no special software coding is required; VAX/VMS and standard applications on the non-fault-tolerant VAXes can be run on VAX*ft*s without any code modifications. Currently, VAX*ft*s range from the model 110 rated at 2.5 VAX Units of Processing (VUPs) to the model 612 rated at 12 VUPs.

An example computer is the VAX*ft* Model 310. The computer is rated at 3.8 VAX Units of Processing (VUPs), which means the CPU speed is 3.8 times that of a VAX 11/780 CPU. Each computer includes two sets of components called *zones*. Typically, a zone contains a VAX CPU, memory and controllers. Each zone is in a separate cabinet. The zones are interconnected by high-speed cables that allow the two computers, one in each zone, to run in "lock step." The CPUs in the two zones run synchronously, executing the same instruction at the same time. Failure of a single hardware component in a zone cannot affect an application because the other zone will continue to operate. In fact, a complete zone can fail and still the users will not be affected. Each zone also has an Uninterruptible Power Supply (UPS) that allows the zone to operate for up to 15 minutes in a 24 hour period without any external power supply.

Figure 19.4 shows a VAX*ft* system. Each zone has its own VAX CPU and memory. The disks are shadowed (mirrored), so that a logical disk consists of multiple physical disks with the same data on them. Failure of a disk does not affect running applications because data is then accessed through the other shadow member or members. One Ethernet port in each zone is connected to the Ethernet network. That way, terminals and other Ethernet devices are redundantly connected to the computer. Two separate Ethernet

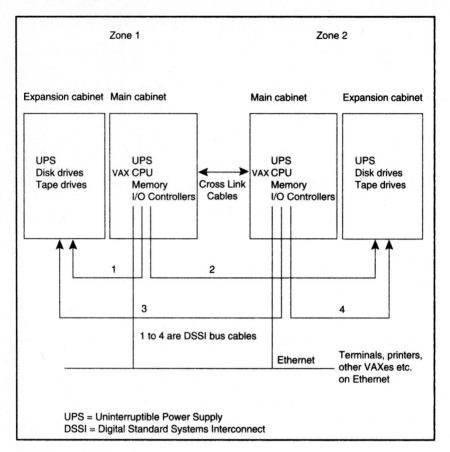

Figure 19.4 A VAXft model 310 system.

segments can be set up, in which case two Ethernet ports from each zone can be connected to the segments. Such a configuration will tolerate failure of an Ethernet segment. The tape drive subsystem is not fault tolerant.

The VAX*ft* systems can be part of a network of VAXes. They can also participate in local area or mixed-interconnect VAXclusters (but not in CI-based VAXclusters).

Here are a few comments on the VAX*ft* systems:

- The systems are relatively expensive because of the hardware redundancy.

- The two CPUs run synchronously (in lock-step). On the Model 310, each CPU is rated at a speed of 3.8 VUPs, and the aggregate throughput is also the same.

- Because the two CPUs run synchronously, a timing-related software bug can cause the CPUs in both zones to crash together.

- The redundancy scheme cannot handle multiple hardware failures of the same type. For example, the computer cannot be configured to accommodate two CPU failures. More than two zones cannot be interconnected to create an even more reliable system.

19.7 SMP—Symmetric Multiprocessing

Many of the high-end VAXes have more than one VAX processor sharing physical memory. The VAX 6000 and 9000 series VAXes support such multiprocessing. For example, the VAX 6000-440 has four processors in the same cabinet enclosure. The VAX/VMS operating system, starting from version 5.0, has been designed to exploit the processing power of all the processors in the VAX. The operating system code and processes can be executed on any processor. The technique is called *symmetric multiprocessing*. An exception: some I/O related low-level code is executed only on one processor, called the *primary processor*. This is because hardware interrupts can be generated only on the primary processor. VAX/VMS uses all the processors when scheduling user programs, however, normally this is transparent to the user. Individual member VAXes on a VAXcluster can have multiple processors.

A single program normally runs on one processor only. The operating system will run multiple programs (within the context of software processes) on multiple processors with each program on one processor. Programmers can write explicit code (with the help of the PPL$ system library routines) to have their programs use multiple processors for faster processing (less elapsed time). Usually, this is cumbersome. Fortunately, the C language compiler generates parallelized code for some sets of statements (typically compute intensive loop statements). It should be noted that multiprocessing has more overhead than single-processor processing for the same program. Hence, on a system running a number of programs, usually, the overall throughput will be less if programs are parallelized than if the programs are allowed to run with each program on only one processor. To parallelize code, the /PARALLEL qualifier is required during compilation. VAX C attempts to parallelize for and while loops (but not do loops).

19.8 Vector Processing

Vector processing is optionally supported on the VAX 6000 and 9000 series systems. The basic VAX architecture has been extended to include about 63 new vector processing instructions and a set of vector registers. Compute intensive applications like scientific, engineering and stock market analytics will run faster if the hardware vector processor is used. Vector processing and multiprocessing is supported within the same processor complex. Individual member VAXes on a VAXcluster can have vector processors (and multiple ordinary processors).

19.9   Macro Output from Compilations

VAX C produces readable assembly language code in the listing file if the /MACHINE_CODE compilation qualifier is specified. Note that the /LIST qualifier is required to produce a listing file. The output may be intimidating to a novice programmer; however, it provides a useful insight into how the program executes at the machine level, and it's a powerful debugging tool. Using such assembly language listings, I've optimized many programs and found why some C statements performed operations that I didn't intend. Figure 19.5 shows a C program that's been used in previous chapters, and Fig. 19.6 shows the program's listing file with machine code. The listing file was produced by the command:

```
$ CC COLLAPSE/LIST/MACHINE_CODE
```

A typical line in the listing is:

```
53 50 8F 9A     00D2     movzbl  #80,r3
```

near line number 962. The code is generated for the C statement:

```
wrap_width=80;
```

In the code line, 53 50 8F 9A is the machine language code for movzbl #80,r3. The code MUST BE READ RIGHT TO LEFT. 00D2 is the (hex) virtual memory location where the code will reside during program execution. The instruction converts the number 80, considered a byte, to a longword by zero-filling the most significant bits, and then moves this longword to CPU register R3. Obviously, R3 corresponds to the variable wrap_width.

Figure 19.5 The program collapse.c.

```
/* File: collapse.c        Author: Jay Shah
 * This program collapses long lines in a file down to 80 columns
 * or any other specified column position. The program can be used
 * when terminals and printers cannot display files with long lines.
 *
 * When the program is run, the user will be prompted for an
```

Figure 19.5 *(Continued)*

```
* input file name, output file name and wrap column number.
*
* Usage of variables:
*
 * infile          - attributes of input file, FILE variable
 * outfile         - attributes of output file, FILE variable
 * line_length     - length of a input line
 * last_line_length - length of last line to be written to
 *                    to output file for each input line
 * current_pos     - current position in input line buffer
 * wrap_width      - width at which lines from input file should
                     be wrapped if the lines exceed this width
 * inp_buffer      - buffer for each line from input file
 * out_buffer      - buffer for each line for output file
 * inp_filename    - buffer for input file name
 * out_filename    - buffer for output file name
*/


#include stdio            /* for the standard I/O performed here */
#include ssdef            /* system error messages */


main()
   {

   FILE *infile;              /* handler for input file */
   FILE *outfile;             /* handler for output file */
   int line_length, last_line_length;
   int current_pos, wrap_width;
  char inp_buffer[10000], out_buffer[10000];
  char inp_filename[80], out_filename[80];


  printf("Program to collapse long lines in a given file\n")


  /* Get input file name and open the file in read mode */
  printf("input file: ");
  if ((infile = fopen(gets(inp_filename),"r")) <= 0)
```

Figure 19.5 *(Continued)*

```
    { perror("fopen:input");exit();
    };


/* Get output file name and open the file in write mode
 * Default file name is same as input file name. */
printf("output file (default %s): ",inp_filename);
gets(out_filename);
if (strlen(out_filename) == 0)
    { strcpy(out_filename,inp_filename);
    };
if ((outfile = fopen(out_filename,"w")) <= 0)
    { perror("fopen:output");exit();
    };


/* Get column at which to wrap around long lines */
printf("Wrap at column (default 80): ");
wrap_width=atoi(gets(inp_filename));
if (wrap_width<=0) wrap_width=80;


/* Now process the input file */


/* Repeat for each line in input file */
while (fgets(inp_buffer,10000,infile) != 0)
    {

    /* linefeed at end of input line is ignored */
    line_length = strlen(inp_buffer) - 1;
    current_pos = 0;

    /* Repeat for each line to be output,
       except for last output line */
    while (current_pos+wrap_width  < line_length)
        {
        strncpy(&out_buffer,&inp_buffer[current_pos],wrap_width);
        fprintf(outfile,"%s\n",&out_buffer);
        current_pos = current_pos + wrap_width;
```

Figure 19.5 *(Continued)*

```
    }; /* end of while */


/* last output line corresponding to the input line */
last_line_length = line_length - current_pos;

    strncpy(out_buffer,&inp_buffer[current_pos],last_line_length);
    out_buffer[last_line_length] = 0;
    fprintf(outfile,"%s\n",&out_buffer);
    } /* end of while */

}
```

Compiler and Linker Options

A1.1 Compiler Options

C source files have a file type of `.c`. The compiler generates an object file of
file type `.obj`. Optionally, a listing file of file type `.LIS` can be produced.
The C compilation command syntax is:

```
$  CC  qualifiers  parameters
```

Examples are:

```
$  CC  myfile
$  CC  /DEBUG  cheaders.tlb/LIBRARY+myfile.c
$  CC  /LIST/SHOW=ALL  myfile1.c+myfile2.c
$  CC  myfile1,myfile2
```

Parameters are file-specs or library-file-specs.

file-specs

One or more VAX C source files separated by plus signs or commas. If
plus signs are used, the input files are concatenated into a single object

file. If commas are used, each file is compiled separately to create separate object files. If the file extension is not specified, .C is assumed.

library-file specs

A text library containing #include modules referenced in one or more of the source files. A library file specification must be concatenated with a file specification with a plus sign and qualified using the /LIBRARY qualifier. If the file extension is not specified, .TLB is assumed.

Qualifiers are preceded by a /. Here are the qualifiers.

Qualifiers

/ANALYSIS_DATA

If specified, a source code analysis file is produced. The file is used by the SCA (Source Code Analyzer) utility. The default filename is the same as that of the source file; the file type is .ANA. A filename can be specified by /ANALYSIS_DATA=filename.type. Default is /NOANALYSIS_DATA.

/CROSS_REFERENCE

If specified, all variables are listed along with the line number where the variable is referenced. The output is in the listing file. The /LIST qualifier is required. Also, either /SHOW=BRIEF or /SHOW=SYMBOLS is required. Default is /NOCROSS_REFERENCE.

/DEBUG

If specified, debugging information is included in the object file for use by the VAX Symbolic Debugger. Options can be specified as:

/DEBUG=ALL	Includes all possible debug information.
/DEBUG=INLINE	Tells the compiler to generate debug information to cause a STEP to step into the inlined function call.
/DEBUG=NOINLINE	Tells the compiler to generate debug information to cause a STEP to step over the inlined function call.
/DEBUG=NONE	Do not include any debugging information.
/DEBUG=NOTRACEBACK	Do not include traceback records.
/DEBUG=TRACEBACK	Include only traceback records.

If only /DEBUG is specified then /DEBUG=NOINLINE is assumed
Default is /NODEBUG.

/DEFINE

/DEFINE performs the same function as the #define preprocessor directive. That is, /DEFINE defines a token string or macro to be substituted for every occurrence of a given identifier in the program. Proper syntax is:

```
/DEFINE=(identifier[=definition][,...])
```

An example is:

```
/DEFINE=(var1=5,MACHINE="vaxc")
```

The simplest form of a /DEFINE definition is:

```
/DEFINE=true
```

which is equivalent to:

```
#define TRUE 1
```

Macro definitions must be enclosed in quotation marks, as in:

```
/DEFINE="recip(x)=1/x"
```

which is equivalent to:

```
#define recip(x) 1/x
```

When both /DEFINE and /UNDEFINE are present in a command line, /DEFINE is evaluated before /UNDEFINE. Default is /NODEFINE.

/DESIGN

The /DESIGN qualifier determines whether the compiler processes the input file as a detailed design. If you specify the /DESIGN qualifier, the compiler modifies its parsing and semantics according to keywords you supply. This qualifier is intended for use in conjunction with the VAXset Program Design Facility. The proper syntax is:

```
/DESIGN[=(keyword[,...])]
```

where keywords are:

COMMENTS   Determines whether the compiler searches inside comment for program design information. The default is COMMENTS.

PLACEHOLDERS   Determines whether the compiler treats placeholders within the program as valid syntax. The default is PLACEHOLDERS.

Default is /DESIGN=(COMMENTS, PLACEHOLDERS).

/DIAGNOSTICS

The /DIAGNOSTICS qualifier creates a file containing compiler messages and diagnostic information. The file is used by the Language Sensitive Editor (LSE). The default file extension for a diagnostics file is .DIA. A file can be specified as /DIAGNOSTICS=filename.type. Default is /NODIAGNOSTICS.

/G_FLOAT

Controls the format of floating-point variables. When /G_FLOAT is not specified, double variables are represented in D-float format. When /G_FLOAT is specified, all variables declared as double are represented in G-float format. A program compiled with /G_FLOAT must be linked with the G-float library, VAXCRTLG.OLB. This library must be specified so that it's searched before VAXCRTL.OLB.

/INCLUDE_DIRECTORY

Provides an additional level of search for user-defined include files. The proper syntax is:

```
/INCLUDE_DIRECTORY=(pathname [,pathname...]]
```

The qualifier provides UNIX functionality and allows you to specify additional directories to search for include files. The forms of inclusion are the #include "file-spec" and #include <file-spec>. For the quoted form, the order of search is as follows:

1. The directory containing the source file.

2. The directories specified in the /INCLUDE qualifier.

3. The directory or search list of directories specified in the logical name C$INCLUDE.

For the bracketed form, the order of search is as follows:

1. The directories specified in the `/INCLUDE` qualifier.
2. The directory or search list of directories specified in the logical name `VAXC$INCLUDE`.
3. If `VAXC$INCLUDE` is not defined, then the directory or search list of directories specified by `SYS$LIBRARY`.

Default is `/NOINCLUDE_DIRECTORY`.

`/LIBRARY`

Indicates that the associated input file is a library containing source text modules specified in `#include` directives. The compiler searches the specified library for all `#include` module names that are not enclosed in angle brackets or quotation marks. The name of the library must be concatenated with the file specification using a plus sign. For example:

```
$ CC cheaders.tlb/library+myfile.c
```

`/LIST`

If specified, a listing file is produced. Output file name is same as source file name, file type is .LIS. An output file can be specified by `/LIST=filename.type`. Default for interactive compilations is `/NOLIST`; for batch compilations it's `/LIST`.

`/MACHINE_CODE`

If specified, the listing produced by the compiler includes the machine language code generated during the compilation. The `/LIST` qualifier is required. The proper syntax is:

`/MACHINE_CODE=[option]`, where options are:

AFTER	The machine code produced during compilation prints after the source code listing.
BEFORE	The machine code prints before the source code listing.
INTERSPERSED	The lines of machine code print alternately with the lines of source code.

If `/MACHINE_CODE` is specified, `/MACHINE_CODE=INTERSPERSED` is assumed. Default is `/NOMACHINE_CODE`.

/NAME
Specifies whether the compiler translates all external symbol names to uppercase, lowercase or leaves the case unchanged. Proper syntax is:

/NAME=option
Options are UPPERCASE, LOWERCASE and AS_IS. /NAME=UPPER
CASE causes all external names to be converted to uppercase. /NAME=LOWERCASE causes all external names to be converted to lowercase. /NAME=AS_IS leaves the case of external names unchanged. Default is /NAME=UPPERCASE.

/OBJECT
If specified, an object file is produced. Output file name is the same as source file name;, file type is .OBJ. An output file can be specified by /OBJECT=filename.type. Default is /NOOBJECT.

/OPTIMIZE
If specified, optimization is performed by the compiler. /NOOPTIMIZE turns off the /PARALLEL qualifier. The proper syntax is:

/OPTIMIZE=[option]

The two options are:

DISJOINT   Directs the compiler to optimize the generated machine code.

INLINE   Specifies whether the compiler is allowed to perform inline expansion of functions.

Default is /OPTIMIZE, which is the same as:

/OPTIMIZE=(DISJOINT,INLINE)

/PARALLEL
Specifies whether the compiler should perform dependency analysis on loops in the program and generate optimized code to run on a multiprocessor system for loops with no dependencies. Default is /NOPARAL
LEL.

/PRECISION
If /PRECISION=SINGLE is specified, floating-point operations on float variables are performed in single precision. Double precision is used if the default /PRECISION=DOUBLE is specified.

/PREPROCESS_ONLY
> Causes the compiler to perform only the actions of the preprocessor phase and to write the resulting processed text out to a file with a default file type of .I. A file can be specified as in /PREPROCESS_ONLY=file name.type. Default is /NOPREPROCESS_ONLY.

/SHOW
> This qualifier is used with the /LIST qualifier to set or cancel specific listing options. Proper syntax is:
>
> /SHOW=(option,...)
>
> where options are:

ALL	Print all listing information.
BRIEF	Print a brief symbol table, listing only those identifiers that are referenced in the program.
DECOMPOSITION	Show a summary of the loops that were decomposed. /PARALLEL required.
DICTIONARY	Print Common Data Dictionary (CDD) definitions.
EXPANSION	Print macro expansions.
INCLUDE	Print contents of #include files.
INTERMEDIATE	Print intermediate macro expansions.
NONE	Print no listing information.
SOURCE	Print source file statements. NOSOURCE disables printing of source file statements.
STATISTICS	Print compiler performance statistics.
SYMBOLS	Print symbol table.
TERMINAL	Display compiler messages at the terminal. If NOTERMINAL is specified, only the summary message is displayed.
TRANSLATION	Display the translation of a UNIX system file specification to a VAX/VMS file specification.

Default is /SHOW=SOURCE.

/STANDARD

Specifies whether the compiler is to generate messages to flag VAX C specific constructs and deviation from conventional C constructs and rules (PORTABLE), or not to generate such messages (NOPORTABLE). Default is /STANDARD=NOPORTABLE.

/UNDEFINE

The qualifier performs the same function as the #undef preprocessor directive—it cancels a macro definition. Proper syntax is:

```
/UNDEFINE=(identifier[,...])
```

The qualifier is useful for undefining the predefined VAX C preprocessor constants. For example, if you use a preprocessor constant like de bug_flag, to conditionally compile segments of VAX C specific code, you can undefine constants to see how the portable sections of your program execute. For example:

```
/UNDEFINE="debug_flag"
```

When both /DEFINE and /UNDEFINE are present on the CC command line, /DEFINE is evaluated before /UNDEFINE. Default is /NOUNDE FINE.

/WARNINGS

If specified, compiler prints warning diagnostic messages, informational diagnostic messages, neither, or both. Proper syntax is:

```
/WARNING[=option]
```

where options are NOINFORMATIONALS and NOWARNINGS. The /WARNINGS qualifier alone forces the compiler to print both informationals and warnings (the same as if no qualifier were used on the command line). The /NOWARNINGS qualifier forces the compiler to suppress both informationals and warnings. The /WARNINGS=NOINFORMATION ALS qualifier forces the compiler to suppress the informationals. The /WARNINGS=NOWARNINGS qualifier forces the compiler to suppress warnings. Default is /WARNINGS.

A1.2 Linker Options

The Linker input file is of type `.obj`. The output file from the linker is
`.EXE`. Optionally, the linker may produce a `.MAP` file.
The `LINK` command syntax is:

```
$ LINK qualifiers  parameters
```

Examples are:

```
$ LINK  myfile, sys$library:vaxcrtl.olb/LIBRARY

$ LINK  myfile, sys$input:/OPTIONS
sys$share:vaxcrtl.exe/share

$ LINK  /DEBUG myfile1,myfile2
```

Linker parameters are filenames separated by commas or plus signs.
Both commas and plus signs are equivalent. Some of the commonly used
qualifiers are shown here.

Qualifiers

`/BRIEF`
  If specified, the linker produces a brief map (memory allocation) file; the
  `/BRIEF` qualifier is valid only with the `/MAP` qualifier. A brief form of the
  map contains the following information:

- A summary of the image characteristics.
- A list of all object modules included in the image.
- A summary of link-time performance statistics.

`/CROSS_REFERENCE`
  If specified, the memory allocation listing (map) contains a symbol cross-
  reference list with entries for each global symbol referenced in the image,
  its value, and all modules in the image that refer to it.

`/DEBUG`
  If specified, debugger is included in the output image and the VAX Symbolic Debugger is linked with the image.

/FULL
  Produces a full memory allocation (map) listing; the /FULL qualifier is
  valid only with /MAP qualifier.
  A full listing contains the following information:

- All the information included in a brief listing (see the description of
  the /BRIEF qualifier).

- Detailed descriptions of each program section and image section in
  the image file.

- Lists of global symbols by name and by value.

/LIBRARY
  Indicates that the associated input file is a library (default file type
  .OLB), whose modules should be searched to resolve undefined symbols.

/MAP
  If specified, a memory allocation listing (map) is produced. In interactive
  mode, the default qualifier is /NOMAP; in batch mode, the default qualifier is /MAP.
  You can specify the map's contents using either the /BRIEF, the /FULL,
  or the /CROSS_REFERENCE qualifier. If you do not specify any of these
  qualifiers, the map contains the following information:

- All the information contained in a brief listing (see /BRIEF).

- A list of user-defined global symbols by name.

- A list of user-defined program sections.

/OPTIONS
  Indicates that the associated input file (default file type .OPT) contains
  a list of linking options. If the file is sys$input:, user input is considered
  the options file.

For complete details on the contents of an options file and other linker features see the *VMS Linker Utility Manual*.

Installing the C Compiler

Here's a sample installation of the C compiler. The compiler is installed from tape drive MUA0:, using the VMSINSTAL utility. Default answers have been used for most questions.

```
$ @SYS$UPDATE:VMSINSTAL

        VAX/VMS Software Product Installation Procedure V5.4
It is 24-JAN-1992 at 12:29.
Enter a question mark (?) at any time for help.

* Are you satisfied with the backup of your system disk [YES]?
* Where will the distribution volumes be mounted: MUA2:

Enter the products to be processed from the first distribution volume
set.
* Products: VAXC
* Enter installation options you wish to use (none):
The following products will be processed:

  VAXC V3.2

    Beginning installation of VAXC V3.2 at 12:30

%VMSINSTAL-I-RESTORE, Restoring product save set A ...
%VMSINSTAL-I-RELMOVED, Product's release notes have been moved to
SYS$HELP.
```

```
VAX C V3.2-044 Installation is commencing ...

Product:       C
Producer:      DEC
Version:       3.2
Release Date:  01-JUL-1990
```

* Does this product have an authorization key registered and loaded? Yes

This kit contains an Installation Verification Procedure
(IVP) to verify the correct installation of the VAX C
compiler.

After the installation is complete, you can invoke the
IVP at any time to reverify that VAX C is installed
and working correctly by executing the command:

```
@SYS$TEST:VAXC$IVP
```

* Do you want to run the IVP after the installation [YES]?
* Do you want to purge files replaced by this installation [YES]?
* Do you want to extract .H files from the text library [YES]?
* Do you want to install the DECwindows Compiler Interface for C [YES]?

To allow the use of VAX C to implement portable programming
interfaces that conform to the NAS Architecture, special
VAX C RTL object libraries can be provided as part of this
installation. It is not necessary to install these libraries
if you do not intend to program to the NAS Architecture.

Please see the NAS Application Style Guide for more details
on the NAS Architecture.

* Do you wish to install the RTL object libraries containing NAS sup
port [NO]?

All the questions regarding the installation have
now been asked. The installation will now continue
for between 20 and 60 minutes, depending on your
CPU type and the installation options you have
chosen.

%VMSINSTAL-I-RESTORE, Restoring product save set B ...
   VAX C V3.2-044 : copying images, libraries and release notes.
   VAX C V3.2-044 : Installing DECwindows Compiler Interface for C.
   VAX C V3.2-044 : extracting .H files.

   A summary of the Software Performance Reports (SPRs) for this release
   can be found in the file SYS$LIBRARY:VAXCSPR.DAT.

%VMSINSTAL-I-SYSDIR, This product creates system disk directory
                                    VMI$ROOT:[SYSTEST.VAXC].

   VAX C V3.2-044 Installation is completed.

   Your VMS system will now be updated to include the following new
   and modified files:

```
SYS$SYSTEM:VAXC.EXE              [new]
SYS$LIBRARY:VAXCDEF.TLB          [new]
SYS$LIBRARY:VAXCSPR.DAT          [new]
```

```
SYS$MESSAGE:VAXCERR.EXE                    [new]
SYS$HELP:VAXC032.RELEASE__NOTES            [new]
SYS$HELP:HELPLIB.HLB                       [modified]
SYS$LIBRARY:DCLTABLES.EXE                  [modified]
SYS$COMMON:[SYSTEST]VAXC$IVP.COM           [new]
SYS$COMMON:[SYSTEST.VAXC]VAXCIVPP.C        [new]
SYS$COMMON:[SYSTEST.VAXC]VAXCIVPC.C        [new]
VUE$LIBRARY:CC$DWCI.EXE                    [new]
VUE$LIBRARY:CC$DWCI.UID                    [new]
SYS$HELP:CC$DWCI.HLB                       [new]
```
%VMSINSTAL-I-MOVEFILES, Files will now be moved to their target direc
tories...

VAX C V3.2-044 Installation Verification Procedure commencing ...
****** VAX C Installation Certification Procedure SUCCESSFUL ******
VAX C V3.2-044 Installation Verification Procedure completed suc
cessfully.

Installation of VAXC V3.2 completed at 12:46

3

A Complete Utility

This chapter shows the files used to create a complete, professional-quality utility. The utility is called `SUBSTITUTE`. It allows users to substitute one string of characters for another in one or more files. For example:

```
$ SUBSTITUTE myfile.doc labal label
```

will replace all occurrences of `labal` with `label` in the file `myfile.doc` (a new version of the file is created). The basic files used to install this utility on a VAX/VMS system are:

- `SUBSTITUTE.C`   The C program.
- `SUBSTITUTE.CLD` The DCL command.
- `SUBSTITUTE.HLP` The HELP.

A few other files are required to make a "shrink wrap" product for wide distribution.

- `KITINSTAL.COM`.   Used to create a `VMSINSTAL` tape for the utility. See chapter 2 on how to integrate C applications with VMS.
- `SUBSTITUTE011.RELEASE_NOTES`.   Inserted in `SYS$HELP:` when the

utility is installed. Usually contains information pertaining to the current release or which was not included in the manual.

■ SUBSTITUTE manual.

A3.1 SUBSTITUTE.C

The C program is the most important component of the utility. The SUBSTI TUTE utility consists of one program file; however, most major applications will consist of multiple program modules. The SUBSTITUTE program is shown in Fig. A3.1.

Figure A3.1 SUBSTITUTE.C.

```
/*  SUBSTITUTE.C      Jay Shah      22-Jan-1992

 *

 * Utility to substitute one string by another in a set of

 * files. An example command line is

 *

 * $ SUBSTITUTE  myfile.txt  "oldstr" "newstr"

 *

 * Files can be specified as wildcards.

 *

 ***********************************************************

 * functions in this file:

 *

 * validateusage()       validate usage of this utility by

 *                       checking expiration date.

 * dumpline()            convert non-printable characters to

 *                       mnemonic forms and print line.

 * strnustr()            search for substring in

 *                       sourcestring. Comparison in

 *                       uppercase.

 * strnstr()             search for substring in source

 *                       string.

 * jay_strstr()          Like the C RTL strstr().

 * cpynbyt()             Copy n bytes from source string to

 *                       destination string. Copies NULLs if

 *                       present.

 * cpynbyt_reverse()     Copy n bytes from source string to
```

Figure A3.1 *(Continued)*

```
*                       destination string starting at end
*                       of strings. Copies NULLs if present.
* get_confirm_rep()     get user response on whether a
*                       replacement should be performed.
* get_confirm_file()    get user response on whether
*                       replacements should be performed in
*                       specified file.
* closefiles()          close one input and one output file,
*                       print replacement statistics if flag on.
* performreplace()      perform one replacement
* processonefile()      process one input file for
*                       replacements.
* main()                evaluate all command line
*                       information (like /CONFIRM),
*                       create temporary file containing
*                       list of files to be processed.
*                       Note that program execution starts
*                       at main().
*
************************************************************
* Overall algorithm
* -----------------
*
* Check if utility has expired. (Useful if utility
* is licensed for use upto a specific date).
*
* Current version of utility uses DIRECTORY/OUTPUT
* command to create a file containing list of files
* to be processed by the utility. This is because
* handling wildcards is tricky. (Consider the
* command
*
* $ substitute  ab*.doc,[...bac...]dd%ef*.txt*,[0,0]m.n  -
*               oldstr newstr
*
* where the filespec requires extensive parsing).
```

Figure A3.1 *(Continued)*

```
* You can modify this portion of the utility using
* the system service LIB$FIND_FILE to make it more
* elegant.
*
* In this program, depending on qualifiers
* specified, a command like the following is SPAWNED
* to create a directory file containing a list of
* files to be processed:
*
* DIRECTORY *.LST/BEFORE:TODAY/VERSION=1/NOHEADER/NOTRAILER
* /OUTPUT:SYS$SYSDEVICE:[SHAHJ.SUBST]-
* SUBST_31-OCT-1992_16_57-25_05.LIST
*
* All qualifiers are then processed and the source
* and replacement strings are read in. For each file
* in the directory file, processonefile() is called.
* At end, statistics are displayed.
*
* processonefile() sets up RMS information of input
* file, checks that the file is sequential (and so
* on), opens output file with filename same as
* input file but file type of .REPLACETEMP. When
* substitutions have been performed on the file, the
* output file is renamed as a new version of the
* input file. This is required because a power
* failure (or a control-Y and similar aborts) when
* replacing text in a large file may leave the
* output file incomplete. If this output file were a
* new version of the old file, a subsequent PURGE
* command will cause loss of data.
*
* Other comments
* --------------
*
* A few functions line cpynbyt() are similar to C
* RTL functions, however, C functions have one
```

Figure A3.1 *(Continued)*

```
* severe limitation; they do not handle 0 bytes

* (NULLs). If a line contains a byte with 0, C

* assumes that terminates the line. NULLS as part of

* strings are not handled well by C functions.

*

* The output of the DIRECTORY command which is

* spawned by this program goes into [.SUBST] within

* the users top level directory which is determined

* from the logical SYS$LOGIN.

*/


#include stdio

#include iodef

#include rms

#include climsgdef

#include descrip

#include lnmdef

#include dvidef

#include ttdef

#include tt2def


/*

 * Variables declared here:

 *

 * aclbuf[500]            ACLs from input file copied to output file

 * actual_repstr[255]     replacement string after case conversion

 * bracket_pos            "]" position in file name string

 * chan                   terminal I/O channel

 * confirm_file           user input on whether file should be processed

 * confirm_rep            user input on whether to replace or not

 * datelimit              disable utility if used after this date

 * devchar2               terminal characteristic to see if ANSICRT

 * dirfile_line[255]      filespec for replacements processing

 * dot_pos                position of . in .filetype

 * dump_ascii             array of 256 pointers to printable

 *                        forms of ASCII characters
```

Figure A3.1 *(Continued)*

```
* exact                 substitution is case-sensitive

* expandedstr_inp       complete filespec of input file

* expandedstr_out       complete filespec of output file

* fabinp                RMS FAB of input file

* fabout                RMS FAB of output file

* filename_str          file with output of DIRECTORY command

* files_searched        files searched for substitute source string

* filesopened           not really used

* filesreplaced         number of files in which replacement was made

* init_confirm_rep      value represented by /REPLACECONFIRM on

*                       command line.

* inp_record[32500]     buffer for lines from input file

* itemlist              for terminal channel

* msg_bufadr[255]       used to get message corresponding to

*                       spawn status

* msg_bufadr_str        descriptor for msg_bufadr[255]

* msg_flags             used in sys$getmsg to specify error

*                       message fields to be returned.

* naminp                RMS NAM block of input file

* namout                RMS NAM block of output file

* offset                offset of character after search string

*                       in input line

* outfile[255]          output file with file type .REPLACETEMP

* posptr                current pointer position in input line

* rabinp                RMS RAB of input file

* rabout                RMS RAB of output file

* replace_files         number of files in which replacement

*                       was made, used to displayu statistics

* replacecnt            replacements made in one file

* replaceperformed      flag TRUE if any replacements done on file

* resp_*                possible response to "CONFIRM?"

* response[1000]        buffer for user input

* retlen                part of itemlist sub-variables

* rms_status            status of RMS calls

* rsiz                  size of input line

* spawn_outfile         NULL file for SPAWN output
```

Figure A3.1 *(Continued)*

```
* src_upper            not really used
* statistics           flag indicating whether statistics
*                      should be displayed
* status               status of system calls
* stringrep[255]       replacement string
* stringrep_len        replacement string length
* stringrep_lower[255] lowercase form of replacement string
* stringrep_upper[255] uppercase form of replacement string
* stringsize_diff      difference in size between source and
*                      replacement strings
* stringsrc[255]       source string
* stringsrc_len        source string length
* stringsrc_upper[255] uppercase form of source string
* terminal             descriptor for sys$input
* timadr1[8]           Next four variables for date & time
*                      in binary form for comparison
* timadr[8]
* timbuf1[7]
* timbuf[7]
* timeok               flag signifying if utility has expired
* tmpbyte              local byte variable
* tmppos               local short variable
* tmppos1              local short variable
* tmpptr               local character pointer
* tmpvar               local short variable
* total_replacecnt     replacements made in all files
* vfc_area[255]        Fixed area of RMS file copied to output
* vtterm               flag TRUE if terminal is ANSICRT
* xabproinp            RMS XABPRO of input file to handle ACLs
*/


/*beep rings bell on terminal */
#define beep printf("%c",'\07');
unsigned char dirfile_line[255], outfile[255];
int filesopened = 0, filesreplaced = 0;
unsigned char stringsrc[255], stringrep[255];
```

Figure A3.1 *(Continued)*

```
unsigned char stringsrc_upper[255], stringrep_upper[255],
            actual_repstr[255];
unsigned char stringrep_lower[255];
unsigned char src_upper;
short stringsrc_len, stringrep_len, stringsize_diff;


unsigned char filename[255];
char msg_bufadr[255];
struct    {
    unsigned short    length;
    unsigned char    dtype;
    unsigned char    dclass;

    char        *str;
    }
    filename_str = { 0, 14,1, filename},
    msg_bufadr_str  = {255,14,1, msg_bufadr};


short msglen;
int msg_flags = 7; /* message  text,identifier,severity */
$DESCRIPTOR (spawn_outfile,"NL:");


static struct FAB fabinp,fabout;
unsigned char inp_record[32500];
static struct RAB rabinp,rabout;
static struct NAM naminp,namout;
unsigned char aclbuf[500];
static struct XABPRO xabproinp;
unsigned char expandedstr_inp[NAM$C_MAXRSS];
unsigned char expandedstr_out[NAM$C_MAXRSS];
unsigned char vfc_area[255];
int rms_status, status;
short bracket_pos,dot_pos, tmppos, tmppos1, tmpvar;
unsigned char tmpbyte;
unsigned char *posptr,*tmpptr;
unsigned char response[1000], init_confirm_rep,
            confirm_rep, confirm_file;
```

Figure A3.1 *(Continued)*

```
unsigned char resp_yes[] = "YES", resp_no[] = "NO",
     resp_end[] = "END THIS FILE",
     resp_all[] = "ALL FILES", resp_last[] = "LAST",
     resp_cancel[] = "CANCEL THIS FILE", resp_quit[] = "QUIT";
unsigned char exact=FALSE, statistics=TRUE;
short rsiz, offset;


/* all this to check if we have a VT terminal */
$DESCRIPTOR (terminal,"sys$input");
short chan;
long devchar2,retlen;
struct       {
   short buflength;
   short item_code;
   long  devchar2adr;
   long  retlenadr;
   long  dummy;
   }
   itemlist = {4,DVI$_DEVDEPEND2,&devchar2,&retlen,0};
unsigned char vtterm;



unsigned char replaceperformed;
int replacecnt,total_replacecnt=0,replace_files=0,files_searched=0;
static unsigned char *dump_ascii[256] =
    {
    "<NUL>", "<SOH>", "<STX>", "<ETX>", "<EOT>", "<ENQ>", "<ACK>",
    "<BEL>", "<BS>", "<HT>", "<LF>", "<VT>", "<FF>", "<CR>",
    "<SO>", "<SI>", "<DLE>", "<DC1>", "<DC2>", "<DC3>", "<DC4>",
    "<NAK>", "<SYN>", "<ETB>", "<CAN>", "<EM>", "<SUB>", "<ESC>",
    "<FS>", "<GS>", "<RS>", "<US>", " ", "!", "\"",
    "#", "$", "%", "&", "'", "(", ")",
    "*", "+", ",", "-", ".", "/", "0",
    "1", "2", "3", "4", "5", "6", "7",
    "8", "9", ":", ";", "<", "=", ">",
    "?", "@", "A", "B", "C", "D", "E",
```

Figure A3.1 *(Continued)*

```
    "F", "G", "H", "I", "J", "K", "L",
    "M", "N", "O", "P", "Q", "R", "S",
    "T", "U", "V", "W", "X", "Y", "Z",
    "[", "\\", "]", "^", "_", "\", "a",
    "b", "c", "d", "e", "f", "g", "h",
    "i", "j", "k", "l", "m", "n", "o",
    "p", "q", "r", "s", "t", "u", "v",
    "w", "x", "y", "z", "{", "|", "}",
    "~", "<DEL>", "<x80>", "<x81>", "<x82>", "<x83>", "<IND>",
    "<NEL>", "<SSA>", "<ESA>", "<HTS>", "<HTJ>", "<VTS>", "<PLD>",
    "<PLU>", "<RI>", "<SS2>", "<SS3>", "<DCS>", "<PU1>", "<PU2>",
    "<STS>", "<CCH>", "<MW>", "<SPA>", "<EPA>", "<x98>", "<x99>",
    "<x9A>", "<CSI>", "<ST>", "<OSC>", "<PM>", "<APC>", "<xA0>",
    "¡", "¢", "£", "¤", "¥", "¦", "§",
    "¨", "©", "ª", "«", "¬", "", "®",
    "¯", "°", "±", "²", "³", "´", "µ",
    "¶", "·", "¸", "¹", "º", "»", "¼",
    "½", "¾", "¿", "À", "Á", "Â", "Ã",
    "Ä", "Å", "Æ", "Ç", "È", "É", "Ê",
    "Ë", "Ì", "Í", "Î", "Ï", "Ð", "Ñ",
    "Ò", "Ó", "Ô", "Õ", "Ö", "Œ", "Ø",
    "Ù", "Ú", "Û", "Ü", "Ÿ", "Þ", "ß",
    "à", "á", "â", "ã", "ä", "å", "æ",
    "ç", "è", "é", "ê", "ë", "ì", "í",
    "î", "ï", "ð", "ñ", "ò", "ó", "ô",
    "õ", "ö", "œ", "ø", "ù", "ú", "û",
    "ü", "ÿ", "þ", "<xFF>"
    };


unsigned char timadr[8],timadr1[8],i,timeok;
short timbuf[7],timbuf1[7];
$DESCRIPTOR (datelimit,"05-SEP-1999 12:00:00.00");


/**************************************************/
validateusage()
{
```

Figure A3.1 *(Continued)*

```
sys$gettim(timadr);              /*current time*/
if (status!=1) exit(status);
status= sys$numtim(timbuf,timadr);
if (status!=1) exit(status);


status = sys$bintim(&datelimit,timadr1);         /*limit time*/
if (status!=1) exit(status);
status= sys$numtim(timbuf1,timadr1);
if (status!=1) exit(status);
timeok=TRUE;
for (i=0;i<3;i++)
        {
        if (timbuf[i]>timbuf1[i])
                {
                timeok=FALSE;
                break;
                };
        if (timbuf[i]<timbuf1[i]) break;
        }
if (timeok==FALSE)
        {
        printf("Unauthorized usage of this package\n");
    beep;beep;
        exit();
            };


};


/*************************************************/
dumpline(lin,cnt)
unsigned char lin[];
short cnt;
{
/* print a line on terminal. Convert non printable
 * characters to mnemonic ASCII form as shown in the
 * array dump_ascii[256].
```

Figure A3.1 *(Continued)*

```
*/

    static short i,outlinesize;
    static unsigned char outline[2005];
    outlinesize = 0;

    for (i = 0; i<cnt; i++)
        {
        strcpy(&outline[outlinesize], dump_ascii[lin[i]]);
        outlinesize += strlen(dump_ascii[lin[i]]);
        if (outlinesize > 1999)
            {
            outline[outlinesize]=0;
            printf("%s\n(continued)\n",outline);
            outlinesize = 0;
            };
        };
    outline[outlinesize]=0;
    printf("%s",outline);
};


/***********************************************/
unsigned char *strnustr(srcstr,srcsize,substr,substrsize)
unsigned char *srcstr,*substr;
short srcsize,substrsize;
{
/* uppercase search for substring in sourcestring.
    sourcestring is converted to uppercase for comparison.
*/
    unsigned char *srcptrtmp,*subptrtmp;
    static short i,j;
    static unsigned char found;

    found = FALSE;
    for (i = 0; i < (srcsize - substrsize + 1); i++)
        {
```

Figure A3.1 *(Continued)*

```
        subptrtmp = substr;
        srcptrtmp = srcstr;
        for (j = 0; j < substrsize; j++)

            {
            if ( (unsigned char)toupper(*srcptrtmp) != *subptrtmp )

                break;
            subptrtmp++;srcptrtmp++;

            };
        if (j == substrsize)

            {
            found = TRUE;

            break;

            };
        srcstr++;

        };
    if (found == FALSE) return(0); else return(srcstr);

};


/**************************************************/
unsigned char *strnstr(srcstr,srcsize,substr,substrsize)
unsigned char *srcstr,*substr;
short srcsize,substrsize;
{
/* similar to strstr() except that input and output

 * string length is given. This way NULLs can also be

 * compared.

*/
    unsigned char *srcptrtmp,*subptrtmp;
    static short i,j;
    static unsigned char found;


    found = FALSE;
    for (i = 0; i < (srcsize - substrsize + 1); i++)

        {
        subptrtmp = substr;
        srcptrtmp = srcstr;
```

Figure A3.1 *(Continued)*

```
for (j = 0; j < substrsize; j++)
    {
    if ( (*srcptrtmp) != (*subptrtmp) ) break;
    subptrtmp++;srcptrtmp++;
    };
if (j == substrsize)
    {
    found = TRUE;
    break;
    };
srcstr++;
};
    if (found == FALSE) return(0); else return(srcstr);
};


/************************************************/
unsigned char *jay_strstr(srcstr,substr)
unsigned char *srcstr,*substr;
{
/* strstr is not present in all c rtls so this function*/
    unsigned char *srcptrtmp,*subptrtmp;
    static short srcsize,substrsize;
    static short i,j;
    static unsigned char found;

    found = FALSE;
    srcsize=strlen(srcstr);
    substrsize=strlen(substr);

    for (i = 0; i < (srcsize - substrsize + 1); i++)
        {
        subptrtmp = substr;
        srcptrtmp = srcstr;
        for (j = 0; j < substrsize; j++)
            {
            if ( (*srcptrtmp) != (*subptrtmp) ) break;
```

Figure A3.1 *(Continued)*

```
            subptrtmp++;srcptrtmp++;
            };
        if (j == substrsize)
            {
            found = TRUE;
            break;
            };
        srcstr++;
        };
    if (found == FALSE) return(0); else return(srcstr);
};


/************************************************/
cpynbyt(outstr,instr,count)
unsigned char *outstr,*instr;
short count;
{
    static short i;
    for (i=0;i<count;i++) *outstr++ = *instr++;
};


/************************************************/
cpynbyt_reverse(outstr,instr,count)
unsigned char *outstr,*instr;
short count;
{
    static short i;
    for (i=0;i<count;i++) *outstr-- = *instr--;
};


/************************************************/
get_confirm_rep()
{
    while (TRUE)
    {
        printf(
```

Figure A3.1 *(Continued)*

```
    "Confirm (Yes, No, All, Last repl, End file or Cancel file): "
          );
    gets(response);
    for (tmppos=0,tmpvar=strlen(response); tmppos<tmpvar; tmppos++)
        response[tmppos] = toupper(response[tmppos]);
    if (strlen(response) == 0) strcpy(response,"X");
    if (jay_strstr(resp_yes,response) == resp_yes)
                    {confirm_rep = 'Y';return;};
    if (jay_strstr(resp_no,response) == resp_no)
                    {confirm_rep = 'N';return;};
    if (jay_strstr(resp_all,response) == resp_all)
                    {confirm_rep = 'A';return;};

      if (jay_strstr(resp_last,response) == resp_last)
                      {confirm_rep = 'L';return;};
      if (jay_strstr(resp_end,response) == resp_end)
                      {confirm_rep = 'E';return;};
      if (jay_strstr(resp_cancel,response) == resp_cancel)
                      {confirm_rep = 'C';return;};
      printf("%%SUBST-W-INVANS, invalid answer\n");
    };
};


/***********************************************/
get_confirm_file()
{
   while (TRUE)
     {
     printf(
     "Confirm file (Yes, No, All files, Last file, Quit): "
          );
     gets(response);
     for (tmppos=0,tmpvar=strlen(response); tmppos<tmpvar; tmppos++)
         response[tmppos] = toupper(response[tmppos]);
     if (strlen(response) == 0) strcpy(response,"X");
     if (jay_strstr(resp_yes,response) == resp_yes)
                    {confirm_file = 'Y';return;};
```

Figure A3.1 *(Continued)*

```
        if (jay_strstr(resp_no,response) == resp_no)
                        {confirm_file = 'N';return;};
        if (jay_strstr(resp_all,response) == resp_all)
                        {confirm_file = 'A';return;};
        if (jay_strstr(resp_last,response) == resp_last)
                        {confirm_file = 'L';return;};
        if (jay_strstr(resp_quit,response) == resp_quit)
                        {confirm_file = 'Q';return;};
        printf("%%SUBST-W-INVANS, invalid answer\n");
        };
};


/**************************************************/
closefiles()
{
    rms_status = sys$close(&fabinp);
    if (rms_status != RMS$_NORMAL)
        { printf(
          "%%SUBST-W-CLSERR, %s close error\n",outfile);
          lib$signal (rms_status);
        };
    if (replaceperformed ==TRUE)
        {
        filesreplaced++;
        rms_status = sys$close(&fabout);
        if (rms_status != RMS$_NORMAL)
            { printf(
              "%%SUBST-W-CLSERR, %s close error\n",
                        outfile);
              lib$signal (rms_status);
            };
        /* remove version number from original filename */
        for (tmppos=0;;) if (dirfile_line[tmppos++] == ';') break;
        fabinp.fab$b_fns = tmppos - 1;
        rms_status = sys$rename(&fabout,0,0,&fabinp);
        if (rms_status != RMS$_NORMAL)
```

Figure A3.1 *(Continued)*

```
       { printf(
         "%%SUBST-W-RENERR, %s rename error\n", outfile);
         lib$signal (rms_status);
         lib$signal (fabout.fab$l_stv);
       };
  if (statistics)
       {
       printf ("%d replacement(s)\n",replacecnt);
       total_replacecnt += replacecnt;
       if (replacecnt > 0) replace_files++;
       };
  }
     else
         { /* no replacement, delete tempfile. */
         rms_status = sys$close(&fabout,0,0);
         if (rms_status != RMS$_NORMAL)
             { printf(
               "%%SUBST-W-OUTERR, %s close error\n", outfile);
               lib$signal (rms_status);
             };
         rms_status = sys$erase(&fabout,0,0);
         if (rms_status != RMS$_NORMAL)
             { printf(
               "%%SUBST-W-ERAERR, %s delete error\n", outfile);
               lib$signal (rms_status);
             };
         }
  };


  /************************************************/
  performreplace()
  {
     offset = posptr - &inp_record + stringrep_len;
     if (stringsize_diff < 0)
         {
         /* move left */
```

Figure A3.1 *(Continued)*

```
        cpynbyt(&inp_record[offset],

                &inp_record[offset-stringsize_diff],

                rsiz-offset+stringsize_diff+1);

    }

  else

      {

      /* move right */

      cpynbyt_reverse(&inp_record[rsiz]+stringsize_diff,

              &inp_record[rsiz],

              rsiz - offset +stringsize_diff+1);

      };

  cpynbyt(posptr,actual_repstr,stringrep_len);

  rsiz += stringsize_diff;

  replaceperformed = TRUE;

  replacecnt++;

};


/***************************************************/

processonefile()

{

int currentrec;


  /* open input file */

  fabinp = cc$rms_fab;

  fabinp.fab$l_fna = dirfile_line;

  fabinp.fab$b_fns = strlen(dirfile_line) ;

  fabinp.fab$l_nam = &naminp;

  *(struct NAM *)&naminp = cc$rms_nam;

  naminp.nam$l_esa = expandedstr_inp;

  naminp.nam$b_ess = NAM$C_MAXRSS;

  xabproinp = cc$rms_xabpro;

  xabproinp.xab$l_aclbuf = aclbuf;

  xabproinp.xab$w_aclsiz = 500;

  fabinp.fab$l_xab = &xabproinp;


  rms_status = sys$open(&fabinp); filesopened++;
```

Figure A3.1 *(Continued)*

```
if (rms_status != RMS$_NORMAL)
    { printf("%%SUBST-W-OPNERR, %s open error\n",dirfile_line);
      lib$signal(rms_status);
    }
else
    {
    /* check: only sequential files. UDF not allowed */
    /* for SEQ-FIX source and replacement strings must be same size */
    if (fabinp.fab$b_org != FAB$C_SEQ)
        printf("%%SUBST-W-NOTSEQ, %s not sequential\n",dirfile_line);
    else if ((fabinp.fab$b_rfm == FAB$C_FIX) &&
            (stringsrc_len != stringrep_len))
    {
    printf(
    "%%SUBST-W-FIXNEQ, %s has fixed size records and,\n",
                        dirfile_line);
    printf(
    " Source and replacement strings of unequal length\n");
    }
else if (fabinp.fab$b_rfm == FAB$C_UDF)
    printf(
    "%%SUBST-W-NOUDF, %s has undefined record format\n",
                        dirfile_line);
else
    {
    /* create output file with name extension .REPLACETEMP */
    for (bracket_pos=0;;)
        if (expandedstr_inp[bracket_pos++] == ']') break;
    for (dot_pos = bracket_pos -1;;)
        if (expandedstr_inp[dot_pos++] == '.') break;
    strncpy(outfile, expandedstr_inp, dot_pos);
    strcpy (outfile + dot_pos, "REPLACETEMP");

    fabout = fabinp;
    fabout.fab$w_ifi = 0;
    fabout.fab$l_fna = outfile;
```

Figure A3.1 *(Continued)*

```
fabout.fab$b_fns = strlen(outfile);
rms_status = sys$create(&fabout);
if (rms_status != RMS$_NORMAL)
    { printf(
      "%%SUBST-W-OUTERR, %s create error\n",outfile);
      lib$signal (rms_status);
    };
/*connect input file rab*/
rabinp = cc$rms_rab;
rabinp.rab$l_fab = &fabinp;
if (fabinp.fab$b_rfm == FAB$C_VFC)
    {
     rabinp.rab$l_rhb = vfc_area;
    }
rms_status = sys$connect(&rabinp);
if (rms_status != RMS$_NORMAL)
    { printf(
      "%%SUBST-W-CONNERR, %s rab error\n",dirfile_line);
      lib$signal (rms_status);
    };
/*connect output file rab*/
rabout = cc$rms_rab;
rabout.rab$l_fab = &fabout;
if (fabinp.fab$b_rfm == FAB$C_VFC)
    {
     rabout.rab$l_rhb = vfc_area;
    }
rms_status = sys$connect(&rabout);
if (rms_status != RMS$_NORMAL)
    { printf(
      "%%SUBST-W-CONNERR, %s rab error\n",outfile);
      lib$signal (rms_status);
    };
rabinp.rab$b_rac = RAB$C_SEQ;
rabinp.rab$l_ubf = inp_record;
rabinp.rab$w_usz = sizeof inp_record;
```

Figure A3.1 *(Continued)*

```
/*replace text in one file.


while (forever)
     {
     getrec.
     if eof {
             close inputfile
             if replacements-were-made
                     {
                     close outputfile. rename it to input filename.
                     break while.


                     }
             else close outputfile. delete it. break while.
             }
     else perform replace
     } (endof while.)
*/


         currentrec = 0; replaceperformed = FALSE; replacecnt=0;
         files_searched++;
         while (TRUE)
         {
         currentrec++;
         rms_status = sys$get(&rabinp);
         if ((rms_status != RMS$_EOF) && (rms_status != RMS$_NORMAL))
             { printf(
               "%%SUBST-W-GETERR, %s get error\n",outfile);
               lib$signal (rms_status);
               closefiles();
               break;
             };
         if (rms_status == RMS$_EOF)
             {
             closefiles();
             break; /* end of file, break while loop */
```

Figure A3.1 *(Continued)*

```
    } /* end of if RMS$_EOF */
{ /*process replace*/
rsiz = rabinp.rab$w_rsz;
inp_record[rsiz] = 0;
/* all replacements in this line */
for (offset = 0;;)
    {
    if (exact==TRUE) posptr = strnstr(inp_record+offset,rsiz-offset,
                                    stringsrc,stringsrc_len);
    else posptr = strnustr(inp_record+offset,rsiz-offset,
                            stringsrc_upper,stringsrc_len);
    if (posptr == 0) break;
    else
        {
        /* form replace string */
        if (exact == TRUE)
            {
            cpynbyt(actual_repstr,stringrep,stringrep_len);
            }
        else
            {
            /* replace string matches case of input string chars
             * if replace string has more chars then remaining
             * chars will be same as case of last input string
             * char.
             */
            tmpptr = posptr;
            for (tmpbyte=0; tmpbyte<stringsrc_len; tmpbyte++)
                {
                if ((*tmpptr >= 'A') && (*tmpptr <= 'Z'))
                    {
                    actual_repstr[tmpbyte] =
                            stringrep_upper[tmpbyte];
                    }
                else  if ((*tmpptr >= 'a') && (*tmpptr <= 'z'))
                    {
```

Figure A3.1 *(Continued)*

```
            actual_repstr[tmpbyte] =
                   stringrep_lower[tmpbyte];
          }
      else
          {
          actual_repstr[tmpbyte] = stringrep[tmpbyte];
          }
      tmpptr++;
      };
  if (stringsize_diff > 0)
      {
      tmpptr--;
              if ((*tmpptr >= 'A') && (*tmpptr <= 'Z'))
                  {
                  cpynbyt(&actual_repstr[tmpbyte],
                          &stringrep_upper[tmpbyte],
                          stringsize_diff);
                  }
              else if ((*tmpptr >= 'a') && (*tmpptr <= 'z'))
                  {
                  cpynbyt(&actual_repstr[tmpbyte],
                          &stringrep_lower[tmpbyte],
                          stringsize_diff);
                  }
              else
                  {
                  cpynbyt(&actual_repstr[tmpbyte],
                          &stringrep[tmpbyte],
                          stringsize_diff);
                  }
              }
          }


      }
  if (confirm_rep == 'A')
      {
```

Figure A3.1 *(Continued)*.

```
    performreplace();
    }
else
    {
    /*confirm*/
    /*old line*/
    printf("****** Line %d:\n", currentrec);
    dumpline(inp_record,posptr - &inp_record);
    if (vtterm) printf("\x1b[1m");
    dumpline(posptr, stringsrc_len);
    if (vtterm) printf("\x1b[0m");
    dumpline(posptr+stringsrc_len,
             &inp_record + rsiz - posptr - stringsrc_len);
    printf("\n");

    /*line with replacement*/
    printf("****** New line:\n");
    dumpline(inp_record, posptr- &inp_record);
    if (vtterm) printf("\x1b[1m");
    dumpline(actual_repstr, stringrep_len);
    if (vtterm) printf("\x1b[0m");
    dumpline(posptr+stringsrc_len,
             &inp_record + rsiz - posptr - stringsrc_len);
    printf("\n");
    get_confirm_rep();
    if ((confirm_rep == 'Y') || (confirm_rep == 'A')
            || (confirm_rep == 'L'))
        {
        performreplace();
        }
    else if (confirm_rep == 'N')
        {
        offset = posptr - inp_record + stringsrc_len;
        }
    else if ((confirm_rep == 'E') || (confirm_rep == 'C'))
            break;
```

Figure A3.1 *(Continued)*

```
        };
    };
rabout.rab$b_rac = RAB$C_SEQ;
rabout.rab$l_rbf = inp_record;
rabout.rab$w_rsz = rsiz;
rms_status = sys$put(&rabout);
if (rms_status != RMS$_NORMAL)
    {
    lib$signal (rms_status);
    };
};

if (confirm_rep == 'C')
    {
    /* ignore current file */
    replaceperformed = FALSE; replacecnt = 0;
    closefiles();
    break;
    };
if ((confirm_rep == 'L') || (confirm_rep == 'E'))
    {
    /* write out remaining records, skip file */
    while (TRUE)
        {
        rms_status = sys$get(&rabinp);
        if (rms_status == RMS$_EOF)
            {
            closefiles();
            break;
            }
        else if (rms_status != RMS$_NORMAL)
            { printf(
              "%%SUBST-W-GETERR, %s get error (Location 15.)\n"
                                            ,outfile);
              lib$signal (rms_status);
              replaceperformed = FALSE;
```

Figure A3.1   *(Continued)*

```
                                closefiles();
                                break;
                            }
                    else
                            {
                            rabout.rab$w_rsz = rabinp.rab$w_rsz;
                            rms_status = sys$put(&rabout);
                            if (rms_status != RMS$_NORMAL)
                                { printf(
                                    "%%SUBST-W-PUTERR, %s put error (Location 18.)\n"
                                                                    ,outfile);
                                    lib$signal(rms_status);
                                    replaceperformed = FALSE;
                                    closefiles();
                                    break;
                                };
                            };
                    };
                break;
                }
        }; /*end of while*/
        }; /* end of if file ok */
    }; /* end of if for sys$open check */
}; /* end of processonefile */

/**********************************************/
/**********************************************/
main()
{
    FILE *dirfile;
    int status, cli_status, spawn_status;
    unsigned char cli_value[255];
    short cli_val_len;
    struct dsc$descriptor_s cli_value_str = { 255,14,1, cli_value };
    /* DCL parameters */
    $DESCRIPTOR (cli_source, "SOURCE");
    $DESCRIPTOR (cli_stringsrc, "STRINGSRC");
```

Figure A3.1 *(Continued)*

```
$DESCRIPTOR (cli_stringrep, "STRINGREP");


/* possible cli qualifiers*/
$DESCRIPTOR (cli_backup  ,"BACKUP");
$DESCRIPTOR (cli_before  ,"BEFORE");
$DESCRIPTOR (cli_by_owner,"BY_OWNER");
$DESCRIPTOR (cli_confirm ,"CONFIRM");
$DESCRIPTOR (cli_replaceconfirm ,"REPLACECONFIRM");
$DESCRIPTOR (cli_fileconfirm ,"FILECONFIRM");
$DESCRIPTOR (cli_created ,"CREATED");

 $DESCRIPTOR (cli_exact   ,"EXACT");
 $DESCRIPTOR (cli_exclude ,"EXCLUDE");
 $DESCRIPTOR (cli_expired ,"EXPIRED");
 $DESCRIPTOR (cli_log     ,"LOG");
 $DESCRIPTOR (cli_modified,"MODIFIED");
 $DESCRIPTOR (cli_numbers ,"NUMBERS");
 $DESCRIPTOR (cli_output  ,"OUTPUT");
 $DESCRIPTOR (cli_since   ,"SINCE");
 $DESCRIPTOR (cli_statistics,"STATISTICS");


int nextptr;
unsigned char dir_command[255];
struct    {
    unsigned short     length;
    unsigned char      dtype;
    unsigned char      dclass;
    unsigned char         *str;
    }
    dir_command_str = { 0, 14,1, dir_command};
/* for sys$login translation and [subst] */
$DESCRIPTOR (normaltables,"LNM$DCL_LOGICAL");
$DESCRIPTOR (syslogin     ,"SYS$LOGIN");
unsigned char syslogin_value[100];
short syslogin_len;
```

Figure A3.1 *(Continued)*

```
struct { short buflen; short itemcode; int bufadr;
        int retlenadr; long dummy;
      }
    itmlst = { 100, LNM$_STRING, syslogin_value, &syslogin_len, 0 };
unsigned char repl_work_area[110];


struct    {                    /* replace directory descriptor*/
    unsigned short    length;
    unsigned char     dtype;
    unsigned char     dclass;
    unsigned char       *str;
    }
    repl_work_area_desc = { 0, 14,1, repl_work_area};


int spawn_flags;


unsigned char timadr[8];
unsigned char timbuf[24];
struct dsc$descriptor_s  timbuf_str = { 23,14,1, timbuf };


/* Check utility has not expired. Can be used if package is
licensed to for use upto a specific date */
validateusage();
 /* get sys$login translated */
status = sys$trnlnm( 0, &normaltables, &syslogin,
                    (unsigned char) 0, &itmlst);
if (status != 1) {printf("Location 10. SYS$LOGIN translation error");
               lib$stop(status);};


/* if sys$login:[subst] not created then create it */
strncpy ( repl_work_area, syslogin_value, syslogin_len - 1);
strcpy ( &repl_work_area[syslogin_len - 1], ".SUBST]");
repl_work_area_desc.length = syslogin_len + 6;
status = lib$create_dir (&repl_work_area_desc);
if (status == 1561) {/*dir created*/}
else if (status != 1) {printf(
```

Figure A3.1 *(Continued)*

```
            "Location 20. [SUBST] sub-directory creation error");

            lib$stop(status);};


/* spawn dir command with all qualifiers */

strcpy (dir_command, "DIRECTORY ");

/* filename(s) */

nextptr = 10;

cli_status = cli$get_value(&cli_source, &cli_value_str, &cli_val_len);

cli_value[cli_val_len]= 0;

if (strchr(cli_value, ';') != 0)

    { printf("%%SUBST-E-VERSINV, Version cannot be specified.\n");


      printf("\\%s\\",cli_value);

      exit();

    };

strncpy (&dir_command + nextptr, cli_value, cli_val_len);

nextptr = nextptr+ cli_val_len;


cli_status = cli$present(&cli_backup);

if (cli_status == CLI$_PRESENT)

    {

    strcpy ( &dir_command + nextptr , "/BACKUP");

    nextptr= nextptr + 7;

    };

cli_status = cli$present(&cli_before);

if (cli_status == CLI$_PRESENT)

    {

    strcpy (&dir_command + nextptr,  "/BEFORE:");

    nextptr = nextptr + 8;

    cli_status = cli$get_value ( &cli_before, &cli_value_str, &cli_val_len);

    strncpy (&dir_command + nextptr, cli_value, cli_val_len);

    nextptr = nextptr + cli_val_len;

    };

cli_status = cli$present(&cli_by_owner);

if (cli_status == CLI$_PRESENT)

    {
```

Figure A3.1 *(Continued)*

```
    strcpy (&dir_command + nextptr,  "/BY_OWNER:");

    nextptr = nextptr + 10;

    cli_status = cli$get_value

        ( &cli_by_owner, &cli_value_str, &cli_val_len);

    strncpy (&dir_command + nextptr, cli_value, cli_val_len);

    nextptr = nextptr + cli_val_len;

    };

cli_status = cli$present(&cli_created);

if (cli_status == CLI$_PRESENT)

    {

    strcpy ( &dir_command + nextptr , "/CREATED");

    nextptr= nextptr + 8;

    };

cli_status = cli$present(&cli_exclude);

if (cli_status == CLI$_PRESENT)

    {

    strcpy (&dir_command + nextptr,  "/EXCLUDE:");

    nextptr = nextptr + 9;

    cli_status = cli$get_value

        ( &cli_exclude, &cli_value_str, &cli_val_len);

    strncpy (&dir_command + nextptr, cli_value, cli_val_len);

    nextptr = nextptr + cli_val_len;

    };

cli_status = cli$present(&cli_expired);

if (cli_status == CLI$_PRESENT)

    {

    strcpy ( &dir_command + nextptr , "/EXPIRED");

    nextptr= nextptr + 8;

    };

cli_status = cli$present(&cli_modified);

if (cli_status == CLI$_PRESENT)

    {

    strcpy ( &dir_command + nextptr , "/MODIFIED");

    nextptr= nextptr + 9;

    };

cli_status = cli$present(&cli_since);
```

Figure A3.1 *(Continued)*

```
if (cli_status == CLI$_PRESENT)

    {

    strcpy (&dir_command + nextptr,  "/SINCE:");

    nextptr = nextptr + 7;

    cli_status = cli$get_value ( &cli_since, &cli_value_str, &cli_val_len);

    strncpy (&dir_command + nextptr, cli_value, cli_val_len);

    nextptr = nextptr + cli_val_len;

    };

strcpy ( &dir_command + nextptr , "/VERSION=1/NOHEADER/NOTRAILER/OUTPUT:");

nextptr = nextptr + strlen("/VERSION=1/NOHEADER/NOTRAILER/OUTPUT:");


/*


output file name based on current time. Example filename:

SYS$SYSDEVICE:[TECH4.SUBST]SUBST_31-OCT-1989_16_44-41_32.LIST;1

*/

strncpy ( filename , repl_work_area, repl_work_area_desc.length);

filename[repl_work_area_desc.length] = 0;

status = sys$gettim(timadr);

if (status != 1) {printf("Location 30."); lib$stop(status);};

status = sys$asctim(0, &timbuf_str, timadr, 0 );

if (status != 1) {printf("Location 40."); lib$stop(status);};

if (timbuf[0] == ' ') {timbuf[0] = '0';};

timbuf[11] = '_'; timbuf[14] = '_'; timbuf[17] = '-'; timbuf[20] = '_';

timbuf[23] = 0;

strcpy( filename + strlen(filename), "SUBST_");

strcpy( filename + strlen(filename), timbuf);

strcpy( filename + strlen(filename), ".LIST");

strcpy ( &dir_command + nextptr , filename);

nextptr = nextptr + strlen(filename);


/*

spawn the directory command. example command:

DIRECTORY *.LST/BEFORE:TODAY/VERSION=1/NOHEADER/NOTRAILER

    /OUTPUT:SYS$SYSDEVICE:[TECH4.SUBST]SUBST_31-OCT-1989_16_57-25_05.LIST

*/
```

Figure A3.1 *(Continued)*

```
dir_command_str.length = strlen( dir_command);
status = lib$spawn( &dir_command_str, 0, &spawn_outfile, 0, 0, 0,
                    &spawn_status, (char) 0, 0, 0, 0, 0);
if (status != 1) {printf("Location 50. Spawn error"); lib$stop(status);};
if (spawn_status != 1)
    {
    status = sys$getmsg(spawn_status, &msglen, &msg_bufadr_str,
                                            msg_flags, 0);
    if (status != 1) {printf("Location 55. getmsg error");
                      lib$stop(status);
                     };
    msg_bufadr[msglen] = 0;
    printf("%%SUBST-%s", msg_bufadr+1);


    filename_str.length = strlen(filename);
    status = lib$delete_file(&filename_str);
    if (status != 1)
        { printf("%%SUBST-W-DELERR, %s delete error\n",filename);
          lib$signal(status);
          return;
        };
    exit (spawn_status);
    }
/* open the directory output file to read filenames one by one */
dirfile = fopen (filename,"r");
if (dirfile <= 0)
    {
    perror ("Location 60.\n"); exit();
    };


/* get source and replacement strings, confirm option */
cli_status = cli$get_value(&cli_stringsrc, &cli_value_str, &cli_val_len);
if (cli_val_len == 0)
    { printf("%%SUBST-E-INVSRC, Search string cannot be of size zero.\n");
      exit();
    };
```

Figure A3.1 *(Continued)*

```
cli_value[cli_val_len]= 0;
cpynbyt(stringsrc,cli_value,cli_val_len);
stringsrc_len = cli_val_len;
cli_status = cli$get_value(&cli_stringrep, &cli_value_str, &cli_val_len);
cli_value[cli_val_len]= 0;
cpynbyt(stringrep,cli_value,cli_val_len);
stringrep_len = cli_val_len;
stringsize_diff = stringrep_len - stringsrc_len;


cli_status = cli$present(&cli_exact);
if (cli_status == CLI$_PRESENT)

    {
    exact = TRUE;
    }
else
    {
    for (tmpbyte=0;tmpbyte<=stringsrc_len;tmpbyte++)
        stringsrc_upper[tmpbyte] = toupper(stringsrc[tmpbyte]);
    for (tmpbyte=0;tmpbyte<=stringrep_len;tmpbyte++)
        stringrep_upper[tmpbyte] = toupper(stringrep[tmpbyte]);
    for (tmpbyte=0;tmpbyte<=stringrep_len;tmpbyte++)
        stringrep_lower[tmpbyte] = tolower(stringrep[tmpbyte]);
    };



/*   assign an io channel to terminal. */
if (((status = SYS$ASSIGN(&terminal,&chan,0,0)) & 1) != 1) lib$stop(status);
if (((status = SYS$GETDVIW(1,chan,0,&itemlist,0,0,0,0)) & 1) != 1)
                                        lib$stop(status);
if ((devchar2 & TT2$M_ANSICRT) != 0) vtterm = TRUE; else vtterm = FALSE;


cli_status = cli$present(&cli_statistics);
if (cli_status == CLI$_PRESENT) statistics = TRUE;
else if (cli_status == CLI$_NEGATED) statistics = FALSE;
else
```

Figure A3.1 *(Continued)*

```
    {
    cli_status = cli$present(&cli_log);
    if (cli_status == CLI$_PRESENT) statistics = TRUE;
    else if (cli_status == CLI$_NEGATED) statistics = FALSE;
    };


/* confirm can apply to a file or to each replacement in a file.
   /CONFIRM means confirm file and repl.
   /NOCONFIRM means no confirm for both file and repl.
   /FILECONFIRM  means confirm for file.
   /REPLACECONFIRM means confirm for each replacement. This is set for
   each file.

   A confirm value of X (no value) means confirm, A (all) means no confirm
*/

init_confirm_rep = 'X';
confirm_file = 'X';
cli_status = cli$present(&cli_confirm);
if (cli_status == CLI$_NEGATED)
    {
    init_confirm_rep = 'A';
    confirm_file = 'A';
    }
 else if (cli_status == CLI$_PRESENT)
    {
    init_confirm_rep = 'X';
    confirm_file = 'X';
    }
 else
    {
    cli_status = cli$present(&cli_replaceconfirm);
    if (cli_status == CLI$_NEGATED) init_confirm_rep = 'A';
    cli_status = cli$present(&cli_fileconfirm);
    if (cli_status == CLI$_NEGATED) confirm_file = 'A';
    }
```

Figure A3.1 *(Continued)*

```
while (TRUE)  /* loop until a break is issued on end of file */
    {
    status = fgets (dirfile_line,255, dirfile); /* get one filename*/
    if (status == 0)
        {
        if feof(dirfile) break;
        else {perror("Location 70."); lib$stop(status);};
        };
    dirfile_line[strlen(dirfile_line) - 1] = 0; /*remove line terminator*/
    printf("\n***********\nFile: %s\n\n",dirfile_line);
    confirm_rep = init_confirm_rep;

    if (confirm_file == 'A')
        {
        processonefile (dirfile_line);
        }
    else
        {
        get_confirm_file();
        if (confirm_file == 'A') processonefile(dirfile_line);
        else if (confirm_file == 'Y') processonefile(dirfile_line);
        else if (confirm_file == 'L')
                {
                processonefile(dirfile_line);
                break;
                }
        else if (confirm_file == 'Q') break;
        /* else if (confirm_file == 'N') ; */
        };
    };
if (statistics)
    {
    printf ("\n%d file(s) searched. ",files_searched);
    printf ("%d replacement(s) in %d file(s).\n",
                total_replacecnt,replace_files);
    };
```

Figure A3.1 *(Continued)*

```
    /* delete the DIRECTORY/OUTOUT file */

        filename_str.length = strlen(filename);

        status = lib$delete_file(&filename_str);

        if (status != 1)

            { printf("%%SUBST-W-DELERR, %s delete error\n",filename);

              lib$signal(status);

              return;

            };

};
```

A3.2 `SUBSTITUTE.CLD`

The `SUBSTITUTE` command must be defined in the user's DCL table or the system's DCL table. Figure A3.2 shows the file with the command definition. The command can be defined in the user's DCL table by:

```
$ SET COMMAND SUBSTITUTE.CLD
```

The command has to be executed every time the user logs in. The command can be made available to everyone logged into the system if it's defined in the system DCL table as shown in Fig. A3.2.

The program will not run by:

```
$ RUN SUBSTITUTE !wrong
```

because the program uses the CLI system services, which return values depending on the command line qualifiers. In this case, the command is RUN, which doesn't have the qualifiers and parameters of the `SUBSTITUTE` command, hence the CLI calls will not function properly. The command definition illustrates most of the features of the command definition utility.

A3.3 `SUBSTITUTE.HLP`

Figure A3.3 shows the HELP file for `SUBSTITUTE`, which can be inserted in the system HELP library by the command:

```
$ LIBRARY/INSERT SYS$HELP:HELPLIB.HLB SUBSTITUTE.HLP
```

Once inserted, the HELP command can be used by anyone on the system to see brief information on `SUBSTITUTE`.

Figure A3.2   The DCL command definition file for SUBSTITUTE.

```
!SUBSTITUTE utility DCL command definition.
!The file can be added to the system DCL table by a command
!like:
! $SET COMMAND/TABLE=SYS$LIBRARY:DCLTABLES -
!              /OUTPUT=SYS$LIBRARY:DCLTABLES -
!              SUBTITUTE.CLD
!
define verb substitute
   image substitute
   parameter P1 , label=SOURCE , prompt="Filename(s)"
      value (required,list,type=$infile)
   parameter P2 , label=STRINGSRC , prompt="Search string"
      value (required)
   parameter P3 , label=STRINGREP , prompt="Replacement string"
      value (required)
   qualifier BACKUP
   qualifier BEFORE
      value (default="TODAY",type=$datetime)
   qualifier BY_OWNER
      value (type=$uic)
   qualifier CONFIRM
   qualifier FILECONFIRM
   qualifier REPLACECONFIRM
!CONFIRM is same as FILECONFIRM and REPLACECONFIRM
   disallow CONFIRM and FILECONFIRM
   disallow CONFIRM and REPLACECONFIRM
   qualifier CREATED
   qualifier EXACT
   qualifier EXCLUDE
      nonnegatable
      value (required,list)

      qualifier EXPIRED
      qualifier LOG
      qualifier STATISTICS
    ! /LOG is equivalent to /STATISTICS
```

Figure A3.2 *(Continued)*

```
disallow LOG and STATISTICS
qualifier MODIFIED
qualifier SINCE
   value (default="TODAY",type=$datetime)
```

A3.4   The SUBSTITUTE Manual

Manuals from Digital have a consistent style. Whether this style is considered good or bad, when writing manuals it may be a good idea to adhere to the "look and feel" of Digital manuals because the reader saves time when using the manual. Digital uses VAX DOCUMENT to produce its manuals.

Figure A3.3   Help for SUBSTITUTE.

```
1 SUBSTITUTE

   Searches one or more files for the specified string and replaces all

   matched strings with the replacement string specified. New versions

   of the files are created. The command format is:


     SUBSTITUTE  file-spec[,...]  search-string  replacement-string


   Uppercase and lowercase characters must be specified exactly in the

   search string unless the /NOEXACT qualifier is used.


   The command will operate on sequential files only. The command uses the

   sub-directory [SUBST] under the login directory as a work area.


   Non-printable characters are displayed as mnemonics. Control characters,

   except NULL, can be specified in the source and replacement strings.



2 Parameters


   file-spec[,...]
```

Figure A3.3 *(Continued)*

Specifies the names of one or more files to be searched. You must
specify at least one file name. If you specify two or more file
names, separate them with commas.

Wildcard characters are allowed in the file specification.

search-string

Specifies one or more strings to search for in the specified files.

Matched strings will be considered for replacement by the
replacement-string. The search is case-sensitive. If uppercase and
lowercase characters are to be considered equivalent then the /NOEXACT
qualifier must be used.

replacement-string

Specifies the string which replaces the string searched for by the
search-string.

2 Command_Qualifiers

/BACKUP
 /BACKUP

Selects files according to the dates of their most recent backup.
This qualifier is only relevant when used with the /BEFORE or /SINCE
qualifier. Use of the /BACKUP qualifier is incompatible with
/CREATED, /EXPIRED, and /MODIFIED. The default is /CREATED.

/BEFORE
 /BEFORE[=time]

Selects only those files that are dated before the specified time.

You can specify either an absolute time or a combination of absolute

Figure A3.3 *(Continued)*

```
and delta times. See the VMS DCL Concepts Manual for complete

information on specifying time values. You can also use the keywords

TODAY, TOMORROW, and YESTERDAY. If no time is specified, TODAY is

assumed.


/BY_OWNER
 /BY_OWNER[=uic]


  Selects one or more files only if their owner user identification

  code (UIC) matches the specified owner UIC.


  Specify the UIC using standard UIC format as described in the VMS

  DCL Concepts Manual.

  If the /BY_OWNER qualifier is specified without a UIC, the UIC of

  the current process is assumed.


/CONFIRM
 /CONFIRM    (default)
 /NOCONFIRM


  /CONFIRM is equivalent to specifiying the two quailifiers /FILECONFIRM and

  /REPLACECONFIRM.


/CREATED
 /CREATED (default)


  Selects files based on their dates of creation. This qualifier is

  relevant only when used with the /BEFORE or /SINCE qualifier. Use

  of the /CREATED qualifier is incompatible with /BACKUP, /EXPIRED,

  and /MODIFIED.


/EXACT
 /EXACT    (default)
 /NOEXACT


  Controls whether the search string is matched exactly, or uppercase
```

Figure A3.3 *(Continued)*

```
and lowercase letters are equivalent. The default qualifier, /NOEXACT,
causes SUBSTITUTE to ignore case differences in letters within the search
string. But the replacement is performed by converting each character
in the replacement string to the case of the corresponding character in
the search string to be replaced in the file. If the searched string is
shorter than the replacement string, the case of the remaining characters
is the same as the last character of the source string in the file. For
example, if the command specified is:


$ SUBSTITUTE  test.file  abcd  pqrst


and the file contains ABcd, the replaced string will be PQrst.


If /EXACT is specified, the search string is searched for exactly as
specified and the replacement string is used exactly as specified. Note
that DCL will convert all input to uppercase unless specified within
quotes.


/EXCLUDE
 /EXCLUDE=(file-spec[,...])


Any files that match the listed file specifications are excluded from
the TYPE operation. If you specify only one file, you can omit the
parentheses.
Wildcard characters are supported for file specifications. However,
you cannot use relative version numbers to exclude a specific version.
The file specification can contain a directory specification, but you
cannot include the device in the file specifications you supply with
the /EXCLUDE qualifier.


/EXPIRED
 /EXPIRED


Selects files according to the dates on which they will expire. This
qualifier is relevant only when used with the /BEFORE or /SINCE
qualifier. Use of the /EXPIRED qualifier is incompatible with /BACKUP,
```

Figure A3.3 *(Continued)*

```
    /CREATED, and /MODIFIED. The default is /CREATED.



/FILECONFIRM

  /FILECONFIRM


  Controls whether a file is to be processed for the replacement

  operation.


  When the system issues the prompt, you can issue any of the

  following responses:

    Yes  No  All  Last "End This file"  "Cancel file"  <RET>


  YES or <RET> will cause the replacement to be effective.

  NO will cause that file to be skipped.

  ALL will cause replacements for all further matches in all files

  without any confirmations.

  LAST will cause the SUBSTITUTE session to terminate after the current

  file is processed. Further files, if any, are ignored.

  "End this file" will cause the current file to be closed without the

  last replacement being performed.

  "Cancel file" will cause the current file to be ignored. None of the

  replacements specified will be performed.


  See /CONFIRM and /REPLACECONFIRM also.


/LOG

  /LOG

  /NOLOG (default)


  Controls whether the SUBSTITUTE command produces a line containing the

  file name and the number of records and matches for each file searched

  The log information is output to the current SYS$OUTPUT device.

  /LOG and /STATISTICS are equivalent.


/MODIFIED
```

Figure A3.3 *(Continued)*

```
/MODIFIED


    Selects files according to the dates on which they were last modified.

    This qualifier is relevant only when used with the /BEFORE or /SINCE

    qualifier. Use of the /MODIFIED qualifier is incompatible with /BACKUP,

    /CREATED, and /EXPIRED. The default is /CREATED.


/REPLACECONFIRM

 /REPLACECONFIRM


    Controls whether replacement should be performed.


    When the system issues the prompt, you can issue any of the

    following responses:


      Yes  No  All  Last Quit  <RET>


    YES or <RET> will cause the replacement to be effective.

    NO will cause that file to be skipped.

    ALL will cause replacements for all further matches in the file

    without any confirmations.
    LAST will close the current file after the current replacement is

    performed.

    QUIT will cause the file to be excluded from replacements.


    See /CONFIRM and /FILECONFIRM also.


/SINCE

 /SINCE[=time]


    Selects only those files that are dated after the specified time.


    You can specify either an absolute time or a combination of absolute

    and delta times. See the VMS DCL Concepts Manual for complete

    information on specifying time values. You can also use the keywords

    TODAY, TOMORROW, and YESTERDAY. If no time is specified, TODAY is

    assumed.
```

Figure A3.3 *(Continued)*

```
/STATISTICS

 /STATISTICS

 /NOSTATISTICS (default)


   Controls whether SUBSTITUTE displays statistics about the replacements.

   The statistics displayed are:

   o  Number of files searched

   o  Number of replacements made


   /LOG and /STATISTICS are equivalent.


2 Examples


   1.   $ SUBSTITUTE TEST.COB,PAYROLL.COB    comput   compute


   Each line containing "comput" in the files TEST.COB and PAYROLL.COB will

   be displayed along with the line with the search string replaced by

   "compute". Each replacement will be confirmed. (/NOCONFIRM can be used if

   the replacements are to be made without confirmations).


   2.   $ SUBSTITUTE  BOOK.CHAPTER1  "in the case of"/NOEXACT  "for"


   If a line containing "in the case of" is found, the line will be

   displayed followed by the line with the replaced string. The replacement

   will be confirmed. Uppercase and lowercase characters are considered

   equivalent when searching for the specified search-string.
```

TEX can also be used. It will be difficult to produce manuals with Digital's style using other packages. Briefly, to produce a postscript file, an .SDML file is created with the appropriate typesetting information, and then the file is run through the DOCUMENT program. The DOCUMENT package cannot be described here; instead, let's look at an example that shows how the SUBSTITUTE manual is produced.

Figure A3.4 shows the `.sdml` file for the SUBSTITUTE manual (with some repetitive text replaced by ellipses to reduce size). The file is processed by a command like:

```
$ DOCUMENT/CONTENTS SUBSTITUTE.SDML SOFTWARE.REFERENCE PS
```

Here, /CONTENTS indicates that a table of contents is to be produced; SOFTWARE.REFERENCE is the design of the document, and PS indicates that the output should be printable on a postscript printer. The output file is SUBSTITUTE.PS. The contents of this file are shown in Fig. A3.5 (with Table 2-1 truncated).

Figure A3.4 The VAX Document source file: SUBSTITUTE.SDML.

```
<FRONT_MATTER>(front)

<DEFINE_BOOK_NAME>(Subst_book\The Substitute Utility)


<TITLE_PAGE>

<TITLE>(<REFERENCE>(Subst_book))


<ABSTRACT>

A string replacement facility for VAX/VMS files.

<P>

<P>

August 1991

<P>

<P>

<P>

Operating System: VMS V5.0 through V5.4-2


<P>

Software Version: SUBSTITUTE V1.1

<P>

<P>

<P>

<P>
```

Figure A3.4   *(Continued)*

```
<P>

<P>

<P>

<P>

<P>

<P>

<P>

<P>

<P>

<P>

<P>

Copyright (c) 1991 Your Company Name

<ENDABSTRACT>

<ENDTITLE_PAGE>


<CONTENTS_FILE>


<PREFACE> <P> This is a minimal manual for the
<EMPHASIS>(substitute\BOLD) utility. The commands should be
practised before using them on critical files.

<P> It may be helpful to see the VMS documentation on the
<EMPHASIS>(search\BOLD) command as <EMPHASIS>(substitute\BOLD) bears
some resemblance with it.


<ENDPREFACE>


<ENDFRONT_MATTER>


<CHAPTER>(Using Substitute)


<P> The <EMPHASIS>(substitute\bold) utility is a powerful facility for string
replacements in one or more sequential files. For example to replace
<EMPHASIS>(DISK$DUA2:\BOLD) by <EMPHASIS>(DISK$DUS4:\BOLD) in all
COBOL files in the current directory, the command would be:


<P>
```

Figure A3.4 *(Continued)*

```
<EMPHASIS>($ SUBSTITUTE  *.COB  DISK$DUA2:  DISK$DUS4:\small_boldcaps)


<P>
In this substitution, the case of the replaced characters is the
same as the source characters. Hence, uppercase source strings are
replaced by uppercase replacement strings while lowercase source
strings are replaced by lowercase replacement strings. The
<EMPHASIS>(/EXACT\BOLD) qualifier should be used if the new string
should be used exactly as specified on the command line.
.

.

.

<P> A work directory, [.SUBSTITUTE] is created under a user's login
directory when he or she first uses the <EMPHASIS>(substitute\bold)
command. This directory contains temporary files created by the
utility. Normally, these files are deleted before the command
execution completes. But in case of system failures or other
instances, some temporary files may remain. These files can be
deleted by the user. <emphasis>(Note that the utility uses the
logical name SYS$LOGIN to determine the user's login
directory\italic). For example, if a user's login directory is
defined as
<P>
SYS$LOGIN = DISK$USERS:[MARY]
<P>
then the <EMPHASIS>(substitute\BOLD) work directory will be
<P>
DISK$USERS:[MARY.SUBSTITUTE].
<P>

If, for any reason, SYS$LOGIN is not properly defined when the
system creates the user process, it can be defined within the user's
LOGIN.COM.


<EXAMPLE_SEQUENCE>
<EXC>
```

Figure A3.4 *(Continued)*

```
<EMPHASIS>($ substitute  test_file.dat  second  2nd\small_BOLDCAPS)


************
File: SYS$SYSDEVICE:[MARY]TEST_FILE.DAT;1


Confirm file (Yes, No, All files, Last file, Quit): <EMPHASIS>(Y\ITALIC)
****** Line 2:
This is the <EMPHASIS>(second\BOLD) line.


****** New line:
This is the <EMPHASIS>(2nd\BOLD) line.


Confirm (Yes, No, All, Last repl, End file or Cancel file): <EMPHASIS>(Y\ITALIC)
1 replacement(s)


1 file(s) searched.
1 replacement(s) in 1 file(s).

<EMPHASIS>(The file used in this example ·is:\bold)


This file contains three lines to test the SUBSTITUTE utility.
This is the second line.
This is the third line.
<EXTEXT>


In this example, <EMPHASIS>(substitute\bold) will replace all

occurrences of the word <EMPHASIS>(second\italic) by the word

<EMPHASIS>(2nd\italic) in the file TEST_FILE.DAT. A new version of

the file will be created.


<EXC>
<EMPHASIS>($ substitute/noconfirm test_file.dat  second  2nd\small_boldcaps)


************
File: SYS$SYSDEVICE:[MARY]TEST_FILE.DAT;1


1 replacement(s)
```

Figure A3.4 *(Continued)*

```
.
 .
  .
<ENDEXAMPLE_SEQUENCE>


<CHAPTER>(Substitute Command Reference)
<COMMAND_SECTION>


<COMMAND>(SUBSTITUTE)
<OVERVIEW>
   Searches one or more files for the specified string and replaces all
   matched strings with the replacement string specified.
<ENDOVERVIEW>
<FORMAT>
<FCMD>(SUBSTITUTE)
<FPARMS>(file-spec[,...]  search-string  replacement-string)
<ENDFORMAT>


<PARAMDEFLIST>
<PARAMITEM>(file-spec[,...])
<PARAMDEF>
   Specifies the names of one or more files to be searched. You must
   specify at least one file name. If you specify two or more file
   names, separate them with commas.
<P>
   Wildcard characters are allowed in the file specification.
<PARAMITEM>(search-string)
<PARAMDEF>
Specifies one or more strings to search for in the specified files.
<P>
   Matched strings will be considered for replacement by the
   replacement-string. The search is case-sensitive. If uppercase and
   lowercase characters are to be considered equivalent then the /NOEXACT
   qualifier must be used.


<PARAMITEM>(replacement-string)
<PARAMDEF>
```

Figure A3.4   *(Continued)*

```
   Specifies the string which replaces the string searched for by the
   search-string.
<ENDPARAMDEFLIST>


<DESCRIPTION>
The utility is useful for global replacements in multiple files,say,
when, the name of a variable is changes and all source files have to
be modified. When one or more substitutions are performed in a file,
a new file is created. The file-spec of the new file is the same as
the old file except that a new version is created.
<P>
   Uppercase and lowercase characters must be specified exactly in the
   search string unless the /NOEXACT qualifier is used.
   The command will operate on sequential files only. The command uses the
   sub-directory [SUBST] under the login directory as a work area.
<P>
   Non-printable characters are displayed as mnemonics. Control characters,
   except NULL, can be specified in the source and replacement strings.
<ENDDESCRIPTION>



<QUALDEFLIST>
<QUALITEM>(/BACKUP)
<QUALDEF>
   Selects files according to the dates of their most recent backup.
<P>
   This qualifier is only relevant when used with the /BEFORE or /SINCE
   qualifier. Use of the /BACKUP qualifier is incompatible with
   /CREATED, /EXPIRED, and /MODIFIED. The default is /CREATED.
<P>
<QUALITEM>(/BEFORE=[time])
<QUALDEF>
   Selects only those files that are dated before the specified time.
<P>
   You can specify either an absolute time or a combination of absolute
   and delta times. See the VMS DCL Concepts Manual for complete
   information on specifying time values. You can also use the keywords
```

Figure A3.4 *(Continued)*

```
   TODAY, TOMORROW, and YESTERDAY. If no time is specified, TODAY is
   assumed.
<P>
 .

 .

 .
<QUALITEM>(/STATISTICS (default)\/NOSTATISTICS)
<QUALDEF>


Controls whether <emphasis>(substitute\bold) displays statistics
about the replacements. The statistics displayed are:


<P>
  o  Number of files searched
  o  Number of replacements made
<P>
  /LOG and /STATISTICS are equivalent.
<ENDQUALDEFLIST>
<EXAMPLE_SEQUENCE>
<EXC>
<EMPHASIS>($ SUBSTITUTE  TEST.COB, PAYROLL.COB   comput   compute\small_boldcaps)
<EXTEXT>
  Each line containing "comput" in the files TEST.COB and PAYROLL.COB will
  be displayed along with the line with the search string replaced by

  "compute". Each replacement will be confirmed. (/NOCONFIRM can be used if
  the replacements are to be made without confirmations).
<EXC>
<EMPHASIS>($ SUBSTITUTE  BOOK.CHAPTER1  "in the case of"/NOEXACT  "for"\small_boldcap:
<EXTEXT>
  If a line containing "in the case of" is found, the line will be
  displayed followed by the line with the replaced string. The replacement
  will be confirmed. Uppercase and lowercase characters are considered
  equivalent when searching for the specified search-string.


(default qualifiers)
<ENDEXAMPLE_SEQUENCE>
```

Figure A3.4   *(Continued)*

```
<ENDCOMMAND_SECTION>


<TABLE>(The character set and its display form)

<TABLE_ATTRIBUTES>(MULTIPAGE)

<TABLE_SETUP>(5\7\7\7\7)

<TABLE_HEADS>(Decimal\Hex\Octal\ASCII\As displayed)

<TABLE_ROW>(000 \ 00 \ 000 \        \ <LITERAL>(<NUL>))

<TABLE_ROW>(001 \ 01 \ 001 \        \ <LITERAL>(<SOH>))

        .

        .

        .

        .

        .

        .

<TABLE_ROW>(255 \ FF \ 377 \        \ <LITERAL>(<xFF>))

<ENDTABLE>


<CHAPTER>(Installation Guide for the Substitute Utility)


For those who have performed VMSINSTALs before, this is a fairly

simple installation. The installation takes less than 5 minutes on

most VMS systems. During the installation, 400 blocks of disk space

on the system disk is required. After the installation, the utility

occupies about 200 blocks.

<P>

<head1>(Using VMSINSTAL)


To install the utility, mount the product tape on a tape drive. Here,

MUA0: is the assumed to be the tape drive. Log into the SYSTEM

account and run the procedure SYS$UPDATE:VMSINSTAL. All the questions are

require simple answers. For more information see the <EMPHASIS>(Guide to

VAX/VMS Software Installation\italic). Here is an example run of the

installation:


<CODE_EXAMPLE>(WIDE)
```

Figure A3.4 *(Continued)*

```
$ <EMPHASIS>(@sys$update:vmsinstal\bold)


   VAX/VMS Software Product Installation Procedure V5.4



It is 28-AUG-1991 at 10:16.


Enter a question mark (?) at any time for help.


* Are you satisfied with the backup of your system disk [YES]? <BOX>(<EMPHASIS>(return\bo
ld))
* Where will the distribution volumes be mounted: <EMPHASIS>(MUA0:\bold)


Enter the products to be processed from the first distribution volume set.
* Products: <EMPHASIS>(SUB\bold)
* Enter installation options you wish to use (none): <BOX>(<EMPHASIS>(return\bold))


The following products will be processed:

   SUB V1.1


   Beginning installation of SUB V1.1 at 10:17


%VMSINSTAL-I-RESTORE, Restoring product save set A ...
%VMSINSTAL-I-RELMOVED, Product's release notes have been moved to SYS$HELP.

* Do you want to purge files replaced by this installation [YES]? <BOX>(<EMPHASIS>(return
\bold))
%VMSINSTAL-I-MOVEFILES Files will now be moved to their target directories...
   Installation of SUB V1.1 completed at 10:18


Enter the products to be processed from the next distribution volume set.
* Products: <BOX>(<EMPHASIS>(control-z\bold))
   VMSINSTAL procedure done at 10:18
$
<ENDCODE_EXAMPLE>


<head1>(Files Created or Modified by the installation)
```

Figure A3.4 *(Continued)*

```
The following table shows the files created or modified by the installation
procedure.


<TABLE>(Files created or modified by the installation)

<TABLE_ATTRIBUTES>(keep)

<TABLE_SETUP>(3\15\20)

<TABLE_HEADS>(File name\Location\Description)

<TABLE_ROW>(DCLTABLES.EXE\SYS$COMMON:[SYSLIB]

              \Modified file. With the SUBSTITUTE DCL command)

<TABLE_ROW>(HELPLIB.HLB\SYS$COMMON:[SYSHLP]

              \Modified file. With HELP for this utility)

<TABLE_ROW>(SUBSTITUTE011. RELEASE_NOTES\SYS$COMMON:[SYSHLP]

              \New File.)

 <TABLE_ROW>(SUBSTITUTE.EXE\SYS$COMMON:[SYSEXE]

              \New File. The executable image of the utility)

 <ENDTABLE>
```

Figure A3.5 The Substitute Utility.

The Substitute Utility

A string replacement facility for VAX/VMS files.

February 1992

Operating System: VMS V5.0 through V5.4-2
Software Version: SUBSTITUTE V1.1

Copyright (c) 1992 Your Company Name

Figure A3.5 *(Continued)*

Contents

Figure A3.5 *(Continued)*

Preface

This is a minimal manual for the **substitute** utility. The commands should be practised before using them on critical files.

It may be helpful to see the VMS documentation on the **search** command as **substitute** bears some resemblance with it.

v

Figure A3.5 *(Continued)*

1   Using Substitute

The **substitute** utility is a powerful facility for string replacements in one or more sequential files. For example to replace **DISK\$DUA2:** by **DISK\$DUS4:** in all COBOL files in the current directory, the command would be:

$ SUBSTITUTE *.COB DISK\$DUA2: DISK\$DUS4:

In this substitution, the case of the replaced characters is the same as the source characters. Hence, uppercase source strings are replaced by uppercase replacement strings while lowercase source strings are replaced by lowercase replacement strings. The /**EXACT** qualifier should be used if the new string should be used exactly as specified on the command line.

By default, the utility will prompt to confirm if substitution should be in a file. The /**NOFILECONFIRM** qualifier can be used if no confirmation is required before a file is considered for substitutions. Similarly, the utility will prompt to confirm if each substitution should be performed. The /**NOREPLACECONFIRM** qualifier can be used if no confirmation is required before each substitution. As a convenience, the /**NOCONFIRM** qualifier can be specified in place of the two qualifiers, /**NOFILECONFIRM** and /**NOREPLACECONFIRM**. The /**NOCONFIRM** qualifier should be used with extreme caution as it can potentially perform unexpected replacements when a set of files are specified for the replacement.

When the utility prompts for confirmation of a substitution, the original line and the line with the substitution are displayed. As a convenience to locating a line when similar lines are present at many locations in the file, the line number of the source string within the file is also displayed.

The utility creates a new version of a file in which substitutions have been made. If a file is selected for substitutions but no substitutions have been made, a new version of the file is *not* created. The output file (or files) cannot be specified as a parameter to the command. The **substitute** utility always operates on the latest versions of specified list of files. *Version numbers cannot be specified for input files.*

When lines from the files are displayed, control characters are displayed in angle brackets. The ascii codes of the characters and their display form are shown in the table at the end of this book. Note that the multinational character set is supported. The source and replacement strings can contain any control characters with the exception of the NULL character (ASCII 0). Normally, control characters cannot be entered from a terminal so when control characters need to be substituted, a DCL command file containing the **substitute** command should be created.

Figure A3.5   *(Continued)*

Using Substitute

The utility will perform substitutions in sequential files with any of the record format: FIX, VARIABLE, VFC, or Stream. For FIX record format files the search and replacement strings must be of the same size. The output files will have the same record formats as the input files. Sequential files with the Undefined (UDF) record format are not supported. Relative or Indexed files are also not supported.

A work directory, [.SUBSTITUTE] is created under a user's login directory when he or she first uses the **substitute** command. This directory contains temporary files created by the utility. Normally, these files are deleted before the command execution completes. But in case of system failures or other instances, some temporary files may remain. These files can be deleted by the user. *Note that the utility uses the logical name SYS$LOGIN to determine the user's login directory.* For example, if a user's login directory is defined as

SYS$LOGIN = DISK$USERS:[MARY]

then the **substitute** work directory will be

DISK$USERS:[MARY.SUBSTITUTE].

If, for any reason, SYS$LOGIN is not properly defined when the system creates the user process, it can be defined within the user's LOGIN.COM.

Examples

1

```
$ SUBSTITUTE  TEST_FILE.DAT  SECOND  2ND
************
File: SYS$SYSDEVICE:[MARY]TEST_FILE.DAT;1

Confirm file (Yes, No, All files, Last file, Quit): Y
****** Line 2:
This is the second line.

****** New line:
This is the 2nd line.

Confirm (Yes, No, All, Last repl, End file or Cancel file): Y
1 replacement(s)

1 file(s) searched.
1 replacement(s) in 1 file(s).

The file used in this example is:

This file contains three lines to test the SUBSTITUTE utility.
This is the second line.
This is the third line.
```

In this example, **substitute** will replace all occurences of the word *second* by the word *2nd* in the file TEST_FILE.DAT. A new version of the file will be created.

1–2

Figure A3.5 *(Continued)*

Using Substitute

2

```
$ SUBSTITUTE/NOCONFIRM  TEST_FILE.DAT  SECOND  2ND
************
File: SYS$SYSDEVICE:[MARY]TEST_FILE.DAT;1

1 replacement(s)

1 file(s) searched.
1 replacement(s) in 1 file(s).
```

> This example is similar to the one above except that there is no prompting to confirm the file to be worked on or to confirm whether each replacement should be performed.

3

```
$ SUBSTITUTE/NOCONFIRM/NOSTAT  TEST_FILE.DAT  SECOND  2ND
************
File: SYS$SYSDEVICE:[MARY]TEST_FILE.DAT;1
```

> In this example, no statistics is displayed after each file is processed and at the end of execution. The /NOSTAT should be used with caution as the statistics displayed can be used to cross check expected substitutions.

4

```
$ SUBSTITUTE/NOFILECONFIRM  TEST_FILE.DAT  SECOND  2ND
************
File: SYS$SYSDEVICE:[MARY]TEST_FILE.DAT;1

****** Line 2:
This is the second line.

****** New line:
This is the 2nd line.

Confirm (Yes, No, All, Last repl, End file or Cancel file): Y
1 replacement(s)

1 file(s) searched.
1 replacement(s) in 1 file(s).
```

> In this example, there is no prompting to confirm the file to be worked on but each replacement is being confirmed.

5

```
$ SUBSTITUTE  *.DAT  INP_STRING  OUTPUT_STRING
************
File: SYS$SYSDEVICE:[MARY]INDEXED_FILE.DAT;1

Confirm file (Yes, No, All files, Last file, Quit): A
%SUBST-W-NOTSEQ, SYS$SYSDEVICE:[MARY]INDEXED_FILE.DAT;1 not sequential
************
File: SYS$SYSDEVICE:[MARY]RELATIVE_FILE.DAT;1

%SUBST-W-NOTSEQ, SYS$SYSDEVICE:[MARY]RELATIVE_FILE.DAT;1 not sequential
************
File: SYS$SYSDEVICE:[MARY]SEQUENTIAL_FIX.DAT;1

%SUBST-W-FIXNEQ, file SYS$SYSDEVICE:[MARY]SEQUENTIAL_FIX.DAT;1
 has fixed size records and,
 Source and replacement strings of unequal length
************
File: SYS$SYSDEVICE:[MARY]SEQUENTIAL_STREAM_CR.DAT;1

************
File: SYS$SYSDEVICE:[MARY]SEQUENTIAL_VFC.DAT;1
```

1–3

Figure A3.5 *(Continued)*

Using Substitute

```
2 file(s) searched.
0 replacement(s) in 0 file(s).
```

This example shows the messages when attempting to perform
substitutions in the various types of files. Note that RELATIVE and
INDEXED files are not supported. For sequential files with FIX record
format, the search and replacement strings must be of the same length.

6

```
$ SUBSTITUTE *CHAR*.DAT ASCII DECIMAL
************
File: SYS$SYSDEVICE:[TECH4]CONTROL_CHARS.DAT;1

Confirm file (Yes, No, All files, Last file, Quit): Y
****** Line 2:
This line has a control-d (ascii 4) here:<EOT>.

****** New line:
This line has a control-d (decimal 4) here:<EOT>.

Confirm (Yes, No, All, Last repl, End file or Cancel file): N
****** Line 3:
This line has ascii 0, 8, and 12 here:<NUL><BS><FF>.

****** New line:
This line has decimal 0, 8, and 12 here:<NUL><BS><FF>.

Confirm (Yes, No, All, Last repl, End file or Cancel file): N
1 file(s) searched.
0 replacement(s) in 0 file(s).

The file used in this example is:
This file contains two lines to test the SUBSTITUTE utility.
This line has a control-d (ascii 4) here:?.
This line has ascii 0, 8, and 12 here:???.
```

This example shows what is displayed when control characters are
encountered in a file. The table at the end of this book shows display
forms of all characters.

1–4

Figure A3.5 *(Continued)*

2   Substitute Command Reference

2–1

Figure A3.5   *(Continued)*

SUBSTITUTE

SUBSTITUTE

Searches one or more files for the specified string and replaces all matched strings with the replacement string specified.

FORMAT   **SUBSTITUTE**   *file-spec[,...] search-string*
                                   replacement-string

PARAMETERS   *file-spec[,...]*
Specifies the names of one or more files to be searched. You must specify at least one file name. If you specify two or more file names, separate them with commas.

Wildcard characters are allowed in the file specification.

search-string
Specifies one or more strings to search for in the specified files.

Matched strings will be considered for replacement by the replacement-string. The search is case-sensitive. If uppercase and lowercase characters are to be considered equivalent then the /NOEXACT qualifier must be used.

replacement-string
Specifies the string which replaces the string searched for by the search-string.

DESCRIPTION   The utility is useful for global replacements in multiple files, say, when, the name of a variable is changes and all source files have to be modified. When one or more substitutions are performed in a file, a new file is created. The file-spec of the new file is the same as the old file except that a new version is created.

Uppercase and lowercase characters must be specified exactly in the search string unless the /NOEXACT qualifier is used. The command will operate on sequential files only. The command uses the sub-directory [SUBST] under the login directory as a work area.

Non-printable characters are displayed as mnemonics. Control characters, except NULL, can be specified in the source and replacement strings.

QUALIFIERS   */BACKUP*
Selects files according to the dates of their most recent backup.

This qualifier is only relevant when used with the /BEFORE or /SINCE qualifier. Use of the /BACKUP qualifier is incompatible with /CREATED, /EXPIRED, and /MODIFIED. The default is /CREATED.

2–2

Figure A3.5 *(Continued)*

SUBSTITUTE

/BEFORE=[time]

Selects only those files that are dated before the specified time.

You can specify either an absolute time or a combination of absolute
and delta times. See the VMS DCL Concepts Manual for complete
information on specifying time values. You can also use the keywords
TODAY, TOMORROW, and YESTERDAY. If no time is specified, TODAY is
assumed.

/BY_OWNER[=uic]

Selects one or more files only if their owner user identification code (UIC)
matches the specified owner UIC.

Specify the UIC using standard UIC format as described in the VMS DCL
Concepts Manual.

If the /BY_OWNER qualifier is specified without a UIC, the UIC of the
current process is assumed.

/CONFIRM (default)
/NOCONFIRM

/CONFIRM is equivalent to specifiying the two quailifiers /FILECONFIRM
and /REPLACECONFIRM.

/CREATED

Selects files based on their dates of creation. This qualifier is relevant only
when used with the /BEFORE or /SINCE qualifier. Use of the /CREATED
qualifier is incompatible with /BACKUP, /EXPIRED, and /MODIFIED.

/EXACT (default)
/NOEXACT

Controls whether the search string is matched exactly, or uppercase and
lowercase letters are equivalent. The default qualifier, /NOEXACT, causes
substitute to ignore case differences in letters within the search string.
But the replacement is performed by converting each character in the
replacement string to the case of the corresponding character in the search
string to be replaced in the file. If the searched string is shorter than
the replacement string, the case of the remaining characters is the same
as the last character of the source string in the file. For example, if the
command specified is:

$ SUBSTITUTE TEST.FILE ABCD PQRST

and the file contains ABcd, the replaced string will be PQrst.

If /EXACT is specified, the search string is searched for exactly as specified
and the replacement string is used exactly as specified. Note that DCL
will convert all input to uppercase unless specified within quotes.

2–3

Figure A3.5 *(Continued)*

SUBSTITUTE

/EXCLUDE=(file-spec[,...])

Any files that match the listed file specifications are excluded from the TYPE operation. If you specify only one file, you can omit the parentheses.

Wildcard characters are supported for file specifications. However, you cannot use relative version numbers to exclude a specific version. The file specification can contain a directory specification, but you cannot include the device in the file specifications you supply with the /EXCLUDE qualifier.

/EXPIRED

Selects files according to the dates on which they will expire. This qualifier is relevant only when used with the /BEFORE or /SINCE qualifier. Use of the /EXPIRED qualifier is incompatible with /BACKUP, /CREATED, and /MODIFIED. The default is /CREATED.

/FILECONFIRM

Controls whether a file is to be processed for the replacement operation.

When the system issues the prompt, you can issue any of the following responses:

Yes No All Last "End This file" "Cancel file" <RET>

YES or <RET> will cause the replacement to be effective. NO will cause that file to be skipped. ALL will cause replacements for all further matches in all files without any confirmations. LAST will cause the **substitute** session to terminate after the current file is processed. Further files, if any, are ignored. "End this file" will cause the current file to be closed without the last replacement being performed. "Cancel file" will cause the current file to be ignored. None of the replacements specified will be performed.

See /CONFIRM and /REPLACECONFIRM also.

/LOG
/NOLOG (default)

Controls whether the **substitute** command produces a line containing the file name and the number of records and matches for each file searched. The log information is output to the current SYS$OUTPUT device.

/LOG and /STATISTICS are equivalent.

/MODIFIED

Selects files according to the dates on which they were last modified. This qualifier is relevant only when used with the /BEFORE or /SINCE qualifier. Use of the /MODIFIED qualifier is incompatible with /BACKUP, /CREATED, and /EXPIRED. The default is /CREATED.

2–4

Figure A3.5 *(Continued)*

SUBSTITUTE

/REPLACECONFIRM
Controls whether replacement should be performed.

When the system issues the prompt, you can issue any of the following responses:

Yes No All Last Quit <RET>

YES or <RET> will cause the replacement to be effective. NO will cause that file to be skipped. ALL will cause replacements for all further matches in the file without any confirmations. LAST will close the current file after the current replacement is performed. QUIT will cause the file to be excluded from replacements.

See /CONFIRM and /FILECONFIRM also.

/SINCE=[time]
Selects only those files that are dated after the specified time.

You can specify either an absolute time or a combination of absolute and delta times. See the VMS DCL Concepts Manual for complete information on specifying time values. You can also use the keywords TODAY, TOMORROW, and YESTERDAY. If no time is specified, TODAY is assumed.

/STATISTICS (default)
/NOSTATISTICS
Controls whether **substitute** displays statistics about the replacements. The statistics displayed are:

o Number of files searched o Number of replacements made

/LOG and /STATISTICS are equivalent.

EXAMPLES

1 $ SUBSTITUTE TEST.COB, PAYROLL.COB   COMPUT COMPUTE

Each line containing "comput" in the files TEST.COB and PAYROLL.COB will be displayed along with the line with the search string replaced by "compute". Each replacement will be confirmed. (/NOCONFIRM can be used if the replacements are to be made without confirmations).

2 $ SUBSTITUTE BOOK.CHAPTER1 "IN THE CASE OF"/NOEXACT "FOR"

If a line containing "in the case of" is found, the line will be displayed followed by the line with the replaced string. The replacement will be confirmed. Uppercase and lowercase characters are considered equivalent when searching for the specified search-string. (default qualifiers)

2–5

Figure A3.5 *(Continued)*

Substitute Command Reference

Table 2–1   The character set and its display form

Decimal	Hex	Octal	ASCII	As displayed
000	00	000		<NUL>
001	01	001		<SOH>
002	02	002		<STX>
003	03	003		<ETX>
004	04	004		<EOT>
005	05	005		<ENQ>
006	06	006		<ACK>
007	07	007		<BEL>
008	08	010		<BS>
009	09	011		<HT>
010	0A	012		<LF>
011	0B	013		<VT>
012	0C	014		<FF>
013	0D	015		<CR>
014	0E	016		<SO>
015	0F	017		<SI>
016	10	020		<DLE>
017	11	021		<DC1>
018	12	022		<DC2>
019	13	023		<DC3>
020	14	024		<DC4>
021	15	025		<NAK>
022	16	026		<SYN>
023	17	027		<ETB>
024	18	030		<CAN>
025	19	031		<EM>
026	1A	032		<SUB>
027	1B	033		<ESC>
028	1C	034		<FS>
029	1D	035		<GS>
030	1E	036		<RS>
031	1F	037		<US>
032	20	040		
033	21	041	!	!
034	22	042	"	"
035	23	043	#	#
036	24	044	$	$
037	25	045	%	%

2–6

Figure A3.5 *(Continued)*

Substitute Command Reference

Table 2–1 (Cont.)   The character set and its display form

Decimal	Hex	Octal	ASCII	As displayed
228	E4	344	ä	ä
229	E5	345	å	å
230	E6	346	æ	æ
231	E7	347	ç	ç
232	E8	350	è	è
233	E9	351	é	é
234	EA	352	ê	ê
235	EB	353	ë	ë
236	EC	354	ì	ì
237	ED	355	í	í
238	EE	356	î	î
239	EF	357	ï	ï
240	F0	360	ð	ð
241	F1	361	ñ	ñ
242	F2	362	ò	ò
243	F3	363	ó	ó
244	F4	364	ô	ô
245	F5	365	õ	õ
246	F6	366	ö	ö
247	F7	367	÷	÷
248	F8	370	ø	ø
249	F9	371	ù	ù
250	FA	372	ú	ú
251	FB	373	û	û
252	FC	374	ü	ü
253	FD	375	ý	ý
254	FE	376	þ	þ
255	FF	377		<xFF>

Figure A3.5   *(Continued)*

---

3   Installation Guide for the Substitute Utility

For those who have performed VMSINSTALs before, this is a fairly simple installation. The installation takes less than 5 minutes on most VMS systems. During the installation, 400 blocks of disk space on the system disk is required. After the installation, the utility occupies about 200 blocks.

3.1   Using VMSINSTAL

To install the utility, mount the product tape on a tape drive. Here, MUA0: is the assumed to be the tape drive. Log into the SYSTEM account and run the procedure SYS$UPDATE:VMSINSTAL. All the questions are require simple answers. For more information see the *Guide to VAX/VMS Software Installation*. Here is an example run of the installation:

```
$ @sys$update:vmsinstal

VAX/VMS Software Product Installation Procedure V5.4

It is 28-AUG-1991 at 10:16.
Enter a question mark (?) at any time for help.

* Are you satisfied with the backup of your system disk [YES]? return
* Where will the distribution volumes be mounted: MUA0:

Enter the products to be processed from the first distribution volume set.
* Products: SUB
* Enter installation options you wish to use (none): return

The following products will be processed:

  SUB V1.1

  Beginning installation of SUB V1.1 at 10:17

%VMSINSTAL-I-RESTORE, Restoring product save set A ...
%VMSINSTAL-I-RELMOVED, Product's release notes have been moved to SYS$HELP.
* Do you want to purge files replaced by this installation [YES]? return
%VMSINSTAL-I-MOVEFILES Files will now be moved to their target directories...
  Installation of SUB V1.1 completed at 10:18

Enter the products to be processed from the next distribution volume set.
* Products: control-E
  VMSINSTAL procedure done at 10:18
$
```

3.2   Files Created or Modified by the installation

The following table shows the files created or modified by the installation procedure.

3–1

Figure A3.5 *(Continued)*

Installation Guide for the Substitute Utility

Table 3–1   Files created or modified by the installation

File name	Location	Description
DCLTABLES.EXE	SYS$COMMON:[SYSLIB]	Modified file. With the SUBSTITUTE DCL command
HELPLIB.HLB	SYS$COMMON:[SYSHLP]	Modified file. With HELP for this utility
SUBSTITUTE011. RELEASE_NOTES	SYS$COMMON:[SYSHLP]	New File.
SUBSTITUTE.EXE	SYS$COMMON:[SYSEXE]	New File. The executable image of the utility

3–2

Input and Output Data Conversion

Formatted output allows for the conversion of internal data to a readable ASCII form. The piece of code:

```
int x;
x = 5;
printf("Value of x is %d\n",x);
```

prints the following text:

```
Value of x is 5
```

In this example, `%d` specified that a decimal number is to be printed. The variable to be printed is specified as a parameter in `printf()`. In effect, the internal binary format of data item x was converted to a readable form.

Formatted input allows for the conversion of ASCII input to an internal form. For example, `scanf()` takes input from standard input (the terminal when the program is run interactively) and converts the ASCII text entered into data to be put into C variables. The piece of code:

```
int x;
scanf("%d", &x);
```

will accept decimal input like "12645" or "0" (followed by a RETURN) from the terminal and convert it to a binary 32-bit integer and store the result in x. Note that scanf() accepts the address of the variable as a parameter.

A formatted input and output specifier begins with a % sign. A number of I/O functions process format specifiers. Possible format specifiers are listed in Table A4.1.

TABLE A4.1 Output format specifier characters

Character	Use
Number output	
d	Convert to decimal.
o	Convert to octal.
X or x	Convert to hexadecimal. Output digits A to F are uppercase if X is specified, lowercase if x is specified.
u	Convert to unsigned decimal.
E or e	Convert float or double to the format [-]m.nnnnnnE[+/-]xx n's are 6 digits unless a precision modifier is specified. The E is upper- or lowercase depending on the specifier's case. m is 1 digit.
f	Convert float or double to the format [-]m...m.nnnnnn n's are 6 digits unless a precision modifier is specified
G or g	Convert float or double to d, e, or f format, whichever is shorter. If E is printed, the case is same as that of the input G.
i	Convert to unsigned decimal.
n	Not actually an output formatter. Write count of characters output as an integer into the location given as a parameter. %n must be at end of the output format string. For example, int cnt,x,y; printf("x=%d,y=%d\n%n",x,y,&cnt)
Character output	
c	Output one character.
s	Write characters until NUL is encountered. If modifier has count then print specified number of characters or until NUL is encountered. Modifiers are shown in a later table.
%	Output the % sign.

Here's an example program using the format specifiers:

```
/* Program demonstrating the format specifiers for output */

main()
{
unsigned int cnt ,x = 516, y = -12;
int z = -3831345;
char c ='A';
```

```
char *s = "test string";
float f = -51.32e2;

printf("x=%d, y=%d\n",x,y);

printf("x=%d, y=%d (again)\n%n",x,y,&cnt);
printf("output chars in previous print statement, cnt=%d\n",cnt);

printf("x=%x (hex)\n",x);

printf("float f = %e (e format)\n",f);
printf("float f = %G (G format)\n",f);

printf("char c = %c\n",c);
printf("string s = %s\n",s);

printf("percent sign = %% \n");
}
```

The output of this program is:

```
x=516, y=-12
x=516, y=-12 (again)
output chars in previous print statement, cnt=21
x=204 (hex)
float f = -5.132000e+03 (e format)
float f = -5132 (G format)
char c = A
string s = test string
percent sign = %
```

A set of modifier characters can be specified between the % and the format specifier character. For example, a number between the % and the format character specifies the width of the output field. The piece of code:

```
int x;
x = 75;
printf ("[%6d]",x);
```

prints the following text:

```
[    75]
```

TABLE A4.2 Format modifier characters

Character	Use
–	Hyphen (minus sign). Left justify output
n	Field width. If output is wider, write beyond field width. If output is shorter, pad with spaces or zeros; zeros if n has a leading 0. Pad at right if hyphen is also specified else pad at left.

TABLE A4.2 Continued

Character	Use
.n	Period followed by precision. For s format, this is number of characters from input string to be printed. For f or e format, this is number of fraction digits to be printed. Example: %7.4s. Field width is 7. 4 characters from input string are printed. Example: %8.2f. Field width 6, 2 fraction digits of floating point number.
1	Long output. For d, o, x, or u formats, input is treated as long. This is the default on VAX so it is redundant.
*	Asterisk. Field width or precision is passed as a parameter. For example, printf ("*.*s", src, width, precision);
+	+ or – sign must be output for a signed data.
#	For e, f, or g formats, the output will have a decimal point even after integer output.

The `%6d` specifies decimal output in a field of width 6. The square brackets indicate the field width. Table A4.2 lists what can be specified between the % and format character.

Here's an example program using format modifiers:

```
/* Program demonstrating the format modifiers for output */

main()
{
int inum = -45, inum2 = 327;
char *str = "test string";
float   fnum = 4.272693e2;

printf ("%16s [%6d]\n",      "%6d:",        inum);
printf ("%16s [%-6d]\n",     "%-06d:",      inum);
printf ("%16s [%06d]\n",     "%06d:",       inum);
printf ("%16s [%-6d]\n",     "%-6d:",       inum);
printf ("%16s [%-06d]\n",    "%-06d:",      inum);

printf ("%16s [%7.4s]\n",    "%7.4s:",      str);
printf ("%16s [%16.4s]\n",   "%16.4s:",     str);
printf ("%16s [%20.18s]\n",  "%20.18s:",    str);

printf ("%16s [%10.2f]\n",   "%10.2f:",     fnum);

printf ("%16s [%6d]\n",      "%6d:",        inum2);
printf ("%16s [%+6d]\n",     "%+6d:",inum2);

printf ("%16s [%*s]\n",      "%*s (%7s):",    7, str);
printf ("%16s [%*.*s]\n",    "%*.*s (%7.4s):", 7, 4, str);
}
```

The output of this program is:

```
      %6d: [   -45]
    %-06d: [-45    ]
```

```
     %06d:   [-00045]
     %-6d:   [-45   ]
    %-06d:   [-45000]
     %7.4s:  [   test]
    %16.4s:  [              test]
   %20.18s:  [          test string]
    %10.2f:  [     427.27]
      %6d:  [    327]
     %+6d:  [   +327]
  %*s (%7s): [test string]
%*.*s (%7.4s): [   test]
```

Table A4.3 shows the format characters when inputting data from a terminal, file or string. A white-space (tab, space, newline) terminates format interpretation. If a no-white-space character is present in the format specifier string, it must be present in the input string also. A white-space in the format specifier string matches a white-space in the input string.

TABLE A4.3   Input format specifier characters

Character	Use
*	Read input as specified, however, suppress assignment to an argument. Effectively, the field is skipped.
Number input	
d	Read decimal integer. Argument must point to an int.
o	Read octal integer. Argument must point to an int.
x	Read hexadecimal integer. Argument must point to an int.
e or f	Read floating-point number. Argument must point to a float. Input format is [+/–]n[.d] [(E/e} [+/–]n] Examples are: 3.4 and –24.563e–4
i	Read integer. Type is determined by leading characters, 0 for octal, 0X for hexadecimal, decimal otherwise. Argument must point to an int.
ld, lo	Read long integers. The 1 is redundant for VAX which reads long integers anyway.
le, lf E or F	Reads double floating point numbers. Argument must point to a double.
hd,ho or hx	Read short integer. Radix is decimal, octal or hexadecimal. Argument must point to short.
Character input	
c	Read one character. Argument must point to a char. White spaces are ignored. %1c reads any character, including a white space. %nc reads n characters Argument must point to array of char.
s	Read string. Argument points to array of char. Argument will hold string plus NUL. Input field is terminated by a space, tab or newline.
[...] or [^...]	Read string of characters as long as Characters in input stream are part of the set specified by ellipses.If the brackets contain an ^ as the first character, then read string of characters until one of the characters specified by the ellipsis is encountered. A white space terminates the input.

Here's an example program using input format specifiers:

```
/* Program doing formatted input*/

main()
{
int inum;
char str[255];
float  fnum;

scanf ("%d %f",  &inum, &fnum);
scanf ("%*d, %f", &fnum);
scanf ("%6d",    &inum);
scanf ("%3d%5c",  &inum, str);
}
```

The program will accept the following input:

```
432 342.3
323, 34         (323 is ignored)
325678
123 abcdef     (inum=123, str[] = " abcd")
```

Getting input through the means of format specifiers is not elegant in C because if the input format does not match the format specifier string, the program either crashes or, worse, the program performs a wrong conversion. The alternative is to read complete lines of input and write code to perform formatting.

VAX C RTL Functions

Note: prototypes that do not end in a semicolon are actually DEFINE macros defined in the header file.

abort   Terminates the process.

                        prototype declared in: stdlib.h
                        prototype: void abort(void);

abs   Returns the absolute value of an integer.

                        prototype declared in: stdlib.h
                        prototype: int abs(int integer);

access   Checks a file to see if a specified access mode
                        is allowed.

                        prototype declared in: stdio.h
                        prototype: int access(char *name, int
                                mode);

acos   Returns a value in the range 0 to π, which is the arc cosine of the radian argument.

prototype declared in: math.h
prototype: double acos(double x);

[w]addch   Curses Screen Management function and macro that add the character ch to the window at the current position of the cursor.

prototype declared in: curses.h
prototype: addch(char ch)
            int waddch(WINDOW *win,
            char ch);

[w]addstr   Curses Screen management function and macro that add the string pointed to by str to the window at the current position of the cursor.

prototype declared in: curses.h
prototype: addstr(char *str)
            int waddstr(WINDOW *win,
            char *str);

alarm   Sends the signal SIGALRM to the invoking process after the number of seconds indicated by its argument has elapsed.

prototype declared in: signal.h
prototype: int alarm(unsigned int
            seconds);

asctime   Converts a broken-down time into a 26-character string in the following form:

Sat JAN 18 02:04:24 1992\n\0

All fields have a constant width.

prototype declared in: time.h
prototype: char *asctime (const tm_t,
            *timeptr);

asin

Returns a value in the range $-\pi/2$ to $\pi/2$, which is the arc sine of its radian argument.

prototype declared in: `math.h`
prototype: double asin(double x);

assert

Puts diagnostics into programs.

prototype declared in: `assert.h`
prototype: void assert (int expression);

atan
which

Returns a value in the range $-\pi/2$ to $\pi/2$, is the arc tangent of its radian argument.

prototype declared in: `math.h`
prototype: double atan(double x);

atan2

Returns a value in the range $-\pi$ to π, which is the arc tangent of x/y, where x and y are the two arguments.

prototype declared in: `math.h`
prototype: double atan2(double x,
            double y);

atexit

Registers a function that's called without arguments at program termination.

prototype declared in: `stdlib.h`
prototype: int atexit (void (*func)
            (void));

atof

Converts an ASCII string to a numeric value. The ASCII string has the following form:

```
[white-spaces][+|-]digits[.digits]
[e|E[+|-]integer]
```

The first unrecognized character ends the conversion. The string is interpreted by the same rules that are used to interpret floating constants.

prototype declared in: `stdlib.h`
prototype: double atof (const char
            *nptr);

atoi   Converts strings of ASCII characters to the appropriate numeric values. The ASCII string has the following form:

```
[white-spaces][+|-]digits
```

The function does not account for overflow resulting from the conversion. In VAX C, `atoi` is the same as `atol`.

prototype declared in: `stdlib.h`
prototype: int atoi(const char *nptr);

atol   Converts strings of ASCII characters to the appropriate numeric values. The ASCII string has the following form:

```
[white-spaces][+|-]digits
```

The function does not account for overflow resulting from the conversion. In VAX C, `atol` is the same as `atoi`.

prototype declared in: `stdlib.h`
prototype: long int atol(const char
                              *nptr);

box   Curses Screen Management function that draws a box around the window using the character ı as the character for drawing the vertical lines of the rectangle, and - for drawing the horizontal lines of the rectangle.

prototype declared in: `curses.h`
prototype: box(WINDOW *win, char
                              vert, char hor);

brk   Determines the lowest virtual address that is not used with the program.

prototype declared in: `stdlib.h`
prototype: void *brk(unsigned long int
                              addr);

bsearch   Performs a binary search. It searches an array
                             of sorted objects for a specified object.

                             prototype declared in: `stdlib.h`
                             prototype: void *bsearch (
                                          const void *key,
                                          const void *base,
                                          size_t nmemb,
                                          size_t size,
                                          int (*compar)
                                          (const void *,
                                          const void *));

cabs   Computes the Euclidean distance between
                             two points as the square root of their respec-
                             tive squares. This function returns `sqrt`
                             `(x*x + y*y)`.

                             prototype declared in: `math.h`
                             prototype: double cabs(cabs_t z);

calloc   Allocates an area of memory.

                             prototype declared in: `stdlib.h`
                             prototype: void *calloc(size_t number,
                                          size_t size);

ceil   Returns (as a double) the smallest integer
                             that is greater than or equal to its argument.

                             prototype declared in: `math.h`
                             prototype: double ceil(double x);

cfree   Makes available for reallocation the area allo-
                             cated by a previous `calloc`, `malloc`, or `re`
                             `alloc` call.

                             prototype declared in: `stdlib.h`
                             prototype: void cfree(char *pointer);

chdir   Changes the default directory.

                             prototype declared in: `stdlib.h`
                             prototype: int chdir(char *name);

chmod

Changes the file protection of a file.
prototype declared in: `stdlib.h`
prototype: int chmod(char *name,
            unsigned int mode);

chown

Changes the owner UIC of a file.

prototype declared in: `stdlib.h`
prototype: int chown(char *name,
            unsigned int owner,
            unsigned int group);

[w]clear

Curses Screen Management function and macro that erase the contents of the specified window and reset the cursor to coordinates (0,0). The clear macro acts on the `stdscr` window.

prototype declared in: `curses.h`
prototype: clear( )
            int wclear(WINDOW *win);

clearerr

Resets the error and end-of-file indicators for a file (so that `ferror` and `feof` will not return a nonzero value).

prototype declared in: `stdio.h`
prototype: void clearerr(FILE
            *file_pointer);

clearok

Sets the clear flag for the window.

prototype declared in: `curses.h`
prototype: clearok(WINDOW *win, int
            boolf);

clock

Determines the amount of CPU time (in 10-millisecond units) used since the beginning of program execution. The time reported is the sum of the user and system times of the calling process and any terminated child processes for which the calling process has executed wait or system.
prototype declared in: `time.h`
prototype: clock_t clock(void);

close   Closes the file associated with a file descriptor.

                       prototype declared in: `unixio.h`
                       prototype: int close(int file_descriptor);

[w]clrattr   Curses Screen Management function and macro that deactivate the video display attributes boldface, blinking, reverse video, and underlining within a specified window on the terminal screen. The attributes are represented by `_BOLD`, `_BLINK`, `_REVERSE`, and `_UNDERLINE`.

                       prototype declared in: `curses.h`
                       prototype: clrattr(attr);
                                     int wclrattr(WINDOW *win,
                                     int attr);

c[w]clrtobot   Curses Screen Management function and macro that erase the contents of the window from the current position of the cursor to the bottom of the window. The `clrtobot` macro acts on the `stdscr` window.

                       prototype declared in: `curses.h`
                       prototype: clrtobot(void);
                                     wclrtobot(WINDOW *win);

[w]clrtoeol   Curses Screen Management function and macro that erase the contents of the window from the current cursor position to the end of the line on the specified window. The `wclr toeol` macro acts on the `stdscr` window.

                       prototype declared in: `curses.h`
                       prototype: clrtoeol( );
                                     int wclrtoeol(WINDOW *win);

cos   Returns the cosine of its radian argument.

                       prototype declared in: `math.h`
                       prototype: double cos(double x);

cosh   Returns the hyperbolic cosine of its argument.

prototype declared in: math.h
prototype: double cosh(double x);

creat

Creates a new file.

prototype declared in: unixio.h
prototype: int creat(char *file_spec,
                unsigned int mode,...);

[no]crmode

Curses Screen Management macros that set
and unset the terminal from cbreak mode.
This mode of single-character input is only supported with the Curses input routine getch.
It also applies to any of the UNIX I/O, Terminal I/O, or Standard I/O routines.

prototype declared in: curses.h
prototype: crmode( )
                nocrmode( );

ctermid

Returns a character string giving the equiva-
lence string of SYS$COMMAND. This is the
name of the controlling terminal.

prototype declared in: stdlib.h
prototype: char *ctermid(char *str);

ctime

Converts a time in seconds to the following
form:

wkd mmm dd hh:mm:ss 19yy\n\0

prototype declared in: time.h
prototype: char *ctime(const long
                *bintim);

cuserid

Returns a pointer to a character string containing the name of the user initiating the
current process.

prototype declared in: stdlib.h
prototype: char *cuserid(char *str);

[w]delch

Curses Screen Management function and macro that delete the character on the specified
window at the current position of the cursor.

prototype declared in: `curses.h`
prototype: delch( )
                  int wdelch(WINDOW *win);

delete   Causes a file to be deleted.

prototype declared in: `stdio.h`
prototype: int delete(const char
                  *file_spec);

[w]deleteln   Curses Screen Management function and
                              macro that delete the line at the end of the
                              current position of the cursor. The `deleteln`
                              macro acts on the `stdscr` window.

prototype declared in: `curses.h`
prototype: deleteln( )
                  int wdeleteln(WINDOW
                  *win);

delwin   Deletes the specified window from memory.

prototype declared in: `curses.h`
prototype: int delwin(WINDOW *win);

difftime   Computes the difference in seconds between
                              the two times specified by the time1 and
                              time2 arguments.

prototype declared in: `time.h`
prototype:
double difftime (time_t time2,
                  time_t time_1);

div   Returns the quotient and remainder after the
                              division of its arguments.

prototype declared in: `stdlib.h`
prototype: div_t div(int numer, int
                  denom);

dup   Allocates a new file descriptor that refers to a
                              file specified by a file descriptor returned by
                              open, creat, or pipe.

prototype declared in: `unixio.h`
prototype: int dup(int file_desc1);

dup2

Makes `file_descriptor_2` point to the same file as `file_descriptor_1`.

prototype declared in: `unixio.h`
prototype:
int dup2 (int file_descriptor_1,
          int file_descriptor_2);

[no]echo

Curses Screen Management macros that set the terminal so that characters may or may not be echoed on the terminal screen. This mode of single-character input is only supported with Curses.

prototype declared in: `curses.h`
prototype: echo( )
            noecho( )

ecvt

Converts its argument to a NUL-terminated string of ASCII digits and returns the address of the string. The strings are stored in a memory location created by the functions.

prototype declared in: `unixlib.h`
prototype: char *ecvt(double value,
                       int ndigit,
                       *decpt,
                       int *sign)

endwin

Curses Screen Management function that clears the terminal screen and frees any virtual memory allocated to Curses data structures.

prototype declared in: `curses.h`
prototype: void endwin(void);

[w]erase

Curses Screen Management function and macro that erase the window by "painting" it with blanks. The erase macro acts on the `stdscr` window.

prototype declared in: `curses.h`
prototype: erase( )
      int werase(WINDOW *win);

execl

Passes the name of an image to be activated on a child process.

prototype declared in: `processes.h`
prototype: int execl (char *file-spec,
      char *argn,...);

execle

Passes the name of an image to be activated on a child process.

prototype declared in: `processes.h`
prototype:
int execle (char *file-spec,
      char *argn,..., char *envp[ ]);

execlp

Passes the name of an image to be activated on a child process.

prototype declared in: `processes.h`
prototype: int execlp (char *file-spec,
      char *argn,...);

execv

Passes the name of an image to be activated on a child process.

prototype declared in: `processes.h`
prototype: int execv (char *file-spec,
      char *argv[ ]);

execve

Passes the name of an image to be activated on a child process.

prototype declared in: `processes.h`
prototype:
int execve (char *file-spec,
      char *argv[ ], char *envp[ ]);

execvp

Passes the name of an image to be activated on a child process.

prototype declared in: `processes.h`
prototype: int execvp (char *file-spec,
                        char *argv[ ]);

exit,
_exit

Terminate the calling process. The `exit` function flushes and closes all open files before terminating the process; the `_exit` function does not.

prototype declared in: `stdlib.h`
prototype: void exit(int status)
                    void _exit(int status);

exp

Returns the base e raised to the power of the argument.

prototype declared in: `math.h`
prototype: double exp(double x);

fabs

Returns the absolute value of a floating-point value.

prototype declared in: `math.h`
prototype: double fabs(double x);

fclose

Closes a file by flushing any buffers associated with the file control block and freeing the file control block and buffers previously associated with the file pointer.

prototype declared in: `stdio.h`
prototype: int fclose(FILE
                       *file_pointer);

fcvt

Converts its argument to a NUL-terminated string of ASCII digits and returns the address of the string.

prototype declared in: `unixlib.h`
prototype:
char *fcvt(double value, int ndigit,
                     int *decpt, int *sign);

fdopen	Associates a file pointer with a file descriptor returned by an `open`, `creat`, `dup`, `dup2`, or `pipe` function. prototype declared in: `stdio.h` prototype: FILE *fdopen(int file_descriptor, char *a_mode);
feof	Tests a file to see if the end-of-file has been reached. prototype declared in: `stdio.h` prototype: int feof(FILE *file_pointer);
ferror	Returns a nonzero integer if an error occurred while reading or writing to a file. prototype declared in: `stdio.h` prototype: int ferror(FILE *file_pointer);
fflush	Writes out any buffered information for the specified file. prototype declared in: `stdio.h` prototype: int fflush(FILE *file_pointer);
fgetc	Returns characters from a specified file. prototype declared in: `stdio.h` prototype: int fgetc(FILE *file_pointer);
fgetname	Returns the file specification associated with a file pointer. prototype declared in: stdio.h prototype: char *fgetname(FILE *file_pointer, char *buffer,...);
fgetpos	Stores the current value of the file position indicator for the stream pointed to by the stream into the object pointed to by pos.

prototype declared in: `stdio.h`
prototype: int fgetpos(FILE *stream,
                    fpos_t *pos);

fgets

Reads a line from a specified file, up to a specified maximum number of characters or up to and including the newline character, whichever comes first. This function stores the string in the `str` argument.

prototype declared in: `stdio.h`
prototype: char *fgets(char *str, int
                    maxchar, FILE *file_ptr);

fileno

Returns an integer file descriptor that identifies the specified file.

prototype declared in: `stdio.h`
prototype: int fileno(FILE
                    *file_pointer);

floor

Returns (as a double) the largest integer that is less than or equal to its argument.

prototype declared in: `math.h`
prototype: double floor(double x);

fmod

Computes the floating-point remainder of the first argument to `fmod` divided by the second. If the quotient cannot be represented, the behavior is undefined.

prototype declared in: `math.h`
prototype: double fmod (double x,
                    double y);

fopen

Opens a file by returning the address of a FILE structure.

prototype declared in: `stdio.h`
prototype:
FILE *fopen(const char *file_spec,
                    const char *a_mode ,...);

fprintf   Performs formatted output to a specified file.

prototype declared in: `stdio.h`
prototype:
int fprintf(FILE *pointer,
                const char *format_spec,...);

fputc   Writes characters to a specified file.

prototype declared in: `stdio.h`
prototype: int fputc(int character, FILE
                *file_pointer);

fputs   Writes a character string to a file without
copying the string's null terminator (\0).

prototype declared in: `stdio.h`
prototype: int fputs(const char *string,
                FILE *file_pointer);

fread   Reads a specified number of items from a file.

prototype declared in: `stdio.h`
prototype: size_t   fread
(void *pointer, size_t length,
  size_t nitems, FILE (*file_pointer);

free   Makes available for reallocation the area allocated by a previous `calloc`, `malloc`, or `re`
`alloc` call.

prototype declared in: `stdlib.h`
prototype: void free(void *pointer);

freopen   Substitutes the file, named by a file specification, for the open file addressed by a file
pointer. The latter file is closed.

prototype declared in: `stdio.h`
prototype:
FILE *freopen(const char *spec,
                const char *access_mode,
                FILE (*file_pointer),...);

frexp   Returns the mantissa of a double value.

prototype declared in: `math.h`
prototype: double frexp(double
                value,int *eptr);

fscanf   Performs formatted input from a specified file.

prototype declared in: `stdio.h`
prototype: fscanf(FILE *file_pointer,
                const char *format_spec,...);

Format specifications begin with a percent sign (%) followed by a conversion character and a number indicating the size of the field. Possible conversion characters are:

`d`	Decimal integer
`D`	Decimal long integer
`o`	Octal integer
`O`	Octal long integer
`x`	Hexadecimal integer
`X`	Hexadecimal long integer
`hd, ho, hx`	Short integer of the specified radix
`c`	Single character
`s`	Character string
`e,f`	Floating-point number having the form `[+|-]nnn[.[ddd]]` `[[E|e][+|-]nn]`
`E,F`	Double-precision e and f
`ld, lo, lx`	Long decimal, long octal, and long hexadecimal integer
`le, lf`	Double-precision e and f
`[..]`	Brackets enclosing a set of characters. The set is made up of the characters in the string field. If the first character is an up-arrow (^), the set is made up of the delimiters for the field.

fseek   Positions the file to the specified byte offset in the file.

prototype declared in: `stdio.h`

prototype: int fseek
(FILE *file_pointer, long int *offset,
 int direction);

fsetpos

Sets the file position indicator for the stream according to the value of the object pointed to by pos.

prototype declared in: stdio.h
prototype: int fsetpos (FILE *stream,
               fpos_t *fpos);

fstat

Accesses information about the file descriptor or the file specification.

prototype declared in: stat.h
prototype: int fstat(int file_descriptor,
               stat_t *buffer);

ftell

Returns the current byte offset to the specified file.

prototype declared in: stdio.h
prototype: int ftell(FILE *file_pointer);

ftime

Returns the time elapsed since 00:00:00 January 1, 1970, in the structure pointed at by timeptr.

prototype declared in: time.h
prototype: void ftime(timeb_t
               *timeptr);

fwrite

Writes a specified number of items to the file.

prototype declared in: stdio.h
prototype: size_t fwrite
(void *pointer, size_t size_of_item,
 size_t number_items, FILE
 *file_pointer);

gcvt

Converts its argument to a NUL-terminated string of ASCII digits and returns the address of the string. The strings are stored in a memory location created by the functions.

prototype declared in: `unixlib.h`
prototype: char *gcvt(double   value,   int
ndigit, char *buf);

getc   Returns characters from a specified file.

prototype declared in: `stdio.h`
prototype: int getc(FILE *file_pointer);

[w]getch   Curses Screen Management function and
macro that get a character from the terminal
screen and echo it on the specified window.

prototype declared in: `curses.h`
prototype: getch( )
char wgetch(WINDOW *win);

getchar   Reads a single character from the standard
input (`stdin`).

prototype declared in: `stdio.h`
prototype: int getchar(void);

getcwd   Returns a pointer to the file specification for
the current working directory.

prototype declared in: `unixlib.h`
prototype: char *getcwd (char *buffer,
unsigned int size,...);

getegid   Returns, in VMS terms, the group number
from the user identification code (UIC). For
example, if the UIC is [313,031], 313 is the
group number.

prototype declared in: `unixlib.h`
prototype: unsigned getegid( );

getenv   Searches the environment array for the current process and returns the value associated
with the environment name.

prototype declared in: `unixlib.h`
prototype: char *getenv(const char
*name);

geteuid   Returns, in VMS terms, the member number
                                from the user identification code (UIC). For
                                example, if the UIC is [313,031], 313 is the
                                member number.

                                prototype declared in: `unixlib.h`
                                prototype: unsigned geteuid(void)

getgid   Returns, in VMS terms, the group number
                                from the user identification code (UIC). For
                                example, if the UIC is [313,031], 313 is the
                                group number.

                                prototype declared in: `unixlib.h`
                                prototype: unsigned int getgid(void);

getname   Returns the file specification associated with
                                a file descriptor.

                                prototype declared in: `unixio.h`
                                prototype: char *getname(int
                                            file_descriptor, char
                                            *buffer,...);

getpid   Returns the process `ID` of the current process.

                                prototype declared in: `unixlib.h`
                                prototype: int getpid(void);

getppid   Returns the parent process `ID` of the calling
                                process.

                                prototype declared in: `unixlib.h`
                                prototype: int getppid (void);

gets   Reads a line from the standard input (`stdin`).

                                prototype declared in: `stdio.h`
                                prototype: char *gets(char *string);

[w]getstr   Curses Screen Management function and
                                macro that get a string from the terminal
                                screen, store it in the variable string, and
                                echo it on the specified window. The `getstr`
                                macro works on the `stdscr` window.

prototype declared in: `curses.h`
prototype: getstr(str);
            int wgetstr(WINDOW *win,
            char *str);

getuid

Returns, in VMS terms, the member number from the user identification code (UIC). For example, if the UIC is [313,031], 313 is the member number.

prototype declared in: `unixlib.h`
prototype: unsigned int getuid(void);

getw

Returns characters from a specified file.

prototype declared in: `stdio.h`
prototype   int getw(FILE
            *file_pointer);

getyx

Curses Screen Management function that puts the (x,y) coordinates of the current cursor position on win in the variables y and x.

prototype declared in: `curses.h`
prototype: getyx(WINDOW *win, int y,
            int x);

gmtime

(GMT not supported on VAX)

gsignal

Generates a specified software signal. Generating a signal causes the action established by the ssignal function to be taken.

prototype declared in: `signal.h`
prototype: int gsignal(int sig,...);

hypot

Returns the square root of the sum of two squares of two arguments. For example: sqrt(x*x + y*y).

prototype declared in: `math.h`
prototype: double hypot(double x,
            double y);

[w]inch

Curses Screen Management function and macro that return the character at the current cursor position on the specified window without making changes to the window. The inch macro acts on the stdscr window.

prototype declared in: curses.h
prototype: inch( )
              char winch(WINDOW *win);

initscr

Curses Screen Management function that initializes the terminal-type data and all screen functions. You must call initscr before using any of the screen functions or macros.

prototype declared in: curses.h
prototype: void initscr(void);

[w]insch

Curses Screen Management function and macro that insert the character ch at the current cursor position in the specified window. The insch macro acts on the stdscr window.

prototype declared in: curses.h
prototype: insch(char ch)
              int winsch(WINDOW *win,
              char ch);

[w]insertln

Curses Screen Management function and macro that insert a line above the line containing the current cursor position. The insertln macro acts on the stdscr window.

prototype declared in: curses.h
prototype: insertln( );
              int winsertln(WINDOW *win);

[w]insstr

Curses Screen Management function and macro that insert a string at the current cursor position on the specified window. The insstr macro acts on the stdscr window.

prototype declared in: `curses.h`
prototype: insstr(char *str);
                int winsstr(WINDOW *win,
                char *str);

isalnum

Returns a nonzero integer if its argument is one of the alphanumeric ASCII characters. Otherwise, it returns 0.

prototype declared in: `ctype.h`
prototype: int isalnum(int character);

isalpha

Returns a nonzero integer if its argument is one of the alphabetic ASCII characters. Otherwise, it returns 0.

prototype declared in: `ctype.h`
prototype: int isalpha(int character);

isapipe

Returns 1 if the specified file descriptor is associated with a mailbox, and 0 if it is not.

prototype declared in: `unixio.h`
prototype: int isapipe
                (int file_descriptor);

isascii

Returns a nonzero integer if its argument is any ASCII character. Otherwise, it returns 0.

prototype declared in: `ctype.h`
prototype: int isascii(int character);

isatty

Returns 1 if the specified file descriptor is associated with a terminal, and 0 if it is not.

prototype declared in: `unixio.h`
prototype: int isatty
                (int file_descriptor);

iscntrl

Returns a nonzero integer if its argument is an ASCII DEL character (177 octal) or any nonprinting ASCII character (a code less than 40 octal). Otherwise, it returns 0.

prototype declared in: `ctype.h`
prototype: int iscntrl(int character);

isdigit

Returns a nonzero integer if its argument is a decimal digit (0 to 9). Otherwise, it returns 0.

prototype declared in: `ctype.h`
prototype: int isdigit(int character);

isgraph

Returns a nonzero integer if its argument is a graphic ASCII character. Otherwise, it returns 0.

prototype declared in: `ctype.h`
prototype: int isgraph(int character);

islower

Returns a nonzero integer if its argument is a lowercase alphabetic ASCII character. Otherwise, it returns 0.

prototype declared in: `ctype.h`
prototype: int islower(int character);

isprint

Returns a nonzero integer if its argument is any ASCII printing character (ASCII codes from 40 octal to 176 octal). Otherwise, it returns 0.

prototype declared in: `ctype.h`
prototype: int isprint(int character);

ispunct

Returns a nonzero integer if its argument is an ASCII punctuation character; that is, if it's nonalphanumeric and greater than 40 octal. Otherwise, it returns 0.

prototype declared in: `ctype.h`
prototype: int ispunct(int character);

isspace

Returns a nonzero integer if its argument is a white space; that is, if it is an ASCII space, tab (horizontal or vertical), carriage-return, form-feed, or newline character. Otherwise, it returns 0.

prototype declared in: ctype.h
prototype: int isspace(int character);

isupper

Returns a nonzero integer if its argument is an uppercase alphabetic ASCII character. Otherwise, it returns 0.

prototype declared in: `ctype.h`
prototype: int isupper(int character);

isxdigit

Returns a nonzero integer if its argument is a hexadecimal digit (0 to 9, A to F, or a to f).

prototype declared in: `ctype.h`
prototype: int isxdigit(int character);

kill

Sends a signal to a process specified by a process ID (PID). This function does not support the same functionality supported by UNIX systems.

prototype declared in: `signal.h`
prototype: int kill(int pid, int sig);

labs

Returns the absolute value of an integer as a long `int`.

prototype declared in: `stdlib.h`
prototype: long int labs(long int j);

ldexp

Returns its first argument multiplied by 2 raised to the power of its second argument.

prototype declared in: `math.h`
prototype: double ldexp(double x, int e);

ldiv

Returns the quotient and remainder after the division of its arguments.

prototype declared in: `stdlib.h`
prototype: ldiv_t ldiv(long int numer,
                long int denom);

leaveok

Curses Screen Management macro that signals Curses to leave the cursor at the current coordinates after an update to the window.

prototype declared in: `curses.h`
prototype: leaveok(WINDOW *win, int
                    boolf);

localtime

Converts a time (expressed as the number of seconds elapsed since 00:00:00, January 1, 1970) into hours, minutes, seconds, and so on.

prototype declared in: `time.h`
prototype: struct tm *localtime(const
                    time_t *bintim);

log

Returns the natural (base-e) logarithm of its argument.

prototype declared in: `math.h`
prototype: double log(double x);

log10

Returns the base-10 logarithm of its argument.

prototype declared in: `math.h`
prototype: double log10(double x);

longjmp

Provides a way to transfer control from a nested series of function invocations back to a predefined point without returning normally; that is, by not using a series of return statements. The `longjmp` function restores the context of the environment buffer.

prototype declared in: `setjmp.h`
prototype: void longjmp(jmp_buf env,
                    int val);

longname

Assigns the full terminal name to name, which must be large enough to hold the character string.

prototype declared in: `curses.h`
prototype: void longname(char *termbuf,
                    char *name);

lseek

Positions a file to an arbitrary byte position and returns the new position as an `int`.

prototype declared in: `unixio.h`
prototype: int lseek(int file_descriptor,
                        int offset,
                        int direction);

malloc

Allocates an area of memory.

prototype declared in: `stdlib.h`
prototype: void *malloc(size_t size);

memchr

Locates the first occurrence of the specified byte within the initial size bytes of a given object.

prototype declared in: `string.h`
prototype: void memchr (const void *s1,
                           int c,
                           size_t size);

memcmp

Compares two objects, byte by byte. The compare operation starts with the first byte in each object. It returns an integer less than, equal to, or greater than 0, depending on whether the lexical value of the first object is less than, equal to, or greater than that of the second object.

prototype declared in: `string.h`
prototype: int memcmp (const void *s1,
                         const void *s2,
                         size_t size);

memcpy

Copies a specified number of bytes from one object to another.

prototype declared in: `string.h`
prototype: void *memcpy (void *s1,
                         const void *s2,
                         size_t size);

memmove

Copies a specified number of bytes from one object to another.

prototype declared in: `string.h`
prototype:
void *memmove(void *s1,
         const void *s2,
         size_t size);

memset

Sets a specified number of bytes in a given object to a given value.

prototype declared in: `string.h`
prototype: void *memset (void *s,
         int value,
         size_t size);

mkdir

Creates a directory.

```
# include stdlib
int mkdir (char *dir_spec,
unsigned mode,...);
```

Creates a unique file name from a template that you supply.

prototype declared in: `unixio.h`
prototype: char *mktemp(char
       *template);

modf

Returns the positive fractional part of its first argument and assigns the integer part, expressed as an object of type double, to the object whose address is specified by the second argument.

prototype declared in: `math.h`
prototype: double modf (double value,
       double *iptr);

[w]move

Curses Screen Management function and macro that change the current cursor position on the specified window to the coordinates (y,x). The move macro acts on the `stdscr` window.

prototype declared in: `curses.h`
prototype: move(y,x)

int wmove(WINDOW *win,
int y, int x);

mv[w]addch

Curses Screen Management macros that
move the cursor to coordinates (y,x) and add
the character ch to the specified window.
The mvaddch macro acts on the stdscr
window.

prototype declared in: curses.h
prototype:
mvaddch(int y, int x, char ch)
mvwaddch(WINDOW *win, int y,
       int x, char ch);

mv[w]addstr

Curses Screen Management macros that
move the cursor to the specified string, to
which str points, to the specified window.
The mvaddstr macro acts on the stdscr
window.

prototype declared in: curses.h
prototype:
mvaddstr(int y, int x, char *str)
mvwaddstr(WINDOW *win, int y,
       int x, char *str);

mvcur

Curses Screen Management macro that
moves the terminal's cursor from (lasty,lastx)
to (newy,newx).

prototype declared in: curses.h
prototype: mvcur(int lasty, int lastx,
           int newy, int newx);

mv[w]delch

Curses Screen Management macros that
move the cursor to coordinates (y,x) and
delete the character on the specified window.
The mvdelch macro acts on the stdscr
window.

prototype declared in: curses.h
prototype: mvdelch(int y, int x);
         mvwdelch(WINDOW *win,
       int y, int x);

mv[w]getch

Curses Screen Management macros that move the cursor to coordinates (y,x), get a character from the terminal screen, and echo it on the specified window. The `mvgetch` macro works on the `stdscr` window.

prototype declared in: `curses.h`
prototype:
mvgetch(int y, int x);
        mvwgetch(WINDOW *win,
            int y, int x);

mv[w]getstr

Curses Screen Management macros that move the cursor to coordinates (y,x), get a string from the terminal screen, and echo it on the specified window. The `mvgetstr` macro acts on the `stdscr` window.

prototype declared in: `curses.h`
prototype:
mvgetstr(int y, int x, char *str)
mvwgetstr(WINDOW *win, int y,
        int x, char *str);

mv[w]inch

Curses Screen Management macros that move the cursor to coordinates (y,x) and return the character on the specified window without making changes to the window. The `mvinch` macro acts on the `stdscr` window.

prototype declared in: `curses.h`
prototype: mvinch(int y, int x);
        mvwinch(WINDOW *win,
        int y, int x);

mv[w]insch

Curses Screen Management macros that move the cursor to coordinates (y,x) and insert the character `ch` in the specified window. The `mvinsch` macro acts on the `std scr` window.

prototype declared in: `curses.h`
prototype:
mvinsch(char ch, int y, int x);

mvwinsch(WINDOW *win, int y,
                int x, char ch);

mv[w]insstr   Curses Screen Management macros that move
the cursor to coordinates (y,x) and insert a
string on the specified window. The mvinsstr
macro acts on the stdscr window.

prototype declared in: curses.h
prototype:
mvinsstr(int y, int x, char *str)
mvwinsstr(WINDOW *win, int y,
                int x, char str);

mvwin   Curses Screen Management macro that
moves the starting position of the window to
the specified (y,x) coordinates.

prototype declared in: curses.h
prototype   wvwin(WINDOW *win, int y,
                int x);

newwin   Curses Screen Management routine that
creates a new window with numlines lines
and numcols columns starting at the coordinates begin_y, begin_x on the terminal
screen.

prototype declared in: curses.h
prototype: WINDOW newwin
                (int numlines, int numcols,
                    int begin_y, int begin_x);

nice   Increases or decreases process priority relative to the process base priority by the
amount of the argument.

prototype declared in: stdlib.h
prototype: nice(int increment);

[no]nl   Curses Screen Management function and
macro that unset and set the terminal to
and from newline mode (they start and stop
the system from mapping <RETURN> to
<LINE-FEED>).

prototype declared in: `curses.h`
prototype: nl( )
                  nonl( )

open

Opens a file for reading, writing, or editing. It positions the file at its beginning (byte 0).

prototype declared in: `unixio.h`
prototype:
int open(char *file_spec, int flags,
             unsigned int mode,...);

overlay

Curses Screen Management routine that superimposes `win1` on `win2`. The function writes the contents of `win1` that will fit onto `win2`, beginning at the starting coordinates of both windows. Blanks on `win1` leave the contents of the corresponding space on `win2` unaltered. The overlay function copies as much of the window's box as possible.

prototype declared in: `curses.h`
prototype: int overlay(WINDOW *win1,
                  WINDOW *win2);

overwrite

Curses Screen Management routine that destructively overwrites the contents of `win1` on `win2`.

prototype declared in: `curses.h`
prototype: int overwrite(WINDOW
                  *win1, WINDOW *win2);

pause

Causes its calling process to stop (hibernate) until the process receives a signal.

prototype declared in: `signal.h`
prototype: int pause(void)

perror

Writes a short message to `stderr` describing the last error encountered during a call to the VAX C RTL from a C program.

prototype declared in: `stdio.h`
prototype: void perror(const char *string);

pipe

Creates a temporary mailbox. You must use a mailbox to read and write data between the parent and child. The channels through which the processes communicate are called a pipe.

prototype declared in: `processes.h`
prototype: int pipe(int
                file_descriptor[2],...);

pow

Returns the first argument raised to the power of the second argument.

prototype declared in: `math.h`
prototype: double pow(double base,
                double exp);

printf

Performs formatted output to the standard output (`stdout`).

prototype declared in: `stdio.h`
prototype:
int printf(const char
                *format_specification,...);

A format specification is a character string that states the output format. The string may contain ordinary characters that are copied to the output, or it may contain a format specification. Format specifications begin with a percent sign (%), and end with a conversion character that states the output format. Each format specification must be paired with an output source. Format specifications are matched to output sources in left-to-right order.

[w]printw

Curses Screen Management function and macro that perform a `PRINTF` on the window starting at the current position of the cursor. The `printw` macro acts on the `stdscr` window.

prototype declared in: `curses.h`
prototype:
printw(char *format_spec,...);
int wprintw(WINDOW *win,
                    char *format_spec,...);

putc   Writes characters to a specified file.

prototype declared in: `stdio.h`
prototype: int putc(int character, FILE
                    *file_pointer);

putchar   Writes a single character to the standard output (`stdout`) and returns the character.

prototype declared in: `stdio.h`
prototype: int putchar(int character);

puts   Writes a character string to the standard output (`stdout`) followed by a newline.

prototype declared in: `stdio.h`
prototype: int puts(char *string);

putw   Writes characters to a specified file.

prototype declared in: `stdio.h`
prototype: int putw(int integer, FILE
                    *file_pointer);

qsort   Sorts an array of objects in place. It imple-
ments the quick-sort algorithm.

prototype declared in: `stdlib.h`
prototype: void qsort (
                    void *base,
                    size_t nmemb,
                    size_t size,
                    int (*compar) const void *,
                    const void *));

raise   Generates a specified software symbol.

prototype declared in: `signal.h`
prototype: int raise(int sig,...);

rand

Returns pseudorandom numbers in the range 0 to (2**31-1).

prototype declared in: `stdlib.h`
prototype: int rand(void)

[no]raw

Curses Screen Management functions and macros that set and unset the terminal to and from raw mode. The RAW function performs the same task as CRMODE, except that it doesn't imply NONL. These functions and macros are provided only for portability with programs running on UNIX systems. This routine is available only on VMS Versions 5.0 and above.

prototype declared in: `curses.h`
prototype: raw( )
              noraw( )

read

Reads bytes from a file and places them in a buffer.

prototype declared in: `unixio.h`
prototype: int read(int file_descriptor,
                       char *buffer,
                       int nbytes);

realloc

Changes the size of the area pointed to by the first argument to the number of bytes given by the second argument.

prototype declared in: `stdlib.h`
prototype: void *realloc(char *pointer,
                           size_t size);

[w]refresh

Curses Screen Management function and macro that repaint the specified window on the terminal screen. The `refresh` macro acts on the `stdscr` window.

prototype declared in: `curses.h`
prototype: refresh( )
                      int wrefresh(WINDOW *win);

remove   Causes a file to be deleted.

prototype declared in: `stdio.h`
prototype: int remove (const char
                      *file-spec);

rename   Gives a new name to an existing file.

prototype declared in: `stdio.h`
prototype: int rename (const char
                      *old_file_spec,
                      const char *new_file_spec);

rewind   Sets the file to its beginning.

prototype declared in: `stdio.h`
prototype: int rewind(FILE
                      *file_pointer);

sbrk   Determines the lowest virtual address that is
                           not used with the program.

prototype declared in: `stdio.h`
prototype: void *sbrk(unsigned long int
                      incr);

scanf   Performs formatted input from the standard
                           input (`stdin`).

prototype declared in: `stdio.h`
prototype: int scanf(const char
                      *format_spec,...);

Format specifications begin with a percent
sign (%) followed by a conversion character
and a number indicating the size of the field.

[w]scanw   Curses Screen Management function and
                           macro that perform a scanf on the window. The
                           `scanw` macro acts on the `stdscr` window.

prototype declared in: `curses.h`
prototype:
scanw(char *format_spec,...);
int wscanw(WINDOW *win,
                   char *format_spec,...);

scroll   Curses Screen Management routine that
                              moves all the lines on the window up one line.
                              The top line scrolls off the window, and the
                              bottom line becomes blank.

                              prototype declared in: `curses.h`
                              prototype: int scroll(WINDOW *win);

scrollok   Curses Screen Management macro that sets
                              the scroll flag for the specified window.

                              prototype declared in: `curses.h`
                              prototype: scrollok(WINDOW *win, int
                                          boolf);

[w]setattr   Curses Screen Management function and
                              macro that activate the video display attri-
                              butes boldface, blinking, reverse video, and
                              underlining within the window. The attri-
                              butes are represented by _BOLD, _BLINK,
                              _REVERSE, and _UNDERLINE. The set
                              `attr` macro acts on the `stdscr` window.

                              prototype declared in: `curses.h`
                              prototype: setattr(attr);
                                          wsetattr(WINDOW *win, int
                                          attr);

setbuf   Associates a buffer with an input or output file.

                              prototype declared in: `stdio.h`
                              prototype: int setbuf(FILE
                                          *file_pointer, char *buffer);

setgid   Implemented for program portability and
                              serves no function. It returns 0 (to indicate
                              success).

prototype declared in: `unixlib.h`
prototype: int setgid(unsigned int
            group_number);

setjmp

Provides a way to transfer control from a nested series of function invocations back to a predefined point without returning normally; that is, by not using a series of return statements. The `setjmp` function saves the context of the environment buffer.

prototype declared in: `setjmp.h`
prototype: int setjmp(jmp_buf env);

setuid

Implemented for program portability and serves no function. It returns 0 (to indicate success).

prototype declared in: `unixlib.h`
prototype: int setuid(unsigned int
            member_number);

setvbuf

Associates a buffer with an input or output file.

prototype declared in: `stdio.h`
prototype:
int setvbuf (FILE *file_ptr, char *buffer,
            int type, size_t size);

sigblock

Causes the signals designated in a mask to be added to the current set of signals being blocked from delivery.

prototype declared in: `signal.h`
prototype: int sigblock(int mask);

signal

Allows you to either catch or ignore a signal.

prototype declared in: `signal.h`
prototype:
int (*signal(int sig,
    void (*func)(int,...)))(int,...);

sigpause   Assigns mask to the current set of masked signals and then waits for a signal.

                             prototype declared in: `signal.h`
                             prototype: int sigpause(int mask);

sigsetmask   Establishes those signals that are blocked from delivery.

                             prototype declared in: `signal.h`
                             prototype: int sigsetmask(int mask);

sigstack   Defines an alternate stack on which to process. This allows the processing of signals in a separate environment from that of the current process.

                             prototype declared in: `signal.h`
                             prototype:
                             int sigstack(struct sigstack *ss,
                                             struct sigstack *oss);

sigvec   Assigns a handler for a specific signal.

                             prototype declared in: `signal.h`
                             prototype:
                             int sigvec(int sigint, struct sigvec *sv,
                                             struct sigvec *osv);

sin   Returns the sine of its radian argument.

                             prototype declared in: `math.h`
                             prototype: double sin(double x);

sinh   Returns the hyperbolic sine of its argument.

                             prototype declared in: `math.h`
                             prototype: double sinh(double x);

sleep   Suspends the execution of the current process for at least the number of seconds indicated by its argument.

                             prototype declared in: `signal.h`
                             prototype: int sleep(unsigned seconds);

sprintf   Performs formatted output to a string in
                                memory.

                                prototype declared in: `stdio.h`
                                prototype:
                                int sprintf(char *string,
                                            const char *format_spec,...);

                                A format specification is a character string that
                                states the output format. The string may con-
                                tain ordinary characters that are copied to the
                                output, or it may contain a format specification.
                                Format specifications begin with a percent sign
                                (%), and end with a conversion character that
                                states the output format. Each format specifi-
                                cation must be paired with an output source.
                                Format specifications are matched to output
                                sources in left-to-right order.

sqrt   Returns the square root of its argument.

                                prototype declared in: `math.h`
                                prototype: double sqrt(double x);

srand   Returns pseudorandom numbers in the range
                                0 to (2**31-1).

                                prototype declared in: `math.h`
                                prototype: int srand(int seed);

sscanf   Performs formatted input from a character
                                string in memory.

                                prototype declared in: `stdio.h`
                                prototype:
                                int sscanf(char *string,
                                           const char *format_spec,...);

                                Format specifications begin with a percent
                                sign (%) followed by a conversion character
                                and a number indicating the size of the field.

ssignal   Allows you to specify the action to take when
                                a particular signal is raised.

prototype declared in: `signal.h`
prototype:
void (*ssignal (int sig,
　　　　　void (*func) (int,...))) (int,...);

[w]standend　　　Curses Screen Management function and macro that deactivate the boldface attribute for the specified window. The `standend` macro acts on the `stdscr` window.

prototype declared in: `curses.h`
prototype:　standend( )
　　　　　int wstandend(WINDOW
　　　　　*win);

[w]standout　　　Curses Screen Management function and macro that activate the boldface attribute of the specified window. The standout macro acts on the `stdscr` window.

prototype declared in: `curses.h`
prototype:　standout( )
　　　　　int wstandout(WINDOW
　　　　　*win);

stat　　　Accesses information about the file descriptor or the file specification.

prototype declared in: `stat.h`
　　　　　　　　　`statbuf.h`
prototype:　int stat(int *file_path,
　　　　　stat_t *buffer);

strcat　　　Concatenates `str_2` to the end of `str_1`.

prototype declared in: `string.h`
prototype:　char *strcat(char *str_1,
　　　　　const char *str_2);

strchr　　　Returns the address of the first occurrence of a given character in a NUL-terminated string.

prototype declared in: `string.h`

prototype: char *strchr(const char
                   *string, int character);

strcmp

Compares two ASCII character strings and
returns a negative, 0, or positive integer, indicating that the ASCII values of the individual characters in the first string are less
than, equal to, or greater than the values in
the second string.

prototype declared in: `string.h`
prototype: int strcmp(const char *str_1,
                   const char *str_2);

strcpy

Copies all of `str_2` into `str_1`.

prototype declared in: `string.h`
prototype: char *strcpy(char *str_1,
                   const char *str_2);

strcspn

Returns the length of the prefix of a string
that consists entirely of characters that are
not in a specified set of characters.

prototype declared in: `string.h`
prototype:
size_t strcspn(const char *str,
                   const char *charset);

strerror

Maps the error number in `error_code` to
an error message string.

prototype declared in: `string.h`
prototype: char *strerror (
                   int error_code [,int
                   vms_error_code]);

strlen

Returns the length of a string of ASCII characters. The returned length does not include
the terminating null character (\0).

prototype declared in: `string.h`
prototype: size_t strlen(const
                   char *str);

strncat   Concatenates `str_2` to the end of `str_1`.

                               prototype declared in: `string.h`
                               prototype: char *strncat(char *str_1,
                                            const char *str_2,
                                            size_t maxchar);

strncmp   Compares two ASCII characters and returns a
                               negative, 0, or positive integer, indicating that
                               the ASCII values of the individual characters
                               in the first string are less than, equal to, or
                               greater than the values in the second string.

                               prototype declared in: `string.h`
                               prototype: int strncmp(const char *str_1,
                                            const char *str_2,
                                            size_t maxchar);

strncpy   Copies all or part of `str_2` into `str_1`.

                               prototype declared in: `string.h`
                               prototype:
                               char *strncpy(char *str_1,
                                            const char *str_2,
                                            size_t maxchar);

strpbrk   Searches a string for the occurrence of one of
                               a specified set of characters.

                               prototype declared in: `string.h`
                               prototype:
                               char *strpbrk(const char *str,
                                            const char *charset);

strrchr   Returns the address of the last occurrence of
                               a given character in a NUL-terminated string.

                               prototype declared in: `string.h`
                               prototype:
                               char *strrchr(char *string,
                                            char character);

strspn   Searches a string for the occurrence of a char-
                               acter that's not in a specified set of characters.

prototype declared in: `string.h`
prototype:
size_t strspn(const char *str,
               const char charset);

strstr

Locates the first occurrence in the string pointed to by s1 of the sequence of characters in the string pointed to by s2.

prototype declared in: `string.h`
prototype: char *strstr(const char *s1,
              const char *s2);

strtod

Converts a given string to a double-precision number.

prototype declared in: `stdlib.h`
prototype:
double strtod (const char *nptr,
              char **endptr);

strtok

Locates text tokens in a given string.

prototype declared in: `string.h`
prototype: char *strtok (char *s1, const
              char *s2);

strtol

Converts strings of ASCII characters to the appropriate numeric values.

prototype declared in: `stdlib.h`
prototype:
long int strtol (const char *nptr,
                  char **endptr,
                  int base);

strtoul

Converts the initial portion of the string pointed to by nptr to an unsigned long integer.

prototype declared in: `stdlib.h`
prototype:
unsigned long int strtoul (
                  const char *nptr,
                  char **endptr,
                  int base);

strspn
Returns the length of the prefix of a string that consists entirely of characters from a set of characters.

prototype declared in: `string.h`
prototype:
size_t strspn(const char *str,
             const char *charset);

subwin
Curses Screen Management routine that creates a new subwindow with numlines lines and numcols columns starting at the coordinates (`begin_y`, `begin_x`) on the terminal screen.

prototype declared in: `curses.h`
prototype:
WINDOW *subwin
(WINDOW *win, int numlines,
 int numcols, int begin_y,
 int begin_x);

system
Passes a given string to the host environment to be executed by a command processor.

prototype declared in: `processes.h`
prototype: int system (const
             char *string);

tan
Returns a double value that is the tangent of its radian argument.

prototype declared in: `math.h`
prototype: double tan(double x);

tanh
Returns a double value that is the hyperbolic tangent of its double argument.

prototype declared in: `math.h`
prototype: double tanh(double x);

time
Returns the time elasped on the system since 00:00:00 January 1, 1970 in seconds.

prototype declared in: time.h
prototype: time_t time(time_t
            *time_location);

times

Passes back the accumulated times of the current process and its terminated child processes.

prototype declared in: time.h
prototype: void times (tbuffer_t
            *buffer);

tmpfile

Creates a temporary file that's opened for update.

prototype declared in: stdio.h
prototype: FILE *tmpfile(void);

tmpnam

Creates a character string that you can use in place of the file-name argument in other function calls.

prototype declared in: stdio.h
prototype: char *tmpnam(char *name);

toascii

Converts its argument, an 8-bit ASCII character, to a 7-bit ASCII character.

prototype declared in: ctype.h
prototype: int toascii(char character);

tolower
_tolower

Convert their argument, an ASCII character, to lowercase. If the argument is not an upper-case character, it is returned unchanged.

prototype declared in: ctype.h
prototype: int tolower(char character);
            int _tolower(char character)

(The function is tolower; the macro is _tolower.)

touchwin

Curses Screen Management routine that places the most recently edited version of the specified window on the terminal screen.

prototype declared in: `curses.h`
prototype: int touchwin(WINDOW *win);

toupper,
_toupper

Convert their argument, an ASCII character, to uppercase. If the argument is not a lowercase character, it is returned unchanged.

prototype declared in: `ctype.h`
prototype: int toupper(char character);
                 int _toupper(char character)

(The function is `toupper`; the macro is `_toupper`.)

ttyname

Returns a pointer to the NUL-terminated name of the terminal device associated with file descriptor 0, the default input device (`stdin`).

prototype declared in: `unixio.h`
prototype: char *ttyname(void);

umask

Creates a file protection mask, which is used when a new file is created, and returns the previous mask value.

prototype declared in: `stdlib.h`
prototype: int umask(unsigned int
                 mode_complement);

ungetc

Pushes a character back into the input stream and leaves the stream positioned before the character.

prototype declared in: `stdio.h`
prototype: int ungetc(int character,
                 FILE *file_pointer);

va_arg

Returns the next item in the argument list.

prototype declared in: `stdarg` or
`#include varargs.h`
prototype: type va_arg(va_list ap type);

va_count Returns the number of longwords in the argument list.

prototype declared in: `varargs.h`
prototype: void va_count(int count);

va_end Finishes the `varargs` session.

prototype declared in: `stdarg` or
`#include varargs.h`
prototype: void va_end(va_list ap);

va_start Initializes a variable to the beginning of the argument list.

prototype declared in: `varargs.h`
prototype: void va_start(va_list ap);

va_start_1 Initializes a variable to the beginning of the argument list.

prototype declared in: `varargs.h`
prototype: void va_start_1(va_list
                ap, int offset);

VAXC$CALLOC_OPT Allocates an area memory.

prototype declared in: `stdlib.h`
prototype: void *VAXC$CALLOC_OPT
                (size_t number,
                size_t size);

VAXC$CFREE_OPT Makes available for reallocation the area allocated by a previous VAXC$CALLOC_OPT, VAXC$MALLOC_OPT, or VAXC$REALLOC_OPT call.

prototype declared in: `stdlib.h`
prototype: int VAXC$CFREE_OPT
                (void *pointer);

VAXC$CRTL_INIT Allows you to call the VAX C RTL from other languages. It initializes the run-time environment and establishes both an exit and condition handler.

VAXC$ESTABLISH   Establishes a special VAX C RTL exception handler that catches all RTL-related exceptions and passes on all others to your handler.

prototype declared in: signal.h
prototype:
void VAXC$ESTABLISH(
        int (*exception_handler)(
           void *mecharr,void *sigarr));

VAXC$FREE_OPT   Makes available for reallocation the area allocated by a previous VAXC$CALLOC_OPT, VAXC$MALLOC_OPT, or VAXC$REALLOC_OPT call.

prototype declared in: stdlib.h
prototype: int VAXC$FREE_OPT(void
        *pointer);

VAXC$MALLOC_OPT   Allocates an area of memory.

prototype declared in: stdlib.h
prototype: void
*VAXC$MALLOC_OPT(size_t size);

VAXC$REALLOC_OPT   Changes the size of the area pointed to by the first argument to the number of bytes given by the second argument.

prototype declared in: stdlib.h
prototype: char
*VAXC$REALLOC_OPT(void *pointer,
                size_t size);

vfork   Creates an independent child process.

prototype declared in: processes.h
prototype: int vfork(void);

vprintf,   Print formatted output based on an argument
vfprintf,   list. These functions are the same as the

vsprintf

printf functions, except that instead of being called with a variable number of arguments, they're called with an argument list that's been initialized by the macro va_start.

prototype declared in: stdio.h
                      stdarg.h
prototype:
int vprintf (const char
*format, va_list *arg);
int vfprintf (FILE *file_ptr,
            const char *format,
            va_list *arg);
int vsprintf (char *str,
            const char *format,
            va_list arg);

wait

Checks the status of the child process before exiting. A child process is terminated when the parent process terminates.

prototype declared in: processes.h
prototype: int wait(int *status);

wrapok

Curses macro that, in the UNIX system environment, allows the wrapping of a word from the right border of the window to the beginning of the next line. This macro is provided only for UNIX compatibility.

prototype declared in: curses.h
prototype: wrapok(WINDOW *win, int
            boolf);

write

Writes a specified number of bytes from a buffer to a file.

prototype declared in: unixio.h
prototype:
int write(int file_descriptor,
            void *buffer,int nbytes);

System-Supplied Header Files

The VAX C language compiler is shipped with a number of header files that reside in the directory `SYS$LIBRARY:`. All of them have a file type of `.h`. These files contain symbolic values for constants, function prototypes for supplied functions, and so on. When a function is used and it's declared in one of these files, the file should be included in the C program so that the compiler can check for incorrect usage of the function. Many constants required with various system routines are defined in the header files. These files should be included when the constants are being used, and the symbolic name of the constant should be used for ease of maintenance. At times it's difficult to find out which header files should be included in the program. Including all header files in every program might be an extreme solution because it would increase the compile time of programs. As an aid in determining which files should be included in a program, here's a list of most of the header files in `SYS$LIBRARY:`, along with a brief description of what information the file contains.

Header file	Contains information on
`ACCDEF.H`	Accounting
`ACEDEF.H`	Access control entries

Header file	Contains information on
ACLDEF.H	Access control lists
ACRDEF.H	Accounting file information
ARMDEF.H	Access Rights Mask
ASSERT.H	Assert macro
ATRDEF.H	File attributes
BASDEF.H	BASIC language (error) messages
BRKDEF.H	$breakthru system service
CDA$DEF.H	Compound Document Architecture (CDA)
CDA$MSG.H	CDA (error) messages
CDA$PTP.H	CDA toolkit
CDA$TYP.H	CDA type definitions
CDDTAG4GL.H	CDA 4gl tags
CDDTAGACMS.H	CDA tags for ACMS
CDDTAGDBMS.H	CDA tags for DBMS
CDDTAGDSRI.H	CDA tags for DSRI databases
CDDTAGNAD.H	CDA tags for NAD
CDDTAGPROG.H	CDA tags for programming
CDDTAGRECFLD.H	CDA tags for data
CDDTAGS.H	CDA tags
CHFDEF.H	Condition handlers
CHKPNTDEF.H	Checkpointable processes
CHPDEF.H	Check protection ($CHKPRO) service
CLIDEF.H	Command definition language (CLI)
CLIMSGDEF.H	CLI (error) messages
CLISERVDEF.H	CLI service request codes
CLIVERBDEF.H	CLI verb generic codes
CLSDEF.H	Security classification mask
COBDEF.H	COBOL message codes
CQUALDEF.H	Some CLI qualifiers
CRDEF.H	Card reader
CREDEF.H	Library create options
CRFDEF.H	Cross reference
CRFMSG.H	Cross reference status codes
CTYPE.H	C character types
CURSES.H	Screen management package
DCDEF.H	Device adapters
DDIF$DEF.H	DDIF routines

Header file	Contains information on
`DECW$CURSOR.H`	DECwindows cursor
`DECW$DWTDEF.H`	DECwindows toolkit
`DECW$DWTENTRY.H`	DECwindows toolkit
`DECW$DWTMSG.H`	DECwindows toolkit messages
`DECW$DWTSTRUCT.H`	DECwindows toolkit structures
`DECW$DWTWIDGETDEF.H`	DECwindows widgets
`DECW$DWTWIDGETSTRUCT.H`	DECwindows widget structures
`DECW$XLIBDEF.H`	DECwindows Xlib
`DECW$XLIBMSG.H`	DECwindows Xlib messages
`DECW$XPORTCOM.H`	DECwindows transport
`DECW$XPORTDEF.H`	DECwindows transport
`DESCRIP.H`	String and other descriptors
`DEVDEF.H`	Device characteristics
`DIBDEF.H`	Device information block
`DMPDEF.H`	System Dump file header
`DMTDEF.H`	Flags for $DISMOU (dismount) service
`DNSDEF.H`	Distributed Naming Services (DNS)
`DNSMSG.H`	DNS messages
`DSTDEF.H`	Data stack
`DTIF$DEF.H`	DTIF routines
`DTK$ROUTINES.H`	DECtalk
`DTKDEF.H`	DECtalk
`DTKMSG.H`	DECtalk (error) messages
`DVIDEF.H`	Device and Volume information
`DVR$CC_DEF.H`	CDA viewer
`DVR$CC_PTP.H`	CDA viewer callable routines
`DVR$DECW_PTP.H`	CDA viewer routines for DECwindows
`DVR$MSG.H`	CDA viewer (error) messages
`ENVDEF.H`	Environment definition
`EOMDEF.H`	End of module record
`EOMWDEF.H`	End of module record with word of psect
`EPMDEF.H`	Entry point, normal symbols
`EPMMDEF.H`	Entry point, version mask symbols
`EPMVDEF.H`	Entry point, vectored symbols
`ERADEF.H`	Erase type codes
`ERRNO.H`	UNIX-style error codes
`ERRNODEF.H`	VMS equivalents for UNIX-style error codes

Header file	Contains information on
FAB.H	RMS File access block
FALDEF.H	DECnet File Access Listener
FCHDEF.H	DEC/Shell file characteristics
FDLDEF.H	File Definition Language interface
FIBDEF.H	File identification block layout
FIDDEF.H	Structure of a FID
FILE.H	Constants used by file OPEN function
FLOAT.H	Floating point numbers
FORDEF.H	FORTRAN (error) messages
FSCNDEF.H	$filescan routine
HLPDEF.H	HELP processing
IACDEF.H	Image activation control flags
INET.H	Internet
IODEF.H	I/O function codes
JBCMSGDEF.H	Job controller messages
JPIDEF.H	Process information codes
KGBDEF.H	Key Grant Block (Rights identifiers)
LADEF.H	LPA-11 characteristics codes
LATDEF.H	LAT messages
LBRCTLTBL.H	Library control table
LBRDEF.H	Types of libraries
LCKDEF.H	Lock manager codes
LEPMDEF.H	Module local entry points
LHIDEF.H	Library header information
LIB$ROUTINES.H	LIB$ routines
LIBCLIDEF.H	LIB$ CLI callback procedures
LIBDCFDEF.H	LIB$DECODE_DEFAULT codes
LIBDEF.H	LIB$ calls return codes
LIBDTDEF.H	LIB$ date/time package
LIBVMDEF.H	LIB$VM package (virtual memory)
LIMITS.H	Highest/lowest values of constants
LKIDEF.H	Lock information
LMFDEF.H	License Management facility
LNKDEF.H	Linker Options Record
LNMDEF.H	Logical names
MAILDEF.H	Callable MAIL codes
MATH.H	RTL math declarations

Header file	Contains information on
MNTDEF.H	Flags for $MOUNT service
MSGDEF.H	Mailbox messages
MT2DEF.H	Extended magtape codes
MTADEF.H	Magtape accessibility routine codes
MTDEF.H	Magtape status bits
MTHDEF.H	MTH$ routine codes
NAM.H	RMS Name block
NCS$ROUTINES.H	National character set routines
NCSDEF.H	NCS (error) messages
NETDB.H	Structures returned by network database libraries
NSARECDEF.H	Security audit record definitions
OPCDEF.H	Operator Communications services codes
OPDEF.H	VAX machine opcodes
OPRDEF.H	Operator Communications messages
OTS$ROUTINES.H	OTS$ routine definitions
OTSDEF.H	OTS$ (error) messages
PCCDEF.H	Printer/terminal carriage control specifiers
PERROR.H	VAX C RTL variables used by the PERROR routine
PLVDEF.H	Privileged library vector definition
PPL$DEF.H	Parallel processing library (PPL$) routines constants
PPL$ROUTINES.H	PPL$ routines
PPLDEF.H	PPL$ (error) messages
PQLDEF.H	Process quota codes
PRCDEF.H	$CREPRC service codes
PRDEF.H	VAX processor register names
PROCESSES.H	Subprocess function declarations
PRTDEF.H	Protection field codes
PRVDEF.H	Privilege bit definitions
PSLDEF.H	Processor Status Longword fields
PSMMSGDEF.H	Print Symbiont messages
PSWDEF.H	Processor Status Word fields
QUIDEF.H	$GETQUI definitions
RAB.H	RMS Record Access Block
RMEDEF.H	Nonstandard RMS functions
RMS.H	All RMS data structures
RMSDEF.H	RMS return codes
SBKDEF.H	File statistics block

Header file	Contains information on
SCRDEF.H	Screen package codes
SECDEF.H	Private/Global Section Definitions
SETJMP.H	Buffer codes for the setjmp/longjmp environment
SIGNAL.H	UNIX Signal Value Definitions
SJCDEF.H	$SNDJBC service definitions
SMG$ROUTINES.H	Screen management routines (SMG$)
SMGDEF.H	SMG$ constants
SMGMSG.H	SMG$ return codes
SMGTRMPTR.H	Terminal Capability codes for SMG$ facility
SMRDEF.H	Symbiont Manager request codes
SNALU62DF.H	SNA LU6.2 codes
SOCKET.H	Berkeley UNIX socket definitions
SOR$ROUTINES.H	Sort
SORDEF.H	Sort codes
SSDEF.H	System (error) codes
STARLET.H	System service entry point descriptions
STAT.H	The stat/fstat UNIX emulation functions
STDARG.H	Access to variable-length argument lists as specified with an ellipsis in a function prototype
STDIO.H	Standard UNIX I/O definitions
STDLIB.H	VAX C RTL general utility functions
STR$ROUTINES.H	STR$ routines
STRDEF.H	STR$ return codes
STRING.H	C (str) string manipulation functions
STSDEF.H	System service return codes
SYIDEF.H	System information codes
TIME.H	C RTL time routines
TIMEB.H	The ftime() routine return structure
TPADEF.H	LIB$TPARSE routine codes
TRMDEF.H	QIO item list symbols for terminals
TT2DEF.H	Terminal constants for QIOs
TTDEF.H	Terminal constants for QIOs
TYPES.H	C RTL typedef definitions
UAIDEF.H	Authorize file fields
UICDEF.H	User Identification Code information
UNIXIO.H	Declarations for UNIX I/O emulation functions

UNIXLIB.H	Declarations for UNIX emulation functions

Header file	Contains information on
USGDEF.H	Disk usage accounting file produced by the `Ana lyze/disk_structure` command
VARARGS.H	Definitions for variable-length argument lists
XAB.H	RMS extended control block
XWDEF.H	DDCMP constants

Index

ABOUT THE AUTHOR

Jay Shah is with the Systems Integration Services Department of Chase Manhattan Bank, New York. He has more than 10 years experience in systems software development and management, with particular strength in VAX systems programming. He is the author of VAX/VMS Concepts and Facilities (McGraw-Hill, 1991) and VAXClusters: Architecture, Programming and Management (McGraw-Hill, 1991). He has a BSEE from the Indian Institute of Technology, Bombay, India, and an M.S. in Technology Management from the Stevens Institute of Technology, Hoboken, New Jersey.